CW00730219

# Ring of Fire

The ring of fire 'stands for the life cycle of both the universe and each individual being: the circular dance of nature in the eternal process of creation and destruction. At the same time, the light radiated by the ring of flames symbolizes eternal wisdom and transcendental illumination.'

J.E. Cirlot, *A Dictionary of Symbols*

The circular form in which the group is seated symbolizes its unity, connectedness and cohesion as well as its microcosmic relation to the larger world of human evolution, culture and the life cycle. Foulkes, Bion and others have identified primitive layers of affect and object relations where universal collective themes and early infantile object relations are re-experienced and repeated in the meeting place for healing called the therapy group. In this context, very profound emotions and energies are released which have deep implications for change and growth, provided the therapist can manage and respond to them effectively.

This book brings together a collection of new and original contributions to an understanding of primitive object relations and intensely critical emotional states which present the maximum challenge to the group psychotherapist: the 'Ring of Fire'. An international group of colleagues, based primarily in Great Britain and the United States, address areas of special interest to them and to which they have devoted considerable research and therapeutic effort. They provide insights into the dynamics of these issues and guide the therapist in the management and interpretation of the group events as they unfold.

While much has been written on primitive group states, the information is scattered throughout many journals and books and all too often does not address the practical problems faced by the group therapist in practical terms. Furthermore, there have been significant developments in affect theory and object-relations theory which have yet to be assimilated sufficiently into the theory and technique of group psychotherapy. This book attempts to reduce that gap as it concentrates on the relevance of concepts to treatment in accordance with Kurt Lewin's maxim, 'There is nothing so practical as a good theory'.

*Ring of Fire* will be invaluable to group psychotherapy supervisors, beginning and experienced group therapists, students and supervisors of group psychotherapy and group dynamics, and organizational consultants who utilize group dynamics principles in their work.

**Victor L. Schermer** is a clinical psychologist in Philadelphia. He is Executive Director of the Study Group for Contemporary Psychoanalytic Process and Director of the Institute for the Study of Human Conflict.

**Malcolm Pines** is a founding member of the Group-Analytic Institute and a Member of the Group-Analytic Practice, London. A consultant psychiatrist, he is Editor of the International Library of Group Psychotherapy and Group Process.

# The International Library of Group Psychotherapy and Group Process

General Editor: Dr Malcolm Pines

*Institute of Group-Analysis, London, and formerly of the Tavistock Clinic, London.*

The International Library of Group Psychotherapy and Group Process reflects the group-analytical approach to psychotherapy from both practical and theoretical viewpoints. It takes into account developments in related areas and includes important works in translation.

## Other titles in the series

# Ring of Fire

Primitive affects and object relations in group psychotherapy

Edited by Victor L. Schermer and Malcolm Pines

London and New York

First published 1994
by Routledge
11 New Fetter Lane, London EC4P 4EE

Simultaneously published in the USA and Canada by Routledge
29 West 35th Street, New York, NY 10001

© 1994 Selection and editorial matter, Victor L. Schermer and
Malcolm Pines; individual chapters, the contributors.

Typeset in Times by
NWL Editorial Services, Langport, Somerset

Printed and bound in Great Britain by
Mackays of Chatham PLC, Chatham, Kent

All rights reserved. No part of this book may be reprinted or
reproduced or utilized in any form or by any electronic,
mechanical, or other means, now known or hereafter invented,
including photocopying and recording, or in any information
storage or retrieval system, without permission in writing from
the publishers.

*British Library Cataloguing in Publication Data*
A catalogue record for this book is available from the British
Library

*Library of Congress Cataloging in Publication Data*
Ring of fire: primitive affects and object relations in group
psychotherapy/edited by Victor L. Schermer and Malcolm
Pines.
p. cm. – (The International Library of Group Psychotherapy
and Group Process)
Includes bibliographical references and index.
1. Group psychotherapy. 2. Regression (Psychology).
3. Small groups – Psychological aspects. 4. Object relations
(Psychoanalysis). I. Schermer, Victor L. II. Pines,
Malcolm. III. Series.
[DNLM: 1. Psychotherapy, Group. 2. Affect. 3. Object
Attachment.
WM 430 R581 1994]
RC488.R54 1994
616.89'152 – dc20
DNLM/DLC                                        93–34089
for Library of Congress                         CIP

ISBN 0–415–06681–6 (hbk)
ISBN 0–415–06682–4 (pbk)

# Contents

# Contributors

**Yvonne M. Agazarian**, EdD, is a psychologist in private practice and Consultant Affiliate to Friends Hospital, Philadelphia, PA. She has developed a Theory of Living Human Systems; founded System-centered Group and Individual Psychotherapy; co-authored *The Visible and Invisible Group* in the International Library of Group Psychotherapy and Group Process series and co-sponsored the System-centered Group Psychotherapy videotape series. She is a fellow of the American Group Psychotherapy Association and a board member of the International Association of Group Psychotherapy.

**Harold S. Bernard**, PhD, is a psychologist in private practice in New York City. He is Clinical Associate Professor of Psychiatry and Chief of the Group Psychotherapy Program, Division of Ambulatory Services, NYU/Bellevue Medical Center, President of the Eastern Group Psychotherapy Society, 1991–3, and Member of the Board of Directors of the American Group Psychotherapy Association, 1991–4. Dr Bernard is book review editor of the *International Journal of Group Psychotherapy*, and co-editor of the *Handbook of Contemporary Group Psychotherapy* and of the *Manual of Group Psychotherapy*.

**John Gordon**, BA, is a psychoanalytic psychotherapist and group analyst in private practice and Principal Psychotherapist in the Department of Psychotherapy, St Bernard's Hospital, London, where he organizes the outpatient service in group psychotherapy. He is a Full Member of the British Association of Psychotherapists, a Member of the Institute of Group Analysis and co-author of *Group Approaches in Psychiatry*.

**Robert D. Hinshelwood**, PhD, is a British psychoanalyst and consultant psychotherapist who has contributed greatly in object-relations theory and group analysis. He is the author of *What Happens in Groups?* and *A Dictionary of Kleinian Thought Analysis*, and the forthcoming *Clinical*

*Klein.* He is Clinical Director of the Cassel Hospital, and the founder of the *British Journal of Psychotherapy.*

**Jeffrey Kauffman**, MA, MSS, is a clinical social worker and psychotherapist specializing in bereavement therapy in suburban Philadelphia, PA. He is founder and Director of the Institute for Spirituality and Psychological Healing and a consultant for nursing homes, hospices and other organizations.

**Robert H. Klein**, PhD, is a psychologist in private practice in Connecticut. He is Clinical Associate Professor of Psychiatry at both Yale University School of Medicine, New Haven, and Albert Einstein College of Medicine, New York. A Fellow of the American Group Psychotherapy Association, Dr Klein is a frequent lecturer, workshop leader and contributor to the group therapy literature. He is co-editor of the *Handbook of Contemporary Group Psychotherapy.*

**Malcolm Pines**, MLB, FRCPsych is a founding member of the Group-Analytic Institute and former consultant at the Tavistock Institute. Author of numerous books and articles in the fields of group psychotherapy and psychoanalysis, he has served as President of the International Association of Group Psychotherapy.

**Salomon Resnik**, MD, is a psychoanalyst, group analyst and author of several works on psychoanalysis and art which have been published in English, French, Italian and Spanish. He has special experience in the treatment of chronic psychotic patients, both in individual psychoanalysis and in group analysis.

**Victor L. Schermer**, MA, CAC, is a psychologist, consultant and supervisor in private practice and clinic settings in Philadelphia, PA. He is Executive Director of the Study Group for Contemporary Psychoanalytic Process and Director of the Institute for the Study of Human Conflict. He is co-author of *Object Relations, the Self and the Group*, and contributes to the psychotherapy literature with an emphasis on object relations theory, self psychology, and group systems theory.

**Marvin R. Skolnick**, MD, is a psychiatrist in private practice in Alexandria, VA. He is a Faculty Member of the Washington School of Psychiatry, Fellow of the A.K. Rice Institute and Clinical Professor of Psychiatry at George Washington University.

**Saul Tuttman**, MD, PhD, is a psychiatrist, psychoanalyst, psychologist and group psychotherapist in private practice in New York City. Dr Tuttman is Clinical Professor of psychiatry at Albert Einstein College of Medicine, New York; President, 1994–5, the American Academy of Psychoanalysis; and President-elect, 1996–8, the American Group Psychotherapy Association.

# Foreword

*Otto Kernberg*

The psychoanalytic exploration of the dynamics of small groups and their therapeutic utilization is a rich, still significantly unexplored territory. The path-breaking findings of Freud, Bion, Turquet, and Anzieu have been only partially integrated with the mainstream of psychoanalytic thinking. As the contributions to this volume demonstrate, even the fundamental developments in other areas of the psychoanalytic domain brought about by the major contributors to the psychoanalytic studies of group processes have not been fully deployed to develop further the understanding of group processes *per se*. Psychoanalytic group therapy has already served as an experimental laboratory for psychoanalytic object relations theory concepts, for the exploration of character pathology and its changes through treatment, and for the study of how individual psychopathology and the unconscious group processes that emerge in the group's interaction impact on each other.

The editors of this book have undertaken an important and challenging task: the study of the mutual influence of the explosive developments in psychoanalytic theory and technique of individual treatment, on the one hand, and on the other, the theoretical and technical innovations in psychoanalytically orientated group psychotherapy. By bringing together leading exponents of various approaches to psychoanalytically orientated group psychotherapy, and encouraging contributors to focus on this central question of the mutual interaction of the two fields, the editors of this book have provided us with a rich and thought-provoking book.

One major danger of trying to integrate various theories is the possibility of creating the appearance of an eclecticism that would do injustice to the competing theoretical models, blur the different concepts, and interfere with raising crucial questions, and with scientific research. This danger has been successfully avoided by the clear differentiation of the various perspectives reflected in the contributions to this book.

Contemporary developments in psychoanalytic technique are

characterized by the tendency to focus increasingly on the 'here-and-now' unconscious developments before attempting genetic reconstructions; on formulating unconscious conflict in object relations terminology, on a growing attention to detection and management of the countertransference, and on the consideration of the centrality of patients' affective experiences. Similarly, psychoanalytic group psychotherapy as exemplified in this volume also focuses more sharply on these issues.

It is now well known that even mature and successfully analysed individuals may present strikingly regressive reactions in unstructured groups. These phenomena point to particular temptations to regression in groups in contrast to what takes place in ordinary dyadic and triadic interactions. The nature of these regressions, their causes, treatment, and the window they provide for the study of mass psychology, ideology, and organizational behaviour warrant further exploration. Indeed, the study of group behaviour may provide new contributions to psychoanalytic theory as well as to the technique of psychoanalytic psychotherapy. The present book takes us a significant distance in the direction of exploring these issues, and does so with commendable clarity and open-endedness.

This book will not provide any particular resolution to the controversies in contemporary psychoanalytic thinking, but it will acquaint the reader with the implications of such new psychoanalytic thinking for the understanding of group processes, and stimulate him or her to explore further the relationship between theory and technique in clinical practice.

New York
1994

# 1 An editorial introduction

Silence = death

*Malcolm Pines and Victor L. Schermer*

The ring of fire 'stands for the life cycle of both the universe and each individual being: the circular dance of nature in the eternal process of creation and destruction. At the same time, the light radiated by the ring of flames symbolizes eternal wisdom and transcendental illumination.'

J.E. Cirlot, *A Dictionary of Symbols*

To everything there is a season, and a time for every purpose under heaven.

*Ecclesiastes*

Group psychotherapy, like the human life cycle, has its universal ongoing themes punctuated by periods of intense emotionality, crisis, regression and transformation. The circular form in which the group is seated symbolizes its unity, connectedness and cohesion as well as its microcosmic relation to the larger world of human evolution, culture and the life cycle. Foulkes, Bion, Ezriel and others have identified primitive layers of affect and object relations where universal collective themes and early infantile object relations are re-experienced and repeated in the meeting place for healing called the therapy group. In this cauldron of group emotionality, profound energies are released which have a wide range of implications for change and growth.

This book brings together a collection of new and original contributions to an understanding of primitive object relations and of those highly charged emotional states which present the maximum challenge to the group psychotherapist: the 'Ring of Fire'. In the present volume, an international group of colleagues, based in Great Britain, France and the United States, address areas of special interest to them and to which they have devoted considerable research and therapeutic effort. They will provide insights into the dynamics of these issues and guide the therapist in the management and interpretation of the group events as they unfold.

When *Ring of Fire* was initially conceived, and each of the contributing authors was contacted, the editors specifically asked him or her to provide, in effect, a teaching and supervisory experience about a particular group issue or set of issues which had been of special interest for an extended time period. We think that the reader will find this goal of such an intimate learning experience with each author at the helm has been largely fulfilled. Certainly, a passionate and important 'message' about the conduct of group therapy is conveyed by each author, yet within the framework of careful observation and scholarly integration, and, thanks to some detailed vignettes and protocols, the reader gets a clear sense of what goes on in actual, 'live' group therapy sessions.

While much has been written about primitive group states, there have been recent developments in psychoanalytic ego psychology, self psychology and object-relations theory which cry out to be assimilated into the theory and technique of group psychotherapy. This book attempts to partially close that gap by emphasizing the relevance of newer concepts to treatment.

## CURRENT DILEMMAS AND ISSUES IN THE FIELD OF GROUP PSYCHOTHERAPY

The incentive for bringing together this collection of articles and essays stems from the striking developments and changes in the context and the practice of group psychotherapy over the past ten to fifteen years, some of which are indeed heartening, but many of which have proved troubling to the serious and dedicated psychotherapist.

A matter of great concern to today's therapist and, for that matter, any human being who inhabits this planet, is the increasing and sometimes traumatic impact of individual and group regressive phenomena on our lives. One could cogently argue that we are currently witnessing a global primitiv- ization of emotional experience as a result of the population explosion, the catastrophic destructive power of modern weapons of war, and the overwhelming quality of advanced technology and modern self- consciousness with a backlash tendency towards primitive splitting, denial, avoidance and pathological narcissism.

Social observers have pointed out the extreme, psychotic-like nature of war in this century; the genocidal leadership pathology of Hitler, Stalin, Saddam Hussein, and so on, the collective paralysis and unresponsiveness to atrocities in the Holocaust and more recently in Serbo-Croatia; and the alienation and anomie of contemporary culture. More proximal to group treatment, numerous therapists have noted the increased influx of borderline and narcissistic patients into their practices. In many ways, life has always been difficult and conflictful, even violent, but these times do seem to be especially so, placing severe stresses on the personality and the social group. It is perhaps encouraging that, in small ways, therapists, negotiators and diplomats are beginning to join forces to apply psychotherapy principles to diplomacy and intergroup conflict resolution (cf. Volkan, Ettin and others).

Whether such primitivization is a result in part of the observer-influenced outcome of enhanced theoretical and observational skills which allows us to perceive the pre-oedipal layers below the oedipal complex, or whether it is the increasing impact of regression due to global communication, powerful technologies and population increase, the reality is that *primitive regression is an increasingly impinging and insistent aspect of the ongoing context within which all group psychotherapy is conducted.* The group therapist who does not attend to the primitive layers either engages in 'whistling in the dark', ignoring and not treating defects and deficits in the self and object relations which underlie the presenting symptoms, or at times sets up the group for catastrophic situations of acting out, loss of group cohesion and failure to thrive as a group. So many patients have been affected by regressive psychocultural and traumatic processes as they operate in childrearing practices, neglect and abuse; substance abuse, and other regressive expressions of culture and society. To be effective psychotherapists, we must be able to accompany such patients and groups through these very painful layers of experience.

An additional concern of far-reaching importance for the environment in which group therapy is conducted is the precipitous change in the health care systems and funding streams which support the therapy process. In the 1960s and 1970s, there was enormous enthusiasm for insight-orientated psychotherapy. Scholarship and research abounded, and public and private grants supported and encouraged pure and applied research, pioneering efforts in individual, family and group psychotherapy, and the start up of new mental health and addictions treatment programmes. Both patients and insurance companies were ready and willing to pay for long-term outpatient treatment, and even long-term hospital stays. In that context, a variety of group therapies thrived and proliferated and had social impact well beyond the professional and treatment sectors.

More recently, a number of trends have militated against dedicated, humanistic and psychodynamic long-term therapy efforts. The most clear-cut force against such work has come from so-called 'third party' funding sources, whether private insurance companies or government-provided health care. In efforts to stem the tide of astronomically increasing health care costs, an admittedly necessary goal, the funding sources have undercut and undermined effective treatment efforts. They have fostered the belief that treatment can be done quickly, and they have done so without the careful research and 'hands on' experience necessary to justify changes in practice where human lives are concerned. The more extreme and poorly thought through of these 'utilization review' and 'managed care' efforts have already had a devastating impact on treatment and research. In England, for example, the Cassel Hospital, the Tavistock Clinic and the Henderson Hospital, world-renowned centres for treatment and research in group psychotherapy, have only barely survived, despite vehement public agitation, the changed climate of the late 1980s and early 1990s. Similar stories could be provided for some of the most prestigious institutions in the United States.

This volume implicitly argues for and is a testimony to longer-term treatment efforts which consider the dynamics of the whole person and wrestle with the deeper levels of difficulty beyond the surface symptoms and which have to do with the quality and durability of treatment efforts rather than patching up and covering up the disorders. We all need to work together to make *proper and appropriate* intensive psychotherapy available and affordable to those who need it.

Such social and economic forces impacting upon the treatment process are further reinforced by the overall societal increase in pathological narcissism discussed by Christopher Lasch and others. Excessive self-centredness reinforced by social norms of isolation leads severely distressed and disturbed people either to avoid treatment entirely on account of the human contact and the admission of shortcomings it entails, or else to make demands for quick, painless 'cures' rather than self-explorations which uncover defences, resistances and areas of vulnerability in the self. The positions of both the psychoanalyst and the group analyst, looking objectively at individual and group phenomena yet with a deep concern for the patients' well-being, is not easily maintained when people in increasing numbers are seeking 'warm, fuzzy' therapy experiences, self-appointed gurus who promise instant transformation, and medications which provide instant escape and relief.

Thus, the present volume, coming to publication as it does in the 1990s is at one level almost a cry in the wilderness, asking that, as therapists, we have the courage to stand up to some of these onslaughts. One place to begin doing this is in the consulting room itself, by practising better therapy, and by asserting the power of our work once again, the power to help persons change by achieving greater self-insight through the nurturing and developmental capacities of the group process. Each chapter of this volume seems to say that it is possible and necessary to dare to go with the group into the primitive realms, mindful of course of the defences, and, through the therapeutic alliance, to learn with the group what we are all made of.

## THE NEED FOR A SCIENTIFIC FRAMEWORK INTEGRATING THEORY AND PRACTICE

The role of theory and a scientific framework for group psychotherapy has found proponents as well as opponents. It is certainly possible to justify, from both existential and phenomenological standpoints, that theory and empirical investigation can both cloud the therapist's perception and potential for relating in an 'I–thou' relationship to the group members, a relationship which promotes 'agape', genuineness, positive self-regard and inner change. The existential approach focuses on our human condition of absurdity and aloneness. Phenomenology says, 'What you see (or, more recently in self psychology, what you empathically understand) is what you get.' In both views, 'experience-distant' theory is believed to interfere with the direct linkage in the here-and-now between patient and therapist. The French existentialist philosopher Jean-Paul Sartre once said, 'The worst crime is to make abstract that which is concrete', by which he meant that abstraction distances us from the human condition and causes us to ignore forceful realities. There is much truth in these words, but we must remember that Sartre is referring to a *misuse* of abstraction to avoid painful realities and human compassion.

Psychoanalytic, group-dynamic, and group-analytic approaches have consistently emphasized the importance of theory in consolidating and systematizing data from human development and from the consulting room. Today, however, we are increasingly aware that theory does not entirely stand for 'truth' as such or for unchangeable patterns of events. As Werner Heisenberg, a founder of quantum theory, pointed out, scientific theory and the observations on which it is based are a function of the observer as well as the observed. In therapeutic parlance there is no observation, inference or theory that is without the subjective bias of countertransference.

So, in the present view, theory and the scientific frame of reference are an inherently paradoxical blend of the subjective and objective, like an Escher print; yet theory is necessary, as are the birds and the fish in one of Escher's drawings. The latter are necessary, though neither 'birds' nor 'fish' 'exist' as such. What exists is the paradox. Modern physicists, with their quantum theory and chaos theory, would heartily agree with us. The symbolism of the 'Ring of Fire' reflects this paradox. The ring is the most perfect, aesthetic, parsimonious figure, representing the unity of thought which scientists seek. Yet it is burning, dissolving.

## GROUP THERAPY SITUATIONS AND POPULATIONS OF THE 'RING OF FIRE'

When the co-editors of this book explored possible themes, the one which stood out as the focus was the following: to examine the most difficult situations and dynamics in group psychotherapy and depict how particular therapists, each from his or her own perspective on primitive affects and object relations, deals with these situations and dynamics. If we were to take a survey of what therapists at various levels of training and experience found 'most difficult', we would undoubtedly find individual and subgroup differences as well as commonalities. A beginning therapist, for example, might say that 'screening for a proper mix of group members' or 'developing a cohesive group' are the most difficult tasks. A therapist working with a population of severely depressed patients might say, 'a suicidal crisis'.

One criterion used in the present volume has been the sorts of difficulties which are not only of interest to beginners but continue to be of ongoing concern to therapists who have completed basic training sequences in group psychotherapy and have honed their group skills with some supervised group therapy experience. For example, the 'perpetual motion' of separation, loss, grief and mourning which characterizes groups, and especially 'bereavement groups', may distress and baffle the therapist. Jeffrey Kauffman holds that such mourning processes are the very 'Rosetta Stone' of what propels groups in the first place, offering for our consideration a new group psychology based on mourning as the central process.

Another instance of a 'primary preoccupation' of the group therapist is the intense aggression which may occur in almost any group, and the management of which most therapists find of great concern. Saul Tuttman, although he focuses primarily on patients we would consider 'character disordered', discusses ways that an object-relations/ego psychological model might be applied in almost any group therapy context to manage and work through severe anger and hostility.

*Ring of Fire* addresses such issues of ongoing concern. Further examples include pressure on the therapist to join in collusive, projective and scapegoating events and processes (Hinshelwood), attacks on thought and emotional growth (Gordon), group treatment of borderlines (Pines) and psychotic patients (Resnik), problems of the co-therapy dyad (Klein and Bernard), and difficulties that come up in milieu therapy situations (Skolnick).

A second criterion for the choice of situations and populations for this volume is the usefulness of contemporary theoretical perspectives in addressing the problem. Self psychology and object-relations theory, for example, have proved very helpful in working with borderline, narcissistic and psychotic patients. As we have said, Malcolm Pines focuses on borderline and narcissistic patients in outpatient open-ended therapy groups. Harold Bernard and Robert Klein delve into the co-therapy issues attendant on work with such patients, utilizing what they term an integrated 'systems/developmental' perspective, emphasizing 'boundary and decider subsystems' of the group along with developmental insights on borderline and narcissistic personality from Kernberg, Masterson and others. Salomon

Resnik and Marvin Skolnick each independently address issues centring around the most profoundly difficult patients' intensive group and milieu treatment: chronically mentally ill borderline and psychotic patients. Resnik is indebted to Bion's work on both group assumptions and on psychosis. Skolnick applies the A.K. Rice 'Systems of Organization' model to the therapeutic community. Yvonne Agazarian uses a synthesis of systems theory and object-relations theory to provide a schema for therapeutic interventions in each phase of group development. One of the editors, Victor Schermer, has contributed a chapter on theory, which will take the reader on a 'guided tour' of such conceptual developments in group psychology and psychoanalysis.

A third and quite unavoidable criterion of chapters for *Ring of Fire* has, like it or not, turned out to be Darwinian natural selection! There were profound and precious time and space constraints imposed on putting together a collection of articles for a book such as this. If time had permitted the sifting, sorting and soliciting of more material, and if the size of the volume were considerably larger, the editors would almost certainly have included topics additional to those which finally have gone to press. For example we would definitely have included a chapter on group psycho-therapy with victims of severe trauma and/or abuse, another on dissociative and multiple personality disorders, and another on the management of shame and shame-based behaviour in group therapy (although Kauffman here places great emphasis on shame as a regulator of mourning processes in groups). Perhaps a second or related volume might take up such areas of great interest in the future. For the nonce, practical necessity forced our hand.

The editors would like to express their appreciation and gratitude to the contributors who have taken time from numerous professional commitments and responsibilities to write the new and original essays which comprise *Ring of Fire*. In addition, special thanks are due to Edwina Welham, editor at Routledge, for her support and encouragement of this volume at its inception, and her ongoing assistance and patience with the complex editorial process of collating a variety of new material into a coherent whole. Thanks also to Michael Graves, poet, writer, teacher and critic, New York City, for his thoughtful comments on readability and style.

We do believe that we have brought together a collection of representative themes which should whet the appetite and address the concerns of almost any group therapist, supervisor or student of group therapy. We invite the reader to read the chapters in whatever order occurs to him or her: each is intended to be a self-sufficient contribution of its own. There is, none the less, a certain logic in the order in which the chapters are presented, moving in a certain respect from the general to the specific, and from a theoretical and process focus to a 'population' focus. Further, each chapter is preceded by a brief 'editors' introduction', to alert the reader to some key points and to give the totality of *Ring of Fire* the sense of a journey through the realm of primitive group regressions. Read, learn, grow and enjoy!

V.L.S. and M.P.
Philadelphia, USA
London, England

# 2 Between theory and practice, light and heat

## On the use of theory in the 'Ring of Fire'

*Victor L. Schermer*

## EDITORS' INTRODUCTION

Co-editor Victor Schermer offers in what follows a guided tour and critique of the variety of theoretical constructs utilized in *Ring of Fire*. Schermer argues that the 'modernist' view in which logical and consistent scientific theory reflects the nature of an orderly, lawful universe is being supplanted by a 'postmodernist' emphasis on diversity, incompleteness, uncertainty, chaotically disorganized elements and catastrophic change and transformation. In group theory and therapy, global theoretical frameworks and schools of thought are being replaced by the use of multiple theories to achieve perspective and containment within the living group.

Schermer first examines several group-as-a-whole theories. He reviews the seminal contributions of Freud, Bion, Foulkes, Lewin and Miller and Rice and then looks at contemporary systems theory.

There follows a perspective on contemporary schools of psychoanalysis: Kleinian, British Independent school, Kohutian self psychology, and the psychoanalytic contributions of Bion. Emphasis is placed throughout on the way each chapter of *Ring of Fire* employs group-as-a-whole and psychoanalytic concepts to elucidate specific group situations.

---

As co-editor of this volume with Malcolm Pines, it is my opinion that readers will be impressed with the diversity of concepts and theories which the contributors have brought to bear upon group psychotherapy, as well as their combination of clinical sophistication and empathic attunedness to be seen in the way each author has used his or her theoretical frame in the treatment context. Such themes, variations, and applications of conceptual schema have called, in my view, for a commentary on the current multiplicity of theories and their relationship to the practice of group psychotherapy.

What follows is an attempt to provide such an orientating framework. I would like briefly to review and examine the various authors' key theoretical constructs, an assessment which I am hopeful will help the reader, in the words of Winnicott (1969), to place the 'object in the setting', that is, to understand each chapter in the context of its theoretical orientation as well as by virtue of its contrast with other alternative contrasting and complementary vantage points. In addition, and in combination with the brief editorial commentaries at the beginning of each chapter, such an overview may serve as a guide to the interrelationships among the chapters and to recent developments in group dynamics and in psychoanalysis.

We begin with a look at a global (in the sense both of worldwide and of extensive import) cultural and scientific change which has occurred in the last several decades, which in some ways demarcates the significance of twentieth-century intellectual life, and which has, I believe, impacted on the theory and practice of group psychotherapy almost without our knowing it.

## THE SHIFTING CONTEXT OF THEORY IN GROUP PSYCHOTHERAPY: FROM MODERNISM TO POSTMODERNISM

In my view, there has been a significant development in group therapists' understanding and utilization of theoretical constructs over the past several decades, a change which reflects a shift in cultural patterns and intellectual trends.

Earlier on, at mid-century, as it were, in those exciting decades (the 1930s through the 1970s) when group psychotherapy and group dynamics came into their own as distinct and innovative disciplines, theories were regarded from the standpoint of 'objective' science as large-scale schema incorporating working models which could generate hypotheses to be tested in the somewhat scientifically controlled settings of therapy groups, training groups and organizational and training conferences. Students, researchers and practitioners would often find themselves attracted to a particular school of thought and its guru/mentor(s), exploring various ramifications of that point of view and modifying theory on the basis of experience. Theory was regarded as a mental 'map' whose logic captured the phenomena being observed. Some of the powerful and empowering mentor figures who generated global theoretical and practical frameworks about groups and the members who comprise them included Bion, Lewin, Bales, Foulkes, Moreno, Miller and Rice, Maslow, and so on. Each of these pioneers sired a school of thought, in some instances fostered the establishment of training institutes, and inspired one or more generations of followers, dissidents and practitioners. Among the organizations which fostered the development of group dynamics and group psychotherapy were the Group-Analytic

Institute, the National Training Laboratories, Esalen Institute, Tavistock Clinic, the A.K. Rice Institute, and the Moreno Institute.

The intellectual current of the western world to which the notion of objective and progressively advancing science is associated, is what some writers have called 'modernity' (cf. Rosenau, 1992, pp. 5–6), rooted in the belief, which emerged in full force in the eighteenth-century Enlightenment with such philosophers and scientists as Newton, Descartes and Spinoza, that the natural world is coherent, causally interactive, and inherently logical, comparable, for example, to a huge clockwork mechanism or, in an analogy often used in group and family systems, a series of springs representing a set of inexorable forces. Such a world, the view of which evolved within a mechanistic techology, can be mastered and understood by comprehensive world-views and theories which themselves are internally consistent, each within its respective 'universe of discourse'. The modernist world-view may have been what supplanted the notion of Greek antiquity that the natural world was governed by the work and play of the gods, or, during the Middle Ages, that there existed a hierarchical order of beings and society under a regulating spiritual power. The conviction of order is deeply embedded in the human psyche.

I would contend that today, within the fields of group psychotherapy and psychoanalysis, as in all the social sciences, there has been a shift away from such a modernist, objectivist view to what has been called by some 'post-modernism'. There is an emphasis now on diversity and on the integration of diverse perspectives into one's own personal 'style' and perceptual gestalt. Today, more than ever, we know that there is no one truth, no 'single thread' (Lewis, 1976), and we seek to find ways to understand phenomena from a variety of perspectives or 'tracks' (Grotstein, 1986). We intuitively grasp the significance of systems paradox (Korzybski, 1948) and complementarity (Ashbach and Schermer, 1987, pp. 20–5) in our work by utilizing contrasting and even mutually contradictory theories to grasp different sides of the complementarities. We use theory to achieve containment and 'pattern recognition' amidst the rush of myriad events that occur within each group session. We accept and work with the possibility that chaos may be part of group experience. Such a *modus operandi* is especially applicable with regard to the highly energized and shifting flux of reality and phantasy to be found both in primitive group regressions and in character-disordered patients. In a certain respect, order and coherence are illusions, albeit very important and necessary ones, reflecting the 'aesthetics', 'autopoeisis' (autonomy), and development of living systems (cf. Maturana, 1980).

Among the scientific and intellectual currents of the twentieth century which have contributed to a more flexible, multi-perspective, paradoxical understanding of nature and the theories which purport to represent it are (a) quantum theory, with its uncertainty and complementarity principles; (b) general systems and gestalt approaches, which emphasize interconnections and wholes; (c) chaos theory, with its thesis that organized 'realities' are merely fractal moments and spaces of order within the incomprehensible, the irretrievable and the disruptive (Gleick, 1987; Lewin, 1993); and (d) deconstructionism, emerging not so much within science as within literary and artistic currents, which points out the contradictions within a 'text', thereby radically attacking theories and ideologies, while at the same time revealing their underlying structure and structural deficiencies (Rosenau, 1992, pp. 120–2; Derrida, 1978). A nineteenth-century 'harbinger' of such world-views was Gödel's incompleteness theorem, which demonstrated that all logical systems must have internal inconsistencies. There are thus a number of recent intellectual trends which argue for the necessity of the use of multiple perspectives in understanding phenomena.[1]

If we think for the moment of theory, not as a cognitive schema per se, written concretely in stone, but more in terms of a *functional object relationship* used by the group therapist to negotiate the forces, situations and dilemmas of the group and his or her own position within it, we can see that theory serves functions similar to a transitional object function (Winnicott, 1971) in bridging the inner world of the therapist with the ongoing life of the group and vice versa. Theory serves to translate inner experience into communicative acts and vice versa. Furthermore, theory helps the therapist and the group contain and modify powerful, even chaotic, affects by facilitating interpretations, symbols, myths and stories about inchoate emotionalities occurring in the group. Thus, theory has a boundary function in the group, defining systems, limits, risks and extents of group events (Ettin, 1992). In a very important way, theory forms part of the ongoing phenomenological intersubjective matrix of transference and countertransference in the life of the group (Atwood and Stolorow, 1984). Theories are not hardbound truth, but shared, interactive constructions which emerge and have a utility in certain situations.

Keeping in mind such a 'postmodernist' shift in the way theory is regarded and utilized, I want to address two aspects of theoretical developments relevant to group psychotherapy: group dynamics and psychoanalysis. I should like to discuss: (1) the historical evolution of *group* theory from Freud's group psychology and Bion's early work on groups, to the 'field', 'systems' and 'matrix' formulations of the group-as-a-whole, as well as some related and more recent understandings of the group, particularly as they are used in the present volume; and (2) the diversity of *psychoanalytic* self, ego and object-relations theories which pervade clinical work today and which are manifest in virtually all the contributions to this book. Although group psychology and psychoanalysis, as I shall suggest, are no longer such completely separate viewpoints as in the past, it is nevertheless convenient and practical to take them up separately from one another, at least to begin with.

## THE EVOLUTION AND CONTEMPORARY ROLE OF GROUP-AS-A-WHOLE PSYCHOLOGY

In the present context I can only skim the surface of a complex subject about which much has already been articulated and much more remains to be said. What I can offer here is a brief narrative (perhaps, with an appropriate scepticism about its 'truth value' – one could call it a 'folk tale' or a 'myth') of how we came to think in 'group-as-a-whole' terms. A thorough history of the evolution of group dynamics has yet to be written and would indeed be an exciting and fascinating story, disclosing extraordinary personalities, intergroup relations and conceptual break-throughs. What follows is merely a sketch designed to bring out a few salient points. I am aware that I am omitting many important personages and developments in group psychology and apologize to those I may have offended by such omission.

### Freud as a group psychologist

A pioneering work on groups written early in the twentieth century and reflecting a shift of interest from the individual to the group was Freud's *Group Psychology and the Analysis of the Ego* (1921), in which, in conjunction with other works such as *Moses and Monotheism* (1939) and the recently discovered *A Phylogenetic Fantasy* written in 1915 (cf. Grubrich, 1988), he explored the connections between the individual, the group, history and society. Unfortunately, in the *Group Psychology* essay Freud created some misunderstanding by utilizing the German word *Massenpsychologie* which could be translated alternatively as 'group' or as 'mass' psychology. While Freud's discussion of the work of LeBon on crowd behaviour suggests that he was referring to the 'mass', 'the crowd', 'the horde', his reference to various cultural groupings and to the re-evocation of parent–child feelings and sibling rivalry in the transference indicate he was speaking generically of any group, large or small, in which primitive regression takes place.

Although Freud was in principle a 'reductionist', explaining group processes in terms of individual transference to the leader, the quality of this particular essay and the way it has been subsequently understood, clearly mark it as a milestone in the study of group and social phenomena. A (1989) film from the former Soviet Union, entitled *The Interpretation of Dreams*, portrays Freud's major interest in his later work as group and cultural psychology. This film offered a specifically Soviet perspective of belated revelation regarding Freud, since knowledge of his work had been repressed there for several decades prior to the Glasnost period. Such an emphasis, on Freud as a social theorist, is vastly underplayed in the training of psychoanalysts in the West.

The feature of Freud's *Group Psychology*, which makes it appealing to psychodynamically based group therapists, is its application of unconscious dynamics, which has relevance both to the group and to individual transference and psychopathology. Indeed, in that essay Freud himself for the first time regarded psychoanalysis as a dualistic individual and group psychology. We can see in the seminal contributions of such group therapists as Scheidlinger (1952, 1964), Helen Durkin (1964) and others how psychoanalytic theory has been fruitfully applied in the domains of group dynamics, interpersonal relations and individual dynamics in the group *qua* group.

In *Group Psychology*, Freud pointed out the importance of transference and identification in group formation, the nature of group regression and its impact on impulse control and the thought process, the processes of introjection and projection, the relationship of group psychology to the super-ego and the ego-ideal, and the dynamics of special group formations: the army, the Church and the state (to which Bion [1959b] later added the aristocracy). Today, we would agree with Jaques (cf. Gibbard *et al.*, 1974, pp. 277–9) that Freud here anticipated Melanie Klein's (1977b, pp. 1–24) concept of 'projective identification', whereby unwanted or disavowed mental content and parts of the self are deposited in a container object, the object being for Bion, the group *qua* group and for both Freud and Jaques, the leader. Freud thus gave us a 'first' object-relations and ego-psychological theory of group and leadership dynamics, as well as a way of understanding the transactions between the individual and the group, the dilemma of individual versus group identity.

## Bion and the 'group-as-a-whole'

A further milestone in psychoanalytic group psychology was Bion's (1959b) groundbreaking *Experiences in Groups*, a series of essays first published in the journal, *Human Relations*, and then in collected form. Bion here elaborated on Freud's *Group Psychology*, but more importantly invoked the object-relations frame of reference of Melanie Klein. Bion made object-relations theory and its insights into the paranoid-schizoid and depressive 'psychotic-like' levels of mentation the basis of understanding regressive group phenomena. He thus opened to investigation deeper layers of group dynamics, the primitive, pre-oedipal, 'part-object' phenomena of anonymous action, fusion and primitive phantasy. He recognized the critical importance for group formation of primitive defences such as splitting and projective identification, and he discussed how unconscious phantasy contributed to the group members' transference relations with the leader and the 'group-as-a-whole'.

Bion accomplished several additional aims in *Experiences in Groups*. He was careful to point out that the group mentality was related to but essentially *different from* individual psychology, something at which Freud (1921) had merely hinted when he speculated that group psychology may have preceded individual psychology in the evolution of the species. Bion's 'basic assumptions' are clearly dynamics which can only occur in and through groups. Bion also postulated a 'work group', a group formation which was task bound and reality-orientated. He thus suggested that groups need not always be regressive, but elaborated little about mature and/or self-actualizing groups, a task reserved for Miller and Rice (1967) and others.

It is important to emphasize that Bion made his extremely brief observations on groups during a short tour of duty as an army psychiatrist at Northfield Hospital in England during the Second World War, and then in further work at Tavistock Clinic in London. As a result of undergoing his own training analysis and supervision with Melanie Klein, Bion then quickly shifted his career trajectory to individual psychoanalysis. The Bion whom group psychologists know well is the one who wrote *Experiences in Groups* and impacted on the Tavistock and A.K. Rice conferences, while the Bion who has had an intense and, as always, controversial impact on psychoanalysis is the one who later focused on borderline and psychotic phenomena and wrote a series of remarkable theoretical and philosophical works which are now being studied intensively by the psychoanalytic community in London and elsewhere (Bollas, personal communication).

In the present volume, both Robert Hinshelwood and John Gordon bring aspects of Bion's later work on thinking processes and containment into focus for group therapists. Furthermore, in the emphasis on containment of group states and on primitive group phantasy, we can see that Bion *qua* psychoanalyst has influenced all of our authors. It was indeed Bion (1959a, 1962, 1970, 1977a) who elaborated Melanie Klein's notion of projective identification into the broader perspective on containment of primitive mental states and unconscious communication. We can see this contemporary emphasis on group containment reflected in virtually all the chapters of *Ring of Fire*. Bion's *Experiences in Groups* served as a mandate to investigate primitive affects and object relations in groups, while his later work on mentation and psychopathology has more subtly infiltrated our thinking in recent years, as both Gordon and Hinshelwood amply illustrate.

## Developments in field theory and general systems theory

The work of Kurt Lewin (1951) in the United States and of S.H. Foulkes (1948) in England provided transatlantic parallel frameworks for an extraordinary expansion of research, training and psychotherapy based on the group-as-a-whole. It may be recalled that Lewin strenuously eschewed the psychoanalytic emphasis on the past, arguing that the sum total of the forces acting on the individual in the group were in the here-and-now, while Foulkes accepted the insights of psychoanalysis in the realm of the individual, but hoped that group analysis would take on its own separate character, reflecting the distinct nature of group dynamics over and above that of the individual.

Lewin's work has had an especially significant impact on the work of one of our own contributors, Yvonne Agazarian, and it is important to see her efforts against the backdrop of Lewinian field theory, although she has gone well beyond Lewin in her recent systems theorizing. Lewin, who was educated in the tradition of Wertheimer's (not Fritz Perls's!) gestalt psychology, the psychology of wholes and patterns, articulated from that tradition how, in groups, 'the whole is greater than and different from the sum of its parts'. He saw the group as a force-field forming an integral whole in which the individual participated and negotiated. He encouraged us to look in the present moment to discover the forces which influenced both the individual's and the group's behaviour, forces which were a function of the group *qua* group, such as group goals, cohesiveness, roles, leadership styles, and so on.

The impact of Lewin on Agazarian can be seen in a number of ways. Most importantly, Agazarian is always and insistently focusing on the group and its subsystems (Agazarian and Peters, 1981). She has an implicit faith, which derives from Lewin, that individual pathology will receive proper attention if the group dynamics are addressed. She thus focuses *away* from the individual members, a strategy which she maintains is less intrusive and less pathologizing (less conducive to iatrogenic illness via self-fulfilling prophecy) than individual-focused methods of group treatment.

Second, Agazarian's view of group development owes a major debt to Bennis and Shepard's (1956) theory of group development. Bennis and Shepard studied *changes* in the group field (as formulated by Lewin and by Bion) *over time*. For Bennis and Shepard it is the group *system* which evolves, and in that ever-changing context, the person grows, resolves conflict, adapts to shifting norms. This view is in sharp contrast to both Bion and Freud, who saw group formations as inherently static and change almost exclusively as a modification of the psychical structure and function of the members of the group. Freud held out little hope that a group could actually develop to higher levels, although he did acknowledge the importance of mature groups which carry out appropriate social functions. Bion, as mentioned earlier, did postulate a mature, 'work group' but said little about its dynamics.

Agazarian, perhaps more than any of her predecessors, has elaborated on how a therapy group 'works', that is, processes information, integrates new members, develops over time, and so on. Further, Agazarian does not appear to make the sharp dichotomy between primitive basic-assumption groups and work groups, which characterize the Bion-related approaches of Tavistock and of Miller and Rice. For her, even primitive group behaviour is group 'work', that is, negentropy. She seems to use the term 'work' in the physicist's sense of 'generating energy and information', defusing the super-ego valuation on work that is sometimes known as the 'Puritan ethic'.

Having myself followed in some measure the development of Agazarian's thinking since around 1975, it seems to me that she has moved from Lewinian field theory, which she had utilized extensively in combination with her own system of analysis of interpersonal communication entitled 'SAVI' (cf. Simon and Agazarian, 1967) to integrate Lewin with a living systems theory incorporating the ideas of von Bertalanffy (1968) and of James Durkin (1980, 1981). Early on, she focused on how groups achieved their goals and how individuals negotiated in the group to overcome obstacles, meet needs and resolve conflicts. She also used information and communication theory models to understand body language, misperceptions and interpersonal pathology as they emerged in the group (Agazarian, 1989). Clinically, she has always been heavily steeped in psychoanalysis, emphasizing individual and group object relations and defence mechanisms.

More recently, Agazarian has developed a point of view which she calls 'systems-centred group psychotherapy' (cf. her chapter in this volume) and which emphasizes such processes as communication between subgroups, parallel processes occurring at different levels and systems ('systems isomorphisms') and group roles as systemic structures. At the risk of oversimplication, we could say that Dr Agazarian has shifted her focus from individuals interacting in a group matrix to an emphasis on the boundary phenomena occurring between and among group subsystems. One has the impression that through a focus on systems boundaries, she has found a practical way to enhance the information flow across boundaries, through the regulation of subgroups, roles and defence mechanisms, thereby giving greater power to the group therapy process as such, while the therapist becomes more of a group facilitator and less directly a modifier of personal and interpersonal psychopathology as such.

If there is a shortcoming in Agazarian's profound, thoroughly researched, increasingly popular and useful model of group therapy, it is, in my opinion, her mixture of categories of concepts which, in my view, do not mix very well. In particular, she moves rather too loosely back and forth between groups as forces, groups as information exchanges, groups as object relationships, and groups as fields. Further, it is sometimes difficult to tell whether she is talking about groups as subjective, phenomenological experiences, or groups as objective, consensually validated configurations of matter and energy. It is of course not just Agazarian who has this problem of a consistent vocabulary and meaning context. Indeed the entire field of group theorizing lacks a common language of discourse. In my opinion, a key to a newer, more internally consistent view of group functioning would be a study of the group as narrative, dialogue and myth (cf. Ettin, 1992, pp. 365–425).

It seems to me that the Foulkesian group-analytic approach, to which we now turn, has just the potential to view group events as dialogue.

## Foulkes's group analysis

A British parallel to Lewinian theory emerged (independently from Lewin) with Foulkes's 'group analysis'. Group analysis has been slow to come to the United States, probably because it is experienced as a competitive foreign import overlapping with the 'native' approaches, but it does appear to be becoming increasingly impactful in the States as evidenced for example by regular, ongoing representation of the Group-Analytic Institute at the annual meetings of the American Group Psychotherapy Association.

The key concept in Foulkes's approach is that of a communications network or 'group matrix' which evolves in the group and takes on varied traits and characteristics over time (cf. de Maré, 1972). Each communication and transaction alters the overall matrix as well as what happens between particular individuals. The individual is seen as a 'nodal point' within the matrix, a social psychological view which contrasts sharply with the conventional idea that the group is the aggregate of the persons who compose it.

Foulkes's theory has an important and as yet little exploited advantage over field theory in that it explains how a group 'field' is constructed as an outcome of the communications among the members. Sometimes the communications occur so rapidly, anonymously and non-verbally as to make the field appear *sui generis*, self-generated. Foulkes termed this a 'condenser effect' and elsewhere used the term 'resonance' (de Maré, 1972, p. 174). Foulkes made communication and interaction central to understanding groups.

In this volume, Foulkes's group analysis is exemplified and utilized most clearly in the contributions of Pines, Gordon and Hinshelwood. Pines focuses on each borderline and narcissistic patient in his therapy group as a 'nodal point' who has potentially both a disruptive and a constructive effect on the group matrix. He lucidly illustrates how the distorted and defective body images of each patient become part of his or her self-system and then translate symbolically into difficulties in empathy and communication. For example, the body image of the borderline is something of a 'leaky vessel', which leads to the inability to contain and communicate affects and develop group boundaries. Conversely, the group matrix has the potential to repair the defective body images through reality-testing, healthy introjection and resolution of primitive defences such as splitting and projective identification. Pines is aware of the slowness of these positive changes over time, and also of the severe countertransference pressures on the therapist who is equally part of the matrix. Pines exemplifies the sensitivity, empathy and tact of the group analyst, reflecting the humanistic orientation of Foulkes's teachings, which genuinely embodied Winnicott's concept of the 'capacity for concern'.

Bob Hinshelwood emphasizes the impact of the contagion and social obedience and conformity effects on the group matrix and on the therapist. He suggests how the therapist must counteract this effect within her- or himself in order to restore her or his leadership and interpretive functions, helping to contain the primitive affects for the group. John Gordon, from a slightly different perspective, achieves an exciting integration of intrapsychic and interpersonal linkages, of Foulkes's 'group free association' (de Maré, 1972, p. 155) and Bion's (1959a) 'attacks on linking', showing how group defence and resistance can entail an active attack on mental processes and on the connections between the group members which form the group matrix. For both, the primary aspect of group life is communication and interrelationship, the 'who-to-whom' of group interaction. They see resistances and acting out as disruptions of that communication process. In their case examples, one finds meticulous attention to who said what to whom and when, consistent with Foulkes's notion of a network or matrix.

### The 'systems of organization' model: Miller/Rice and Tavistock

Particular applications of general systems theory evolved in the context of the so-called 'conferences', i.e. large organizational meetings convened to examine their own group and institutional processes. Such conferences appear to have begun at the Tavistock clinic and then been adapted in various contexts worldwide. One of the main offshoots of the Tavistock conferences has been the A.K. Rice Institute, which stresses its differences from the Tavistock approach, yet has many commonalities with it.

The theoretical rationale for the A.K. Rice group relations conferences have always seemed to me to be anachronistic in comparison with their advanced and sophisticated group methodology. Miller and Rice (1967) regard group relations rather like a large manufacturing company which takes in natural resources – matter, information and energy – processes them in different procedures and departments, and has an output or product. This way of thinking reflects models of economics and assembly-line production as well as the mechanistic biology of the nineteenth century, harking back even further to Descartes, who saw the mind and body as complex machines. It seems to me that contemporary systems theory has gone well beyond such a mechanistic model and that the A.K. Rice proponents should forthrightly address their need for a more sophisticated systems viewpoint and philosophy of human interaction.

Despite this shortcoming, the Miller and Rice 'systems of organization' approach has a distinct advantage over traditional group psychotherapy 'schools' in simultaneously addressing small-group dynamics, intergroup relations, large-group and institutional dynamics.

The key functional elements in the A.K. Rice model include: (a) the primary task; (b) the nature of authority; and (c) the boundary function, with its tasks of import and export, limits and risk-taking. The primary task resembles the 'mission statement' of a corporation, but on a psychosocial plane it is often harder to define and sometimes takes on a metaphysical connotation. Self-study is a common primary task, but there are differences of opinion about who is studying what, and who defines the focus of observation. The authority relation involves organizational hierarchies, such as the relationship between the group therapist and the group members. The boundary function has to do with transactions at junctures between person and group, one group and another, and so on.

The psychological frame for the A.K. Rice approach has been an eclectic borrowing from object-relations theory, ego psychology, and self psychology.

In the present volume, Marvin Skolnick has made excellent use of the A.K. Rice model in his evolution and depiction of a therapeutic community/ day treatment centre for the chronically mentally ill for which he has served and continues to serve as chief psychiatrist and an inspirational force. Skolnick defines the primary task of this therapeutic community as the 'promotion of healing and psychosocial development of psychiatric patients in the least restrictive environment'. The way in which he defines 'healing' and 'least restrictive environment' sets the tone for a synthesis of three perspectives: (a) the A.K. Rice model of group relations; (b) a reconsideration of the social definition of madness; and (c) the use of object-relations constructs to define a holding and containing environment based on ongoing dialogue and problem solving between staff and patients.

Skolnick explicitly acknowledges the social and political nature of 'mental illness' and of 'madness'. He emphasizes the distinction for therapists and institutions between the authority relationship of social control and the healing role of providing a holding and containing 'maternal' environment. Citing the work of Michel Foucault (1965), Erving Goffman (1961) and others suggesting that 'madness' is socially defined, he emphasizes that mental patients have areas of extraordinary insight and true self-awareness which are threatening to society. He distinguishes between the use of psychiatric intervention to suppress these insights from interventions which promote holding and containment of primitive unmetabolized emotional states.

By so defining the primary task of the treatment centre as a dialogue between staff and patients which promotes holding and containment, Skolnick provides a frame of reference for observing and modifying the interactions between staff, patients and their various groups and subgroups according to the primary task definition. In effect, he thus draws a boundary which to some extent shields the community from external and internal pressures which militate towards social control and medical 'overkill'. He illustrates how events at the boundaries between the various groups within the institution, as well as the input of the entire community, can be used as supports for containment and holding. Finally, in the context of discussing group systems, it is appropriate to interject a reminder of the very fruitful models and insights about small groups and group psychotherapy which emerged in the 1950s through the 1970s. Saul Tuttman's chapter in this volume, for example, makes use of Scheidlinger's formulations of group identifications and the positive group transference. Scheidlinger (1955, 1964) held that many of the benefits of group therapy derive from the mutual identifications of the members with one another which can serve as a source of both self-insight and new introjections. He also recognized that the group evokes a benign maternal transference object for the members, which gives them a sense of support, hope, and caring (Scheidlinger, 1974). Scheidlinger's views provide a necessary antidote to Bion's view of the group *qua* group as a threatening phantasy object which has to be defended against by the membership. Tuttman (this volume) utilizes Scheidlinger's (1974) perspective on the group-as-mother to delineate how the group can provide a 'second chance' for the patients to work through their childhood derailing of the symbiosis/separation–individuation process.

## Interpretations of group dynamics based on mourning

Freud, in *Totem and Taboo* and *Moses and Monotheism*, set the stage for an understanding of group mourning by speculating that the primal group originated with the murder of the father-leader by the siblings. According to Freud, the act of parricide not only represented the oedipal dynamics of identification and competition, love and hate, but also established the newly formed group's need to cope with the loss, to make reparation for the associated guilt, and so on. Thus, a group can be said to form in a state of mourning a lost object.

A different but not incompatible way of looking at the problem is to note that entry into any group entails sorting out and mourning those aspects of self and of past group identifications which are not consistent with the new group goals and norms. Relinquishing these attachments and identifications is a *sacrifice* which establishes a need to grieve and also, *pari passu*, establishes group cohesion. Group development is thus a reworking of the self in the group and thus parallels the separation–individuation process (Mahler *et al.*, 1975), which itself requires mourning the separation from the primal mother of symbiosis.

Aspects of such ubiquitous mourning dynamics can be seen, for example, in Bion's (1959b) basic-assumption 'pairing', where a messianic couple appears to restore hope to the group (implying that there has been a loss of hope), in the 'disenchantment' subphase following the group revolt or 'barometric event' of Bennis and Shepard (1956) and which directly parallels the act of parricide of which Freud wrote, and in the variety of externalization mechanisms such as projective identification and scapegoating used by the group to ward off the 'depressive anxiety' of owning one's own aggression and 'bad' part-self elements.

Such formulations are thus far consistent with the mainstream of group theory and do not require assumptions beyond the 'traditional' psychoanalytic metapsychology. However, it is possible to expand upon Freud's (1920) *Beyond the Pleasure Principle* where he suggests an entirely new dimension of a death drive. The cultural anthropologist, Ernest Becker, in a groundbreaking book entitled *The Denial of Death* (1973), held that the structure of the personality is founded on the characterological and symptomatic mechanisms the individual develops to cope with mortality and death.

Jeffrey Kauffman's chapter in this volume articulates the radical proposition that what Becker said of the individual can also be said of the group, that group development is rooted in the pervasive significance of death (what Kauffman calls 'thanatropics'). He attempts to develop an understanding of groups as a function of omnipresent mourning processes and defences against mourning. Kauffman's work echoes a prescient but little-known treatise by the Italian analyst, Franco Fornari, entitled *The Psychoanalysis of War* (1974) which postulates that war phenomena are the consequence of misdirected, regressive mourning processes, what Fornari calls a 'paranoid elaboration of mourning'.

Kauffman relates his theory to the Kleinian depressive position, which holds that the infant develops precursors of mourning in order to manage the imagined risks to the primary caregiver stemming from the infant's own aggressive drive. Kauffman also sees the importance of Bion's (1970, 1977a) work on the hitherto neglected aspects of catastrophic change, chaos and transformation in individual and group life. The dynamics of mourning are a response to the catastrophe of death and allow for radical, even mystical, experience and transformation of the self.

The key question raised by such a 'thanato-centric' view of groups is not whether mourning is a key dynamic of groups – that is well documented – but whether a radically new group psychology is necessitated to account for the data. Following Kuhn's (1970) criteria for the emergence of a new scientific paradigm, are there indeed anomalous phenomena which cannot be accounted for by extant theory, or is a new theory simply a matter of old wine in new bottles? Do we need a radical theoretical revision emphasizing death awareness to account for group mourning or other behaviour in groups? Further, an important question which Kauffman needs to consider relates to the nature of primary narcissism and omnipotence. That is, can loss and death awareness be experienced before there is a primary object relation and the possibility of loss? How can the fear of death precede either ontologically or developmentally the existence of a primary attachment and narcissistic cathexis of both self and object? Kauffman, in a personal communication (1993), acknowledged his position: 'The possibility for loss is an existential condition of attachment. It is copresent with primary bonding and with the earliest incipient self.' The more traditional view has been that awareness of loss is an acquired response to the absence of the caregiver.

Thus far I have focused attention on a variety of formulations about the group-as-a-whole. By my frequent references to psychoanalytic theory, I have illustrated how, in the present context, group psychology and psychoanalysis are intimately intertwined. Since the contributors to this volume all utilize psychoanalysis in different ways to grasp the intrapsychic, interactive and group-systems processes which take place within the group, and since developments in psychoanalytic theory and practice are regularly 'inputting' to group therapy on an ongoing basis, I shall turn now to some contemporary psychoanalytic formulations for understanding the personality, psychopathology and transactions with the group.

## PSYCHOANALYTIC PERSPECTIVES ON SELF, OBJECT AND MIND

Although virtually all the authors of this volume are steeped in the psychoanalytic models of the mind, there is considerable variation in the way each uses psychoanalytic perspectives. This book clearly reflects the current state of psychoanalysis for which Wallerstein (1992, pp. 3–62, 203–4) has used the apt phrase, 'psychoanalytic pluralism'. Ego psychology, self psychology, Kleinian, Bionian and British Independent school object-relations theories are absorbing one another's insights and are employed in a flexible, adaptive way by clinicians. Furthermore, one can see that 'anomalous' perspectives on attachment, loss, catastrophic change and the so-called 'death instinct', as well as other vantage points hitherto 'outside the fold' of traditional psychoanalysis, are beginning to knock more insistently on the door of psychoanalytic and group theory. One can see the influence of such controversial perspectives in the way that Kauffman (this volume) attempts to formulate a group psychology based on the pervasive human experience of death and dying, loss and grief.

Similarly, the perspectives of Bion on thought disorder, of Lacan on language and the unconscious (Sarup, 1992) and of Kohut (1971, 1977) on the self are beginning to impact upon object-relations theory (Schermer, 1993), creating a stimulating dialogue which in turn can be expected to impact upon group psychotherapy.

In what follows, I want to try to provide a short 'pluralistic' discussion of the varied psychoanalytic concepts which the contributors to *Ring of Fire* have brought to their work. Although clinical psychoanalysis focuses on the intrapsychic dimension of experience rather than the group-as-a-whole, recent work in psychoanalysis has reinforced the earlier held view of Harry Stack Sullivan (1953) that the primary dynamic dimension is interpersonal in nature. Langs (1976), for example, postulated a 'bipersonal' field for understanding the patient's productions. Atwood and Stolorow (1984) have elaborated upon the 'intersubjective' phenomenology of all mental life and communications. Mitchell (1988) argued for a 'relational' understanding of psychoanalytic constructs and process. Daniel Stern (1984) has researched the 'interpersonal world' of the infant. Christopher Bollas (1987, pp. 173–276; 1989, 1992) understands how all that occurs in a therapy session has a contribution from both the analyst and the patient. Bollas (1992) further elaborates that an internal object is a creative, idiomatic use of the external object, and so in a manner not unlike that stated by Guntrip, each personality has an 'inner group' consisting of his or her introjects in dialogue with one another, contributing to the idiom or 'valence' (Bion, 1959b) which partly defines how the person interacts with others. Psychoanalytic theory has definitely 'come of age' as an interactional psychology.

## Current trends combining object-relations theory, self psychology and ego psychology

In recent years, four perspectives or schools of thought have come to dominate psychoanalytic theory and practice: Kleinian object-relations theory; the British Independent school of object relations; ego psychology; and self psychology. Today, we are witnessing a period of dialogue, cross-over, synthesis, and integration of these perspectives.

Kleinian theory (Klein, 1977a and b; Segal, 1974) brought into focus the primitive, pre-oedipal layers of the psyche, emphasizing the role of unconscious phantasy, the anxieties and defences of the paranoid-schizoid and depressive positions and the infant's struggles to manage anxiety, guilt and 'bad' internal objects. The 'British school', sired by Fairbairn (1952), Winnicott and others, shifted attention to the quality of the interaction between mother and infant. Modern ego psychology is a functionalist, biologically rooted psychology emphasizing the mechanisms of adaptation and defence and therapeutically working to strengthen these functions (cf. Blanck and Blanck, 1974). Self psychology (Kohut, 1971, 1977; Chessick, 1985) has emphasized the narcissistic sector of the personality and the way in which self-cohesion and self-esteem are developed, maintained and restored by significant others who are known in self psychological parlance as 'selfobjects'. Because self psychology emphasizes the relational connection between the self and its selfobjects, Bacal (1992) contends that it is, *de facto*, an object-relations theory, although others (e.g. Stone, 1992) hold that self psychology offers a distinctly different model from object relations. In truth, self psychology emphasizes relational aspects of the mother–infant dyad, but its way of understanding how such a relationship is incorporated in the psyche is quite different from object-relations theories; and the self psychologist operates therapeutically in a manner that differs markedly from, say, a Kleinian, and is more subtly different from a Winnicottian or Fairbairnian.

In *Ring of Fire*, several of our authors, specifically Pines, Tuttman and Skolnick, utilize various combinations and permutations of these theoretical schools to achieve their own particular syntheses and 'self-conscious pluralism'. On the whole, it is my impression that they avoid the danger of a hodgepodge mixture of constructs but that it is clinical acumen rather than theoretical integration which keeps them away from the 'primrose path' of conceptual confusion. Almost despite the differences, the authors keep returning to their observational data base and use concepts which emphasize the overlapping areas of diverse theories. For example, Pines uses concepts such as 'sense of self' and 'self-image' in a way which is not unrelated to Tuttman's discussion of 'identifications' and ego functions. These writers seem to perceive commonalities among theories more than differences, and there is very little contentiousness in their views. On the other hand, neither do they try to debate the very significant differences between the theories.

Malcolm Pines has been strongly influenced by both object-relations theory and self psychology. Group analysis, of which Pines is one of the seminal and central figures, emphasizes the nature of the self as a social process in a manner similar to George Herbert Meade's 'symbolic inter-actionism' (de Maré, 1972, pp. 32–3) in sociology and Harry Stack Sullivan's 'interpersonal relations' and 'self-system' in psychiatry (de Maré, 1972, pp. 59–60). The self is defined by its social interactions, and so, in this view, is predominantly social in nature, even in schizophrenic isolation, narcissistic grandiosity or idiosyncratically expressed neurosis. Historically, an early monograph by the nineteenth-century French psychiatrists Lasegue and Falret (see Michaud, 1964) on the *folie à deux* seems to have presaged such a perspective, a century before it had become part of the psycho-dynamic *Zeitgeist*.[2]

As a result of such a view of the self as socially defined, Pines is able to see the vicissitudes of the self-deficits in borderlines in groups. In an earlier paper (1982), Pines explored how mirroring in the Kohutian sense of reflecting the child's budding narcissism is also mirroring in the group sense of accurate empathy, feedback, identity formation and role definition. In his contribution to the present volume, Pines shows in detail how such mirroring and related processes operate in a therapy group to heal the deficient structures of the borderline patient.

Kohut strived for a psychological approach which concentrated on the 'experience near' phenomenology of the patient's self, as accessed by the therapist's empathy (Kohut, 1977, pp. 302–4). For that reason, he tended to reject instinctual and object-relations interpretations of internal experience as too abstract to be utilized by the patient with a self-deficit. Stone (1992) has applied Kohut's model in this rigorous mode to group psychotherapy. Pines, however, seems to suggest that object relations and ego inter-pretations need not be 'distant' from the patient's and group's experience. For example his emphasis on boundaries and the polarity of fusion and individuation, coincides with the patients' experience of their own body images, their frustrations in relating to other group members, and their need to extrude their own sense of shame and 'badness'. Thus, as the group boundaries become sharper yet realistic, 'semi-permeable', flexible and adaptive, so the members' internal perceptions and defences achieve higher levels of functioning, and the patients gradually internalize these boundary shifts into their self- and body images. This process well exemplifies what is meant by the use of the group process as the medium of treatment, of psychotherapy '*by* the group'.

A developmental linkage among the different schools of thought comes from Daniel Stern's research on the infant's 'sense of self' (Stern, 1984; Lichtenberg, 1983). Stern notes that the infant constructs out of his interpersonal experience what he calls RIG's, 'representations of interactions that have been generalized', which in turn foster an ever-developing and ever-expanding awareness and representation of a 'sense of self' (Lichtenberg, 1983, pp. 29–39). Stern's concept of self seems deliberately designed to be equally compatible with self psychology, ego psychology and object-relations theory. Self psychology emphasizes narcissistic mirroring and idealization processes in the sense of self. Ego psychology points to the adaptive context of the symbiosis/separation–individuation process. Object-relations theory focuses on projective/ introjective processes and the management of primitive anxieties involving internal and external objects. Stern's 'sense of self' incorporates these varied dimensions, regarding them as simultaneously ongoing relational processes.

Finally, the vital function of 'soothing' and 'holding' introject (Buie and Adler, 1982) relates to the self psychology formulation of empathy and the amelioration of narcissistic injury, the ego psychology emphasis on optimal frustration and tolerance of separation, and Winnicott's object-relations concepts of 'holding' and the use of the transitional object.

With such connections between the schools of thought, Pines is able to attune to his patients' inner worlds while having a conceptual schema which he can translate into affectively meaningful terms. He appears to use theory to remain connected to his patients *even when they attack the empathic function*. This represents an important function of theory as a container within the countertransference.

## The significance of the therapist as an observer and a 'nodal point' in the group matrix

Countertransference, an issue which has received increasing and detailed attention in psychoanalysis (cf. Gorkin, 1987), and which plays a powerful role in group dynamics, since the therapist is the identified and influential leader of the group, is also coming into its own as a topic of concern in group psychotherapy. Klein and Bernard's chapter in this volume brings countertransference into sharp focus, and they do it in an appropriately 'heated' context: co-therapy. The co-therapy dyad creates a vulnerability in the therapists in two respects: (a) they observe themselves and one another in intimate interactions and so are likely to spot (and one hopes address) countertransference difficulties; (b) borderline and narcissistic patients may 'seize the moment' to form a collusive 'divide and conquer' resistance and attack the co-therapy dyad.

Klein and Bernard approach countertransference from the perspective which developed in working with borderline patients: the so-called 'totalistic' view. In this view, countertransference is defined as the sum total of the feelings and reactions of the therapist, so that it may have conscious and realistic components, and not just represent a problem or 'bind' of the therapist. This allows for a less judgemental view of the therapist, and it also regards therapist reactions as potential sources of information about the patients and the group.

Klein and Bernard call their perspective for the co-therapy relationship a 'systems/developmental' view. They emphasize Kernberg's (1975) work on splitting and projective identification as well as the Miller and Rice (1967) systems model as inspirations for their own thinking. Such a way of looking at the group treatment of borderlines is both similar to and different from that of Pines. It would seem to me that Pines would stay in an interpretative and empathic role on a consistent basis, and sort out his countertransference reactions outside the group, while Klein and Bernard would emphasize confrontive interventions, and boundary and limit setting as containers for the borderlines' split-off affects. My impression is also that Klein and Bernard, like Tuttman, would advocate judicious sharing of counter-transference feelings with the group members.

### The role of Bion's later theorizing about psychopathology and mind

Bion has had a pervasive impact on contemporary psychoanalytic thought, yet very few analysts and group theorists have read his later work either in the original or in the several excellent interpretations that are available (e.g. Grinberg *et al.*, 1977). Bion initially followed along the lines of Melanie Klein's investigations of primitive mental states, emphasizing the nature of the psychotic's disordered thinking process. He achieved high stature in the British Psycho-Analytical Society, becoming their president and achieving many other honours. Eventually, he moved to Los Angeles, where he had a major impact on psychoanalytic training there. His work then went well beyond that of Klein, achieving its own theoretical structure. Bion has had a major impact internationally, and there are now institutes, for example in São Paulo, Brazil, which emphasize his teachings. Bion died in 1980. His wife, Francesca, and his publishers have continued to edit and publish his writings after his death. Since several of the contributors to *Ring of Fire*, especially Hinshelwood and Gordon, utilize Bion's 'post-*Experiences in Groups* thinking', an all too brief overview of his theorizing is very much in order.

The central element in Bion's thinking was his use of the philosophical 'idealism' of Plato and of Kant, which postulated 'worlds' beyond the doors of perception, which Plato called 'ideal forms' and

Kant termed 'things-in-themselves'. Bion (1977a and b) recast the notion of ideas beyond or prior to experience into a theory of the unconscious by attempting to explain how 'things-in-themselves', which he viewed as unmetabolized sensory input or 'beta elements', became transformed into perceived images, dreams and internal objects, which he called 'alpha elements'. He termed the process of transformation 'alphabetization', and saw this as a normal mental function, in which beta elements, 'thoughts without a thinker', become alpha elements, the content of dreams, fantasies, imagery, and so on. These are then built up into concepts and abstract systems of thought. Bion held that the psychotic patient suffered from a defect in alphabetization. Consistent with his earlier work on groups, he felt that groups, too, may suffer from such a defect, leading to a type of group psychosis. This could occur in group regression, or when genuinely new and radical ideas, which he called 'messiah thoughts', disrupted the group 'Establishment' (Bion, 1970).

Bion (1959a) had earlier noted a particular type of defect in the psychotic thought process which he termed 'attacks on linking'. Psychotic and schizophrenic images and thought processes not only appear unrealistic, but also often fragmented and bizarre. Examples would include the apparently random associations of the 'word salad' of hebephrenics and the bizarre and dislocated images in psychosis where, for instance, snakes might emerge from the head (for example the Medusa image), and which seem to be made of fragments from other images which had been previously destroyed in some mental catastrophe. Bion speculated that one source of such fragmented and bizarre associations and images was an active mental 'attack' on the original linkages which, for a variety of reasons, were too painful for containment.

A key 'mental health' feature of early mothering which keeps such bizarre images from being 'permanentized' in the infant and allows for proper linkages among thoughts, is the mother's state of attuned 'reverie' whereby she is able to empathize and respond to the infant's internal states. By so doing, she forms a 'thought apparatus' and a container for the infant's inner experience: mother and infant together become a 'thinking couple' (Bion, 1962). There is a parallel between the mother's reverie and the therapist's hovering attention.

John Gordon's chapter in this volume contributes an important work in which he notes and observes the group's 'attacks on linking'. He describes a group session in which the members attack the connections between one another as well as the internal representations; in fact they attack the thought process itself.

With the same general concern for the quality of group mentation, Robert Hinshelwood focuses on the therapist's containment of such attacks and his or her role in restoring the normal group function, a role akin to that of the mother who contains and metabolizes the infant's inner states.

Salomon Resnik emphasizes yet another feature of Bion's theorizing, namely, the 'bizarre objects' and affect states which result from the attacks on linking. Bizarre objects are most clearly evident in schizophrenic patients, but may be present in any group where fragmentation experiences occur. I myself have observed on a number of occasions how co-therapists are fantastically fused into a bizarre object by the group and then collusively manipulated.

In certain of his later writings, especially in *Attention and Interpretation* (1970) and in his autobiographical 'fantasy', *A Memoir of the Future* (1990), Bion concerned himself with the role of leadership and new ideas in group relations. Bion, with both a hint of humour as well as very serious intent, considers the importance of the 'mystic' (himself?) in challenging the assumptions of the 'Establishment' (traditional psychoanalysis?) and provoking transformation and change in the group. Bion suggests that some thoughts which express deep truths come new and unbidden to the group or to some person in the group. He calls these 'messiah thoughts' and questions the dubious ability of the Establishment to assimilate the new ideas. In a way, deep analytic work in the group is likely to unearth these messiah thoughts and create a sense of danger in the therapist, members, or both.

Kauffman's chapter in this volume explores the role of the mystic and of messiah thoughts when he discusses the transformative role of death awareness for the group. He proposes what might be called a psychology of transformation for group work, and this would reflect Bion's considerations on containment, catastrophic change and mysticism. Similarly, but without direct reference to messiah thoughts, Skolnick says that severely mentally ill patients sometimes offer such thoughts to a psychiatric culture which is not prepared to hear them, and he asks that therapists and other caregivers try to acknowledge these underlying messages. This raises the important question of the difference and relationship between delusion and insight.

Bion (1992) increasingly saw truth and psychosis as overlapping processes, and his writings sometimes have the disturbing appearance of psychotic dissociative ramblings, especially the four parts of *A Memoir of the Future* (1990) which is a type of biographical fantasy with some possible implications and 'lessons' within it. In the present volume, the chapters by Agazarian, Kauffman, Skolnick and Resnik in particular bring us very close to this 'primitive edge' of group experience where the border between insight and madness, between order and chaos, is often hard to discern. In the future, it is likely that group therapists who have the courage to do so will be increasingly called upon to enter that realm and to cogitate on how the therapist shall manage events in that 'boundary subsystem' between what

Lacan has called the Symbolic, the Imaginary and the Real (Sarup, 1992), between the symbolic order of language, rules and expectations, the world of images, and the hallucinatory/delusional world of the concretely real. Parenthetically, it could be said that the future of our species may also depend upon our ability to make such a distinction.

## REVIEW AND CONCLUSIONS

At this point, we may complete our tour of the multiple theories and concepts utilized by the contributors to *Ring of Fire* to grasp the difficult layers of disturbance and change in the group regression. It seems to me that the diversity of ideas is more apparent than the areas of convergence and coherence. Yet I believe that we would find consensus among the contributors on the following points:

1  That a group has a life of its own, is a living system that cannot be understood as if it were a simple aggregate or a machine.
2  That psychoanalytic constructs, hitherto regarded as speaking to the intrapsychic life of the 'mind', also refer to interactive and intersubjective features of communication and groups.
3  That so-called 'regressive' group phenomena are not merely 'primitive' or 'distorted' but also possess the potential for self and group transformations. Further, that deep internal changes cannot occur without allowing regressive processes which may at times be quite disturbing and distressing to all concerned.
4  That countertransference feelings and reactions are not merely interferences with the proper conduct of the group, but play important communicative and signalling functions and can help the therapist detect changes in the group system as well as the emotional life of particular members.
5  That the earliest pre-oedipal object relations are evoked in groups and permit opportunities for a 'second chance' to work through such object relations.
6  That groups are not static, but evolve dynamically through various states and conditions which affect how individuals behave in the group.
7  That disorganization, chaos, death, aggression and unknowing are important and hitherto neglected aspects of groups as of all living systems.
8  That no single theoretical frame can explain group phenomena.

I shall end this excursion with a question that will not be answered in this volume, but which I thought about as I read these wonderful and courageous explorations of group psychotherapy. On this issue, I suspect, we would find vastly different views from our authors. It is the question of the extent to which each retains his or her faith in a scientific world-view and understanding of groups, and the extent to which each has gravitated towards a more humanistic, literary-hermeneutic or even mystico-spiritual sense of the way groups operate. To some degree of course, such a spiritual sense goes very deep, even to what Winnicott called the 'incommunicado core' of a person's being. But certain aspects of the question are capable of being spoken, and Kohut's emphasis on 'experience near' subjectivity and empathy (cf. Chessick, 1985, pp. 297–310), Bollas's (1987) discussions of the human 'idiom', and Bion's forays into the realm of transformation and messiah thoughts, among other things, seem a far cry from the Helmoltzian/ Fechnerian physico-chemical psychology of the young Sigmund Freud of one hundred years ago. We are committed to a scientifically based enterprise, yet in the past decade our observations and theories have burst the bubble of mechanistic constructs, even going well beyond social psychology and transactionalism, and so we might want to take some time out to ask, Where are we at the very core of our work?

## NOTES

1  There are major scientific and philosophical differences regarding the extent to which order, structure and unity are present in mind and nature. We can agree with Einstein (Clark, 1971, p. 97) that disorder and chaos merely mean that we haven't yet understood a higher-level order. Einstein said at one point in response to quantum theory's postulate of a degree of randomness in the motion of electrons, 'God does not play dice with the world'. Or, at the other extreme, we can say that order is an illusion which can be deconstructed (Derrida, 1978). A compromise position which has evolved recently in mathematics is 'complexity theory' (Lewin, 1993), which holds that order and chaos are the extremes of a universe whose structure is irreducibly complex. In addition, postmodernism has political and social implications which are highly controversial (Rosenau, 1992) and with which I do not necessarily agree.

2  The author is indebted to John Sonne, MD, for bringing this fascinating document to his attention.

## REFERENCES

Agazarian, Y.M. (1989) 'Group-as-a-whole systems theory and practice', in Y.M. Agazarian (ed.), *Group: Special Issue on the Group-as-a-Whole, Journal of the Eastern Group Psychotherapy Society* 13 (3, 4): 131–55, winter, New York: Brunner/Mazel.

—— and Peters, R. (1981) *The Visible and Invisible Group*, London: Routledge & Kegan Paul.

Ashbach, C. and Schermer, V. (1987) *Object Relations, the Self, and the Group: A Conceptual Paradigm*, London: Routledge & Kegan Paul.

Atwood, G.E. and Stolorow, R.D. (1984) 'Psychoanalytic phenomenology: toward a science of human experience', *Psychoanalytic Inquiry* 4 (1): 87–105.

Bacal, H. (1992) 'Contributions from self psychology', in R.H. Klein, H.S. Bernard and D.L. Singer, *Handbook of Contemporary Group Psychotherapy*, Madison, CT: International Universities Press, 55–86.

Becker, E. (1973) *The Denial of Death*, New York: The Free Press.

Bennis, W.G. and Shepard, H.A. (1956) 'A theory of group development', *Human Relations* 9: 415–37.

Bertalanffy, L. von (1968) *General Systems Theory*, New York: George Braziller.

Bion, W.R. (1959a) 'Attacks on linking', *International Journal of Psycho-Analysis* 40: 308–15. Republished in W.R. Bion (1967) *Second Thoughts*, London: Heinemann.

—— (1959b) *Experiences in Groups*, London: Tavistock.

—— (1962) 'A theory of thinking', *International Journal of Psycho-Analysis* 43: 306–10. Republished in W.R. Bion (1967) *Second Thoughts*, London: Heinemann.

—— (1970) *Attention and Interpretation*, London: Tavistock.

—— (1977a) *Seven Servants*, New York: Jason Aronson.

—— (1977b) *Two Papers: The Grid and Caesura*, Rio de Janeiro: Imago Editora.

—— (1990) *A Memoir of the Future*, London: Karnac.

—— (1992) *Cogitations*, London: Karnac.

Blanck, G. and Blanck, R. (1974) *Ego Psychology: Theory and Practice*, New York: Columbia University Press.

Bollas, C. (1987) *The Shadow of the Object*, New York: Columbia University Press.

—— (1989) *Forces of Destiny*, London: Free Association Books.

—— (1992) *Being a Character*, New York: Hill & Wang.

Buie, D.H. and Adler, G. (1982) 'Definitive treatment of the borderline personality', in R. Langs (ed.) *International Journal of Psychoanalytic Psychotherapy* 9, New York: Aronson.

Chessick, R. (1985) *Psychology of the Self and the Treatment of Narcissism*, New York: Jason Aronson.

Clark, R.W. (1971) *Einstein: The Life and Times*, New York: Avon (reprinted 1972).

Derrida, J. (1978) *Writing and Difference*, Chicago, IL: University of Chicago Press.

Durkin, H. (1964) *The Group in Depth*, New York: International Universities Press.

Durkin, J. (1980) 'Boundarying: the structure of autonomy in living groups', Seventh Annual Ludwig von Bertalanffy Memorial Lecture, Society for General Systems Research Annual Convention, San Francisco, CA.

—— (1981) *Living Groups: Group Psychotherapy and General System Theory*, New York: Brunner/Mazel.

Ettin, M. (1992) *Foundations and Applications of Group Psychotherapy*, Boston, MA: Allyn & Bacon.

Fairbairn, R.W.D. (1952) *Psychoanalytic Studies of the Personality*, London: Routledge & Kegan Paul.

Fornari, F. (1974) *The Psychoanalysis of War*, New York: Anchor Books.

Foucault, M. (1965) *Madness and Civilization*, New York: Pantheon.

Foulkes, S.H. (1948) *Therapeutic Group Analysis*, London: Maresfield Reprints.

Freud, S. (1920) *Beyond the Pleasure Principle, Standard Edition*, 18: 3–66.

—— (1921) *Group Psychology and the Analysis of the Ego*, S.E., 18, 67–135.

—— (1939) *Moses and Monotheism*, S.E. 23, 17–140.

Gibbard, G., Hartman, J. and Mann, R. (eds) (1974) *Analysis of Groups*, San Francisco, CA: Jossey Bass.

Gleick, J. (1987) *Chaos*, New York: Viking.

Goffman, E. (1961) *Asylums*, New York: Anchor Books.

Gorkin, M. (1987) *The Uses of Countertransference*, New York: Jason Aronson.

Grinberg, L., Sor, D. and de Bianchedi, E. (1977) *Introduction to the Work of Bion*, New York: Jason Aronson.

Grotstein, J. (1986) 'The dual-track: contribution toward a neurobehavioral model of cerebral processing', *Psychiatric Clinics of North America* 9: 353–66.

Grubrich, S.I. (1988) 'Trauma or drive–drive and trauma: a reading of Sigmund Freud's phylogenetic fantasy of 1915', *Psychoanalytic Study of the Child* 43: 3–32.

Kernberg, O. (1975) *Borderline Conditions and Pathological Narcissism*, New York: Jason Aronson.

Klein, M. (1977a) *Love, Guilt, and Reparation and Other Works: 1921–1945*, New York: Delta.

—— (1977b) *Envy and Gratitude and Other Works: 1946–1963*, New York: Delta.

Klein, R.H., Bernard, H.S. and Singer, D.L. (1992) *Handbook of Contemporary Group Psychotherapy*, Madison, CT: International Universities Press.

Kohut, H. (1971) *Analysis of the Self*, New York: International Universities Press.

—— (1977) *Restoration of the Self*, New York: International Universities Press.

Korzybski, A. (1948) *Science and Sanity: An Introduction to Non-Aristotelian Systems and General Semantics*, 3rd edn, International Non-Aristotelian Library, distributed by Institute of General Semantics, Lakeville, CT, USA.

Kuhn, T. (1970) *The Structure of Scientific Revolutions*, 2nd edn, *International Encyclopedia of Universal Science* 2: 2, Chicago, IL: University of Chicago Press.

Langs, R. (1976) *The Bipersonal Field*, New York: Jason Aronson.

Lewin, K. (1951) *Field Theory in Social Science*, New York: Harper & Row.

Lewin, R. (1993) *Complexity: Life at the Edge of Chaos*, New York: Macmillan.

Lewis, J. (1976) *No Single Thread: Psychological Health in Family Systems*, New York: Brunner/Mazel.

Lichtenberg, J. (1983) *Psychoanalysis and Infant Research*, Hillsdale, NJ: Analytic Press.

Mahler, M., Pine, F. and Bergman, A. (1975) *The Psychological Birth of the Human Infant*, New York: Basic Books.

Maré, P.B. de (1972) *Perspectives in Group Psychotherapy: A Theoretical Background*, New York: Science House.

Maturana, H. (1980) *Autopoesis and Cognition: The Realization of the Living*, Dordrecht: Reidel.

Michaud, R. (ed.) (1964) Translation and bibliography of Lasegue, C. and Falret, J., *La Folie à deux; ou folie communiquée* (1877), published as a supplement to *The American Journal of Psychiatry* 121.

Miller, E.J. and Rice, A.K. (1967) *Systems of Organization*, London: Tavistock.

Mitchell, S.A. (1988) 'The intrapsychic and the interpersonal: different theories, different domains, or historical artifacts?', *Psychoanalytic Inquiry* 8 (4): 472–96.

—— (1992) 'Contemporary perspectives on self: toward an integration', *Psychoanalytic Dialogues*, 1991, 1 (2): 121–47.

Pines, M. (1982) 'On mirroring in group psychotherapy', *Group Therapy Monograph* 9, New York: Washington Square Institute.

Rosenau, P.M. (1992) *Post-Modernism and the Social Sciences*, Princeton, NJ: Princeton University Press.

Sarup, M. (1992) *Jacques Lacan*, Toronto: University of Toronto Press.

Scheidlinger, S. (1952) *Psychoanalysis and Group Behavior: A Study of Freudian Group Psychology*, Westport, CT: Greenwood Press (reprinted, 1974).

—— (1955) 'The concept of identification in group psychotherapy', *American Journal of Group Psychotherapy* 9: 661–72.

—— (1964) 'Identification, the sense of belonging and of identity in small groups', *International Journal of Group Psychotherapy* 14: 291–306.

—— (1974) 'On the concept of the "mother group"', *International Journal of Group Psychotherapy* 24: 417–28.

Schermer, V. (1993) 'Diversity at the core: the emergence of contemporary variations in the metapsychological "scaffolding" of psychoanalysis', presentation at the Annual Meeting of Division 39 of the American Psychological Association, New York City, 18 April.

Segal, H. (1974) *Introduction to the Work of Melanie Klein*, 2nd edn, New York: Basic Books.

Simon, A. and Agazarian, Y.M. (1967) *SAVI: Sequential Analysis of Verbal Interaction*, Philadelphia: Research for Better Schools.

Speck, R. (1967) 'Psychotherapy of the social network of a schizophrenic family', *Family Process* 6 (2): 208–14.

Stern, D. (1984) *The Interpersonal World of the Infant*, New York: Basic Books.

Stone, W. (1992) 'The clinical application of self psychology theory', in R.H. Klein, H.S. Bernard and D.L. Singer, *Handbook of Contemporary Group Psychotherapy*, Madison, CT: International Universities Press, 177–208.

Sullivan, H.S. (1953) *The Interpersonal Theory of Psychiatry*, New York: Norton.

Wallerstein, R.S. (1992) *The Common Ground of Psychoanalysis*, Northvale, NJ: Jason Aronson.

Winnicott, D.W. (1969) 'The use of an object', *International Journal of Psychoanalysis* 50: 711–16

—— (1971) 'Transitional objects and transitional phenomena', in *Playing and Reality*, New York: Basic Books, 1–25.

# 3 The phases of group development and the systems-centred group

*Yvonne M. Agazarian*

## EDITORS' INTRODUCTION

Yvonne Agazarian is a pioneering figure in the application of General Systems Theory (GST) to group psychotherapy. Here she offers a comprehensive 'systems-centred' theory of the development of the psychotherapy group, rich with theoretical insight, practical exemplification and provocative viewpoints which challenge conventional wisdom regarding group psychotherapy.

Dr Agazarian's theory of group development derives from Bennis and Shepard's (1956) formulation, but goes well beyond it. Agazarian draws on her own theory of living human systems, Lewinian field theory, the notion of 'systems isomorphisms' from GST, Shannon and Weaver's information theory, Anna Freud's classic work on *The Ego and the Mechanisms of Defense*, and the object-relations concepts of splitting, projective identification and containment to provide a unique synthesis and an 'active' systemic approach to group work which has the potential to enhance the power and effectiveness of the group therapy situation.

Anyone who has worked with Dr Agazarian can testify to her extraordinary ability to bring into focus and elucidate the dynamics of groups, as well as her discomfiting capacity to 'disturb the universe' of our cherished belief systems. In the words of T.S. Eliot, as one 'ascends the stair' of her formulations on group development, one will know with clarity how, in the course of group life, 'In a minute there is time / For decisions and revisions which a minute will reverse'. At this edge of chaos and transformation in the group matrix is the potential for change and growth.

## GROUP DEVELOPMENT

a crucible, a relentless, uncompromising,
inexorable pressure on the outer shell of defenses
burning hot and cold
a ring of fire around the inner core of ash
transformation – and the many splendoured phoenix.

## INTRODUCTION

Systems-centred theory approaches all living things, as small as a cell and as large or larger than society, by defining them as systems that are similar in structure, function and dynamics. This then sets up a hierarchy of classes of living systems where each class, and every member in it, has a set of common factors which apply to all classes in the hierarchy; and each class, and every member of each class, is unique unto itself! The advantage of describing all living human systems isomorphically in this way is that what one learns about the dynamics of any one system says something about the dynamics of all the other systems in its hierarchy.

It is through the discrimination and integration of similarities and differences that systems develop from simple to complex (Agazarian, 1989b). The system of the group-as-a-whole develops from simple to complex by splitting into differentiating subgroups which have the potential to remain in communication with one another across their boundaries (Agazarian, 1989b). In a systems-centred group, the basic unit is not the individual member, but the subgroup (Agazarian, 1989a).

In the systems-centred approach to the phases of development in group psychotherapy, the group is not left to develop 'naturally' while the therapist 'contains' the process and judiciously interprets it to make it conscious to the group, as is the case when the approach is primarily psychodynamic. Rather, group forces are deliberately exploited; certain group behaviours deliber-ately encouraged, others discouraged; and all dynamics are legitimized so that they can be explored and understood (Agazarian, 1992c).

### Functional subgrouping

In systems-centred groups, the primary task is to develop an interdependent problem-solving system so that the work of therapy is done in the process of learning how to do the work of therapy. From the first few minutes of the very first group, members are actively discouraged from withdrawing into themselves with their pain – or into fantasy to avoid their pain. Members are encouraged to work interpersonally, to talk to the group or to a particular member and to stay connected to one another. This sets up a work style of supportive mirroring, which is the key to the therapeutic power of functional subgrouping.

The very process of learning to subgroup requires members to relate to others as well as to themselves. Members learn that there is an important difference between encouraging another member's work, paying lip service to subgroup work, and joining the subgroup with heart as well as words. When the members have difficulty working, rather than being encouraged to struggle through their resistances (as in patient-centred therapy) they are encouraged to turn to their subgroup and make space for a fellow-member who has more immediate available salience for (or less resistance to) the next step. In this way, the member who starts to work 'rests' without guilt when he or she can go no further, while others in the subgroup continue to work. Resonating with the subgroup work, the 'resting' member takes his own next step when he or she is ready.

It is important to emphasize, however, that learning to work in subgroups is no easy task. For many members, being required to join a subgroup is experienced as a violation of individuality. Joining a subgroup is like learning a social role. It requires devoting the self to the subgroup goal, selecting from the internal range of responses those that build upon and deepen the experience that is being built and deepened by the work of the subgroup. Spontaneity in resonance with the group is an intimate and healing experience. Failures in resonance result in solo activity. At best, the solo individual relates to the group (or the self) as if to an audience, and at worst re-creates the experience of being forever alienated and isolated, alone. No matter how great the pain and frustration of isolation, however, joining can be experienced as a compromise, or even a violation, of the essential sense of self.

## Containing

'Containment' is a central concept in systems-centred group psychotherapy. Differences generate conflict yet systems mature and transform through recognizing and integrating differences. When differences are similar enough, they are integrated with less conflict. When differences are too different, however, they are split off and projected into *containing* subsystems. This resolves one level of the conflict and creates another.

The simplest management of differences in human systems is to contain them in stereotype subsystems with stereotype communications. This is easily done when differences are manifestly obvious, as in gender, race, age or status. Dynamic differences however, cannot be so easily stereotyped. The most predictable 'containers' of dynamic differences, manifest at every level in the hierarchy of human systems, from individuals to societies, are the containing subsystem roles of the identified patient and the scapegoat.

In groups, there is great resonance between the delegation of containing roles – such as the scapegoat or the identified patient – and the individual member salience for playing the roles. Perhaps it has always been too much to expect individual group members to contain their impulses to act out, when their own conflicts in development are re-aroused and aggravated by the conflicts in the developing group.

In systems-centred groups, it is the subgroup, not the individual member, that is required to contain different sides of predictable 'splits' around difference. When the group-as-a-whole works to 'contain' the conflict consciously as a working task, then it is no longer necessary to delegate conflicting differences to a scapegoat, an identified patient or a deviant pair. In this way, the group learns to exploit the natural tendency to split the 'like me and good' from the 'not like me and bad'. By *deliberately* containing the good/bad split in different subgroups, each side of the split can be explored with less conflict than when contained as different parts of the inner self. By employing the technique of functional subgrouping, the mechanisms of splitting and projection are utilized rather than pathologized. When these mechanisms are seen as functional, there is less pressure to deny or repress their manifestations (Agazarian and Janoff, 1993).

## PSYCHODYNAMICS WITHIN THE SYSTEMS FRAME

Systems theory is a meta-theory (von Bertalanffy, 1969; Agazarian and Janoff, 1993). Thus, framing dynamics from a systems-centred point of view adds an additional dimension to the psychodynamic framework. There is a significant compatibility between psychodynamic and systems constructs. Psychodynamic constructs of the ego, the id and the super-ego, for instance, can be redefined as interdependent subsystems without changing the frame. Both psychodynamic and systems therapists would agree that therapeutic outcome results from modifications of the 'communications' across the boundaries between the ego, the id and the super-ego 'subsystems'. Dynamically monitoring 'transactions across the boundaries' results in: changes in the *permeability* of the boundary between the super-ego and the ego; changes in selectivity in the transfer of information across the boundary between the ego and the id; and changes in the 'ability' of the ego to discriminate, process and integrate information across the boundaries, within, between and among systems at all levels of the abstraction hierarchy. Importing systems thinking imports clear guidelines for structural and functional interventions that may complement and strengthen the effectiveness of dynamic interventions.

Similarly, Anna Freud's work on the ego mechanisms of defence translates directly into the operational definitions for restraining forces at boundaries between, within and among systems (Agazarian, 1988). Jung's 'collective unconscious' is implicit in any understanding of the system of the group-as-a-whole. Melanie Klein's (Hinshelwood, 1989) important work on splitting and containing and projective identification is fundamental, both to understanding the human dynamics underlying the systems perspective, and to the generalization of the systems framework to object-relations theory. And of course, Bion's (1959) 'basic assumptions' of flight and fight, dependency and pairing not only generalize to, but also enrich and deepen, the understanding of system dynamics as applied to systems of human beings (Agazarian, 1989b).

What the systems-centred orientation introduces to the psychodynamic approach is not a competing theory, but different strategies, theoretically derived from hypotheses about how human systems function, that may well provide a more efficient way of developing the structure for regressions 'in the service of the ego'.

However, although the psychodynamic constructs are compatible with systems constructs, they may conflict when used as a language for interpreting the development of the group system. What becomes abundantly clear, is that the human tendency to discharge hostility in punitive language can find an easy expression by pathologizing normal system dynamics. In the early phases of group development almost all therapist communications, however descriptive, are experienced as super-ego injunctions. Inevitably, before the modification of the relationship with authority, interpretations of unconscious motives, however empathic, vastly increase group anxiety, defensiveness and dependency. What is worse, when the members imitate the intervention style of the therapist (as all members do before they gain autonomy in the group) their interpretative style is not only an identification with the aggressor, but also an effective method of turning communication into ammunition in the power, control and status fights of the first phase of group life (Agazarian, 1989b).

It is for this reason that systems-centred therapists talk, not in the language of pathology, but in terms of difficulties, inherent to the human condition, that are general manifestations of developmental issues aroused by the phases of group development, and dynamics that are central to the development of all living human systems. It is also for this reason that the focus of attention is not on *interpretation* but on *communication*: not on *content* but on *context*.

## Context vs content

A focus on the context and function of communication rather than its content is an acquired skill. The systems-centred therapist neither interprets individual dynamics, nor attends to the denotations and connotations of the content in the communications of the individual members. Rather, the focus of attention is on the communication transactions between subgroups. Just as in the early days of psychoanalysis, it became necessary to learn how to understand communication in relationship to its unconscious meanings, so now, in the early days of systems analysis, it is necessary to learn to understand communications in relationship to their potential for transferring information across the boundaries in space and time; among, within and between systems in the hierarchy.

This requires understanding communications as driving and restraining forces that balance the system in relationship to its goals (Agazarian, 1989b). Reducing restraining forces in communication is achieved by reducing the defences in sending and receiving. Reducing defences in the sending and receiving transaction involves influencing the permeability of boundaries to the information contained in the communication. Influencing boundaries entails, not only the management of boundaries in time and space but also between reality and unreality. Reducing the restraining forces to communication transactions across the boundaries within, between and among all systems in the hierarchy *is* therapeutic change!

Lewin's force-field (1951) serves as an excellent model of the relationship between driving and restraining forces to communications at the boundary. Lewin recognizes these forces as 'vectors', which have direction, velocity (energy) and a point of application. As a dynamic concept, he defines tension as oppositely directed vectors, which is also his understanding of conflict. Communication transactions across systems boundaries, therefore, can be understood as forces in conflict, and the drive to communicate and the defences against communication can be defined in a force-field of the group's behaviour.

At the level of interpersonal communication this is isomorphic to the psychodynamic attention of managing the permeability of the boundaries between the conscious and the unconscious: increasing boundary permeability when obsessive defences predominate, decreasing permeability when there are regressive defences. Decreasing or increasing the permeability of boundaries depends upon the relationship between conflict and context. This has great significance when applied clinically to the fragile or brittle patient 'as systems'. When there is poor discrimination between the boundaries within the system, as well as between the system and the environment, as there is with many regressive patients, it becomes important to increase the *awareness of context* before any change in the fluidity or rigidity of boundaries are made, so that internal boundary management is developed *in the context of the environment.*

It has been emphasized that transformation occurs as a function of both the system's ability to integrate discriminations of similarity and difference, and the time it takes for this process to take place. In groups where boundary permeability is a major problem, the speed in which discriminations are made and integrated becomes an important factor. System goals are primary and secondary: primary are the goals of survival and development; secondary are the goals of environmental mastery. When boundary management is related to survival and developmental goals, the process of rediscrimination and reintegration takes more time.

Monitoring boundary permeability does not mean that the systems-centred approach represses the underlying primal experience of the underworld of the unconscious which arouses such annihilating terror and primitive defences in the group. But rather than allowing the underworld to surface in the early phases of group, the systems-centred focus ensures that the group first builds a structure so that regressions are in the context of group development. In each phase a different structure is generated as a containing context for the individual confrontation of the terror engendered, both from primitive conceptions and also from the primitive defences against them.

In the first phase of development, when the group makes the transition from the good to the bad leader, the individual members also struggle with annihilating fantasies towards the therapist: in the unconscious displacements to the group's identified patients and scapegoats: as well as towards the therapist. The primitive experiences of murderous rage towards the therapist occur in the controlled regression of the authority issue in the group-as-a-whole. The nightmare fantasies in the underworlds of human experience are brought to light in a context where they can be modified in here-and-now reality.

In the clinical field we are increasingly paying attention to the difference that our clinical orientation makes to how dynamics manifest in groups. Take for example the differences in approach to the 'identified patient' and 'scapegoat' roles. One approach will analyse the unconscious motives of the individuals; another the interpersonal repetition compulsions or the role suction; another the games people play; and still another will focus on the here-and-now function of the behaviour for the developing system. As the twig is bent so the bough grows. Even more important to our field is the question of how we tell the difference, in our work in therapy, between when we address issues that are generic to treating human ills, and when what we address are iatrogenic, regressive or defensive constellations elicited by our own clinical interpretations (Agazarian, 1989b). In other words, when is our practice a function of our own rationalized projective identifications which require human containers for the differences that we and our society cannot bear, and when a function of enabling us to cross the boundaries between our different human systems so that we can work together towards our therapeutic goals? Looking at our work through systems eyes, and understanding the immutable influence of phases in the development of human group systems, may be a step towards this important discrimination.

## DISCOVERING THE GROUP-AS-A-WHOLE

Bion (1959), a pioneer in thinking about the group-as-a-whole as a system independent of the people who were its members, lived at a time when either/or thinking was the norm. Bion observed the familiar defensive responses of the individual members to each other, to authority and to the internal conflicts that exist in a group. He also observed consistent defensive responses to group conflicts that did not appear to be the property of individual members but rather to be a property of the group-as-a-whole. He failed to observe that these conflicts tended to occur in a sequence. As Bion spent a relatively short time actually working with groups, the marvel is not that he did not see phases of group development, although it would have been a useful influence on the development of group-dynamic theory and practice if he had, but that he saw as much as he did.

In order to apply systems thinking to groups it takes the ability not only to quantum jump levels of abstraction – which Bion certainly must have possessed in order to formulate his basic assumptions as properties of the group-as-a-whole rather than the individual – but also the willingness to think about human beings beyond the psychoanalytic definitions for being human. Bion certainly possessed the background. Bion was acquainted with Lewin's field theory and von Bertalanffy's general systems theory, each of which offer objective, dispassionate models for human behaviour. Bion, however, chose to frame his thinking about the group-as-a-whole through Klein's concepts of psychotic anxieties and the defences against them. Hence his basic assumptions of fight and flight, pairing and dependency, and hence, also, his all too brief relationship with the dynamics of groups. Ganzarain (1989) reports Bion's rueful reply when questioned on this: 'Paula Heimann and Melanie did not like analysts working with groups!' Then, 'That sounds pretty childish!' And, 'I guess I had already made my contribution . . . hence, I moved on, to explore another topic . . . psychotic thought.'

The consequences for Bion, and for the new group-centred paradigm in group psychotherapy, was a focus on psychopathology and psychosis, in contrast to an exploration into dynamic formulations compatible with, for example, the principles of field theory and general systems theory. I was perhaps luckier than Bion in that my first analyst introduced me to Shannon and Weaver's information theory and thus to the concept of 'noise': defined as the entropic resultant of the ambiguities, contradictions and redundancies inherent in man's communication with man.'

There is an inverse relationship between the ambiguities, redundancies and contradictions (noise) in the communication process and the potential for transferring information in the process (Shannon and Weaver, 1964; Simon and Agazarian, 1967). The greater the noise the less predictive probability and, therefore, the greater the chaos. Chaos is defined in terms of 'noise': random or uncoded information. Reframing chaos in terms of noise frames chaos as a researchable construct which reflects the universal rhythm of organization and disorganization, matter and mass, entropy and negative entropy. Noise is assumed to be inherent in the input and output communication transactions that cross system boundaries. Communication transactions occur across boundaries at all levels of the system hierarchy and reflect, on the one hand, the inner state of the system and the primary system goals (survival and development), and on the other hand influence the system's relationship with its environment, the environment itself and the attainment of the systems' secondary goals (environmental mastery) (Agazarian, 1986).

Thus in formulating the dynamics of groups, I had available to me the concept of noise to make sense of the primal forces underlying group experience. I understood the dynamics of primal forces to be, not kin to psychosis as they are so often interpreted, but as de-differentiated information: chaos, in the sense that the manifestations of the dynamics of groups cannot be predicted although their principles can be hypothesized.[2] It can be assumed that human beings have an instinctive compulsion to 'make sense' of the unknown. Primary 'sense' is primitive sense: archaic, anthropomorphizing, primordial, chaotic, often experienced as psychotic. Thus each new experience arouses the terror of the unknown combined with curiosity about it, which fuels the impulse to explore, organize and master.

## DISCOVERING PHASES OF GROUP DEVELOPMENT

An intensive comparison of the different theories of group development, in both social psychology and in psychology, has been made by Ariadne Beck (1981). She found that although different authors had different labels for the different events that they observed in groups, the sequence and description of those events were consistent across writers. However, even though phases of group development have been discussed in the literature since the

1950s, they are still not a commonly accepted reality among group psychotherapists.

There is an evident and predictable sequence of phases in group development to be seen if the therapist knows where to look. Seen or unseen, each phase has a different and forceful impact on what happens to a group. When seen and understood, these forces can be deliberately harnessed in the service of the therapeutic goals; when not, the impact of these forces go unidentified and unaddressed. Hence the stereotypic and repetitive creation of the roles of the identified patient and scapegoat in therapist-orientated and patient-orientated, and even in some group-orientated, psychotherapy groups.

Bennis and Shepard (1956) did the original work that resulted in the sequence of group developmental phases described in this chapter. Their work on group development was based on their observations of repeated and consistent sequences of individual behaviour that occurred in groups of university students that they observed over a period of more than five years. They categorized these predictable sequences of events into phases of group development. Theoretically, they were influenced by Sullivan and Bion, particularly by Bion's basic assumptions about group defences of dependency, flight–fight and pairing. Bion, in his turn, had been greatly influenced by his analyst, one of the pioneers in the development of object-relations theory, Melanie Klein. Thus the concepts of 'containment' and 'projective identification' are implicit in Bennis and Shepard's group developmental theory, and so, by implication, are the underlying dynamics of Klein's depressive and paranoid-schizoid positions, which were subsequently addressed in detail by Bennis (1961).

Bennis and Shepard (1956) observed two discrete phases in group development. They called the first phase 'Dependence–power relations' and the second phase 'Interdependence–personal relations'. They noted that the leader-orientated *phase one* gave way to the group-orientated *phase two*: separated by an important transformational 'barometric event'. They noted two predictable subphases in phase I, the first a more passive phase of flight, and a second more active fight phase during which the group progresses from passive stereotyping to active scapegoating, first of one another and then of the leader. Scapegoating the leader is not always overtly hostile. It can be manifested by covertly seducing the leader into membership or denigrating the leader as an incompetent. In fact, in therapy groups, as distinct from training groups, it is often easier for the group covertly to seduce authority than to challenge it overtly.

When the group successfully overthrows authority, the group temporarily resolves the conflict around good and evil by splitting: locating 'evil' in the 'bad-leader', and 'good' in the 'group-as-a-whole'. Bennis and Shepard called this 'barometric', in that after a successful confrontation of the leader, the group energy is freed from the compelling struggle with authority and is turned, instead, towards issues of intimacy. Bennis and Shepard noted that in the five years that they observed their student groups it was not unusual for the group to remain in the first phase of development throughout the seventeen-week term, either failing to reach, or aborting, the direct confrontation with the leader. Unfortunately, it is not unusual for the therapy group to remain in the first phase of development throughout its entire life. In systems-centred terms, there has not been sufficient system development for the 'transformation' to occur.

## INDIVIDUAL AND GROUP DEVELOPMENT

Before describing the phases of group development from the systems-centred point of view, it is important to point out that whereas there are many similarities between the phases of the development of a group and an individual, there are also important differences.

For example the developmental phases of a group parallel but do not correspond with the developmental phases of an individual at the manifest level. The dynamics of the human baby can be described (for instance) as characterizing first a paranoid-schizoid developmental position and second a depressive position in the important process of separating and individuating into a differentiated human being. Group dynamics can be described as manifesting behaviour more typical of the depressive position in the struggles for power and control in the first phase of group development, and moving into (regressing into) the paranoid-schizoid position in the second phase when individuals in the group attempt to develop intimacy with one another. This does not deny that the fragmenting terror of the world of partial objects is lurking beneath the more manifest struggles for power and control. (So too, in human development, the dynamics of the paranoid-schizoid phase lurks under the depressive in the socializing development of the child.) It is axiomatic that the terror present in the beginning moments of a beginning group is a nameless rather than an un-named dread, well understood by Ashbach and Schermer (1987): 'The void . . . is the *absence* of information, direction, connectedness . . . which attends a situation where structure is minimal.' Although the authors are referring to individuals, their words apply equally well to all human systems. Notwithstanding the presence of these dynamics in the first phase of group development, the paranoid-schizoid dynamics are not *manifest* until the second phase of development.

In the first phase, the group first denies its paranoid rage and, in a reaction formation familiar to every therapist, creates a patient to cure of the dependency hunger that is feared in the self. This is the solution of compliance with authority with the hope that in passive followership the self may be actualized – thus the identified patient, who contains for the group the anguished cry for someone to be able to depend upon, and who is offered up to the therapist by the group for an analysis interminable. When this solution fails, the defiant, rebellious, paranoid rage breaks through the reaction formation, targeted first towards the scapegoat and ultimately towards the therapist. It is the whole object that the group wishes to destroy. From the depths of the experience it is true that the fantasies in the group are primal and bloody. The cry is that there is room for one object only: it is either you or I. When these dynamics are acted out in society, leaders are murdered, and so are the followers in the ghettos; and when society's reaction formation turns their identified patients into scapegoats, the pogroms are directed towards society's helpless and homeless as well.

Being able to discriminate between the initial power/control phase and the later intimacy phase of a developing group can be clinically important for the individual patient. For example insight for individual members into individual dependency and counterdependency, relationships to authority and work with their underlying depressive dynamics occur most easily in the first phase of group development; and insight into individual issues of interpersonal closeness and distance, love addiction, loneliness, alienation, despair and work with the underlying paranoid-schizoid dynamics occur most easily in the second phase of group development.

When individual work is 'in phase' members in the group spontaneously access memories and feelings that serve as stimuli that are relevant to the general work and specific to their own. The loss of an apparently appropriate new member, however, may well bewilder a therapist who does not 'match' the member to the developing group phase. In a developing group, the dynamics of each phase of development are available as a major force that has impact upon the individual experience. Within each member, salient developmental issues are aroused that resonate with the issues that the group is in the process of mastering. Thus, groups provide the context in which individual developmental issues are revisited. Group members mature as the group learns to work and to love and to play.

The issues on the surface in the first phase of group development have to do with members' dependency upon the therapist and competition with one another. Therefore it appears that the manifest human dynamics in the first phase of group development are developmentally equivalent to the struggle for individual autonomy. Indeed, the behaviour and content in the group reflects this. The projections in the interactions between the members in the group are fully object-related, in spite of the fact that the projections also contain dynamics that are not. The creation of the identified patient and scapegoat are certainly a function of projective identification, the splitting off from the self of the unacknowledged and unconscious parts of the self, projected into another. However, the group roles themselves are a function of the repetition compulsion, and the group work with the *people* who are volunteered into these roles is object-related. The communication patterns between the group and the identified patient or deviant, for example, are *socially* stereotypic, as is the content.

Underlying system dynamics are no different whether the 'groups' observed are therapy groups, training groups or groups of people working on a board or in committee; no different in organizations nor even in nations! What makes the difference to the work of any group system is not group dynamics but the clarity of the relationship between the dynamics and the goals. Group structure is related to function, and group function is related to group goals. Appropriate boundaries, therefore, are boundaries that are both permeable to information and able to contain the information so that it can be organized into a driving force in relationship to the group goals (Agazarian, 1992b). The major difference between training groups and therapy groups in this task is that the task of the training groups is most often to make boundaries more permeable; whereas in the therapy groups the task is often to make them appropriately permeable. The more inappropriately permeable the boundaries, the greater the danger that undifferentiated information will flood the system.

In systems-centred group therapy, therefore, group-as-a-whole boundaries are developed to *contain* the regression in the *group* before any regression in function takes place. Thus some facility in opening or closing boundaries at all system levels has been developed *before* the group works on the goals that have brought the members into therapy. Before the group addresses the issues of organizing the information stored in the chaos of the primary process, skills in information-organizing have already been acquired. That this structural work in no way dilutes the experience of the primary process, but rather increases both access and insight, is illustrated later in this chapter.

## PHASES OF DEVELOPMENT IN THE SYSTEMS-CENTRED GROUP

There are many paths to a goal. The goals in systems-centred therapy are the same as the goals of psychodynamic therapy, but the ways of reaching them are different. The development of a group results from an interplay of the same forces that characterize the process of development of any human system: separation, individuation, integration and transformation. All human systems move from primal dependence to independence and interdependence, and the course is determined by successive integrations of approach and avoidance forces (Agazarian, 1988). From the systems-centred perspective, the relationship between developmental forces and the developmental goals are related to systems, and are manifested in 'roles', not in 'people'. The 'people' who occupy these roles are 'transients' playing a part in the work of the group.

## Roles as subsystems

For example, developmental dynamics around dependency are not interpreted as a property of 'dependent' or 'counterdependent' *individuals* but rather as approach and avoidance forces. These forces are manifested in roles. (Agazarian and Peters, 1981). 'Roles' are subsystems, characterized by boundaries and goals, that serve a dynamic system function. Roles maintain a system equilibrium while the system develops interdependence. For example, in the passive phase of *flight*, the group 'identified patient' role is created to contain the group's passive and helpless dependency, offered to the 'good' leader to nurture and cherish. In the active *fight* phase, the group 'scapegoat' role is created to contain the active deviance, in an attempt to bind the murderous rage so that the bad leader is not destroyed. However, which members will occupy these roles is not predetermined. Many will volunteer, but few will be chosen! Thus dependent or counterdependent forces are contained in subsystems of systems – isomorphic (similar in structure and function) – and can be observed simultaneously at the system levels of member, subgroup and the group-as-a-whole. Compliant over-dependent and defiant counterdependence roles are a constant in the first phase of group development, and perform a special containing function in the development of functional dependency. Similarly, in the second phase, containment of blind trust and fusion on the one hand, and mistrust and alienation on the other, are not the property of 'over-personal' and 'counter-personal' individuals, but roles that are in service of functional separation and individuation.

In systems-centred groups, the norms of working, not alone but always in a subgroup, make it more difficult for the group to create either an identified patient or a scapegoat, and easier for the group to subgroup around understanding the conflict that the group is attempting to master by setting up the roles. The identified patient, for example, contains for the group both the wish to be helped and to help, as a defence against helplessness and in the service of masochism. The scapegoat, on the other hand, contains for the group both the wish to victimize and to be a victim, as a defence against differentiating and in the service of sadism. In both cases, promoting functional subgrouping to explore the issues contained in the roles is rewarding for the members and resolving for the group-as-a-whole. This is particularly important in the case of the vulnerable patients. In the containing structure of a subgroup, for example the patient who does not yet have the ability to feel compassion for either him- or herself or for others can be 'held' while the subgroup contains the regression necessary to understand the impulses involved in scapegoating or creating the identified patient. When the vulnerable patient expresses, for example, sadism without the expected retaliation, and at the same time can listen to other members explore, compassionately, both the experience of being sadistic and being the target of sadism, the potential for future interpersonal connections are made.

In the pages that follow, I address the expected course of development as outlined by Bennis and Shepard (1956) and my own earlier work (Agazarian and Peters, 1981) as well as the modifications that are introduced by the systems-centred techniques of functional subgrouping. When subgroups contain different sides of the group 'splits' and the group-as-a-whole 'contains' the conflict as a working task, it is no longer predictable that conflicts will be projected into a scapegoat, an identified patient or a deviant pair. In systems-centred theory, system development results in an interplay of forces inherent in separation, individuation, integration and transformation.

## PHASE I: LEADER-ORIENTATED

When social behaviour fails, as it must in a therapy group, the group first coalesces around creating a deviant role as a container for the projectively identified aggression. This first takes the form of creating an identified patient, later a scapegoat, a hero or a cause. Creating an identified patient or a scapegoat is often considered a difficult but inevitable event in group psychotherapy. Indeed, in some forms of therapy, putting people on the 'hot seat' or encouraging the group to use scapegoating to promote interpersonal insight is seen as a useful form of therapy (Agazarian, 1992b). The systems approach in family therapy (Bateson, 1972) and the group-as-a-whole work in Tavistock (Coleman and Bexton, 1975) did much of pioneer work in recognizing that the system creates specific roles to serve containing functions for group projections. It is relatively easy to recognize the phenomenon when the group creates the role of scapegoat; not so easy to recognize that the role of the 'identified patient' serves the same containing function for the projective identifications of the group, and often also for the leader!

In Phase I, the preoccupation with the politics of power and control are the resultant of defensive manoeuvres that protect the system from the frustrations that are inherent in dependency, and the deeper annihilation anxiety that is aroused in the separation–individuation struggle. The multi-dimensional dynamics of the early days of a new group are familiar to all psychodynamic therapists. Which level of regression is salient to the work of the developing group in this phase is a matter of some controversy, and has been discussed in this chapter under the section 'Individual and group development' (pp. 46–8).

From the systems point of view the major force to be contended with is the flight from functional dependency into the defences against impulses to be dependent. As this dynamic flight is common to therapists as well as patients, *dependency* is often given a bad name in groups. Indeed, Bion claims 'dependency' as one of the basic assumptions. Few interpret his basic assumption of dependency as a defence *against* dependency; many interpret that dependency *is* the defence. Much work in the beginning of a systems-centred group is directed towards legitimizing dependency and the exploration of the consequences of the defences that make it difficult to depend on either the self or others. The ability to subgroup depends upon it. As will be explored in much greater depth later, there is a relationship between the ability to develop some functional dependency upon the therapist and upon the process of subgrouping, and how virulent the paranoid threshold will be as the group works through Phase II, and how usefully its members can use the group as a transitional space in the Winnicottian sense (1974).

The systems-centred goal of phase one development, therefore, is to undo the defences against dependency disappointment and restore the ability to be functionally dependent. Nothing human can be achieved unless a functional dependency can be developed among the members, in relationship to the therapist and to the group process, for the life and work of the group. This is well understood by others in the field, although they may not use the label 'functional dependency'. Fairbairn (1952) spoke of the human movement and growth from 'dependence' to 'independence' to 'interdependence'. Ganzarain (1992) noted, with respect to the development of a therapy group, that 'this group displayed appropriate dependency, which led to the members realistically assimilating the help I offered and integrating it to foster their further emotional growth.'

How painfully vulnerable the group is in its first attempts to be compliantly dependent upon the therapist is shown in the excerpt below:

*Fern:* Well, I don't exactly know what you mean by work in here, can you explain that to me?

*Therapist:* So you have a question that you're not quite sure how to answer. Is anyone else in that boat?

*Group:* Silence.

| | |
|---|---|
| *Fern:* | Mm. |
| *Group:* | Silence. |
| *Fern:* | Well, what am I supposed to do? |
| *Mark:* | Yeah! (Mark joins the subgroup.) |
| *Fern:* | What exactly am I supposed to do? |
| *Mark* | |
| *(to Fern):* | I want to know the answer to your question. |
| *Annie:* | Yeah! (Annie joins the subgroup.) |
| *Fern:* | Well, I don't have the answer. |
| *Annie:* | I don't have the answer. |
| *Mark:* | I was kind of wanting her (the therapist) to answer. She didn't really answer. |

(Agazarian, 1991a)[3]

## PHASE I: SUBPHASE IA
## FLIGHT AND THE IDENTIFIED PATIENT

The flight subphase of Phase I is characterized by group behaviour that is predominantly dependent, stereotypic and conforming. Members come together around similarities that are mainly irrelevant to the goals of the group but are highly relevant to political survival. The following doggerel caricatures the stereotype responses to authority that are obvious to the observer but not to those members who are caught up in acting them out.

### Passive compliance

'Tell us to jump and we'll ask you how high,
We promise we'll never question you why.'

### Active compliance

'We'll stand on your shoulders and speak with your voice;
Make them do what you say, and give them no choice.'

### Defiance

'Whatever you say we will do the reverse,
And dare you to say that we are perverse.
We'll always know better and tell everyone so,
So "off with your head" and away we all go.'

Insight into these responses comes relatively easily in subgroup work around passive compliance, less easily in the work around active defiance. The passively compliant part of the self emerges as obedient, conforming, pleasing, adaptive, and lovingly merging with blind trust: given to flight and avoidance and addictive 'love'. Members, with most salience for this response, recognize how easily and spontaneously they subgroup around their similarities, and how difficult it is to tolerate differences. It comes as useful insight, as members explore the passive and compliant aspect of their responses to authority, how easy it is for them to volunteer as the identified patient in the group, and how often the group volunteers them. The compliant subgroup often recognizes a consistent and debilitating underlying depression which defends them against the full experience of both their disappointment and aggression when the 'identified patients' are not cured. It is more difficult for the compliant subgroup to experience the aggression that they defend against and their tendency is to act out the aggression by sabotaging themselves, the therapist and the group by following the letter of the law but not the spirit.

In the early phases of group development, the group-as-a-whole can suddenly turn on an active member, and either scapegoat him or her or elect him or her as a surrogate leader! Most active members can tell tales of the suddenness of their rise to power, followed by an equally swift descent when their leadership did not provide the solution to the problems they had been elected to solve.

The role of the identified patient is a stabilizing solution to the tensions in the flight subphase. When it manifests, it is like a 'play within the play': a pairing that both creates a patient for the therapist to cure, and provides the therapy that the group feels the therapist is failing to provide. Understanding this, enables the group to understand their attempt to create an isolated subgroup to act out the wish for therapy – and enables the group to do the first important learning in how to take back whatever conscious projections are available to them.

Below is a good example of how the group-as-as-whole dynamics of creating the 'identified patient' are isomorphic to the individual dynamics that create the 'premature adult' or 'parentified child'.

*Maggie:* So why are you here, why are you here?

*Carrie:* ... feel like, I feel scared to say it like, uh, well, it's just that, it's just that I'm not very happy and I find like I work a lot, I work very hard. And uh ...

*Maggie:* What do you do?

*Carrie:* I do counselling, with kids, in schools.

*Mark:* In schools?

*Carrie:* Yeah, I work a lot and I just don't feel very good, about, I don't know what. And then I have times when I just don't feel like doing anything and I wake up at night, and I can't sleep, and I really feel weird sometimes when I wake up. I don't feel very happy. And that's why I'm here.

*Mark:*       Mm.

*Maggie:*   I know what that's like. (Joins the subgroup.)

*Annie:*     Well, how long have you felt that way? (Takes on the role of the authority.)

*Carrie:*    I don't know, my whole life.

*Annie:*     When you wake up sometimes, you said you felt weird. What's that like?

*Carrie:*    Um, I don't know, why do you want to know? (Resisting the role suction.)

*Annie:*     Well, this is a self-help group obviously so the best we can do is to try and help each other, I think. I want to help you. (This affords an opportunity, if the climate is right, to point out to the group that the therapeutic attention to Carrie, as a potential identified patient, is at the same time a reproach to the 'bad' therapist.)

*Carrie:*    Well, that's nice.

*Annie:*     I don't want to put you on the spot.

(Agazarian, 1991a)

## TRANSITION: FROM SUBPHASE IA TO SUBPHASE IB FLIGHT INTO FIGHT

The transition from flight to fight is the transition from passive to active. The actively compliant subgroup learns about their identification with the aggressor, and their tendencies to try to bully other members into compliance with authority. The actively and passively defiant subgroups explore the many manifestations of their overt and covert sabotage of authority.

It is commonly understood by therapists that without insight, human systems are doomed to repeat rather than to change. However, as in all human dynamics, nothing is quite that black and white. In every repetition there is the potential for development. The example below shows how spontaneous subgrouping enables the members to support one another as they move towards tentative defiance, on the brink of exploring the depth of their disappointment in the therapist.

*Fern:*      I'm still waiting to hear from her. I mean how do I know just talking about my problems is the job? I've been talking about my problems for years and nothing's ever happened.

| | |
|---|---|
| *Sally:* | Yeah, right. |
| *Annie:* | Well, we can talk about her (the therapist's) problems but I don't think that's going to help. |
| *Carrie:* | Whose problems? (Giggles.) |
| *Annie:* | Her problems! |
| *Mark:* | (Laughs.) |
| *Annie:* | That's not going to help. |
| *Adam:* | Group therapy . . . we'll all be the therapists . . . |
| *Annie:* | I love it! |
| *Adam:* | . . . and she can be the patient! |
| *Group:* | (Whole group laughs spontaneously.) |
| *Annie:* | Love it! |
| *Sally:* | This is how to have fun! |
| *Mark:* | Pick on somebody bigger than you! |
| *Sally:* | Bigger than you, right! |
| *Mark:* | Fine. I like that! |
| *Adam:* | But if we're all together then she's not bigger. |
| *Annie:* | I'm not sure about that. |
| *Carrie:* | This makes me nervous, now, because I'm afraid we made her mad. |

(Agazarian, 1991a)

In the systems-centred group, the transition into the fight phase marks the transition from work that is primarily targeted at the cognitive defences against anxiety into work that targets the character defences against impulse. In the subphase of flight, the group learns to tell the difference between the feelings that arise from their conflicts, and the symptoms that result from the defences against the anxiety, tension and irritability that is engendered by the frustration that these conflicts arouse. It is in this phase that members learn that tantrums and acting out and depression are defensive expressions of anger, not the anger itself. That the experience of anger is quite different from the experience of anger mixed with defences against anger.

In the fight subphase, role relationships are identified. The role relationships in the first phase of development are a repetition of those originally developed in earlier struggles with authority. Typically, these role solutions fall into relationships of either compliance or defiance, and occur between peers as well as with authorities. Exploring these role relationships brings to light the related character defences: like the passive-aggressive aspect of compliance; the aggressive activity of defiance. Character defences are ego-syntonic in a way that tactical and social defences are not. In making the character defences manifest, the systems therapist also encourages the group to look at what they are likely to cost the group in its development. This is the first step in making character defences ego-alien. Through subgroup work, the consequences of the compliant and defiant roles are experienced as giving power to others while keeping powerlessness for the self.

The strongest character defence against impulse is stubbornness. Stubbornness is characteristically evoked in the group whenever there is a power struggle between the group and the therapist. The tragedy of stubbornness is that, while on the one hand it saves the inner life, on the other hand it makes it impossible to live it. Stubbornness makes it impossible to experience any inner life relationship with either the self or other. It is particularly important to the development of systems-centred groups that the therapist draws the group's attention (and his or her own!) to both the survival function of stubbornness and also to its cost. Characteristic defences unwittingly replicate, in the presence of the group, the role relationships learned in the past. The work of identifying the function of the containing role of victim for the group in the first subphase leads to a better understanding of the function of the scapegoat role in the second subphase.

## PHASE I: SUBPHASE IB
## FIGHT AND SCAPEGOATING

The predictable course of the subphase of fight manifests in group behaviour that is predominantly contentious with members pairing politically for control. Defiant subgroups explore their tendencies to be rebellious, nonconforming, resistant to influence, stubborn, individualistic, contentious and authoritarian throughout. The defiant subgroup battle consistently with the impulse to take a stand against group issues. In groups, it is the defiant subgroup that creates the safety that ultimately enables the shift from the therapist to the group.

In psychodynamic groups, relationships shift constantly as the tides change in the group. Scapegoating a member (usually initiated by the aggressive and active compliants) makes for group cohesion in relationship to a common enemy; therefore the scapegoat is an integrative agent for the group in the dynamics of the fight subphase, in the same way that the identified patient was in the flight subphase. Scapegoating also serves as a trial run. The group, discovering that it can survive scapegoating, and coming together as a group-as-a-whole around the resolution of scapegoating, does the necessary membership work to enable it to take on the therapist.

But group scapegoating is by no means a benign experience, even when it is used as a therapeutic method. Anyone who has been in a group on the brink of scapegoating knows the 'feel' – reminiscent of *Lord of the Flies*. It is true that the surviving scapegoat often makes the first major strides in therapy of all the members of the group. It is also true that sometimes the scapegoat does not survive and leaves therapy.

Techniques derived from the systems-centred view provide alternatives to acting out group tensions in scapegoating. From the beginning of the first subphase of group development, systems-centred members are introduced to the idea that they project into others that which they are not able to address in themselves, and are encouraged to work to 'take back' their projections. They learn that it is the hurt self that is projected into the 'identified patient' to be cured; that it is the unacceptable self that is projected into the scapegoat and treated as unacceptable.

## TRANSITION FROM PHASE I TO PHASE II LEADER-ORIENTATED TO GROUP-ORIENTATED

> a crucible, a relentless, uncompromising,
> inexorable pressure on the outer shell of defences
> – burning hot and cold –
> a ring of fire around the inner core of ash

### The barometric event

The 'barometric event' is the fulcrum that marks the transition from Phase I and Phase II. In a systems-centred group, it is also the transition between the 'training phase', in which the group-as-a-whole acquires the skills to undo the defences and 'contain' frustration, and a second phase, in which the conflicts in primary experience are experienced and explored. Throughout this transitional phase, and indeed, throughout the life of the group, the therapist's responsibility is to contain the group projective identifications until the group-as-a-whole can contain those dynamics itself. The therapist role serves as a container for the group-as-a-whole good/bad split: while the group crosses the boundary between fantasy and reality: the fantasy of the good/idealized and bad/de-valued therapist into the reality of the de-idealized function of the therapist.

In the first phase of group, the underlying fears of dependency are expressed in terms of annihilation – kill or be killed – with resultant guilt and blame. Murderous rage 'turned in' relates to the 'overdependent' depressive, guilty, compliant, passive response to dependency disappointment. Rage 'turned out' relates to the 'counterdependent', counter-phobic, blameful, rebellious, active response to dependency disappointment. In the heat of the barometric transition, these fears are expressed openly. Members, in different groups, will express the same sentiments, in a varying range and intensity of grief, guilt and fear. 'There is only room for one of us!' 'It's either you or me!' This will be familiar to individual therapists in the heat of the negative (essentially paranoid) transference where the belief is that only the patient or the therapist can survive and there cannot be room for both.

Whereas the basic work of recognizing and struggling with defences is done in the earlier stages of the group, it is the authority issue that puts the work to the test. The early work on containment enables the group to regress within its group-generated structure. It is within the safety of this group 'surrogate ego' that the regression in the service of therapy is done, with little risk that the group will actually act out the sadism. Typically, of course, the more available and primitive and bloody and savage the primary images, the easier it is for the group to move past the sadistic fantasies, and the more relief the group experiences and the more wholeheartedly they move on to the next phase. This is compatible, of course, with the understanding that the deeper the unconscious access, the less denial, repression, reaction formation and paranoid ideation will distort the inner experience, and the greater the potential for transformation.

The most difficult experience of the barometric event (more likely in a group-as-a-whole approach that does not include systems training) is when the sadism that underlies the murderous rage breaks through the 'containment' in the group-as-a-whole and expresses itself as a group-level paranoid delusion, generating a 'real' experience of the therapist as toxic and destructive, with concomitant threats, either of real murder or symbolic character assassination. This can also take the form of the group unconsciously electing a member with salience for the role to express sadistic virulence for the group without the group being able to subgroup functionally. In both cases, the steady insistence of subgrouping around the issues, and a consistent emphasis on the containment of boundaries and a focus on goals, increases the likelihood that sooner or later, the group-as-a-whole will be able to 'contain' the dynamics so that they be made conscious and integrated.

The management of levels of regression is an important factor through this phase. As long as the work is contained in subgroups, even the most fragile patient is also 'contained', and the different levels in the regressive experience can occur at a pace within which they can be integrated. However, when the pace is mismanaged, or when a member reaches a level of experience from which the group withdraws, a decompensation of the group-as-a-whole can occur. The probability for this increases when the group contains fragile patients who have not yet learned how to work in a subgroup, or with whom the subgroups have not achieved valid communication. Both of these conditions are red flags for the therapist. The stability of fragile patients in a group-as-a-whole regression depends upon the supportive environment of a subgroup. In the worst case, the patient who is 'too open' to the virulence of disappointment and hatred, is split off by the group and 'paired' with the therapist, and each becomes the other's paranoid object in a mutual and reciprocal projective identification. This experience, for the therapist, is very different from the relatively benign and heroic 'David and Goliath' pairing that the group often sets up in the earlier stages of the barometric event. This is a mutual pairing of assassins!

We have already discussed the role suction for the therapist in relationship to the identified patient and the scapegoat and the threat it carries for group fixation. It is through learning not to act out these earlier role relationships that the therapist develops the ability to contain and understand the impulse and there is therefore some preparation for the powerful role suction of the barometric event. The hatred towards authority experienced in the barometric event springs, not only from the object-related defiant and compliant transferences of the first phase of group development, but also from the objectless transferences of the second phase. Thus the therapist's countertransference response is both to the role transferences and the pervasive transferences. The therapist's own therapy is likely to have familiarized him or her with his or her vulnerability to reciprocal role transferences with which he will be challenged throughout Phase I. The sources of pervasive transference responses, however, are always unconscious, and the work of making the unconscious conscious never ends. Thus the therapist will always be more vulnerable to the transferences in the work of Phase II, and never more so than in the crucible of the barometric event.

Working through the vicissitudes of the transition in the barometric event is dependent upon the therapist being able to maintain the role boundaries in the group, and to maintain subgroups as containers for the work. It is easy enough for a systems-centred therapist to mistake a 'pair' that is a look-alike for a subgroup, but is functionally a split-off container for a group projective identification. When the therapist is one of the pair, it is even more difficult to maintain objectivity. The way out for the therapist is to rely on the group-level process of subgrouping. With subgroups working around similarities and identifying differences, there is an ongoing opportunity for the group to reabsorb the split off pair and restore a working environment.

What the group-as-a-whole has to become ready to contain are the regressive, primitive, and often very bloody and violent fantasies of the destruction of the therapist. 'These many individuals eventually banded themselves together, killed (the father) and cut him in pieces. . . . They then formed the totemistic community of brothers, all with equal rights and united by the totem prohibitions which were to preserve and to expiate the memory of the murder' (quoted by Bennis and Shepard [1956] from Freud, 1922).

Sometimes the therapist is seen as some animal, murdered and thrown into the middle of the group, and savaged. Sometimes the members experience themselves as violent and bloody animals feeding on the carcass, with blood dripping from their faces. Other times the therapist is thrown on to a fire, a pyre, danced around, roasted and eaten. Sometimes a duality is experienced: the impulse to rend and tear at flesh in savage hunger, and at the same time, to swallow and digest and be satisfied and full inside. Often, the work is followed by a rush of gratitude and love that the therapist can contain so much hate. And afterwards, in the relief, there can be a profound feeling of group communion. These developments can be grasped in terms of the dynamics of guilt and reparation in the depressive position (Klein, 1977).

In groups that access less primal levels, seduction or devaluation is used to undermine the authority of the therapist. There can be a symbolic communion around the therapist as an alternative to the underlying savagery. Once a group passed around one small peppermint patty, which the group managed so that each of its members broke off a piece (Agazarian and Peters, 1981). Devaluation can defeat authority by rendering it bumbling and incompetent. One group became convinced that I was ageing beyond reason, and held no future for them. Another decided that I did not know enough about groups to help, and seriously considered the task of trying to train me, and yet another wanted to keep me around affectionately as a pet.

The example that follows illustrates several aspect of the systems-centred approach to the barometric event. The group is much stronger than it was in the earlier illustration when it joked about 'picking on someone bigger than you . . .'

In the first part of the episode there is a transitional quality in which it can be seen how the group builds, through some defensive somatizing, to a collective wish to murder the 'battleaxe' with an axe!

The second part of the episode illustrates how the subgroup work resonates throughout the group, across the boundaries between the present and the past, and certainly for Carrie, into an eruption of a spontaneous insight at the end.

| | |
|---|---|
| *Annie:* | I think she's a battleaxe, a crazy battleaxe . . . |
| *Fern:* | It makes me so angry. (Then to therapist:) Why won't you help? (The voice of the subgroup where active rage has replaced the helplessness of frustrated dependency.) |
| *Annie:* | It makes me sad. (The voice of the subgroup that contains the yearning for dependency.) |
| *Fern:* | It makes me so angry. I feel so sick. I feel just sick. It's like if you're not going to help I want you out. |
| *Adam:* | While everybody else has been talking about being sick, I've |

been sitting here worried that I am the one in the group that's going to have to run to the bathroom and throw up. (Somatic defence.)

*Mark:* Feels like I'm going to get rid of something. (The group is already familiar with somatizing defences against feelings, and Mark is spontaneously reversing the somatization for the group.)

*Carrie:* Throw up Yvonne.

*Mark:* Like I shouldn't have it inside me so get it out.

*Carrie:* That's the first time I've called her 'Yvonne' instead of 'Dr Agazarian'. (Shift from passive to active – a change in subgroups.)

*Annie:* I have such a worry that I have to kill her.

*Mark:* Have to?

*Annie:* There isn't going to be any way out. The idea of doing it is really horrible.

Later:

*Sally:* There's only one thing to do it with, with a hatchet. (The group is working closer, with analogy and metaphor.)

*Mark:* Right.

*Adam:* I've turned it into a big long hatchet with about a 20-ft handle and we all have part of the handle.

*Carrie:* We'll do it all together.

*Annie:* I can't get that, it feels like shirking. If I hold on to the handle with everybody then it feels like I'm not doing my job.

*Mark:* We could each take a shot.

*Annie:* We each all have to take a shot.

*Sally:* Murder on the Orient Express.

*Fern:* You said there was only one thing to do with a hatchet, though I got confused because the only thing you can do with a hatchet is bury it.

*Carrie:* Yeah.

*Annie:* Or cut your own foot off.

*Carrie:* That's what I was thinking, bury the hatchet.

*Fern:* Bury the hatchet and . . .

*Carrie:* . . . and I'm just stuck with whether to bury it in Yvonne's head. Or whether to bury it somewhere else.

*Group:* (Pause.)

*Carrie:* I just had an idea that is sort of scary to me, Adam's idea that we would have a long battleaxe that everyone could hold on to and – this is connected to tightness (points to her chest) – and I suddenly realized that together we are physically stronger than you are. We *are* stronger, and that just suddenly became real. And that only, like for a moment, the only protection for you is the fact that we can't get together.

Fern:   I feel a little frightened because I'm sitting so close. Mine isn't the axe it's just wanting to choke you anytime you say anything. (Shifting from metaphor to direct experience.)

Carrie:   I mean, I mean it's like I could just tear this place apart. I could tear the chairs apart. I could tear the furniture apart, I could tear the pictures off the walls, I'm just so mad, just furious, I could. . . . It's like this, the feeling that was in my chest that felt like anxiety is just getting bigger. I just really am. I keep seeing my mother's bedroom, my mother's room and I could just tear it apart. I could tear this room apart and you're supposed to see it. You're supposed to stop me. If I get really mad, if I get really mad. (Carrie has led the group away from the underlying sadistic fantasies of murdering the leader to the underlying impulses that are fuelling her individual transference to the leader.)

Therapist:   What's the experience? (The therapist is encouraging Carrie to contain and complete her experience, both for her individual therapy and also for the group experience that rage is not dangerous when it is a 'contained' experience.)

Carrie:   If I get really mad. You're supposed to stop me and for once, God damn, you're supposed to notice me.

Therapist:   Let your experience grow, have your experience. What's it like?

Carrie:   I'm all filled with it.

Therapist:   What's it like, to be so filled with rage, to be so full? What's it like?

Carrie:   I still want to break things. It's now, and it's still up to you. (Still wanting the therapist to contain the acting out.)

Therapist:   What's it feel like inside as you want to break?

Carrie:   I feel something coming all up in here. (Points to abdomen.)

Therapist:   Let yourself fill up with it.

Annie:   I'm filled with 'No!' (Intensely experiences and expresses the impulse that erupts in the 'No!'.)

Fern:   I felt angry and then I felt this. (Makes a fist.) (Others in the group are now accessing the physical aspect of their experience. The members' work is deepening in resonance to the deepening of the subgroup work.)

Adam:   It's like screaming in the middle of the desert and there is no

one there to hear me and no matter how much I scream it's just
... myself. Nobody notices, nobody responds, I can go 'Aagh!'
until I wear out. (Adam has the urge to discharge the anger in a
scream and then defends against the urge with an 'explanation'
that renders the discharge futile – he is now two defences away
from his original experience. Technically, Adam is accessing
the objectless alienation, which belongs, not in the
object-related experience of the barometric event but in the
partial-object world of the second phase of development. Being
out of phase does, in fact, leave him alone in a desert.)

*Therapist:* How do you feel about me leaving you screaming in the desert
and not hearing? Leaving you out there and not responding?
(This is the therapist's attempt to reconnect him to the
here-and-now of the object-related world of the barometric
event.)

*Adam:* It feels like beyond Rage.

*Therapist:* How do you feel about me, leaving you in that state?

*Adam:* I want to strangle you.

*Therapist:* How?

*Adam:* By jumping up and grabbing you and grabbing you so hard that
we both go right through the window. And then just taking you
like a rag doll and then beating you and beating you and beating
you on the sidewalk ... (The primary impulse has broken
through. Adam's hands are outstretched and his body charged
with energy. He experiences a moment of potency.) ... No
matter what I do: scream, rage, grab you, beat you, you are not
going to respond. (Adam is now 'undoing' his primary
experience by making a negative prediction. This then relates
his feelings to an explanation, which creates a secondary
experience, complete with secondary affect, which then serves
as a barrier to continuing to access his primary experience. This
is an excellent example of how defensive explanation aborts the
experience that is being explored and reinforces the compulsion
to repeat – in Adam's case, to repeat both the impotence of his
rage and his alienation.)

*Therapist:* So how do you get even? (Therapist attempts to reconnect to the
primary experience through accessing the primitive affect
around the Law of the Talion.)

*Adam:* I can't – that's the rage – that's the frustration, there's nothing
I can do to get even. (A graphic example of the secondary
feelings of impotent rage that are generated by the defence
against primary affect.)

*Therapist:*    Find your subgroup. (The therapist turns to the group, and by putting the conflict back in the group hopes to reconnect Adam to his primary experience through resonance.) Get help from your subgroup, the group can help you get even. It's here in the group, the wish. (As you will see, although members of the subgroup carry on the work, Adam does not. It is possible that Adam will resonate more easily with the work of the next phase.)

*Fern:*    Oh I know, I know exactly how you feel. It's a very unusual . . . everything you have described has gone on inside of me – I've never heard it outside – had anyone say it. (There is subgroup resonance!)

*Sally:*    Something's happening and I really – I need help . . .

*Carrie:*    Well, I've got another piece from what Adam said. I've got a sense that it's not . . . that nobody's there – it's just *this* room – but I'm not very big – but it's your legs I'm kicking (to therapist) – it's – you've got something – you're going to pay attention to me (with increasing emphasis) you're going to pay attention to me – it's not that you're not there – you're gonna pay attention to me – Ah! – (rise in intensity) – it's a baby! (clutching her abdomen – staring across at the therapist's abdomen) – just out of the way – it's me! And if tearing up the room isn't enough – I'll kick and I'll scream!

## PHASE II: GROUP-ORIENTATED

Intimacy engenders more complex dynamics than issues with authority in that the dynamics are more primal and therefore the defences against the primary dynamics are more complex. The major split is into 'passive merging' and 'actively alienated' subgroups organized around over-personal, counter-personal and interpersonal forces. In this second phase, subgroups balance closeness: too far for some; too close for others. Enchantment and disappointment, suspicion, alienation, despair and the emptiness of being together alone!

The experience of paranoid suspiciousness in the second phase of development is not the rationalized paranoid world of the first phase which is no more or no less difficult to endure than the French Revolution. The suspicious, paranoid world of the second phase is the objectless world of Kafka – where the location of threat is nowhere and everywhere. It is the world familiar to every adult who remembers what every child forgets: where intuitions of reality make no external sense; where interpretations from reality make no internal sense; and nowhere is the language for making sense spoken.

Taking flight from confusion into a sceptical suspicion or a despairing and isolated alienation and despair is an organized world compared to the nameless dread of this boundless unknown. In the therapy group, the repair of the relationship with the self and the other and the group is the final work of the group: a stark search through the world of the fragmented self.

The inner journey to the lost parts of the self is the challenge to every member and is the challenge to every therapist too. The temptation is to defend against helplessness by 'helping', to intervene with therapeutic words; or to interpret the experience in terms of the individual childhood self instead of joining in the transformation experience of the adult membership in the here-and-now: a solo and silent journey. To explain or interpret instead of to accompany is again to contaminate and disconfirm essential reality.

Thus, from the systems-centred point of view, the introjective and projective dynamics of both the first and second phase of group development are defensive solutions to the annihilation anxiety aroused when the boundary is breached between the undifferentiated world of fragments and the constructs of reality.

Just as in the 'dependency' first phase, the dynamics of the struggle with authority is influenced by the balance in the conformist (overdependent) and rebellious (counterdependent) subgroups who contain for the group the split between defiance and compliance; so, in the second 'interdependent' phase, the outcome of the dynamics in intimacy are influenced by the balance between counter-personal and over-personal subgroups, that contain for the group the split between blind trust and blind mistrust.

In systems-centred group development, encouraging the group to split into two containing subgroups – one containing the salience for closeness and the other containing the salience for distance – permits both sides of the experience to be explored simultaneously, and makes it unnecessary to work through the second phase in two separated phases of enchantment and disenchantment. Thus 'blind trust' can be explored in relationship to 'blind mistrust'; the wish for merging and fusion and togetherness can be explored in relationship to the fear of engulfment, the retreat into isolation and alienation. As the exploration of the experiences deepen and differentiate, the different issues can be recognized, contained, integrated and reintegrated through the many levels of work that are required in this phase.

## PHASE II: SUBPHASE IIA
## ENCHANTMENT AND BLIND TRUST

In the symbiotic ambience of this phase, members experience a euphoric relief. It is as if the dreams of mirroring have become a reality, and that the group is truly a holding environment. This is the phase in which the group subgroups around learning to experience pleasure fully: to experience it in relationship to the self without shame, and to experience it in relationship to others without embarrassment or shyness.

It is an interesting fact that there are many more descriptive words in our language for unpleasure than there are for pleasure. It is perhaps not surprising, therefore, that this is often reflected in the focus of group psychotherapy, where there is often a tendency to encourage a wide range of exploration into the realms of unpleasure and of pain. The exploration of the *pain* of masochism, for example, is 'group-syntonic' in most psychodynamic groups, whereas the exploration of the *pleasure* in sado-masochism is not. The same kinds of conflicts around opening the boundaries to spontaneous experience exist, however, whether the experience feels good or bad. For this reason, there is a lot of attention paid, in systems-centred groups, to enabling the full experience of the range of pleasure, with much subgrouping around both the wish for the full experience of good feelings and the inhibitions to it.

Throughout this phase there is also the underlying motif that not close enough for some ('you seem so far away') is too close for others ('a little too gooey'). In the following example, there is a group-as-a-whole solution to the conflict around the experience of pleasure in the 'tribe', a metaphor that is apparently acceptable.

| | |
|---|---|
| *Annie:* | Well, last week was such a great session for me. I just made all kinds of contact and it felt wonderful. |
| *Sally:* | I feel full, warm. Hi Adam, glad to see you there. |
| *Adam:* | Good to be here. |
| *Annie:* | You seem so far away (too far for some!). |
| *Adam:* | I'm off this kick that going through rough times together is a terrible thing! It's not so bad. |
| *Carrie:* | It's like a wagon-train going across the plains and the prairies with other people in it and the storms. |
| *Sally:* | Yeah! |
| *Mark:* | We haven't seen Indians in months. |
| *Sally:* | I was in another desert actually. It was in Egypt but it was good that I wasn't alone. It was nice to be with the tribe. |
| *Mark:* | The tribe! |
| *Sally:* | Right! |
| *Mark:* | The tribe! |
| *Carrie:* | The tribe! |
| *Mark:* | The tribe! |
| *Carrie:* | That feels great. When the two of you were talking it was a little bit too close (pointing to Sally and Annie). A little too gooey. I thought well that's you guys (too close for others!). But a tribe. |

| | |
|---|---|
| *Mark:* | A tribe! |
| *Carrie:* | But a tribe! |
| *Annie:* | It was hard. |
| *Mark:* | A tribe! |
| *Carrie:* | But a tribe, I can get into that! |
| *Mark:* | Tribe is cool! |
| *Fern:* | Tribe is all right! |

The enchanted, merging subgroup above contains the blind trust of the group and one another. For the enchanted subgroup, relationships can never be too close. Differences, when they intrude into the enchantment of similarity, can be experienced with all the pain of a break in mirroring as is seen below:

| | |
|---|---|
| *Maggie:* | This feels real nice for me. I felt myself in the beginning sort of like I'm not sure I want to be part of this tribe – but that's a bunch of bull. |
| *Sally:* | God, I really feel good. I mean it. |
| *Mark (sarcastic):* | |
| | No shit, Sally. You mean you really feel good? |

When, in disappointment, the group is 'dropped', the pain precipitates the group into the phase of disenchantment, full of despairing mistrust of one another, the group and the self.


## TRANSITION: FROM SUBPHASE IIA TO IIB
## ENCHANTMENT TO DISENCHANTMENT

Too close to you I disappear,
Too far away and you're not here.

Not close enough for some is too close for others, irreconcilable subgrouping that inevitably plummets the group into disenchantment.

There is a relationship between the ability to develop some functional dependency upon the therapist and how virulent the paranoid threshold will be as the group moves into disenchantment. Suspiciousness and the 'paranoia' eject the group from its somewhat 'manic' heaven of enchantment. Suspicious, persecutory fantasies are also a last-ditch stand against shame and humiliation and the underlying underworld: the dungeons and dragons world of half-formed monsters. When the projective defences do not hold, there is the experience of unbearable shame and humiliation, which is retreated from in a painful withdrawal. The group is no longer full of warm interpersonal affective responses. Instead, there is a grim, 'responsible' joyless knowledge that survival is at the price of being for ever alone.

## Depression vs despair

The systems-centred approach makes an important distinction between the depression which occurs in the first phase of development, and despair which underlies the second. Depression is dynamically related to disappointment and rage in relationship with another; while in the isolation of despair, there is no relationship, there is no other, only the fragmented emptiness that results from the loss of the self.

Depression uses the language of complaining and blaming – a litany bemoaning fate and crying out to God. 'Out of the depths I cry to thee, Oh Lord, Lord hear my voice' says the 130th psalm. The voice of depression, reaching out in guilt; a sinner in repentance; justifiably abandoned; seeking forgiveness and love and bemoaning fate. But forgivenness and repentance bring, at best, only temporary relief. The crime of the depressed does not exist in reality. Relief comes only when the depressed gains access to the primitive violence in the retaliatory fantasies that are the reality of the unconscious. In the unconscious, where there is no distinction between thought and word and deed, the crime has already been committed. When the unconscious is made conscious, there is no crime.

Depression is a manifestation of super-ego pathology. A reintrojection: the Law of the Talion turned back on the self; murderous rage denied and turned back on the self. Depression is essentially object-related. Despair is not. Despair has no object; there is no God.

Despair is the cry of the hopeless. It is the cry that knows there is no one. Like Thomas Wolfe, in *Look Homeward Angel*, the despairing know that

> naked and alone we came unto exile. In her dark womb we did not know our mother's face. From the prison of her flesh have we come unto the unspeakable prison of this earth. . . . Which of us has known his brother? Which of us has looked into our father's heart? Which of us has not remained forever prison pent? Which of us is not forever a stranger and alone? . . . Lost! Remembering speechlessly we seek the great forgotten language . . .
> (Wolfe, 1929)

Despair is not only a matter of accessing unconscious fantasy, but also a matter of finding the way to the lost self and to the forgotten language. To face the valley of death requires the courage to follow dread's lead. Through loneliness and alienation and pain; from emptiness into the fear of fragmentation and the fragmented horrors of the underworld; re-experiencing the annihilating memories of shame and the shaming; and finally rediscovering the hidden self and life with spontaneity and joy.

'I thought it was my wish to fly – and now I understand that it was just the wax', said one member; who for many years had felt like Icharus, doomed to earth's darkness for the hubris of daring to fly too near the sun and suddenly understanding that it was not hubris, not her essential spirit that was at fault, but the reality that she needed to develop wings that were held together with something more practical than wax if she was to fly towards the sun.

## PHASE II: SUBPHASE IIB
## DISENCHANTMENT, SUSPICION, DESPAIR AND ALIENATION

*Adam:*  I've had the music of *Camelot* going through my head – 'For one brief shining moment that was known as Camelot'.

*Maggie:*  Gone so fast!

*Annie:*  Yeah!

*Adam:*  I have a sense that we were a tribe. We were great. We could do anything and you could pick a person out of a hat and any one of us could lead us anywhere . . .

*Group:*  Uh huh!

*Adam:*  We were that powerful. That everyone of us had enough resources to lead us anywhere. And that was just a wonderful feeling for us to have together for a while and now somehow the foundations, I wouldn't say crumbling, but certainly being shaken . . .

*Sally:*  I feel very alone.

*Mark:*  Well, I'm used to going it on my own.

### Disenchantment 1: disappointment and suspicion

First comes the suspiciousness which makes for distance and reduces intimacy – thus requiring the system to shift from the phase of enchantment to the phase of disenchantment. There is great disappointment in the transition work, when the group is working hard to deny the conflicted feelings in relationship to one another.

Potentially, the group can take advantage of the emerging feelings of disappointment by learning to own some of the more difficult of the interpersonal feelings, like jealousy or envy, which, when defended against, make for alienation and distance. When this work is kept in focus, as it is in systems groups, then the transition into alienation and despair does not become an overwhelming and alienating experience and can be explored and contained by functional subgrouping.

Suspiciousness disrupts the climate of the group and at the same time increases the need to develop reality-testing mechanisms – thus shifting from the phase of disenchantment to the phase of consensual validation. Suspiciousness 'denied' leaves the system doomed to the homeostatic mechanism of blind trust and fixated in the phase of disenchantment. In systems-centred group work, mechanisms of reality-testing have been developed from the inception of the group. Thus, if the salience for suspicion is not too great in the group, this work is done with relatively little difficulty.

Suspiciousness and paranoia protect against shame and humiliation by projection. When this defence does not hold, there is the experience of unbearable shame and humiliation, which is retreated from in a painful withdrawal. The group is no longer full of warm interpersonal affective responses and instead a grim, 'responsible' joyless knowledge that survival is at the price of being for ever alone. Suspicion defends, by the projection of blind mistrust, against the bitter, cold and empty despair of betrayal. When the cohesiveness in the group is strong, the sense of interpersonal betrayal is less, but the sense of intrapersonal betrayal more, and suspicion is weighed under by the sense of disappointment. Painful though it is, this is a good time to do interpersonal work. As is illustrated below, the conflict, when accessed, is painfully simple and painfully human: and simply, humanly, acceptable.

*Therapist:*   And we don't talk about the cynicism that we are withholding right here and now which keeps us running and running in an apparent closeness but in fact we can't get past that barrier. So what are the feelings that we are not being public about, that are getting in the way of our being honest with one another?

*Sally:*   I have some stuff. I do know that when you started talking I felt left out and I didn't want to be left out. I didn't want to be left out.

*Therapist:*   In what way were you dishonest?

*Sally:*   By not saying anything.

*Therapist:*   What exactly did you withhold?

*Sally:*   Jealousy.

*Therapist:*   So how would you have said that?

*Sally:*   Ugh.

*Therapist:*   Honestly.

*Sally:*   I don't know.

*Therapist:*   About the envy and the jealousy that was in your relationship honestly.

*Sally:*   I don't know. My heart's racing right now. I wanted to be in on something nice. I didn't want to just watch it. I want to be part of it. (To Adam and Carrie:) You were talking to one another – ugh – I just wanted it to be a three-way talk.

*Maggie (to Adam and Carrie):*

        I wanted to break up the contact that you two had.

*Therapist:*  How?

*Maggie:*    How? I wanted to get in the middle. I wanted to be me. I wanted it to be me! I want it with you – just for me – with everyone else out . . . everybody else out. That feels better now it's out!

*Carrie:*    It's very funny, very uncomfortable. I can only talk to one person at a time right now.

*Maggie:*    Well, mine was envy and jealousy. Because Adam and I had completed something and you (to the therapist) were wanting to talk to me and Adam at the same time and I wanted you to talk to me. I want you to talk to me. So . . . I wanted to cut across, that you wanted to talk to Adam.

*Adam (to the therapist):*

        And when you confronted me with reality, my immediate response was, Hey, I'd rather live in unreality and enjoy it, than settle with reality. Who wants to settle for reality when I can have the solution that I was enjoying so much?

*Therapist:*  What is the cost?

*Adam:*     What is the cost for hanging on to the illusion rather than facing the truth?

*Sally:*     Empty core.

*Adam:*     Yeah.

*Annie:*    The truth that I feel worried and dissatisfied.

*Carrie:*    The truth . . .

## Disenchantment 2: alienation

Within the schizoid withdrawal there is the association to the black hole (Grotstein, 1990) – being in outer space without a life line – cold – in the ice age – empty – hollow – for ever in despair – hopeless. When this defence is threatened there is a desperate 'holding on' so that one does not 'disintegrate', 'fall apart'. When the group is encouraged to regress into and through the feared disintegration, the group reaches an understanding at the group level that there is a 'shared' alienation – and therefore an existential common experience.

    The individual work at this time is the work of 'letting go' and 'falling into the black hole', finding the way by following the affective signal of dread. A further retracing step, past the despair, is the original betrayal of the true self by whatever shaming experience created a split between the spontaneous self and the self that was shamed (probably in the process of being socialized). Thus paranoia and despair are the last ditch defences against the anguish of shame. The consequences of the defences are the permanent absence of that part of the self in intimate relationships, either with the true self or with any significant other, which results in the schizoid feelings of emptiness. (In truth, the self has been 'emptied out', and the inconsolable grief is at its absence.)

This work, of course, is greatly facilitated by the resonance of a subgroup. As was illustrated in the episode around the barometric event, one member's work takes the subgroup forward, and when that individual member can go no further, another member picks up and carries on. When one or two members have survived the fear of disintegration and the loss of the self, and discover the spontaneous experience behind the original shaming, the map is drawn and other members can follow. It is in this phase that members learn that they continue to shame the spontaneous experience that was split off in the original shaming. They learn that they are now shaming themselves as they were once shamed.

In one group, for example, where the group was working with inhibitions around sex, two members were building on one another's childhood experience: one caught showing his penis to another boy, and one caught masturbating. It seemed that it was only the first member who was able to move past the memories of his terrible punishment to the original pleasure and pride in himself and in his younger friends' admiration. When, however, he shyly shared his sudden full experience of physical sexuality with the group, the other member was able to join the work, and own that she too had a full sexual experience and was hiding it behind her shyness.

Working through the phases of leader-centred and group-centred group development, members discover that they are, in truth, self-centred. Confronting the work of membership in themselves, in their subgroups and in their group systems, they confront the many ways that they have compromised, distorted or lost themselves. The journey seems easier when the members learn to work in subgroups and learn to be systems-centred.

## TRANSITION: FROM PHASE II TO PHASE III
## GROUP-ORIENTATED TO CONTEXT-ORIENTATED

From the understanding that the 'whole group' has the potential for an alienated and alone experience comes the gradual testing of reality – the ability to call a spade a spade. In the transition from a developing group to a mature group, the group uses subgrouping as the major developmental force, containing the maturational process of splitting in the group-as-a-whole while the splits are integrated through membership in discriminating subgroups.

The work at the boundary between group-orientated and goal-orientated is the work that affirms individual reality. The following episode illustrates the difficult work of checking out interpersonal impressions, risking that, in spite of one's inner conviction, one has been mistaken.

| | |
|---|---|
| *Fern:* | I feel so attached I feel so attached so attached everyone (looking around). |
| *Annie:* | To me too? (Checking her mistrust.) |
| *Fern:* | Yeah. I keep feeling you want that answer to be 'no', but I do. |
| *Annie:* | Yeah, but . . . |
| *Fern:* | I feel you keep wanting me to say 'no'. |
| *Therapist:* | And you feel? |
| *Fern:* | Angry. I'm angry about that feeling (talking directly to Annie). |
| *Therapist:* | So you've got two feelings. |
| *Fern:* | I do have two feelings. |
| *Therapist:* | And you've only shared one! |
| *Fern:* | Right. |
| *Annie:* | Why are you angry? |
| *Therapist:* | Asking for an explanation stops the exploring! |
| *Annie:* | Thank you, because I pick up a different message. I picked up a different message underneath, and didn't realize it until Yvonne said to explore. Now I know that I believe you – that you were giving me a double message. |
| *Therapist:* | That's the context. Now for the feelings. |

*Annie (looking at Fern):*
> I feel closer to you now that I know you've carried two messages.

| | |
|---|---|
| *Therapist:* | That's an explanation of your feeling of right now. |

*Annie (still talking to Fern):*
> I feel close. I feel close to you now. I am very grateful that you can be that straight. I feel the release of a lot of pain a lot of worry for no reason because I think I know underneath . . .

*Therapist (interrupting):*
> So how does it feel to know you know something, without having to mask it with a protective 'I think'? How does it feel to know what you know whether you're right or wrong?

| | |
|---|---|
| *Annie:* | A little dangerous. |
| *Therapist:* | So how does it feel to own up to what you really feel? |
| *Annie:* | Great! |
| *Therapist:* | So will you do it? |
| *Annie:* | I'm going to do it. I am doing it. |
| *Therapist:* | You need to tell Fern what you know, even though you may be wrong about what goes on with you, and what you think goes on with her. |

| | |
|---|---|
| *Annie:* | (Nods her head.) |
| *Therapist:* | Can you share that? |
| *Annie:* | Yes, sometimes, I think . . . |
| *Therapist:* | Can you tell Fern directly what you know, whether you're right or wrong: how you feel when you think she's sending a double message and only owning one? |
| *Annie:* | When you said you cared, I didn't feel convinced. When you said you thought I was trying to do something, get you to say I didn't like you, I felt trapped. I felt lassoed around the ankles and the rug pulled out from under me. When I owned that you probably had both of those at the same time I feel back in control, and I feel close . . . and I think you were doing it! |
| *Therapist:* | 'I think' is a way of not fully owning what you know, whether right or wrong. Can anyone else help? |
| *Fern:* | I wonder if I can! What's happening for me – I have exactly the same feelings to say back to you. I feel like I'm angry, I'm angry because I felt trapped – I felt trapped in hearing from you a question. What I heard was, 'Do you care about me? And I know you don't!' That's what I heard. |
| *Therapist:* | And you might be right and you might be wrong. Put your whole self on what you know. Abandon your alibi first. |
| *Fern:* | Mm! it's true. |
| *Therapist:* | Can you go from there – can anyone in the group help? Does the group understand what the issue is? |
| *Mark:* | Owning the alibi. |
| *Annie:* | It's giving up a paranoid world. |
| *Fern:* | Checking it out! Boy! |

## PHASE III: GOAL- AND CONTEXT-ORIENTATED

Phase III introduces the phase of work, goal- and context-orientated, where the primary goals of survival and development exist in the context of the secondary goals of environmental mastery. Phase III is containment; the inner balancing of the love, the hate and the many transformations of reality. It is almost as if, once the group has experienced being able to survive as a group, the descent into the primary experience of abandonment of self and other in the black hole of despair, the transformation occurs. The original fear that to grow separate is to die, transmutes to an understanding that to separate is the way to survive and live, in ever-increasing complexity, in the hierarchy of human systems.

There is a major difference between a developing group, developing through the different phases of group development for the first time, and a developed group that can recognize aspects of the developmental phases in the re-experience and reworking of issues that are aroused in group life. It is the difference between the patient in individual therapy who is helplessly tossed on the sea of transference, and the patient who is familiar enough already with the experience to be able to navigate through its shoals. As is shown in the example of Jane.

In a 'look-alike' authority issue, Jane was working in a subgroup that was exploring the trap of passivity that she often fell into in relation to the leader. 'It's like you are looking at me through the wrong end of the telescope', she said. The leader asked her how that felt when she looked through the wrong end of a telescope, and Jane burst out with 'bigger!' at which both she and the group joined in peals of spontaneous laughter.

The experience of being looked at through the wrong end of a telescope or through a microscope is a frequent metaphor when the group is struggling with the feelings of helplessness and powerlessness in relationship to authority (Phase I). Frequently there are sadistic overtones: not only do the members feel small and helpless, like Gulliver with the giants, but they often also feel that they are being scrutinized dispassionately, like bugs under a microscope, or worse, like butterflies being watched fluttering helplessly on the end of a pin. Reversing the image from small to big is another step of shifting both the self-image and the role relationship towards reality.

The work of the mature group is to enable transactions across the boundaries. In the ongoing group life of work, the issues themselves do not change, but the ability to work with them do. This next episode around fears of fusion illustrates the difference between an anxiety-ridden Phase II subgroup exploration and the deeper yet less frightening work of a mature group.

Exploring their fear of being swallowed up – fused – the group teamed up in subgroups around two sides of an issue: the fear of being swallowed and the fear of swallowing. The group-as-a-whole first distanced itself through talk about the difference between activity and passivity. Next, it voiced the voraciousness of appetite, of greed, of the eaters and the eaten. The group was then able to divide into subgroups: the voice of the 'eaten' subgroup saying: 'You'll demand insatiably and you'll always complain . . . I'll never be enough and never do it right enough for you.' And the voice of the 'eaters' subgroup: 'I'll demand and demand and always want more, and there's never enough to fill me up . . .' There was group peace, when the work was finished, a sense of completeness and satisfaction and closeness, without fear.

There are some experiences in mature systems-centred groups which are quite marvellous. For example, mature groups are consistently aware that all group work is done in the context of reality: that the first step in any difficult work is to establish a containing reality (of time, place and person) within which regression to other levels of experience can take place.

In a recent group, Mac was urged by the group not to hurt himself by ripping at his hand, but to choose another member and talk about why he couldn't talk. He said he could not – a field of energy was keeping him out of the group. There was a startled silence and a moment of group-as-a-whole shock. Then Chris, whose relationships are tenuous at best, said: 'Mac is quite right! I've been related to Erica and Betty and that makes a triangle of energy that shuts him out.' Claudia, my co-therapist, and I had been unaware of any such connection – and watched with astonishment as Erica and Betty acknowledged the bond. Mac, contained in this reality, was then able to talk to Chris about the explosive force inside him that he was attempting to discharge by ripping at his hand.

Large groups have not been the focus in this chapter, even though, in my personal experience, I observe the same phases of development, whether the developing human system is as small as a dyad or as large as a medium to large group of 30 or 100 people (Agazarian and Janoff, 1993). However, the work of one large-group leader has had a great influence on what I look for in the dynamics of developing groups. I look for the dynamic development that de Maré calls 'koinonia'. De Maré defines koinonia as 'impersonal citizenship and good fellowship . . . a form of togetherness and amity that brings a serendipity of resources' (de Maré *et al.*, 1991, in Agazarian, 1992a). From his many years of work in the large group, de Maré has hypothesized that koinonia, that can be developed in the large group, can *only* develop in the large group. First, family transferences do not have the tenacious hold on individual experience that they do in the small group. What is more, he says, the large size of the group both elicits and contains the hatred that group experience engenders, but in a less personal focus than in the transference-ridden small group. In his experience, though, even in large groups, he doubts that koinonia can be developed in much less than ten years.

*Koinonia* has been an important book for me. The summer I spent reviewing it brought me to the understanding that it was the containment of hatred without a target that was the nexus of the healing process. This then required me to revise my understanding of the function of the super-ego. Translating the super-ego into a defence against human irritability (the basic human response to differences and also the first sign of life!) brought it into isomorphy with the systems-centred hypothesis that 'containing' energy within the system was the essential task in the work of integration. This enabled me to make operational a formulation of human-system dynamics without pathologizing. This in turn led to the current formulation of defence analysis which is centred around group members taking an executive role in their own therapy (Agazarian, 1992d).

For several years now, we have brought each training group to a close with a review period, as a method of formalizing the executive function of the members. We have recently introduced this 'review' period to our therapy groups. This requires members to change from their 'participant' to their 'observer' roles and to focus on the group as the context of their individual experience. After crossing the time boundary, members are asked, 'Any surprises?', and thus pay attention to what had been the unexpected, and therefore the potentially new, aspects of their group experience that day. We have found that the activity of shifting from one role to another has been particularly useful for our group therapy members, who have taken very seriously the different goals of the different roles, and the different demands that the role shift makes on the way they think and behave. It does, of course, give them an executive function, and the challenge of taking personal experience objectively, that is not only often missing in their attitude to their life, but also, unfortunately, too easily undermined in their therapy.

It is in these review periods that we have learned, from our therapy group members as well as from our training group members, the content of those moments of silence that sometimes occur in group after a completed piece of work: that feel so profound and are so seldom discussed. We have found that for training and therapy groups alike, these moments seem to be what Pat de Maré calls koinonia. In those shared and resonating, though silent, moments, members are experiencing some form of existential reality; able to *be*, freed momentarily from family transferences; related yet separate, intimate and differentiated, and experiencing with awe the working fellowship in the work of the group. Communicating across the boundaries in space and time, within, between and among all systems in the hierarchy of living human systems, modifying defences and working functionally in subgroups, has brought into being a structure that has made it possible to develop koinonia deliberately in small, as well as large groups. In the closed system of a workshop this has been accomplished in less than a day, however hesitantly. The challenge remains to see how koinonia can be functionally integrated as an ongoing working property of the individual human system as well as of the group-as-a-whole.

Human responses develop from simple to complex, and so do human systems. Just as the infant responds to excesses of frustration in random behaviour, so do the responses in the early development of groups. Just as the small child kicks the door, so the older child mentally kicks a human object and adults find a scapegoat. Thus developmentally human systems change from simple random discharge responses, through behavioural discharge responses, to organizing the frustration in blame: either internalized or externalized. Maturation demands that every human system, when frustrated, must contain the tension, anxiety and rage while internal and external reality is remapped and the problems along the path to the goals of transformation are solved. An example:

The group, with great commitment, were struggling to contain their frustration at how difficult group work is – a frustration that was increased by my asking the group to explore the experience of containing their frustration without finding an object to blame. They said 'I don't understand what you mean by "contain the hatred without an object".' And, 'How can I be this angry without either hating you or this group or myself?' Just at that moment, the telephone, usually switched off during the group, rang. There was an instantaneous roar of laughter at just how intensely, and with what relief, everybody instantly *hated* the telephone. Almost immediately afterwards came insight. 'I need a home for my hatred.' 'Now I understand why I keep hating my mother/my parents/my boss/you!' 'Now I understand what you mean when you say that if you don't "contain" frustration, the hatred is fixating!' (Agazarian, 1992c).

It will be clear to theorists that, psychodynamically, what is entailed in the above example is the ongoing task of separation/individuation (Mahler *et al.*, 1975). What may not have been so clear before is that the annihilating rage so often aroused in groups is a *natural stage* in the toleration of frustration, and that too much therapeutic emphasis on the frustrating people or traumatic events in the past fixates the person in the past, rather than directing him or her to work through the past by developing greater tolerance for crossing the boundary from the past to the present and solving the reality problems in the here-and-now.

In the summary table that follows, the phases of group development are presented in a form that makes it easier to compare and contrast some of the dynamic issues that underlie the problems that the group must solve as it travels along the path to the developmental goals.

*Table 3.1* Phases of systems-centred group-as-a-whole development

| PHASE I: LEADER-ORIENTATED | | |
|---|---|---|
| MAJOR GROUP ISSUE: Functional dependence, idealization/de-valuation of leader; power, control, authority, political pairing, good leader/bad leader<br><br>DEVELOPMENTAL DYNAMICS: Splitting into love of leader/hate of leader; good/bad; depression vs murderous rage; acting out/acting in, idealization/de-valuation of good leader into bad leader<br><br>BASIC ASSUMPTION: Fight/flight – approach/avoidance/freeze<br><br>FUNCTIONAL SUBGROUPING: Compliance/defiance around conflicts in functional dependency<br><br>SYSTEM GOAL: Development<br><br>CONTAINING ROLES: Identified patient and scapegoat | | |
| *Leader-orientated Subphase Ia: flight* | *Leader orientated transitional stage flight and compliance: fight and defiance* | *Leader orientated Subphase Ib: flight* |
| MAJOR ISSUE: Idealization of leader: good leader/good member split<br><br>MAJOR GROUP FOCUS: FLIGHT: Dependency, stereotyping and conformity, homogeneous pairing for survival; idealization of leader<br><br>FUNCTIONAL SUBGROUPING: COMPLIANCE: Survival through conformity; communication around similarities<br><br>CONTAINING ROLE: Identified patient | TRANSITION ISSUES: Passivity to Activity; Compliance to Defiance; Ambiguity to Contradictions<br><br>DEVELOPMENTAL DYNAMICS: Shift from communication around similarities to communication around differences | MAJOR ISSUE: De-valuation of leader: bad leader/good member split<br><br>MAJOR GROUP FOCUS: FIGHT: Counterdependency, scapegoating, rebellion, political pairing for control<br><br>FUNCTIONAL SUBGROUPING: DEFIANCE: Survival through conflict; communication around differences<br><br>CONTAINING ROLE: Scapegoat |

---

**TRANSITION FROM PHASE I TO PHASE II:
LEADER-ORIENTATED TO GROUP-ORIENTATED**

MAJOR GROUP ISSUE:
Barometric event – acting out seduction, de-valuation or coup d'état;
Bad leader – Good group

DEVELOPMENTAL DYNAMIC: Acting out
Symbolic acting out of murderous rage;
Relationship to leader transferred to the group;
de-valuation of leader/ idealization of group

| PHASE II: GROUP ORIENTATED |
|---|

MAJOR GROUP ISSUE: Functional independence, idealization/de-valuation of group intimacy, closeness and distance – all-or-nothing pairing: good group/bad group/bad self

DEVELOPMENTAL DYNAMICS: Splitting love of group/hate of self; Idealization/de-valuation of good group/good self into bad group/bad self; Separation/individuation

BASIC ASSUMPTION: Pairing; interpersonal approach/avoidance; enchantment/disenchantment

FUNCTIONAL SUBGROUPING: Blind trust/mistrust – conflicts with functional independence

SYSTEM GOAL: Survival

CONTAINING ROLES: True self/false self

| *Group orientated subphase IIa: enchantment* | *Transitional stage enchantment to disenchantment* | *Group orientated subphase IIb: disenchantment* |
|---|---|---|
| MAJOR GROUP ISSUE: Idealization of group good group/good member | TRANSITION ISSUE: Activity to passivity blind trust to blind mistrust, redundancy | MAJOR GROUP ISSUE: De-valuation of group: bad group/bad member split |
| MAJOR GROUP FOCUS: Symbiotic pairing; overpersonal closeness, merging, fusion, idealizing of group, blind trust, optimism | DEVELOPMENTAL DYNAMICS: Transition from fusion to de-fusion; from denial of differences to denial of similarities | MAJOR GROUP FOCUS: (1) Disappointment and suspicion – blind mistrust (2) No pairing; Alienation, wariness, despair, alienation; Pessimism and counterpersonal despair |
| FUNCTIONAL SUBGROUPING: Enchantment: blind trust, fusion, communication around similarities | | FUNCTIONAL SUBGROUPING: Disenchantment: blind mistrust, isolation, communication around differences |
| CONTAINING ROLE: Hero | | CONTAINING ROLE: isolate |

---

**TRANSITION PHASE II TO PHASE III**
**INTIMACY TO MATURITY**

MAJOR GROUP ISSUE: Separation/individuation; the development of
here-and-now consensually validated communication for reality testing

DEVELOPMENTAL DYNAMICS: Containing alienation 'shared'; development of
interpersonal and interdependent relationships; trust becomes a function of tested
expectations as trust and mistrust tested in group reality

---

**PHASE III: GOAL ORIENTATED**

MAJOR GROUP ISSUE: Functional interdependence, de-idealization
of authority in self and other

DEVELOPMENTAL DYNAMICS: Transformation through simple and
complex discriminations and integrations between, among and within
all systems in the hierarchy

BASIC ASSUMPTION: Fight, flight, pairing related to work

FUNCTIONAL SUBGROUPING: Containing conflicts around boundaries
of time, space, reality and role; containing and directing work energy;
solving problems along the path to primary and secondary goals

SYSTEM GOAL: Survival, development and environmental mastery

CONTAINING ROLES: Participant/observer

WORK: In the context of solving the problems on the path to the explicit
and implicit goals. Containment of conflict in discriminatory sub-systems
for systems-as-a-whole integration.

Communication transactions across the boundaries between, within and among
systems, modified for ambiguities, contradictions and redundancies to increase
the transfer of information in the communication.

## NOTES

1 'Man' is being used here as a generic not a gender description.
2 At the time of writing I was ignorant of chaos and complexity theory. However, there appears to be an isomorphy both in theory and the experience of the theorist.
3 The dialogues in this chapter are taken from the videotape of a training group who put their hearts into 'role playing' the phases of group development in front of the camera. Dialogues referenced (Agazarian 1991a) refer to the videotape cited in the references. Where they are not referenced, the dialogues are taken from the original script which is not yet available on videotape.

## REFERENCES

Agazarian, Y.M. (1986) 'Application of Lewin's life space concept to the individual and group-as-a-whole systems in psychotherapy', in Stivers and Wheelan (eds), *The Lewin Legacy: Field Theory in Current Practice*, New York: Springer-Verlag.

—— (1988) 'Application of a modified force field analysis to the diagnosis of implicit group goals', paper delivered at the Third International Kurt Lewin Conference, sponsored by the Society for the Advancement of Field Theory.

—— (1989a) 'Pathogenic beliefs and implicit goals: discussion of The Mount Zion Group: "Therapeutic Process and Applicability of the Group's Work to Psychotherapy"', paper presented by Harold Sampson and Joseph Weiss, Slavson Memorial Lecture, AGPA, San Francisco, February 1989.

—— (1989b) 'Group-as-a-whole systems theory and practice', in Y.M. Agazarian (ed.), *Group: Special Issue on the Group-as-a-Whole, Journal of the Eastern Group Psychotherapy Society* 13 (3, 4): 131–55, winter, New York: Brunner/Mazel.

—— (1990a) 'A flip-chart of systems-centered thinking and its application to the practice of group therapy', in *Collected Papers: Systems-Centered Workshop* I, Systems Centered Press, Philadelphia.

—— (1990b) 'Systems-centered thinking applied to human systems in general and to systems-centered therapy in particular', in *Collected Papers: Systems-Centered Workshop* II, Systems Centered Press, Philadelphia.

—— (1991a) 'Videotape introduction to group-as-a-whole dynamics, presented by Yvonne M. Agazarian', Agazarian Videotape Series: Systems-centered Group Psychotherapy. Module I. Blue Sky Productions, Philadelphia, PA.

—— (1991b) 'Systems theory and group psychotherapy: from there-and-then to here-and-now', *The International Forum of Group Psychotherapy* 1 (3), Montreal.

—— (1992a) Book review of *Koinonia: From Hate, through Dialogue, to Culture in the Large Group*, by Patrick de Maré, Robin Piper and Sheila Thompson, in *International Journal of Group Psychotherapy* 42 (3).

—— (1992b) 'Contrasting views of a representative group event', discussion of a ten-minute video tape of a psychotherapy group led by Irvin Yalom, Forty-ninth Annual Conference, AGPA, 20–22 February, New York.

—— (1992c) 'A systems approach to the group-as-a-whole', *International Journal of Group Psychotherapy* 42 (2): 177–205.

—— (1992d) 'Systems-centered group psychotherapy: how to get through group defenses', paper written for Friends Hospital Training Series on the systems-centered approach to group-as-a-whole therapy, Friends Hospital.

—— (1992e) 'A systems approach to the group-as-a-whole', *International Journal of Group Psychotherapy* 42 (3).

—— (1993) 'Reframing the group-as-a-whole', in T. Hugg, N. Carson and T. Lipgar (eds), *Changing Group Relations: the Next Twenty-five Years in America, Proceedings of the Ninth Scientific Meeting of the A.K. Rice Institute*, A.K.R. Institute, FLA.

—— and Peters, R. (1981) *The Visible and Invisible Group: Two Perspectives on Group Psychotherapy and Group Process*, London: Routledge & Kegan Paul.

—— and Carter, F. (1994) 'The large group and systems-centred theory', *Journal of the Eastern Group Psychotherapy Society*.

—— and Janoff, S. (1993) 'Systems theory and small groups', in H. Kaplan and B. Sadock (eds), *Comprehensive Textbook of Psychotherapy*, Williams & Wilkins.

Ashbach, C. and Schermer, V. (1987) *Object Relations, the Self, and the Group: A Conceptual Paradigm*, London: Routledge & Kegan Paul.

Bateson, G. (1972) *Steps to an Ecology of Mind*, New York: Ballantine Books.

Beck, A.P. (1981) 'A study of group phase development and emergent leadership', *Group* 5 (4).

Bennis, W.G. (1961) 'Defenses against "depressive anxiety" in groups: the case of the absent leader', *Merrill-Palmer Quarterly* 7: 3–29.

—— and Shepard, H.A. (1956) 'A theory of group development', *Human Relations* 9 (4): 415–37.

Bertalanffy, L. von (1969) *General Systems*, revised edn, New York: George Braziller.

Bion, W.R. (1959) *Experiences in Groups*, London: Tavistock.

Bowlby, J. (1969) 'Instinctive behaviour, an alternative model', in *Attachment and Loss*, vol. 1, *Attachment*, New York: Basic Books.

Coleman, Arthur D. and Bexton, W.H. (eds) (1975) *The Group Relations Reader: I*, Washington, DC: A.K. Rice Institute.

Fairbairn, R.W.D. (1952) *Psychoanalytic Studies of the Personality*, London: Routledge & Kegan Paul.

Freud, S. (1922) *Group Psychology and the Analysis of the Ego*, London: International Psycho-Analytic Press.

Ganzarain, R. (1989) *Object Relations Group Psychotherapy: the Group as an Object, a Tool, and a Training Base*, Madison, CT: International Universities Press.

—— (1992) 'Introduction to object relations group psychotherapy', *International Journal of Group Psychotherapy* 42 (2): 205–23.

Grotstein, J.S. (1990) 'The "black hole" as the basic psychotic experience: some newer psychoanalytic and neuroscience perspectives on psychosis', *Journal of the American Academy of Psychoanalysis* 18 (1): 29–46.

Hinshelwood, R.D. (1989) *A Dictionary of Kleinian Thought*, London: Free Association Books.

Horwitz, L. (1977) 'Group centered approach to group psychotherapy', *International Journal of Group Psychotherapy* 27: 423–39.

—— (1983) 'Projective identification in diads and groups', *International Journal of Group Psychotherapy* 33: 259–79.

Howard, A. and Scott, R.A. (1965) 'A proposed framework for the analysis of stress in the human organism', *Journal of Applied Behavioral Science* 10: 141–60.

Klein, M. (1977) *Love, Guilt, and Reparation and Other Works: 1921–1945*, New York: Delta.

Korzybski, A. (1948) *Science and Sanity: An Introduction to Non-Aristotelian*

*Systems and General Semantics*, 3rd edn. International Non-Aristotelian Library, Institute of General Semantics, Lakeville, CT.

Lewin, K. (1951) *A Dynamic Theory of Personality: Selected Papers*, New York: McGraw-Hill.

—— (1951) *Field Theory in Social Science*, New York: Harper & Row.

Mahler, M., Pine, F. and Bergman, A. (1975) *The Psychological Birth of the Human Infant*, New York: Basic Books.

Maré, P. de, Piper, R. and Thompson, S. (1991) *Koinonia: From Hate, through Dialogue, to Culture in the Large Group*, London: Karnac.

Miller, J.G. (1978) *Living Systems*, New York: McGraw-Hill.

Rothman, M.A. (1992) *The Science Gap: Dispelling the Myths and Understanding the Reality of Science*, Buffalo, NY: Prometheus Books.

Shannon, C.E. and Weaver, W. (1964) *The Mathematical Theory of Communication*, Urbana, IL: University of Illinois Press.

Shengold, L. (1991) *Father, Don't You See I'm Burning?* New Haven, CT: Yale University Press.

Simon, A. and Agazarian, Y.M. (1967) *SAVI: Sequential Analysis of Verbal Interaction*, Philadelphia: Research for Better Schools.

Williams, Tennessee (1955) *Cat on a Hot Tin Roof*, New York: New Directions.

Winnicott, D.W. (1974) 'Transitional objects and transitional phenomena', in *Playing and Reality*, Harmondsworth: Penguin.

Wolfe, T. (1929) *Look Homeward Angel*, London: Charles Scribner.

# 4 Attacks on the reflective space

## Containing primitive emotional states

*Robert D. Hinshelwood*

## EDITORS' INTRODUCTION

What group therapist has not experienced the intense group pressure to join the interpersonal transference matrix of the group, to be pulled into its incestuous ways, its hostile acting out, its resistance to doing the work of the group? Robert Hinshelwood here offers a unique conceptual model which the therapist can use to retain his or her ability to think objectively yet empathically under stress and to create for himself and the group a mental space relatively free of the group contagion effect.

Hinshelwood makes use of a fascinating connection between paranoid projection, group contagion and conformity pressure. Citing Asch's well-known experimental research showing that the subject's objective judgement is markedly influenced and distorted by the judgements of other members of a group, Hinshelwood realizes that due to group pressure, the primitive paranoid-schizoid ideation of a regressed group can distort the thinking even of the group leader. Thus, when scapegoating, for example, takes place, it becomes extremely difficult for the leader to sort out the actual characteristics of the scapegoated member from what the group has projected into him.

Hinshelwood postulates a new concept to account for the way in which the group contains or fails to contain affects and linkages in its interactions: what he calls the group 'reflective space'.

Hinshelwood then exemplifies in detail how the therapist can contain the group's projections and help sort out the cognitive distortions which threaten to disrupt the life of the group.

There is hardly a more frightening appearance than an angry crowd of people, a mob; there can hardly be anything more destructive on this planet than a large group of people armed with the latest military technology; there is nothing more shocking than a gang committing multiple rape on its victim.

The intensity of feelings sweeping the individuals, their weakness to withstand the impulses generated in them by those feelings lead, above all, to the loss of a sense of reality and balance. These are manifestations of the primitive in groups. They all depend on the individuals cohering around grossly polarized, 'good-versus-bad' assessments of their objects of interest. I shall be concerned with these polarized views that groups construct to live in, and the construction in those realities of the personalities of the individuals. These are anti-therapeutic effects of group pressures; and I shall argue that these disrupting pressures work on a specific aspect of the group culture which I call the *reflective space*. I shall argue that a space for reflection forms from the emotional linking between the individuals. Too much fear and intrusiveness destroys a capacity in the group to link and to form the emotional reflective space. The role of the therapist is to attempt to keep his or her own mind sufficiently clear of intrusion to form his or her own space for monitoring emotional linking, and for monitoring the forces that attack the containing links.

## THE GROUP'S AGREED CONSTRUCTION OF REALITY

The most disastrous primitive feature is the individual's hampered sense of reality, the loss of valid testing or balancing of judgements about agreed action. The lynching mob in the deep South that comes across a black whose pick-up truck has broken down, and who castrate him brutally, tie him up in the cab of his vehicle and set fire to it, have certainly lost the capacity to judge the real social significance of their victim, or to judge the real moral justifications of their actions. Football fans from Liverpool who hunted Italian supporters to their deaths at the Heysal stadium in Brussels are equally removed from the world of reality. All the most primitive manifestations of groups are violent; the angry violence of the mob, the triumph of war, the sadism of lust. . . . The most primitive is that which is most dominated by distortion. The black or the Italian is compellingly constructed in a particular sense for each member of the mob.

If, in a group, we agree on a description of an occurrence, how do we know it is valid? There is a sense in which our agreement to agree actually creates a reality we both believe in. In the act of sharing our perceptions and agreeing our descriptions we are also engaged in a group process which can be dominated by similar primitive group processes.

The founding experiments of social psychology proved just how 'relative' the reality of a group is.[1] Asch showed that individuals in a group had great difficulty in standing against a unanimously held opposing view. One individual (the naive subject) was confronted by a whole group who, by prior arrangement, falsified their perceptions of the length of a line drawn on a card. This naive subject, faced with such a united group, tended to conform to the group's (falsified) perceptions, and against the evidence of his own eyes. In a similar experiment on group pressure, Milgram showed that the naive subject could be coerced by group pressure to administer dangerous electrical shocks to a human victim.

## Unconscious group pressures

If group pressures can enforce distorted perceptions of a line then they can surely enforce distorted perceptions of the members themselves. We know this goes on – the well-known forms of scapegoating, stereotyping, and so on. And we know that there are hidden sources of these pressures – the unconscious forces deeply hidden within each individual.[2] These forces derive from the intrapsychic processes of the individuals, their unconscious phantasies and impulses and the way they cohere through processes of identification;[3] and they become manifest as the group-as-a-whole (Lewin's 'social field', Foulkes's 'matrix' and Bion's 'group mentality').[4]

If an individual appears in the group in a certain way – as angry, for example, or provocative, or sentimentally charming – how do we know that it is him or her, as opposed to a socially constructed version, a distorted reduction of that individual to a single dimension (a stereotyped cardboard cut-out)? This is a real problem. It is highly dubious whether scapegoating and stereotyping activity is therapeutically useful.[5] A depressed patient with low self-esteem may have his/her esteem reconstructed by the group in more normal ways; or the converse, his/her wingeing can lead the group to progressively alienate that person into a worthless category for the group: 'Oh, Mabel is off again!'

Let us address the question: When does a group, its processes and pressures, *enhance* someone's personality, enabling an individual to redefine him- or herself more accurately? And when do they distort the personality? For instance someone may lack control of his/her own aggressiveness; a group may then: (a) give him/her a more complete sense of him- or herself as having an understandable form of temper; or (b) set him or her up as 'the aggression' in the group to be separated off from the others, perhaps pilloried and in one way or another discarded (a constructed stereotype). These are two different processes.

## CONSTRUCTION OF GROUP MEMBERS

I shall describe a group (whose sessions will illustrate points throughout this chapter) in which one person, Jeff, is constructed by unconscious group pressures.[6]

*Jeff*, an only child, had lost both parents before the age of 5 years. In the group, Jeff's loneliness was a persistent topic of conversation. He frequently held forth in long-winded and tedious monologues, sometimes for as long as half an hour of the group's time. This was difficult for other members of the group who developed angry reactions to him.

*Simon*, a languid, cultured man who in his late thirties was a virgin and felt tortured by his unacceptable homosexual fantasies, took a quizzical stance as if to convey that it was perfectly obvious why no one befriended Jeff.

*Jennifer*, a rather obsessional woman who pulled her hair out, tended to keep herself to herself and retreat from any confrontation with Jeff but, when she did, it was with a sweet reasonableness so inoffensive that Jeff had no trouble apparently ignoring her.

*Tom* was a burly man, lonely like Jeff, but who had achieved a marriage of sorts which had not produced children. He tackled Jeff incessantly in a way that was often tactless and sometimes provocatively aggressive.

*Pauline* attended irregularly and dramatically demanded to be a centre of attention herself and controlled others by offering or withdrawing her own attention; she distracted by intrusive physical activity – for example elaborate procedures for finding a cigarette from her bag, asking for a light and an ashtray – or she might engage in a comment in an undertone to her neighbour.

There were other reactions in this group which comprised ten members, though rarely more than seven on any one occasion. Jeff had been quickly isolated within the group, tolerated rather than included. The particular aspect of his loneliness that tended to be picked out for discussion was his aggressiveness to others, usually at his workplace. Mostly half-hearted attempts to point out his aggression were made which usually subsided quickly in the face of his indifferent response. 'Jeff' was constructed as a separated element that stood for the 'problem' of the group, a problem that could not be adequately dealt with. Partly it was on the basis of his angular, self-involved personality, and partly on the basis of other group members' need to discover the problem in someone else (a group collaboration in a common psychological defence).[7] He had some potential to fill the stereotyped role; and he accepted it. The following sequence illustrates this at a point some eighteen months into the life of the group.

### Session 1: a constructed personality

Jeff complained of his grinding unhappiness about his inability to have friends and he had spent the week without contact, except at his routine clerical work, and then he did not really get to know people. Jennifer had been looking very strained, which she often did. In order to try to divert from

Jeff's self-involvement, Simon turned to her and said she looked pale. She confided that things were difficult at home. The group knows very little about Jennifer's life which is obscured behind her rather brittle social manner, just as she conceals her hair-pulling by wearing a wig. She offered no more information. Jeff resumed with his difficulties at work, but turning to face more in Jennifer's direction as he spoke. He had become stuck in his efforts to study as a quantity surveyor and he described the hopelessness of progressing when he was not allowed to have experience of certain kinds of work. I pointed to Jeff's feeling interrupted by Simon, which led him to express his frustration in terms of his blocked career. This led him to greater efforts to repeat his complaints. Simon looked sulky, but eventually managed to find an opening in Jeff's monologue to tell me that he had intended only to change the subject slightly. He said this in a charming and long-suffering way as if forgiving me for unjustly chastising him. I thought he was right. I interpreted that he and Jennifer and perhaps others felt dominated and chastised by myself, and felt that they could not be more forthcoming at present in the group. I said that they might perhaps feel that Jeff was a favourite of mine, whereas he was not a favourite of theirs.

This rather clumsy interpretation resulted I think from the continual perplexity we all had over how to deal with Jeff's dominance. However, Simon responded, as if accepting my interpretation as an apology, by turning again to Jennifer and politely inviting her to continue. This she did by telling us that her recent marriage was in difficulties because her husband turned out to require her to act out certain sexual fantasies in which she had to use ropes and chains to restrain him while she made love to him. She found this disagreeable, but felt she had no alternative but to acquiesce. She stopped, having delivered the story in an unemotional manner. However, the emotion was elsewhere. Simon became tense and withdrew from the discussion in embarrassment. Tom seemed excited by it and began to fire questions at Jennifer aimed at trying to help her to be tolerant of her husband. Pauline who had arrived late needed to be filled in on the story. I pointed out the emotion had been redistributed through the group members, and went on to suggest that like Jennifer there were others here who, in the group, preferred to be dominated by someone else's personality and demands. Though there may have been some developing awareness of the significance of my comments within the group, Jeff came in, on cue.

He talked of sexual perversions in a declamatory way, as reprehensible, but in a manner to suggest that the world is an evil place, with evil people, about which he can do nothing except suffer it.

The insight about relations of power in the group now turned to a kind of knowingness about Jeff. Tom took issue with Jeff, and described him as the pervert in the group because he dominated everyone in the group with his talking. Jeff dolefully quarrelled with Tom; he claimed that if the rest of the group allowed him to dominate them then they were perverts like Jennifer's husband. Jennifer became tense and Simon giggled, looking at her. Tom's aggressiveness picked up, on behalf of Jennifer, and her husband. Jeff was now quite alone fighting his own corner. Tom described a list of complaints against Jeff and demanded that his effect on the group was such that he should leave it so the rest of the members could get on with group therapy without interruption. I had often wondered much the same, whether I had made a mistake taking Jeff into the group, and should now ask him to leave. I felt considerable responsibility at that moment. Tom's rage began to escalate and to my dismay, and the group's, he stood over Jeff with his finger pointing at him, as if firing bullets into him: 'You have no sensitivity for any of us. You've upset Jenny. Why don't you apologize to her – to all of us. You're the pervert here, you wind us all up. You're . . .'

I told Tom to sit down. He turned to me his finger ready to fire bullets into me then. I tried to interpret that the group felt I had made the group impossible for them by accepting Jeff into the group, and that I was being asked to take him out of it. I conceded that this must be a possibility and that I would have to take some time to consider it. Tom sat down at this point, the group fell silent and I felt uncertain about what effect I had just had on the process that had been going on. After a couple of minutes I added that although there was a reality to be considered here, perhaps they had fallen silent because the thought of the group without Jeff was similar to Jennifer considering life without her husband – it would be impossible. Tom snorted but said nothing. Simon admitted that if he had a choice between the arguments with Jeff or discussing Jennifer's husband he would probably choose Jeff.

The particular disturbed features of Jeff's personality led him into an isolated position in which he can be regarded as *the* problem of the group; the rest of the group formed up around this plausible construction. Excluding him would seem to solve the group's problem. We were all caught up in this. It had become the group reality. It was almost as an afterthought that I could recognize the link with the marriage Jennifer needed. It was clear that her enchained personality, stiff and unemotional, requiring others to express her emotions, was enacted within her marriage. Simon's comment at the end clearly showed that Jeff's presence in his role as the group problem was *required* in order to deal with other more difficult problems. These are projective processes, exploiting Jeff's character to make him a scapegoat of the group with an easy apparent solution to the group's difficulties.

Thus the social construction of 'Jeff' on the basis of his character has good reason to it: it relieves the individuals of seeing themselves as 'a problem', and offers itself as an easy solution – to get him out of the group.

Unconsciously, in fact, certain aspects of Jeff's personality are interwoven with other sado-masochistic elements in the group.

There is a sequence in the session which I want to emphasize:

- First, primitive processes of splitting and projective identification operate.
- They create distorted perceptions (scapegoating, stereotyping) of the individual – in this case Jeff as 'the problem'.
- 'Jeff' as a problem becomes an actual reality in the group.

This sequence risks anti-therapeutic, distorting influences bearing upon Jeff and the other individuals.

I shall now trace this sequence to an underlying process in which emotional links between group members are attacked. In the next illustration note a series of discontinuities which isolate one communication from another, and thus each group member from the others. It is not just Jeff who is an isolate. In an important emotional sense all the members are isolated, and isolate one another as their potential emotional linking is repeatedly attacked.

It is not enough that contributions in the group come freely; it is important how, in detail, one follows another. The capacity to link emotion to emotion, and thereby member to member, *can* be tracked in the group process; and the group therapist's task is primarily to be responsible for seeing this is done. This is the criterion that I am putting forward for keeping one's feet firm in the shifting sands of the group pressures. The next illustration attempts to show the therapist's stance in tracking these processes – either the creating or the destroying of potential links between members at the emotional level. These patterns result in the constructed reality, or culture, of the group and comprise: (a) disconnection of the individuals one from another (a failure to link between individuals); (b) no proper accommodation of the emotional life of each individual (a severely restricted reflective space); and (c) a resort to the typical stereotyping of one isolated person, Jeff.

## Session 2 – breaking the communicational linking

In a session a few weeks after the one reported in the first illustration, Jeff was describing a familiar situation in which he sat alone at work in the coffee break, wrapped in his sense of loneliness. In a brief pause for breath, Pauline brightly remarked on her own work and the various attractive features of her boss for whom she was an efficient personal assistant. He had taken the trouble to make her a cup of coffee when she was typing some urgent letter for him. This was a little provocative as Pauline was normally supercilious about her boss whom she regarded as rather useless. Simon was amused and ironic about her change of view. Before Jeff could resume his complaints about his own lack of friendship, Tom pointed out how Simon trivialized

Pauline's communication with his irony. Simon reacted in a mock-startled fashion as if he was bewildered by such a construction of his comment. Jeff eventually intruded in characteristic fashion: starting with quite an insightful view of Pauline's overtly sexual slaving for her boss, he immediately described one of the secretaries at work – Jeff often told us that the secretaries were sexually tantalizing for him – who had refused to do anything for him when he had an urgent report to do. This led on to his moroseness about his own lack of success with the secretaries – either sexually or in the work.

At this point, I interpreted because I felt the patterns of communication invited, in fact put pressure on, me to do something about the way in which Jeff dominated the proceedings, and left so little chance for interaction and communication between the other members. I was familiar with this pressure on me to rescue the group from Jeff, and had made many attempts to help the group to see something of Jeff's masochistic posturing, and his covert excitement at getting everybody else in a state of exasperation with him. Such remarks of mine had tended only to raise the frustration towards Jeff as his behaviour was made clearer and more obvious to them. In contrast, Jeff invariably responded as if my remarks had gone straight through him and out again without leaving any trace. I did not want to continue this kind of interpreting which left me as frustrated as the rest of the group, and to no apparent avail.

On this occasion I reflected on my impressions in this and in recent meetings of the group. I realized that it was not just Jeff's method of communication but many of the communications from others could also be equally unconnected. In particular, in this sequence:

1  Pauline made a comment about her boss to distract from Jeff and as a way of boasting unkindly about her working relations thus dissociating herself from him;
2  Simon sidestepped Pauline's intention of feeling satisfied with her own 'success' with the boss and instead referred to her contradictions about her boss (in reality his own preoccupation with satisfactory sexual coupling);
3  Then Tom pointed out how Simon had devalued Pauline's communication, as if protesting, and thus blocking any possible recognition of Simon's hidden fears;
4  Simon then overtly dismissed Tom's irritable comment with a mild mockingness; and
5  Jeff diverted from his own insightful link with Pauline's covert sexual flaunting, and returned to his own maudlin preoccupations.

I also noticed the withdrawal and isolation of a couple of other members who were silent throughout this sequence – one was a woman who is working through the possibilities of divorce from a husband with whom there is no adequate communication, overt or emotional.

I pointed out these observations to demonstrate the way in which each of the communications, though conveying some content on the surface, was *doing* something else; that is, they were leaving the last person's comments hanging unheard in some essential and emotional way: Pauline's interruption rather cruelly triumphed over the pain of Jeff's loneliness; Simon's rational pointing to Pauline's contradiction; Tom's protest at Simon's rational trivializing; Simon's mocking sidestep of the punch in Tom's protest; and Jeff's further retreat into his masochistic misery. Each time an attempted emotional link was brought to a halt. In short, each participant was emotionally abandoned in turn. They were each, in a significant way, left alone in the group. Jeff could be speaking about his unhappiness at work; but he equally represented the loneliness of each (or most) members of the group at this time, in the self-perpetuating process of emotional disconnection.

My intervention along these lines may well have been less systematic and less clear than the presentation here, but I experienced a significant change in the atmosphere of the group after I had finished speaking. My attention was particularly drawn to Jeff who was looking directly at me by the time I had finished. The eye contact between us was most unusual for him since he typically looked at the floor throughout the sessions. Jeff said, 'You mean that the others are as bad as me?' It was clearly an arresting thought.

There was then only a very brief moment to reflect on the account I had given, and Jeff's response to it, before Simon turned rather quizzically to Pauline to ask what she thought of my 'accusation' that she had interrupted Jeff. Before she replied, I felt the need to come in to defend what I had said, as it seemed to me that Simon's question would lead (and was probably intended to lead) back to what Pauline had interrupted and thus to give the floor to Jeff again. I tried to convey this and point out that Simon's question seemed to be designed to restore the old pattern by making sure that my interpretation could not be taken up and thought about, and would be left as another unheard communication in the group. Simon sat back with an amused smile on his face as if I was simply being mischievous, and that he would in a good-natured way allow me to be so. I felt my efforts had been lost and I felt unhappy at the way I had tried to defend my interpretation which had cost so much thought on my part. I realized that my impulse to rescue my comments had fed into the culture of the group at that time by allowing myself to be the one who 'carried' the need to communicate. I now carried the frustration at all the broken links. This led me to feel the wish to make a further interpretation along these lines. However, now I realized that I was in a dilemma: if I followed my impulse to speak further I would collude further with the polarization in which I carried everyone's frustrated wishes for the group, and if I did not I would allow the group to fall back into its self-perpetuating debility.

During these moments of time out from the group while I was reflecting on this, there was further talking going on which, when my attention returned to them, seemed to be in the familiar pattern. Simon was recounting in his amused way some incident in the school where he teaches a class of backward children and his efforts to make these unwilling children read. The group seemed to be enjoying this anecdote for its own sake without any recognition of how it applied to themselves as recalcitrant learners. I decided I might be able to show them the dilemma I had been reflecting upon: if anyone said anything in the group with the intention that their emotional state would be taken seriously, then they were immediately left on their own with it, while the others would dissociate from it by feeling dominated by a barrage of words, feeling accused, or by being blithely amused. I used the example of my own interpretation to show how I too had been left on my own to be serious and then frustrated. There were blank stares as if children had been caught talking in class.

But Jeff, suddenly out of the blue, made a most untypically direct remark. He said he often thought that Pauline tried to flirt with Dr Hinshelwood. This seemed to me so apt that I felt it to be quite clarifying for myself. Pauline went pink, and Simon went white. For once an intense emotional contact between two of us had been overtly recognized. Tom began to talk about jealousy he had experienced with a girlfriend before his marriage. The quality of the discussion at this point had changed radically. Various members could allow some immediate emotional link to go on *within* the group – though not necessarily an easy linking. This capacity for connection between us was in sharp contrast to the prevailing culture of largely disconnected personal contributions delivered in sequence.

These last moments of this material demonstrate the construction of a group space in which the persons are much more linked together emotionally.

## Linking and group culture

It is not difficult to see that the intensity of the felt emotions can lead to attacks upon emotional linking, and a culture in the group that was determined *not to know* about such links. The lack of linking then leaves each of the members isolated; and the group culture is coloured by a frustrating irritation, due to the repetition of the old stereotyped roles and subjects. There is an important conjunction of features:

- contributions that attack the links that could have been made between individuals and their emotional states;
- polarizations of the exaggerated good-versus-bad kind;
- a restriction of mental space within the group for reflection.

This conjunction is important. The group therapist must be especially concerned with these attacks on the links between members and, most noticeably, between the emotional content of their communications. The therapeutic or anti-therapeutic nature of the group culture depends on the extent of these attacks, and the consequent restriction of the reflective space. When the group culture displays constructions due to primitive processes we need as therapists to *attend continually to the nature of the reflective space* – the quality of the linking processes, and whatever restricts it.

I want in the rest of this chapter to concentrate on the capacity in a group to reflect, and interactions with the primitive processes of violence and paranoia which interrupt the reflective mental space of the group.

## THE REFLECTIVE SPACE

The term 'reflective space' indicates that aspect of the group in which members link emotionally and from which the personalities can emerge. In contrast, primitive states reveal themselves in attacks on the capacities for thinking, for reflecting and for making emotional links.

The capacity groups have to reflect has been emphasized by Foulkes, who adapted Freud's notion of free association of the individual to the equivalent idea of free-floating discussion in the group (Foulkes, 1964). The communication between members of the group gradually, he observed, developed patterns within a particular group into which the members slowly settle. They may then sustain, on the whole, a congenial attitude towards one another and towards exploring their own feelings. Various phenomena of a specifically group kind grew out of his observations on free group discussion – resonance, mirroring and the idea of a network of communication among the individual group members, which he called the 'matrix'. De Maré, in turn, extended the idea of free discussion to the larger group, where he employs the terms 'dialogue' and 'koinonia' to indicate a felt solidarity among the members expressed in a loose form of associative conversing (de Maré *et al.*, 1991). My observations have led me to believe that 'free-floating discussion' and 'dialogue' have to be won against the attacks of primitive aggression, notably intrusive forms of projective identification.

## Structured space

I wish now to describe some of the features of the *reflective space* and how it is disordered by the primitive fears and emotions of the group.

Each individual needs to reflect on his or her own experience, and construct a reflective space in his or her own mind. Any experience is linked to others with the development of phantasies or theories of the person and others. A peculiar noise as one passes a graveyard at night is likely to be construed in a frightening way that derives from personal and social meanings of death, graves, ghosts, and so on, even though the noise may merely be that of an owl. When traffic lights change a driver recognizes a meaning in terms of what he/she is permitted to do. These personal and social meanings are links made within ourselves.

Linking may be reversed, or attacked, and experience is reduced to meaninglessness (Bion, 1957, 1959; Meltzer, 1981). The reflective space is either structured by existing links (theories and phantasies) or populated by their ruined remains following violent attacks upon them. When there is a considerable amount of attacking, then remnants of links accumulate within the space, and it comes to function as a mental organ for the expulsion of this mental refuse; such as Tom's explosive violence or Jeff's inexhaustible stream of frustration.

## Reflective space between minds

I take this model to apply to groups as well. The linking *between* minds undergoes a similar set of vicissitudes. They may interact such that one mind can accept, reflect upon (link up with) and contain the anxiety and emotions of the other. Typically this is expressed as follows:

> When an infant has an intolerable anxiety, he deals with it by projecting it into mother. The mother's response is to acknowledge this anxiety and do whatever is necesary to relieve the infant's distress. The infant's perception is that he has projected something intolerable into his object, but the object is capable of containing it and dealing with it. He can then reintroject not only his original anxiety but an anxiety modified by having been contained. He also introjects an object capable of containing and dealing with anxiety.
>
> (Segal, 1975, pp. 134–5)[8]

The containing of emotional experience by one person for another in the manner of the mother's function with the infant leads to our need to explore the group as such a containing reflective space for the emotional experiences that the members wish or need to put into it. Equally this can go wrong in the manner I have illustrated.

This formulation of human interaction, developed from individual psychoanalysis, leads to a possible reformulation of group material. My second illustration described:

1  a space which was stricken by attacks on the linking function in the group; but
2  towards the end of the illustration the group was a potential mental space, in which the individuals were linked by their emotional experiences impacting on one another.

In general, a therapeutic group functions in so far as it manages to create a culture of emotional linking between individuals so that it becomes a container in which the members' experiences can be formed, reflected upon and more or less protected from attack.

## The reflective space and its contents

There are specific conditions for the relationship between the space and its contents which are reflected upon (the container–contained relationship). Bion (1970) described three particular kinds of relationship:[9]

1  the contents are so vibrant and explosive that the whole container is exploded and disabled with an uncontained result (an example is the way the group fragmented in session 1 with Tom's bullets);
2  the container is so rigid that it does not allow of any real expression of the contents which are then simply moulded to the containing space (Jennifer's particularly controlled unemotional sexual revelations, again in session 1); or
3  both the container and the contents adapt and mould in response to one another, so that both are able to develop and 'grow' (an example of this was the much more accepting but emotionally charged group state at the end of session 2).

These simple phenomenological categories are quite useful in practice. The following three illustrations depict each of these kinds of relationships: fragmented, rigid and flexible (mutual growth). The first two come from very early on in the group:

*Session 3 – the fragmented container*

Tom arrived one evening having crashed his car in the morning. He was rather belligerent towards members of the group without telling them details of what had happened. They mostly failed to respond to him. Eventually, the group put it down to his 'symptom' (aggression). Various methods for controlling his anger were suggested to him based mostly on popular psychology: counting to one hundred before he speaks, cold showers, and so on. There was some humour at times. Tom remained silent and brooding in response to this bouncy helpfulness. He clearly did not like it. I interpreted that there seemed to be various ideas about what is helpful; behind the suggestions being put forward, there seemed to be theories on how group therapy might help. I said I thought that the members of the group were still very perplexed by group therapy and had not grasped from me what they should be doing or what they could expect. I said this left them in a state of insecurity, and therefore of brooding anger which they were scarcely able to keep in check behind their humour; in short, I was an irresponsible 'driver' of the group. Tom exploded, principally at me, telling me I did not know what the hell I was talking about. I made everything so complicated. What he was upset about was not the group therapy, it was his car, and the bloody car driver who had run into him. His fury filled the air in a frightening way. He was a big man and even sitting down he seemed very threatening. I felt he might write me off as he had his car.

The nakedness of his rage startled and terrified the other group members as well. It was the first outburst that this group had had to withstand. Mostly, the members froze in embarrassment and fear, leaving it to me to control this situation which suddenly felt completely out of hand. I paused because I was not sure how to proceed with this sudden injection of uncontained rage into the group, reluctant to engage in a one-to-one dialogue with Tom who I felt could possibly attack me physically. Before I had time to formulate the state of fear which (subsequently) seemed to me the immediate thing to attend to, Jeff had begun to draw the aggression on to himself by a pseudo-understanding comment about the other driver who, Jeff supposed, had not intended to cause the accident. This did not soothe Tom's rage and he turned from me to Jeff with a violent explosive shout which did not seem to be any actual words, but more an ear-splitting noise. Jeff's eyes remained cast downwards submissively. A rather dowdy young woman who had said very little in the group and whose main symptom was premenstrual disturbance, was placed between these two men, one on either side of her. She got up with a jerky movement and plunged for the door to escape. In fact she did not return to the group. The two men then faced one another across the empty chair, which Tom proceeded to lean across and to gesticulate vehemently and to insult Jeff as if he had been the other driver. He described Jeff as an unwanted intrusion in the group, who had no more right to be there than the other driver should be on the road. The ugliness of this incident was not abating. A rather heavy, strong man, Graham, whose complaint was that his wife thought he was too passive (probably impotent though this did not emerge till later), moved across the room and placed his bulk on the empty chair between them. Clearly he intended to use size and bulk as a method of damping out the emotional conflagration. Tom, however, merely leant forward to continue his abuse around Graham's body. Over several minutes he gradually subsided. A new thought seemed to dawn in his eyes, and he looked round at all our shocked, frozen faces. He then seemed suddenly deflated, mumbled a general apology round the room, and left. He, however, did return the following week.

In this incident Tom's primitive anger was triggered by my touching on fury over the mystification that the new experience of the group represented. Although I cannot confirm it, I think that as the 'driver' of the group I had proved myself sufficiently incompetent for Tom to use me as a surrogate for the driver he had run into in the road. The light-hearted response to his aggression on the road was no adequate container for him and he burst. The members, including the therapist, were then also incapable of containing the fearful experience of Tom's anger in words. Inadequate actions and movements were resorted to, and the group literally, in a concrete way, began to break up and fragment as two of its members left.

*Session 4 – the crushed individual member*

The week following the incident described in the last illustration, there were three people missing, though Tom returned. Tom was accepted as part of the group, though he was spoken to very gingerly, and the incident was not referred to directly. There was some discussion about terrorist activities in far-away lands. I pointed out that perhaps there was a nearer, and internal land that needed a better government, that is, the land of the group and of each person's own experience in it. And, with my heart in my mouth, I returned to my interpretation of the week before, and touched on the state of bewilderment and fear which I induced in them through putting them through the experience of this group.

The atmosphere of the group did not thaw, but Jeff, with a seemingly provocative innocence, asked Tom about his car. Tom appeared in turmoil, passing his hand over his forehead, and without looking at Jeff, or anyone, described in a strained and controlled way how he had proceeded to deal with the reporting of the accident to the police and the insurance company, and about his wife's severe lecturing of him over his bad driving habits; he recited each of her complaints, half resentfully and half contritely, rather like a schoolboy writing out lines for punishment. Sitting next to him, Jennifer was scratching the arm of her chair with long, pointed nails. She told him (without justification really) that the group would forgive him but he must not allow an outburst like that to happen again. The session continued in a nervous way, skating over careful, uncontentious subjects. When I interpreted the group's method of re-establishing itself by employing topics on which there was a requirement for unanimous agreement throughout the group, as a method for keeping the group intact, there was an anxious silence eventually broken by Jennifer who asked the stolid Graham some rather unthreatening questions about his marriage. Tom remained silent, and in fact barely took part in the next two groups seeming relieved to be left out.

This group managed to reassemble itself after the explosion. But it did so, through the over-controlled Jennifer leading a heavy, oppressive agreement among the members to limit all topics to an unemotional reciting, and to sustain superficial dialogue, which might be reminiscent of Graham's unconsummated marriage.[10]

To illustrate the third container–contained relationship (mutual growth), I take a session from much later – after some three and a half years. A good deal of work had been done on the primitive explosive quality of the emotional impulses in the group, and on the way the members used one another (projectively) to deal with their intolerable experiences. There had been an attrition of members (Graham for instance), and one or two new members (including Pauline and Simon) had arrived. It now consisted of six, of whom five were present at the session I shall describe next. The members now had a good deal more understanding of the way they avoided emotional contacts and links with one another and with me.

### Session 5 – mutual growth

Simon had taken one of the boys from his school to the cricket nets for some extra coaching. He knew he had felt some excitement, and was pained over the question of what sort of personal link he was trying to establish with the boy. Was it sexual or was it honourable in his terms? He showed moments of the familiar amused innocence. Jennifer told him reassuringly that, however sexual he had felt, she was sure there were honest feelings in Simon for the boy as well. He responded quite smoothly to tease her over her reassurance, asking her how she could possibly see into him with such certainty. She felt upset at this rejection and stayed silent. Pauline asked what was wrong with sexual feelings; they were after all loving feelings, she said. And then, as if aware that she had also rather dismissed the pain of Simon's agony over his sexuality, she told us in a more serious way about a brief encounter she had had in the last week. She had had several brief affairs recently about which she was quite defensive. This encounter had been particularly short-lived and, seemingly to show some support for Simon, she wondered if she was being promiscuous. Partly she was fishing for someone to tell her she was not, but she was also conveying a similar shamefulness to Simon's. I thought there was a fair amount of courageousness in the group, explicitly in Simon and Pauline who were edging towards being able to put across their pain and shame, and in most of the members of the group (except perhaps Jennifer at this stage) in trying to edge towards one another's pain. I said this and described their gratitude to me for providing the group in which they could begin to feel safe; and that the gratitude was a form of loving feelings towards me which could make them feel warm and understanding towards one another. Jeff, who had weathered for so long his unpopularity in the group and was now more in tune with others, surprisingly told us that one of the secretaries had offered to bring back his sandwiches from the canteen for lunch, when she went to get her own.

In this brief excerpt there is a struggle towards locating themselves with one another's pain and an increased feeling of safety in venturing out with their own experiences. The provision of the enhancing quality of this space seemed to me important, and I had pointed it out in terms of myself as a kind of provider and guardian of it for them; their gratitude made them feel further enhanced through experiencing their own capacity for appreciation.

This material from three sessions illustrates the main forms which primitive mental processes take in groups.[11] They indicate to the therapist how much the group has managed to construct a reflective space in the group – or to destroy it.

## CONCLUSION AND TECHNICAL CONSIDERATIONS

Technically one could say that the task is to create a group reflective space which does not become closed off, whether through rigidity or through fragmentation, to the contents that individuals wish to have contained. The therapist needs to bear in mind the various states of the group's, and individuals', capacities to listen in to and link with one another's expressions of feeling, even (and especially) when those expressions are not in the form of words, but are delivered as direct emotional incursions into one another. In the first disastrous illustration, these intrusions took the form of a shower of emotional bullets. These expressions of feeling may be felt as (and at times are intended as) violations, like a physical rape.

When people express their feelings so that others pick them up and can know something of them, the expression may be made in a relatively benign manner as in session 5 (a kind of communication), but it may be resorted to with a *malevolent force*, as Tom and Jeff exemplified at times, Tom intruding guilt and anger, and Jeff intruding frustration. The degree of malevolence of the primitive forces, transforms in the group into a culture in which emotional linking is restricted. Intrusion and the paranoid blocking of intrusion destroy links in the group, and prevent the emergence of the individual personalities. Instead, individuals are severely distorted in the way they are perceived and in the way they are induced to become. These processes are damaging projective ones. The introjective component is equally important, since stereotyped identities may be taken away *inside* the member after the sessions (introjection).

However, introjection, too, may be accomplished in a more benign way; and typically the important introjection that might be hoped for is the appreciative acquisition of the containing mental space for which the group and the therapist both come to stand in the minds of the members. Then, individuals with such an introject inside them can come to reflect frutifully on themselves.

## The therapist's mind

A major resource that a group possesses, is the therapist's own capacity for linking, his/her own internal reflective container. This needs to take the form of linking what is happening in the group process with the material which is being brought. The therapist's technical equipment rests mostly on his/her developed capacity to discern the kinds of links being made in the group.

Now, the problem is that anyone *in* the group who wishes to steer this process therapeutically is, like everyone else in the group, under pressure to accept the group perceptions. If the group pressure is to pillory a member unfairly then the group therapist will find him- or herself going along with that as surely as if he or she were in a lynching mob.[12] If the group pressure is to reassure in a bland and uncomprehending way,[12] the group therapist will likewise tend to find him- or herself accepting and approving of it as therapeutic. How can group therapists find adequate bearings?

Are there any objective aspects with which we might prise ourselves out of this fog? We have to look from inside, since there is no position outside of a group from which to perceive things independent of group pressures. The group and the therapist equally are buffeted by powerful forces while groping in the 'relativity' of the group reality. My argument is that there are certain beacons for finding one's way in the fog. I have begun to indicate in this chapter an outline of some of them.

I shall make three recommendations for the therapist to steady his/her own judgements. *First* is to discard all attempts to focus purely on the characters of the group members, and to turn the spotlight on to the processes going on *between* members. That is to say, the results of the construction of a group member's identity are less certain than the processes involved in the construction. Let the personalities we perceive in the group merely aid thinking about the processes.

*Second* is the therapist's task to follow the group's capacity to reflect, and how it establishes thoughtful links *within* the group. The group's capacity for reflective judgement is not an easy criterion to apply, and of course, in applying it, we can be influenced by group pressures, but its discontinuities are more apparent. It is often a vivid moment for members to have them described.

*Third* is the therapist's role to represent a mental space for enhancing the members' containment of one another's experience and ultimately of their own. It is important for therapists to remember that their reflections do not always have to be correct (though it is best). They have merely to represent the role of attempting reflection of the emotional links, to keep reflection going.

In all this therapists are not neutral bystanders and they cannot represent a space that is completely free from the dynamic conflicts of the group. They are swayed by them and, as often as not, in the full flood of these most primitive processes, they can be put out of action as much as the others. When swept along in the morass of multi-dimensioned material in a group session, we are in an exactly comparable position to the participant in a lynching mob or a football crowd. Certain factors work to our advantage; one is the great ordering power that comes from recalling the fundamental process of containment in the reflective space (the linking structure of emotional contacts between the members, or alternatively their destruction of these potential links). This is a kind of radar beam which can plot out the essential outlines of the important therapeutic dynamics of the group. Therapists need their radar beams, not just for the plethora of cognitive meanings in the members' dialogue but even more for the flood of expressed emotions that invade the reflecting and the linking in the group and in the therapist. We need a simple ground on which to base our observations; and the more primitive and more hostilely enforcing these emotional currents, the more useful is the notion of a reflective containing space as a bearing.

In summary, the capacity to link emotion to emotion, and thereby member to member, *can* be tracked in the group process; and the group therapist's task is primarily to be responsible for seeing this is done. This is the criterion that I put forward for keeping one's feet firm in the shifting sands of the group pressures.

## ACKNOWLEDGEMENTS

I am grateful to John Gordon, Gaili MacArthur and Anne Chancer for their comments on this chapter, as well as those of the editors of this book.

# NOTES

1 Asch, 1952; Milgram, 1964; Festinger, Schacter and Back, 1950; Sherif, Harvey, White, Hood and Sherif, 1961.
2 I exclude for these purposes the social constructions from historical, cultural and economic factors including the views of Berger and Luckman (1967). In this short chapter I do not want to dwell on the forces which underpin group solidarity – neither the external economic and political ones, nor the intrapsychic ones. I shall be concerned here with the manifestations of these forces as they create the realities the group and its individuals live in. Further, I shall limit this chapter to therapeutic groups.
3 Freud, 1921.
4 Lewin, 1947; Foulkes, 1964; Bion, 1961.
5 Similarly, Goffman's work (1961) gave rise to a theory that all psychopathology comes from a process of social *labelling* (Scheff, 1963).
6 I mention only the main protagonists in the sequences of the group that I shall choose for the purposes of this paper.
7 Collective defences of this kind depend on the individuals employing primitive defences – notably splitting, projective identification and denial.
8 Interpersonal linking between mother and infant does occur very early in life as a precursor of the social processes seen in groups (Newson and Newson, 1975; Stern, 1985; Chamberlain, 1987).
9 These views are taken from Wilfred Bion's later work, that which he progressed to after he left the work and the ideas in *Experiences in Groups* (1961).
10 Tom's 'internal' space is equally rigid, shown by his strained, controlled and unemotional manner.
11 I have given a more comprehensive account of these kinds of phenomena elsewhere (Hinshelwood, 1987).
12 Sometimes group therapists cultivate an emotionally distanced position from the members. But in my view they cannot do so without some violence to their link with the group, with its members and with themselves. That kind of therapeutic distance is a 'defence' used by group therapists trying to remain *above* the processes they are trying to describe. But it unfortunately renders them out of reach from the group.

# REFERENCES

Asch, Solomon (1952) *Social Psychology*, Englewood Cliffs, NJ: Prentice-Hall.
Berger, P. and Luckman, T. (1967) *The Social Construction of Reality*, Harmondsworth: Penguin.
Bion, W.R. (1957) 'Differentiation of the psychotic from the non-psychotic personalities', *International Journal of Psycho-Analysis* 38: 266–75.
—— (1959) 'Attacks on linking', *International Journal of Psycho-Analysis* 40: 308–15.
—— (1961) *Experiences in Groups*, London: Tavistock
—— (1970) *Attention and Interpretation*, London: Tavistock.
Chamberlain, David B. (1987) 'The cognitive newborn: a scientific update', *British Journal of Psychotherapy* 4: 30–71.
Festinger, L., Schacter, S. and Back, K. (1950) *Social Pressure in Informal Groups*, New York: Harper & Row.

Foulkes, S.H. (1964) *Therapeutic Group Analysis*, London: Allen & Unwin.

Freud, S. (1921) *Group-Psychology and the Analysis of the Ego, Standard Edition* 18.

Goffman, Erving (1961) *Asylums: Essays on the Social Situation of Mental Patients and Other Inmates*, Harmondsworth: Penguin.

Hinshelwood, R.D. (1987) *What Happens in Groups*, London: Free Association Books.

—— (1989) *A Dictionary of Kleinian Thought*, London: Free Association Books.

Lewin, Kurt (1952) *Field Theory in Social Science: Selected Papers*, London: Tavistock.

Maré, P. de, Piper, R. and Thompson, S. (1991) *Koinonia: From Hate through Dialogue, to Culture in the Large Group*, London: Karnac.

Meltzer, Donald (1981) 'A note on Bion's concept "reversal of alpha-function" ', in J. Grotstein (ed.), *Do I Dare Disturb the Universe?*, Beverly Hills, CA: Caesura Press.

Milgram, S. (1964) 'Group pressure and action against a person', *Journal of Abnormal and Social Psychology* 64: 137–43.

Newson, John and Newson, Elizabeth (1975) 'Intersubjectivity and the transmission of culture: on the social origins of symbolic functioning', *Bulletin of the British Psychological Society* 28: 437–46.

Scheff, Thomas (1963) 'The role of the mentally ill and the dynamics of mental disorder', *Sociometry* 26: 436–53.

Segal, H. (1975) 'A psycho-analytic approach to the treatment of psychoses', in M.H. Lader (ed.), *Studies in Schizophrenia*, Ashford: Headley; reprinted in *The Work of Hanna Segal*, New York: Jason Aronson, 1981.

Sherif, M., Harvey, O.J., White, B.J., Hood, W.T. and Sherif, C.W. (1961) *Intergroup Conflict and Co-operation: The Robbers Cave Experiment*, Oklahoma: Institute of Group Relations.

Stern, Daniel (1985) *The Interpersonal World of the Infant*, New York: Basic Books.

# 5 Bion's post-*Experiences in Groups* thinking on groups
## A clinical example of –K

*John Gordon*

## EDITORS' INTRODUCTION

In what follows, John Gordon presciently applies Bion's work on thought disorder to the group setting. Gordon notes, as part of the group regression, the 'attacks on linking' which Bion originally observed in borderline and psychotic states. He illustrates how the members attack the bonds between them (the group matrix) as well as the thought process. Gordon thus achieves an important integration of Foulkes's concept of 'group free association' and Bion's 'K links'.

## INTRODUCTION

The abiding influence of Bion's *Experiences in Groups* (1961), particularly of the concept of basic assumption group, can be gauged by reference to a number of recent contributions to the group psychotherapy literature. Anzieu (1975), Brown (1985), Schermer (1985), Ganzarain (1989) and Karterud (1990) all discuss basic-assumption functioning; and its appearance in groups has been related to a wide spectrum of issues and anxieties: task breakdown or ambiguity; psychopathology in leaders; oedipal and pre-oedipal, narcissistic and 'psychotic-like' conflicts. Agazarian and Peters (1981) use a modified version of basic assumptions to characterize a fundamental dimension of the 'invisible group', the implied group goal.

The purpose of these representative citations is not to assess or criticize how the authors have understood the concept of basic assumptions but to indicate how frequently it is still applied in discussions of group dynamics and therapy. At the same time, there is a growing awareness that *Experiences in Groups* was not Bion's last word on the subject (James, 1981; Grinberg, 1985; Ashbach and Schermer, 1987), although of the subsequent work only *Attention and Interpretation* (1970) merits a listing in the *Comprehensive Index of Group Psychotherapy Writings* (Lubin and Lubin, 1987).

The area of Bion's thought to which I should like to direct the attention of group psychotherapists is marked out by the two books, *Learning from Experience* (1962b) and *Attention and Interpretation* (1970), and the papers, collected as *Second Thoughts* (1967), which were first published between 1953 and 1962. These papers – among them, 'Differentiation of the psychotic from the non-psychotic personalities' (1957), 'On arrogance' (1958), 'Attacks on linking' (1959) and 'A theory of thinking' (1962a) – address the subject of thought disorder as manifested in individual psychoanalytic treatment of psychotic and other severely disturbed patients. This work has been explored and developed by Kleinian analysts (Meltzer, 1978; Spillius, 1988; Hinshelwood, 1989; Joseph, 1989). Yet throughout his writing, especially in the imaginative 'memoirs' (Bion, 1975, 1977, 1979) of later years, Bion resorted to the use of group fables to illustrate aspects of individual personality functioning, and I think it is illuminating to reverse perspective and to see whether some of the work ostensibly concerned with the individual mind can also be read as fables which represent aspects of group functioning.

In fact, the relevance of extending Bion's post-*Experiences in Groups* thinking beyond the sphere of individual analysis to work with groups was recognized by Schermer (1985) but not theoretically attempted by him until the volume co-authored with Ashbach (Ashbach and Schermer, 1987). Even earlier, James (1981) pointed out the value for an understanding of communication in groups of Bion's theory of thinking and subsequently (James, 1984) applied Bion's concept of containing to groups. Grinberg (1985) highlighted the importance of the concepts I intend to explicate in this chapter, but he did not give clinical examples. The basic formulation of 'container/contained' – the group as a container of the individual, of unconscious experience, of latent emotional turbulence ('genius', or 'messianic idea') – as adumbrated in *Attention and Interpretation* (Bion, 1970) and applied in social contexts by Jaques (1955) and Menzies (1960), has informed the more clinical orientation of Kaës (1976), Hinshelwood (1987), Ganzarain (1989) and Gaburri (1990). Certainly Bion himself was explicit:

> Finally, though I shall not follow it up here, the theories in which I have used the signs K and –K [theories derived from the papers on thought disorder and signs representing the link constituted by emotional understanding and its obliteration, respectively] *can be seen to represent realizations in groups.* In K the group increases by the introduction of new ideas or people. In –K the new idea (or person) is stripped of its value, and the group in turn feels devalued by the new idea. In K the climate is conducive to mental health. In –K neither group nor idea can survive.
>
> (Bion, 1962b, p. 99; italics added)

I believe from my clinical and supervisory experience that there are 'states of group' which resemble –K, a term Bion used in *Learning from Experience* to symbolize the annihilation of the capacity to generate meaning, particularly emotional understanding of oneself and others. The climate or atmosphere of such group sessions is evoked by Thomas Hardy's descriptions of English Christmas mumming, that 'fossilized survival' (Hardy, 1878, p. 128) and mummers, 'the curiously hypnotizing impressiveness of whose automatic style – that of persons who spoke by no will of their own – may be remembered by all who ever experienced it' (Hardy, 1904–08, p. 8).

> [T]he survival is carried on with a stolidity and absence of stir which sets one wondering why a thing that is done so perfunctorily should be kept up at all. Like Balaam and other unwilling prophets, the agents seem moved by an inner compulsion to say and do their allotted parts whether they will or no.
>
> (Hardy, 1878, p. 128)

There is a 'cancellation of relations among people [which alternates] with their futile continuance' (Ellmann, 1987, p. 92, describing the literary 'world' of Samuel Beckett). These are sessions in which there is little evidence of curiosity; when links between people, associations, perceptions and events are destroyed: the group maintains 'a non-position in the null dimension' (Eigen, 1985, p. 323).

I intend to present some extended clinical material to show a –K state in a group session. I think that –K states are frequently encountered in outpatient and private practice groups and are not confined to groups of psychotic, narcissistic or borderline patients. (Resnik [1985], Roth [1990] and Pines [1990] discuss these types of psychopathology and related group dynamics which I would consider examples of –K.) Their recognition and analysis by the group psychotherapist (and increasingly by the group members) can facilitate the working through of an extremely primitive and terrifying internal object relationship, ultimately transferred to the group-as-a-whole. First, however, it is necessary to explain more fully what Bion meant by K and –K.

## WHAT ARE K AND –K?

From an analytic perspective, a crucial issue is how developmental experience is internalized and how internalizations affect subsequent experience. Freud conceptualized this in the structural theory of the mind and illustrated it most convincingly in terms of the super-ego in melancholia. Klein emphasized recurrent processes of projection and introjection through which elements of self and object are mutually constructed, modified and organized. Fairbairn understood the same issue by stating that what is internalized is always an object relationship. In all these theories a link is projected or introjected, a link between properties or qualities or images, however rudimentary, of self and other.

What links the self and the object, internally and externally, what constitutes the 'relationship' between two (or in a group, more) human beings, is affect or simply feelings. Such feeling links are usually variations on love and hate, their shadings, intensifications of one or the other, fusions of or conflicts between them. Stern (1985) calls these categorical affects and suggests another range of vitality affects: explosiveness, exuberance, crescendo/decrescendo, piano, flattening and syncopation. The latter are better understood in terms of analogies from music and dance and can also constitute primary links between infant and mother.

In regard to any group session, for example, statements such as 'Jack became furious with Peter's procrastination', 'Mary spoke softly and affectionately to Frank' or 'A crescendo of excitement ran through the group' manifestly refer to descriptions of a basic link between the people involved. In object relations theory, this link characterizes the conscious and unconscious experience of *both* the external relationship and of its internal precipitate, or alternatively the experience of the internal object relation and of its externalization, depending on the predominance of introjective or projective processes.

Bion hypothesized another fundamental human link, the link formed by 'thinking'. By 'thinking' Bion did not mean an abstract cognitive process, the automatic result of brain development or constitutionally given autonomous ego capacity. There is no doubt, as the results of research into the neonatal period amply demonstrate, that the abilities of the infant to discriminate, remember and abstract are considerable (Lichtenberg, 1983; Stern, 1985). Bion's 'thinking' is that process by which a person attempts to know his own personality or that of another. As O'Shaugnessey has concisely stated: 'His concern is with thinking as a human link – the endeavor to understand, comprehend the reality of, get insight into the nature of, etc., oneself or another. Thinking is an emotional experience of trying to know oneself or someone else' (O'Shaugnessey, 1981, p. 181). Such 'thinking' is doubly emotional because doubly painful. On the one hand, as Bion indicated in *Learning from Experience*, the intrinsic uncertainty in the question, 'How can one know anything?' (Bion, 1962b, p. 48) points to a painful quest in which doubt can never be absent; on the other, the 'thinking' in question must often involve trying to know – to attend to, to represent, to remember – painful emotional experiences.

In order to learn from these emotional experiences and to develop, it is necessary to think about them, to know them; but as Bion put it in a crucial phrase that recurs in many of the papers to which I am referring, '[A]n emotional experience that is felt to be painful may initiate an attempt either to evade or to modify the pain according to the capacity of the personality to tolerate frustration' (Bion, 1962b, p. 48). I shall consider below some factors which may influence the balance between tendencies towards evasion, at the extreme a virtual obliteration of the capacity to know emotional experience, to even 'experience experience', and tendencies towards modification which lead to the development of thoughts through identification with an object who can bear raw emotional experience and think about it. Clearly, according to Bion's account this 'thinking' may never occur at all, whatever the intellectual level of attainment in any personality.

Bion used the letter K to symbolize the emotionally painful and unsettling attempt to know about intrinsically turbulent experiences. In the xKy link, 'x is in the state of getting to know y and y is in a state of getting to be known by x' (Bion, 1962b, p. 47). This getting to know is different from any sense of finally possessing a bit of knowledge; rather, Bion consistently emphasized the active process of engaging in an emotional experience concerned with finding the evolving truth (Bion, 1970, pp. 26–40). And given the doubly painful nature of this link, it is not surprising that a 'determination not to experience anything', in this context a not-K or –K link, 'can be shown to co-exist' (Bion, 1962b, p. 18).

The state of –K, of not knowing or misunderstanding, perhaps anti-understanding (Bion, 1962b, pp. 52, 95–9) can be related by analogy to Freud's concept of the pleasure ego elaborated in 'Formulations on the two principles of mental functioning' (1911), a paper to which Bion frequently turned. In this essay Freud discussed the pleasure principle and the reality principle, and he described how an original pleasure ego maintains its integrity by avoiding and discharging – evacuating into the 'not-me', outside world – all unpleasurable tensions and stimuli. In –K, knowledge of painful external and internal reality is evaded; there is 'a need to be rid of emotional complications, of awareness of life and of a relationship with live objects' (Bion, 1962b, p. 11) and in general a hypertrophied pleasure ego functions 'to disencumber the personality of accretions of stimuli' (Bion, 1962b, p. 13). The reality principle, based on knowing the truth about inner, subjective and external, objective reality and their interrelationship, is eclipsed. All meaning deteriorates; symbolization collapses; states of attention are replaced by states of tension; misunderstanding, failure to remember and stripping emotional experience of significance are held to be superior to understanding, coherent representation and integration of experience.

Bion held that active steps have to be taken to achieve this state of mind

(Bion, 1967, p. 113). Further, such 'pleasure' carries a heavy cost:

> This failure [to K] is serious because in addition to the obvious penalties that follow from an inability to learn from experience there is a need for awareness of an emotional experience, similar to the need for an awareness of concrete objects that is achieved through the sense impressions, because lack of such awareness implies a deprivation of truth and truth seems to be essential for psychic health. The effect on the personality of such deprivation is analogous to the effect of physical starvation on the physique.
>
> (Bion, 1962b, p. 56)

More starkly summarized, 'The attempt to evade the experience of contact with live objects . . . leaves the personality unable to have a relationship with any aspect of itself that does not resemble an automaton' (Bion, 1962b, p. 13).

In short, for Bion the struggle to know and to understand (K) or the opposite, mindless evasion and anti-understanding (–K) are as central for mental life as love and hate. Consequently, attempts to know; anxieties about and defences against that which is known; perversion and obliteration of the truth can be as salient in any group session or series of sessions as efforts to express love and hate and the related anxieties, defences and perversions. The K or –K link may be the 'key' to the material (Bion, 1962b, pp. 42–6; O'Shaugnessey, 1981, pp. 184–5).

## THE DEVELOPED THEORY OF PROJECTIVE IDENTIFICATION

I mentioned above that I would comment on the factors, in Bion's view, which influence whether K or –K develops. Basically, the balance is determined by the fate and the nature of the infant's attempt to evade mental pain. To conceptualize this attempt, Bion put forward an interpersonal account of projective identification.

From the point of view of the infant, tension, anxiety, terror and mental pain might be evacuated into the 'not-me'; but from another perspective these states of mind are put into the mother:

> The broad outline of this theory is that there exists an omnipotent phantasy that it is possible to split off temporarily undesired, though sometimes valued, parts of the personality and put them into an object. . . . It is also possible, and in fact essential, to observe evidence which shows that a patient in whom the operation of this omnipotent phantasy can be deduced is capable of behaviour which is related to a counterpart in reality of this phantasy. The patient, even at the outset of life, has contact with

reality sufficient to enable him to act in a way that engenders in the mother feelings that he does not want, or which he wants the mother to have.

(Bion, 1962b, p. 31)

The notion of an unconscious invasive, evacuative, controlling or communicative phantasy, an interaction with an internal object, is extended to include congruent impacts on external objects; and the stage is set for the application of the theory of projective identification to the infant–mother dyad, to the analytic transference–countertransference and to an understanding of unconscious group dynamics (Gordon, 1991).The mother who can emotionally take in her infant's state of mind; attend to, sustain and think about it; who can understand and know (K) her child and respond appropriately may be introjected as someone who can tolerate pain, imbue it with meaning and thereby modify the 'experience of experience'. However, Bion introduced a complemental series or aetiological equation to comprehend the fate and nature of the infant's projective identification in the case of failure to establish the K link. At one end of the series (environment/ nurture) the infant must deal with a mother who cannot tolerate the feelings which her baby is experiencing, wants not to experience and is attempting to repose in her. She becomes panicked by her baby's panic, terrified by his terror; she 'reacted either by denying them ingress, or alternatively by becoming a prey to the anxiety which resulted from introjection of the infant's feelings' (Bion, 1967, p. 104). The mother is consequently experienced and internalized by the infant as an object which is either destroyed by or totally rejecting of the most important means available for the communication of internal states (Bion, 1967, pp. 90–1). Even 'dutiful' mothers, who do not deprive their children of their physical presence, may be externally and become internally an object which does not adequately provide the K function, the linking between infant, the infant's too powerful emotions and a separate mind which can introject turbulence, bear it and thus become available as a model for processing emotional experience.The aborted K link is a psychic catastrophe; its results include:

[A] severe disorder of the impulse to be curious on which all learning depends . . . the conduct of emotional life, in any case a severe problem, becomes intolerable. Feelings of hatred are therefore directed against all emotions including hate itself, and against external reality which stimulates them. It is a short step from hatred of the emotions to hatred of life itself.

(Bion, 1967, pp. 106–7)

In one of his most telling descriptions of this failure to K, Bion wrote that the baby 'reintrojects, not a fear of dying made tolerable, but nameless dread' (Bion, 1967, p. 116).

At the other end of the complemental series, essentially Bion's aetiological equation for psychosis, is the inborn disposition of the infant which
affects the nature of his projective identifications. Bion singled out primary
aggression and envy which he admitted would be increased in the case of the
unreceptive object (Bion, 1962b, pp. 96–9). But he believed that even the
experience of a containing, balanced mother could trigger in the psychotic
infant (or in the psychotic part of the personality) enraged, envious attacks
on the very ability of the mother simultaneously to bear the (to the infant)
unbearable and to retain 'relative' peace of mind. This dynamic is repeated
in the transference when a patient abuses and resents the therapist or other
group members for not feeling exactly the same turmoil or for 'not having to
go through it' the way the patient does after the session. Many sessions
become precisely devoted to putting the therapist or the group 'through it',
not at all to communicate but to spoil the balance which is envied because it
seems unattainable to the patient. In such a state, when the infant does not
permit the mother to exercise her introjecting, linking function, potential
development and internalization of a K link is not only violently attacked but
transformed. The envious, destructive assaults on the container/mind of the
mother are themselves projected into the mother whose image, altered
through the process, becomes one of an extremely dangerous object that
seeks greedily to devour the infant's psyche or whose peace of mind is
interpreted as hostile indifference (Bion, 1967, pp. 103–7). This is –K: a
rampant, obstructive object (Bion, 1967, pp. 90–2); 'a vagina-like "breast" '
(Bion, 1967, p. 115) seeks to strip all communication of meaning, to
misunderstand and to reduce emotional experience to a nullity (Bion, 1962b,
pp. 96–9).When a relationship to such an object – an object constructed
through experience of a mother who either failed to introject projective
identifications and appeared therefore to be intrinsically antagonistic to
curiosity and to life, or whose basic understanding was projectively
transformed by the infant's hate and envy into rapacious greed and
introjection of projective identifications in order to decimate and degen-
erate their contents – is internalized, the inner world is profoundly changed:

> [T]he ... psyche contains an internal object which is opposed to, and
> destructive of, all links whatsoever from the most primitive (which I have
> suggested is a normal degree of projective identification) to the most
> sophisticated forms of verbal communication and the arts. In this state of
> mind emotion is hated; it is felt to be too powerful to be contained by the
> immature psyche, it is felt to link objects and it gives reality to objects
> which are not self and therefore inimical to primary narcissism.
>
> (Bion, 1967, p. 108)

Identification with such an internal object by an individual, a subgroup or a group leads to virulent –K activity. Victimization by this object can result in numbing torpor, blocking, terror of fragmentation, dense silence and intensified projective processes. As with any internal object relationship, either role may be externalized (projected or projectively identified) in the transference–countertransference which entails corresponding alterations in the perception of individuals, subgroups, elements of the group system (norms, values, goals) and the group-as-a-whole.

## 'THE –K OBJECT AS GROUP'

The following clinical material, an account of a group session immediately preceding a summer holiday break, shows how I try to use the above concepts in my work. A process report of the entire session is presented, rather than a series of vignettes, in order to convey the accumulative impact of turbulence, disjunction and intense disturbance which was so important in finally reaching an understanding of the group members' unconscious communications and experience.

There are four men and four women in the group, but one of the women (Janice) is absent. Alan arrives several minutes late and joins a silent group. He eventually comments on the heat and mentions almost in passing that he nearly didn't come to the session. His computer had 'cut out', certain vital information hadn't been processed, but it didn't matter. After further silence, several people remark tersely on the closeness. Joan complains about biting flies which flourish in this weather and get into the house or threaten to do so. She then notices an empty chair, asks where Janice is and is briefly told by Alan, 'She's away'. 'Oh yes, she told us about that last time, didn't she', replies Joan in a manner that dismisses the issue as a cut-and-dried matter which needs no more exploration. I feel slightly uneasy and wonder if I am in for a session in which I get completely landed with the analytic function and then set upon as if experienced as an obnoxious fly, seeking heat and closeness. James comments on his 'irritability on weekends', and Bert cuts across, 'Sleep, that's what I do'. This reminds me of a recent session in which Bert had extolled the virtues of sleep and had added, 'When I get bad thoughts in my head they just went out of my mind'. An image was evoked of a 'spastic mind', a mind out of control and somehow not experienced as part of the self which just gets rid of painful thoughts in a mysterious way.

James now wishes 'to change the subject' and tells us that he has attended a crisis meeting at work, at the bank where he is an assistant manager. There is only silence in response to James, without even the hint of amusement which is often stirred up in the group by his pompous style of talking. After a further silence which has the effect of stranding James, I suggest that the allusion to his irritability on weekends and to a crisis meeting elsewhere enables us to avoid considering that it might be something to do with us now, but James says, 'No, except that "they" seem to be at sixes and sevens about the holiday'. I said, 'It looks like you're excluding yourself from the sixes and sevens', and James insists that Bert, Mary and maybe absent Janice seemed bothered about the break (he didn't know about Alan) but makes it clear that he is *not* annoyed. If anything, James looks annoyed that I even think he might be annoyed, and in a completely 'rational' tone says, 'Of course it's OK for you to have a holiday'. I become aware that I am working hard to get things going in this desultory atmosphere.

Throughout a silence, punctuated by a few sparse comments, it was possible to gather that there had been some talk about the holiday before the session. It turned out that in the waiting-room Mary had been resentful about the length of the holiday which she now repeats in a stumbling, barely coherent way. A qualified nurse doing further training in psychiatry and recovering from a divorce which had left her and her ex-husband sharing the three children from week to week, Mary murmurs that she has noticed the holiday is six weeks this year, not five like last time. Her manner is confused and conveys an almost depersonalized sense of being out of touch. It is immediately clarified by James that the holiday is five weeks, again as if this should put an end to all discussion. It does and there is a vacant silence for ten minutes; some members sit limply, others with closed eyes. I find myself thinking about a large group of chronic psychotic patients at one of the community mental health centres where I meet the staff for supervision, but soon my mind wanders and I nearly forget the group. Joan suddenly turns and asks me directly why the holiday is six weeks and in August, but she immediately answers herself by stating, 'I suppose it's to do with school and children, but not everyone, even if most, may be covered by that.' Bert has been sitting in a heavy knitted sweater in spite of the heat, and he is clearly boiling away inside but sitting on it. This was as obvious to everyone else in the group as to me, or should have been to anyone with eyes and ears, yet no one has commented. Bert's breathing is like steam coming out of a pressure cooker, but the most he says, as if answering Joan, is 'What's the point?' Mary takes up the theme, attempting now to defend the holiday in terms of 'letting the land lie fallow'. Bert looks at me and demands. 'What's fallow?' I point out that he doesn't ask Mary (he doesn't relate directly to a woman but to a man, a persistent difficulty which keeps him at home, attached to ageing parents, with no relationship since his fiancée died of cancer fifteen years before). Bert continues to glare at me: 'What's the point?' enacted. Nobody defines 'fallow' for Bert, and I decide not to take over this function which would be well within the capacity of this group.

I am aware now that the members of the group are responding to the impending holiday in a 'catastrophic' mode and that I am struggling to try to understand this response in the face of their reluctance, as well as my own, to go further. I want to 'lie fallow' for the rest of the session, think of my holiday and become very uncomfortable which in turn I want to avoid. Mary eventually continues and talks about her own wish to get away and forget everything, although she can see this is really impossible; she sounds slightly more focused. Then she sees, 'irrationally' as she terms it, that she thought I was ditching them, dumping them. I link this feeling to (absent) Janice's motivation in accepting a holiday booked out of the blue and without discussion by her husband, although she had the group times well in advance, and I reflect back Joan's earlier implication that it had been out of Janice's hands.

The group seems poised between two defensive strategies in dealing with feelings of loss: an obliteration of any meaning regarding the holiday and a forceful attack on me, seen as outrageous for daring to go away for so long. Frank weighs in on both sides, angrily asserting that he is not concerned in the slightest that I am going away; it was obvious I would have a holiday and there could consequently be no significance whatever in talking further about it. James looks at me and says he was very angry when I had earlier observed how, in his 'sixes and sevens' remarks, he had left himself out. Joan caps this crescendo with, 'Just looking at you makes people angry'. I felt pleasantly surprised by this extremely rare, nearly direct communication of Joan's own feelings (she chronically somatized her feelings and was initially referred for this) and was just able to hang on to my chair and to contain my experience that I was now being set upon by biting flies and it was certainly close and getting hot. The angry attack also helped me to focus again and to try to formulate some understanding of the group which I could convey before the session ended. It was clear that lying fallow would not be enough. Frank then gets very angry, apparently with the group, for 'not paying attention to me, not asking me last time by what authority I spoke to Gill about her children'. No one, he explains, had asked him if he had kids himself; they didn't want to know him. Frank is disappointed in the group, especially the previous two sessions; it is making him worse and he is going to quit. The others immediately try to reassure Frank that they are happy to hear him speaking up recently, but I notice they are rather off-balance and intimidated. I remind Frank and the others that he told us in his first session some months before that 'trouble would start' for him when he began to feel familiar; before that stage in relationships he experienced no anxiety or interpersonal difficulties. I suggest that the group had noted this and had been slightly scared off by Frank's warning which was now coming home to roost. Bert interjects, 'Familiarity breeds contempt'. Mary says she thinks that is the message they might be giving one another all the time. I reflect to myself how Frank, perhaps on behalf of others in the group, is trying to relate more closely while simultaneously signalling, 'Don't acknowledge my wish for closeness lest it lead to disaster'. I could also see that my holiday was clearly being experienced as contemptuous lack of attention and care and that my active stance so far could be a response to this.

Gill had started to cry, characteristically attempting not to let it show, about half way through these interchanges, and Mary finally remarks on this. Gill tells us that she has miscarried that week, and the emotional atmosphere alters completely. She blames herself even though Tom, her husband, doesn't. (Gill has two sons from a previous marriage. Both she and Tom were very ambivalent about marrying, she because Tom is ten years younger; and Gill felt she had to give Tom a child even though the marriage was recent and they hadn't had much time to settle down.) 'Tom cried and we talked about it together.' Joan, in a tone which combines arrogant, dictatorial certainty with a hint of panic, says, 'You "shouldn't" feel like that, what will be will be.' I see this as both her own defence against childlessness and an expression of the group defence against feelings of loss and grief, an offer to return to Bert's earlier recommendation to ignore thoughts and feelings, to 'go to sleep'. After a silence, I say: 'This is how Gill does feel; the group so far is almost debating whether certain feelings, about how we relate together here or about the holiday and now what Gill has told us, are justified. There is surprise that, for example, Frank is angry or that Gill is very upset or Mary confused. Some of you (I had Alan, silently aloof, and Bert in mind) seem to be afraid of your anger and seem to keep it bottled up.' Gill continues that she'd known the pregnancy wasn't right. As we all knew, there was persistent early bleeding, so in a way Gill felt forewarned. But she feels left with a sense of having let Tom down as well as with the whole issue of putting pressure on herself to become pregnant without working it out in the group. She knows from the doctors that it isn't her age, that they can try again but anticipates great anxiety during the first twelve weeks.

I think to myself that Gill needs to get pregnant in order to stave off longstanding anxieties about her value within her family, in relationship to Tom and to me and the group. I can also see how Gill communicates her conflict that she both has to have a baby and can't have one now, but I wait to see if the group will respond more directly to her sadness. Mary takes a lead in this and the others sympathize with Gill, almost polarizing Joan as the 'unfeeling one'. I continue silently to wonder under the impact of this distress whether what Gill is telling us could also be heard as a metaphor for her own and the others' current experience in the group: is she an insecurely planted egg in a womb which can't or won't hold her and help her to develop, and am I aborting them now? Is their anxiety being 'owned' a bit more, leading to terrifying questions about whether the group can contain what they bring, for example, Frank's anxiety about his 'familiarity' with the group, Joan's anger, Gill's tears, Bert's fury? Her 'messed up, bleeding pregnancy' through which we had accompanied Gill for weeks – was this the group/womb since Joe had left and Frank arrived?

Gill seems to be calmer, but before she can proceed James says he agrees with me about the group's response to Frank: 'We probably did see that he didn't want us to get too close because he might be afraid of that.' This infrequent sign of agreement with me seemed more a way of blaming Frank for the difficulty as if James could only get closer to me by elbowing aside his younger brother in the transference. In combination with its content, I experienced the timing and impact of James's intervention as an unconscious attempt to abort a rival, a miscarriage of understanding and a chilling severance of the group's tenuous contact with Gill. Gill immediately says that, sitting next to Bert, she can feel how tense and angry he is, but she hasn't been able to mention this because she is afraid that Bert might tell her to 'fuck off' and she would. Her comment serves further to deflect attention from what she had been experiencing a few moments before, as well as to push Bert to express tense anger. There is general discussion on what to do when people say 'fuck off': do you go or keep trying and stay involved? Would Janice tell the group to 'fuck off' if the missed session were mentioned when she returns? Frank says, in relation to the uncertainty about Janice, that he feels good when his wife is away. He uses his wife 'like a crutch, but this must stop'. Alan, who has maintained a nearly mute, distanced silence, says that he has again been refusing his wife intercourse. Frank suddenly turns to Bert and in an aggressive tone tackles him 'on your chronic dependency on your mother'. 'My mother is a brick', retaliates Bert. 'Yes, not a woman, you're just like me with my wife, a baby', Frank continues. Bert finally blows: 'I'm fucked, I'm totally fucked!' I immediately ask for his associations to this; if he is 'fucked' who is he and who is doing it to him? He screams that he's 'one out of ten on driving'. (Bert came to the group after he failed his heavy goods vehicle licence; he panicked and fled from the exam, was unable consequently to drive his car and had been 'off sick' from work.) 'I come downstairs in the morning full of beans' – Bert suddenly looks potent and sits straight in his chair, Joan murmurs 'hard' – but he is then deflated by the group with comments like 'What kind of beans?', 'Human beings?' and slumps back, looking at the floor. Frank puts it together: 'You wake up feeling alive, full of feelings [after a dream, I think] but can't keep it up.'

There is silence, and I follow my associations to dreaming. We know that Bert's rarely remembered dreams are about Sharon, his late fiancée who died of cancer fifteen years ago just before they had planned to marry. Sharon's father loomed large in Bert's life and in his inner world. He had been Bert's boss, had in fact got him a job and had introduced Bert to his daughter, thus almost providing a wife as well. But according to Bert this man turned out to be a 'bastard' after the funeral; he took all the couple's furniture and money when Bert had been disorientated and depressed. Bert often felt and said in the group that he could kill this man. I had also previously interpreted Bert's unconscious identification with his would-be father-in-law, his fear that if he were a 'man' he would destroy any woman by his aggressive intercourse. There had been many associations to how, in Bert's opinion, this man had decimated his wife and daughter through womanizing and intemperate language. Bert's anxiety and withdrawal covered an omnipotent sense of himself destroying ('fucking') Sharon. Bert is also consciously afraid of becoming like his uncle, his father's wayward brother who was an alcoholic and had never married. His father's one plea to Bert was not to be like this uncle who, within the family, had achieved almost mythical status as one who could not contain his impulses. Bert turns to me and says that I'd been giving him a rough time in the session, 'fucking me up', and that the whole group had felt intolerable.

The group again lapses into silence. An awful image comes into my mind which I immediately try to wipe out. Bert had once described his fiancée's head, after the surgery for a malignant tumour, as looking like a female baboon's swollen red vulva. I could recognize my own wish to obliterate this image, as though one's mind auto-destructs its capacity to attend to its contents, and I tried to recover to formulate privately how I could understand Bert, what had just gone on within myself and their relation to the total session. At this stage in its history (looking back, I obviously needed to get some distance to get a grip on this emotional turbulence) the group seemed to be at a defensive cusp, a point of potential change. Previous sessions of predominantly –K activity, some of which was startling in this session, when thoughts, feelings and perceptions had been completely obliterated; when the themes had been to do with sleeping and spastic minds; when interactions and relationships seemed to be a series of fragments with sparse acknowledgement of prior contributions; when the structure was one of monologue – this manifest configuration began to reveal the underlying, terrifying sexualized and aggressive phantasies related to catastrophic loss and damage which the configuration had itself both expressed and defended against. My own immediate experience was that an unbearable bit of psychic stuff, condensing a crude, concrete visceral image of animal fertility with an equally primitive image of an utterly attacked and disintegrated human form – mind and womb – had surfaced and become evident momentarily but long enough to be intuited. The group itself, I thought, had been identified with this image. Perhaps throughout the session everyone had been striving to avoid this, but within the boundary of the whole group it had taken form. At first destructive conflict, contempt, confusion, anger, attacks on closeness had been enacted inside the group; the result, expressed with poignant human suffering, was revealed when Gill told us of her miscarriage; this experience in turn was evacuated by James's nullifying intervention and Alan's refusal to connect; finally, Bert is prompted to enact his identification with a destroyed container as well as its miscarried contents, an image of which I had picked up and quickly evaded.

I then said to the group members that I knew how strong some of the feelings were that had been expressed in the session, and I particularly referred to Gill's sadness in losing her pregnancy, 'as if there has been an awful abortion. And Gill's experience, and our involvement in it, may also be showing us something about how it feels to be in this group now. You are all very concerned about the miscarried possibilities and hopes, the aborted closeness in the group, the disrupted contact partly to do with the holiday break. These thoughts are frightening and some of them have to be avoided and not even thought about or noticed. One of these awful thoughts seems to be that it is my fault that Bert is still "fucked" after one year in the group and therefore "retires" from the group here to get back at me. It's as if I'm subjecting him and the group to a cruel and intolerable attack by organizing and bringing you together in this group, by allowing there to be this place where you are then exposed to and spill on to one another such emotion, which you believe is then ignored or worse, stuffed back into you.'

After a short, less oppressive silence, Mary tells us that she has just had a picture in her mind of me sitting under a palm tree; 'in the Caribbean', adds Bert. I use this and continue: 'Frank says he feels left out, maybe speaking for everyone, but he then retaliates, again perhaps for everyone, by threatening to abandon us if it gets too rough and the stakes get too high. You believe I have allowed this chaos to be set loose on you and am now unaffected on an island.' There is another pause, and Joan and Gill begin to talk to Bert more warmly but also without the previous fear. Bert says he feels a little better now, relieved he 'got it out', but that he might dwell on these issues over the break. At this moment I sense that he, on behalf of the group, may be voicing an anxiety that could lead to readopting –K defences. As the session ends, Joan turns to Bert and says, 'You take care of yourself,' adding (to my astonishment), 'but if you just dwell on it that's not thinking'. The members wish one another and me a good holiday, and I leave with the impression that some significant shift has occurred and that the need for primitive defences had been somewhat diminished.

## DISCUSSION

It is well recognized in the group psychotherapy literature that 'the group-*qua*-group transference is a "normal" phenomenon of group life' (Ashbach and Schermer, 1987, p. 183). And as various terms used to describe transferences to the group suggest ('primordial', 'primitive', 'matrix'), the externalized phantasy objects are considered to be aspects of the mother. Anxious separations from or wishes for union with the nurturing 'good mother' group; hatred, sado-masochistic enthralment or terrified fight/flight in relation to the tantalizing or persecuting 'bad mother' group; and defensive splitting and projection of all-good or all-bad images on to the group, the therapist(s) or subsystems of the group (roles, norms, goals, subgroups) have been the focus of both theoretical and clinical interest (Durkin, 1964; Scheidlinger, 1974; Whiteley and Gordon, 1979; Agazarian and Peters, 1981; Ashbach and Schermer, 1987; Ganzarain, 1989). Increasingly, understanding of the transferred internal object has included its containing, environmental (holding) or psychic metabolizing (processing) capacities – or, as I have emphasized, the lack of them. These are qualities of the mother as a transformational object (Bollas, 1987), and I have instanced Bion's concept of K as a salient characterization of this transformational object function and of the internal relationship to it. König (1985) has implicitly linked the nature of the maternal transference to the therapeutic action of group psychotherapy: 'The mother object transferred would then be the chief determinant of the depth of the group's regression' (König, 1985, p. 155) and, therefore, of the level of unconscious experience mobilized and potentially available for working through. To the extent that an internalized –K object relationship can be enacted in the transference, group members are afforded the opportunity to contact, to face and to work through patterns of relating and identification which perpetuate the obliteration of meaning and lie at the root of psychopathology.

The clinical material I have put forward shows how the group came to be experienced unconsciously as an utterly destroyed maternal container which, in retaliation, took on a lethal impetus and threatened to annihilate the minds of the group members. The nature of this object could only be grasped gradually. Initially, I was mostly aware of how the group members were treating one another. I was struck by the extent to which comments (including my own) were not pursued; the meanings of, for example, absence from the group (Janice), words ('lie fallow'), misconceptions about the length of the holiday (all group members had been given a calendar with holiday dates for the several years this group had been meeting) were ignored, denied, explicitly held to be irrelevant, misunderstood.The atmosphere – a vital element of the transference which every group creates in each session – was unusually harsh, uncomfortable and uncaring, interspersed with periods of sluggish, lethargic blankness. The tone in which group members spoke often combined arrogance, omniscience and stupidity: James's, Frank's and Alan's exclusive superiority and dismissiveness towards others; Bert's laudation of sleep and evacuation of painful thoughts; Joan's recommendation to Gill not to feel what Gill obviously could not help but feel.

In my account of the session, I have tried to show the process by which I was affected physically and emotionally, as well as what associations came to mind as I became immersed in the world unconsciously created by this group. I was handled and used by the group members in ways which I attempted to discover but also did not want to know. Countertransference is inevitably concerned with the group psychotherapist's affective experience, but I have included thoughts and images which are essential aids in working through rather than enacting countertransference feelings (Brenman Pick, 1985). In the session described, I consider the evocation of an image, the baboon's vulva condensed with the fiancée's horribly wounded and deformed head after two bouts of major surgery, to have been fundamental in helping me to organize my emotional experience, to integrate it with other material in the session and to formulate my interpretations. The image was a 'selected fact . . . the emotional experience of a sense of discovery of coherence' (Bion, 1962b, p. 73) which enabled me to relate the group interaction; the atmosphere; my personal feeling of being attacked in my mind and succumbing, then shaking free as the anger in the group became more obvious and directly expressed; and the themes of abortion, miscarriage and loss.Only when the −K object could be projected on to the group, and after the anxieties of relating to such an object could be recognized and tentatively formulated in words, was it possible for the individual members to begin to confront how deeply identified with this object they were. There are signs of concern about their treatment of their own experience, of me and of the group time and space, especially the mutually devaluing and wasting attacks on feeling typified by James's abrupt change of subject after Gill had spoken.

The working through of these identifications took months and years but eventuated in many changes, among them: Bert became able to remember his dreams and regularly bring them to the sessions after twenty years of 'amnesia'; Gill, in her own time, conceived and gave birth to a child; Mary contained her confusion instead of projectively identifying it into her children and the other members of the group; James overcame years of schizoid grandiosity and started to share his feelings with the group members and then with his second wife. Slowly the wish and the capacity to know their own and others' personalities began to develop. This was obviously not a magical breakthrough or a straightforward evolution, but I do not believe it could have occurred without attention to the mental realm denominated by Bion as K and −K and to manifestations in the group experience of the −K link. I think that many of the clinical phenomena conceptualized, for example, by Nitsun (1991) as the 'anti-group'[1] and by Roth (1990) as 'a group that would not relate to itself'[2] are dramatizations in the here-and-now of the group sessions of a –K transference, the object alternately projected on to the group and enacted by the members. These transferences can be handled analytically, through interpretation, if they are consistently addressed wherever sufficient evidence exists to demonstrate them to the group members.

## CONCLUSION

Bion clearly expressed his view in *Learning from Experience* (Bion, 1962b, p. 99) that the clinical theories developed in his post-*Experiences in Groups* work with psychotic and other seriously disturbed patients were applicable to groups. He discussed this in *Attention and Interpretation* as container–contained relationships. However, aside from some general examples of commensal (creative: 'two objects share a third to the advantage of all three'); symbiotic (mutually satisfactory: 'one depends on another to mutual advantage') and parasitic (mutually destructive: 'one depends on another to produce a third, which is destructive of all three') (Bion, 1970, p. 95) encounters between the mystic and the establishment, Bion did not offer clinical material from psychotherapy groups to illustrate the application. After considering Bion's concepts of K and –K, I have presented a session to show how I use these in my clinical practice. I have elaborated elsewhere (Gordon, 1987) some of the reasons for thinking that members of a group may be particularly susceptible to an 'experience of gap' – a sudden experience of overwhelming separation, otherness, void (Ashbach and Schermer, 1987, p. 198) or opaque inscrutability which is traumatic in the formative stages of group life, although it may occur in any phase of the developing group; is massively defended against; and often irrupts at times of stress, for example around holiday breaks. I think that the intense feelings of alienation, emptiness and meaninglessness which accompany an 'experience of gap' reflect and express the unconscious effects on the personality of the psychic catastrophe Bion symbolizes by –K. The working through of these issues can be facilitated via the resonating negative transference to the group of what I have called the –K object relationship. This requires close attention to every indication in the group interaction, structure, atmosphere and themes, especially as registered in the countertransference, that a process to reverse K is active: consciously or unconsciously the group members 'for whatever reason of anxiety, perversion, pain or envy' try not to 'think about and keep a truthful and real record of their relationships' (O'Shaugnessey, 1981, pp. 188–9). I have emphasized the technical importance of addressing interpretively both the projection of the –K object on to the group and the profound identification with and enactment of this object role by group members.

## NOTES

1 '[A] construct describing a constellation of destructive fantasies and impulses that may impinge on the group in varying ways and degrees' (Nitsun, 1991, p. 18).
2 Roth discusses deficits in and defences against experience of 'the object relationship from which symbolic meanings arise' (Roth, 1990, p. 145).

## REFERENCES

Agazarian, Y. and Peters, R. (1981) *The Visible and Invisible Group*, London and New York: Routledge & Kegan Paul.

Anzieu, D. (1975) *The Group and the Unconscious*, transl. B. Kilbourne, 1984, London: Routledge & Kegan Paul.

Ashbach, C. and Schermer, V. (1987) *Object Relations, the Self, and the Group: A conceptual paradigm*, London and New York: Routledge & Kegan Paul.

Bion, W.R. (1957) 'Differentiation of the psychotic from the non-psychotic personalities', *International Journal of Psycho-Analysis* 38: 266–75. Republished in Bion, W.R. (1967) *Second Thoughts*, London: William Heinemann.

—— (1958) 'On arrogance', *International Journal of Psycho-Analysis* 39: 341–9. Republished in Bion, W.R. (1967) *Second Thoughts*, London: William Heinemann.

—— (1959) 'Attacks on linking', *International Journal of Psycho-Analysis* 40: 308–15. Republished in Bion, W.R. (1967) *Second Thoughts*, London: William Heinemann.

—— (1961) *Experiences in Groups*, London: Tavistock.

—— (1962a) 'A theory of thinking', *International Journal of Psycho-Analysis* 43: 306–10. Republished in Bion, W.R. (1967) *Second Thoughts*, London: William Heinemann.

—— (1962b) *Learning from Experience*, London: William Heinemann. Second reprinting, 1988, London: Maresfield Reprints. All quotations in the text are from the 1988 edition.

—— (1967) *Second Thoughts*, London: William Heinemann. Reprinted, 1984, London: Maresfield Reprints. All quotations in the text are from the 1984 edition.

—— (1970) *Attention and Interpretation*, London: Tavistock. Second reprinting, 1988, London: Maresfield Reprints. All quotations in the text are from the 1988 edition.

—— (1975) *A Memoir of the Future*, vol. 1 *The Dream*, Rio de Janeiro: Imago Editora.

—— (1977) *A Memoir of the Future*, vol. 2 *The Past Presented*, Rio de Janeiro: Imago Editora.

—— (1979) *A Memoir of the Future*, vol. 3 *The Dawn of Oblivion*, Rio de Janeiro: Imago Editora.

126  *John Gordon*

Bollas, C. (1987) *The Shadow of the Object: Psychoanalysis of the Unthought Known*, London: Free Association Books.

Brenman Pick, I. (1985) 'Working through in the countertransference', *International Journal of Psycho-Analysis* 66: 157–66.

Brown, D.G. (1985) 'Bion and Foulkes: basic assumptions and beyond', in M. Pines (ed.), *Bion and Group Psychotherapy*, London: Routledge & Kegan Paul.

Durkin, H. (1964) *The Group in Depth*, New York: International Universities Press.

Eigen, M. (1985) 'Toward Bion's starting point: between catastrophe and faith', *International Journal of Psycho-Analysis* 66: 321–30.

Ellmann, R. (1987) *Four Dubliners*, London: Hamish Hamilton.

Freud, S. (1911) 'Formulations on the two principles of mental functioning', *Standard Edition* 12: 213–36.

Gaburri, E. (1990) 'Thought disorders and identity disturbances between the individual and the group', in B.E. Roth *et al.* (eds), *The Difficult Patient in Group*, Madison, CT: International Universities Press.

Ganzarain, R. (1989) *Object Relations Group Psychotherapy: The Group as an Object, a Tool and a Training Base*, Madison, CT: International Universities Press.

Gordon, J. (1987) 'The experience of "gap" in group-analytic psychotherapy: reflections on an aspect of psychotic functioning, its manifestation and analysis in the group', paper presented to a seminar at the Institute of Group Analysis, London: IGA Library.

—— (1991) 'Discussion on J.F. Zender's paper "Projective identification in group psychotherapy" ', *Group Analysis* 24: 130–2.

Grinberg, L. (1985) 'Bion's contribution to the understanding of the individual and the group', in M. Pines (ed.), *Bion and Group Psychotherapy*, London: Routledge & Kegan Paul.

Hardy, T. (1904–08) *The Dynasts*, London: Macmillan, 1978.

—— (1878) *The Return of the Native*, London: Macmillan, 1985.

Hinshelwood, R.D. (1987) *What Happens in Groups: Psychoanalysis, the Individual and the Community*, London: Free Association Books.

—— (1989) *A Dictionary of Kleinian Thought*, London: Free Association Books.

James, D.C. (1981) 'W.R. Bion's contribution to the field of group therapy: an appreciation', in L. Wolberg and M. Aronson (eds), *Group and Family Therapy*, New York: Brunner/Mazel.

—— (1984) 'Bion's "containing" and Winnicott's "holding" in the context of the group matrix', *International Journal of Group Psychotherapy* 34: 201–13.

Jaques, E. (1955) 'Social systems as a defense against persecutory and depressive anxiety', in M. Klein, P. Heimann and R. Money-Kyrle (eds), *New Directions in Psycho-Analysis*, London: Tavistock.

Joseph, B. (1989) *Psychic Equilibrium and Psychic Change: Selected Papers of Betty Joseph*, ed. E.B. Spillius and M. Feldman, London and New York: Tavistock/Routledge.

Kaës, R. (1976) 'Analyse inter-transférentielle, fonction alpha et groupe conteneur', *L'Evolution psychiatrique* 2: 339–47.

Karterud, S.W. (1990) 'Bion or Kohut: two paradigms of group dynamics', in B.E. Roth *et al.* (eds), *The Difficult Patient in Group*, Madison, CT: International Universities Press.

König, K. (1985) 'Basic assumption groups and working groups revisited', in M. Pines (ed.), *Bion and Group Psychotherapy*, London: Routledge & Kegan Paul.

Lichtenberg, J. (1983) *Psychoanalysis and Infant Research*, Hillsdale, NJ: Analytic Press.

Lubin, B. and Lubin, A.W. (1987) *Comprehensive Index of Group Psychotherapy Writings*, American Group Psychotherapy Association Monograph no. 2, Madison, CT: International Universities Press.

Meltzer, D. (1978) *The Kleinian Development*, Strath Tay, Perthshire: Clunie Press.

Menzies (Lyth), I. (1960) 'A case study of the functioning of a social system as a defense against anxiety', *Human Relations* 13: 95–121.

Nitsun, M. (1991) 'The anti-group: destructive forces in the group and their therapeutic potential', *Group Analysis* 24: 7–20.

O'Shaugnessey, E. (1981) 'A commemorative essay on W.R. Bion's theory of thinking', *Journal of Child Psychotherapy* 7: 181–92.

Pines, M. (ed.) (1985) *Bion and Group Psychotherapy*, London: Routledge & Kegan Paul.

—— (1990) 'Group analytic psychotherapy and the borderline patient', in B.E. Roth *et al.* (eds), *The Difficult Patient in Group*, Madison, CT: International Universities Press.

Resnik, S. (1985) 'The space of madness', in M. Pines (ed.), *Bion and Group Psychotherapy*, London: Routledge & Kegan Paul.

Roth, B.E. (1990) 'The group that would not relate to itself', in B.E. Roth *et al.* (eds), *The Difficult Patient in Group*, Madison, CT: International Universities Press.

Roth, B.E., Stone, W.N. and Kibel, H.D. (eds) (1990) *The Difficult Patient in Group: Group Psychotherapy with Borderline and Narcissistic Disorders*, American Group Psychotherapy Association Monograph no. 6, Madison, CT: International Universities Press.

Scheidlinger, S. (1974) 'On the concept of the "mother group"', *International Journal of Group Psychotherapy* 24: 417–28.

Schermer, V. (1985) 'Beyond Bion: the basic assumption states revisited', in M. Pines (ed.), *Bion and Group Psychotherapy*, London: Routledge & Kegan Paul.

Spillius, E.B. (ed.) (1988) *Melanie Klein Today*: vol. 1, *Mainly Theory*; vol. 2, *Mainly Practice*, London: Routledge.

Stern, D. (1985) *The Interpersonal World of the Infant: A View from Psychoanalysis and Developmental Psychology*, New York: Basic Books.

Whiteley, J.S. and Gordon, J. (1979) *Group Approaches in Psychiatry*, London: Routledge & Kegan Paul.

# 6 Borderline phenomena in analytic groups

*Malcolm Pines*

## EDITORS' INTRODUCTION

This chapter combines a description of the fundamentals of group-analytic psychotherapy as developed by S.H. Foulkes with an integrated object-relations, self and ego psychological approach to group treatment of patients in the 'borderline spectrum'. It will be seen that, while several other contributors to this volume are interested primarily in the externalization and projection of internal objects and the vicissitudes of mental content and process, Pines further understands the borderline in terms of that elusive but crucial element, the self.

Pines's treatment of borderline patients reflects a shift away from the confrontive and perhaps rather harsh approach which characterized earlier therapeutic efforts – for example, the early work of Kernberg and of Masterson – towards a more empathic view which includes the acknowledgement of real needs, hurts and trauma of the self system. While Pines acknowledges the need for containment and boundaries, he also stresses the importance of empathic mirroring, holding and soothing aspects of the therapist's stance.

---

The group analytic situation as devised by S.H. Foulkes combines strength with sensitivity. The model has been adequately outlined elsewhere and I have described experiences with difficult and borderline patients in other publications as have other group analysts. In this chapter my aim is to describe and to discuss situations that strain and test the capacity of the group-analytic setting to, and sometimes beyond, its limits. Particular to the group-analytic approach is the clarification and emphasis that the group analyst has a dual function as a group leader. First, this is to be the 'dynamic administrator' who has the responsibility for establishing and maintaining the group-analytic setting. After this he can become the 'group conductor'.

As dynamic administrator his/her responsibilities are to select individual patients for membership of the group and for composition of the group so that there is an adequate balance of resources to enable the group to function therapeutically.

The conductor must take into account the psychological strengths and weaknesses of the various members, so that, for instance, if the group includes quite ill patients then there must also be a potential for health in the other members of the group to fulfil what S.H. Foulkes called his 'Basic Law of Group Dynamics'. By this he meant that though each member of the group may themselves represent some form of deviance from the social and cultural norm, together those group members will have a built-in developmental thrust towards regaining that norm. This can be expressed in terms of regression and progression, that the individuals may in different ways show different forms of regression but the group itself will have an inherent move towards higher levels of organization, that is of progression. The exception to this is when there is a homogeneous population who all come from some form of deviant subculture, for instance of psychopaths or other severely deviant characters. Such a group will not have an inherent developmental thrust towards the social norm. The dynamic administrator has responsibility for control of the group boundaries, for determining who enters and exits from the group, for the boundaries of time and place. Any analytic group is at an interface with its surrounding and encompassing environment, a larger group. This can be a clinic, an in- or outpatient service, and so on. The dynamic responses of this wider setting to the dynamics of the analytic group will be especially important when 'boundary' incidents occur – that is, when issues provoked and arising in the group itself impinge on the human and physical surround. In the clinic this can involve the interactions with and responses of other staff, other therapists, administrators, secretaries, domestics, other patients. In private practice this may affect the therapist's own domestic arrangements – his/her family space, privacy. My extensive experience over more than thirty years of psychoanalytic and group-analytic work has been in the setting of the Group-Analytic Practice. This has recently been described in *The Practice of Group Analysis* (1992). In this situation a number of colleagues who know one another well and who share a common group-analytic orientation occupy a physical setting that has been adapted for group psychotherapy. It is a large apartment with several rooms and secretarial staff and there are a large number of groups taking place each day of the week. The members of this Practice combine to make a common waiting list for patients, and by sharing this waiting list they are usually able to place patients in what seems to be an appropriate group, for groups take on a style and culture of their own over time based upon their histories which derive from the style of conductor, the types of patients in the groups, the success or lack of success in helping the patients already in the group or who have left. Our groups are mainly of the 'slow-open' type, where the life of the group extends over several years and there is a slow turnover of patients during that time. Hopefully the therapist remains constant! The combined experience of the Group-Analytic Practice has given a reasonably good sense of what we can do to help patients and which patients may be more suited to individual or marital therapy or family therapy rather than to group analysis.

For many years we have worked with twice-a-week groups, each session lasting ninety minutes. In these twice-a-week groups we are able to place patients who both need and can use the greater frequency and continuity. This includes the more disturbed patients. Notably our groups also often contain persons who are in group-analytic training. Though the presence of these members does offer a level of strength and stability to the group, the trainees themselves are not expected to act as assistant therapists. Indeed, such moves are very quickly recognized and discouraged. In the main the trainees themselves accept and wish to make use of the therapeutic opportunities to a personal degree.

In this book we are looking at various aspects of regression so I shall now briefly discuss some aspects of regression in psychoanalytical psychotherapy. It is useful to think of regression in two senses:

1  The individual who comes for therapy is already in some ways in regression. Here the term is used as representing some backward movement from an assumed norm. Otto Kernberg's (1984) classification is a useful way of identifying forms of regression psychodynamically.

2  A psychotherapeutic situation offers and encourages some regressive moves. In the safety of such a situation we can enable patients to come into contact with earlier forms of experience, through memory, through contact with and release of affect and through the transference relationships that they have with other members of the group, the therapist and with the group-as-a-whole. The psychotherapeutic response, the empathic understanding that is expressed verbally, enables a bridge to be made between these earlier forms of mental functioning and the organizing activity of words and ranges of responses. In a group these can come from the other group members, indeed are more likely to do so than from the group conductor. As Hans Loewald (1980) puts it, a dynamic field develops in the psychotherapeutic situation and the analyst's interpretations help to reorganize the patient's internal world as his/her more primitive modes of experience enter into the dynamic field of the therapist. The same of course applies to the group-analytic situation with some significant differences.

The group-analytic situation has much in common with the dyadic situation (Pines, 1981). Common to both is the creation and opening up of a dynamic force-field. In that force-field there are different levels of organization, different levels of progression and regression, many more so in the group than in the dyad. The organizing effect of responses, verbal and non-verbal, are common to both. In group analysis the verbal responses of the patients to one another are both organizing and disorganizing. In their relationships and in their conversations the group members relate and provoke responses that are disorganizing, releasing transferential levels of object relationships. These experiences which are essential to the therapeutic process are shared and witnessed by the other group members who through their own resonances can help to reorganize through acceptance and understanding the experiences that have disturbed its members. Intrinsic to the notion of the therapeutic function of regression is that contact is made with earlier forms of experience and that these have been blocked from integration with the central self (Fairbairn). These integrations can take place in therapy and thereby the patient is ultimately enriched and strengthened. The setting must be able to allow such regression to take place, to protect the patient from too powerful and primitive a regression and to provide the resources of understanding and responding that make a corrective emotional experience possible. What can affect the possible range of responses?

First, at one extreme is a strongly defensive group that will not allow such re-experiences to occur. Group relationships and discussions remain on a mainly conscious and safe level. This can come about for a variety of reasons such as faulty selection and balance of the group, putting together a group of persons all of whom are strongly defensive and none of whom have the resources or willingness to go beyond such defended areas. This can also occur when there is an obviously disturbed or fragile patient or patients, and in that instance the other members are afraid to open up lest danger erupts.

Second, at the other end of the scale is the group that quickly reaches to regressed levels and will not relinquish them. The group becomes a forum for acting out an avoidance of the painful work of understanding and reintegration. Here again selection is important. Has the therapist as dynamic administrator failed to balance the group? Are there insufficient 'healthy' aspects of personality function to integrate and work with the regressed levels of the other members? See, for example, the work on borderline groups of Kutter (1982) and Roth (1990).

Recently a strong case has been put forward for what Nitsun (1991) has called the 'Anti-Group', in which there exist levels of destructiveness and disorganization that are inherent to the group process and which can obstruct and overwhelm what Foulkes described as the Basic Law of Group Dynamics, that is the move of the group towards higher levels of organization, towards the social and cultural norm. In between these extremes is what is desirable and indeed possible, that is a group selected and composed so that a whole range of resources and responses are present. In such a group regression is understood, accepted and encouraged but the group norm remains that of working with and working through these experiences. This clinical vignette is of such a group.

The group meets again after the long summer holiday break. One member maintains his habitual silence and anxious withdrawn state throughout much of the sessions; another talks in rather vague terms, creating a sense of confusion and uncertainty in other persons. I never quite know what he means and in this way he avoids being fully present, for if he is fully present then he would be more unsafe. The issues in this session, which are clearly presented, have to do with events that took place away from the group and only gradually do they begin to deal with the dynamics of the situation in which they find themselves. One girl is displaced from her usual seat by another member and has brought with her a bag containing knitting. She struggles for sometime not to take up the knitting, her hands being restless and her fingers intertwining. She is able eventually to say that what the knitting does is to give herself a second skin, a sense of containment, and that with this she is then able to relax and to take part in the give and take of the group. When the issue of a new member joining the group comes up her fantasies are clearly that the new person might be a violent, psychotic person, one who will repeat for her the experience of her psychotic younger brother. Another person, a psychotherapist with many years of experience and of personal analysis, speaks of her anxiety whenever she goes through a door because at the other side there may be a disaster and that disaster is a void, an emptiness. She says very firmly that she does not want a new member to join the group and in that way she seems to be taking a firm grasp of the door, the symbolic entrance to the group, and acquiring some sense of control both over herself, of the group situation and of the inner fantasy that she will be lost through the entrance of another person to the group. The only frankly borderline member of the group is away and sent a very polite letter explaining her absence which is due to her going to stay with her father and sending her warm regards to the group. They are rather amazed by the fact that she can go and stay with her father with whom she has the most violent confrontations and that she should actually send her good wishes to the group and it seems that in the absence of this frankly borderline person, they have no receptacle into which to project those aspects of themselves and therefore more primitive experiences come more to the surface.

This is one of the problems that faces the therapist who treats a mixed group of neurotic and borderline patients (Hearst, 1988). Borderline patients can, by the intensity and primitiveness of their emotional reactions, challenge, threaten, stir and stimulate the group into facing those similar aspects of themselves. The patient can however also be used as a dumping ground for unwanted aspects of themselves and become a scapegoat; an expulsion can occur unless this process is understood and worked through. The scapegoating process can involve the therapist as well as the other members of the group and the therapist's incapacity to tolerate and to cope with the violent responses of the borderline patient can bring him or her into collusion with the other group members. On the other hand, if the therapist does not do so, and supports the borderline patient and does not collude with the move towards expulsion, he or she is in danger of feeling scapegoated and made to feel the cause of the group's difficulties.

## CLINICAL PROFILES OF TWO PATIENTS WITH BORDERLINE FEATURES IN GROUP PSYCHOTHERAPY: TWICE-WEEKLY SLOW-OPEN GROUP

### The uncontainable regression

(See the chapters by Hinshelwood and by Gordon, this volume.) Sara is a single woman in her early thirties, tall, quite good looking but very thin looking, as if she had a severe period of anorexia earlier on in life. She walks briskly, seeming to ignore everything around her as she walks purposefully through the environment to her particular goal. She is often very poorly dressed but always appears to be clean. She is a university graduate, speaks very rapidly and explosively with a sharp tongue, a mordant wit and a rather rich yet oblique and difficult-to-comprehend form of symbolic language. Her language is idiosyncratic, but she is very impatient if it is not immediately understood. It is allusive in that she is drawing upon a rich knowledge of the English language and literature in which she is a graduate. She lives a chaotic life and has an obsessive attachment to a married man, who is also in therapy, and she is constantly tormented by her feelings of jealousy and rage.

Most members of the group experience her as disruptive and almost intolerable. She will attack almost anyone in sight mercilessly and will impatiently interrupt anything that she feels does not interest or involve her or will otherwise withdraw into stony silence. Only lately, after about a year in the group, does she sometimes show an interest in other people's problems or respond constructively to some issue that she has not herself initiated. She always sits next to the therapist and at times speaks quietly, almost under her breath, in a way that he alone can hear. What she says at these times is often much more sensitive and constructive than the words that the rest of the group can hear.

Her impact upon the group is very divisive. Most of the members find her very threatening and she provokes enormous rage in them. She can goad people whom she dislikes into declaring their hatred of her and their wish for her to leave the group. Only one man in the group can tolerate her easily, feeling himself to be on the same wavelength and he can deal with her with an easy humour. One very warm and motherly person, who has since left the group, had a positive attitude towards her, despite all the contempt and derision with which she was treated. She admired Sara's qualities of sharpness and directness and felt that she could learn from her. Her principal targets for hostility have been an attractive middle-aged married woman, who is always dressed in a sophisticated manner and uses elaborate make-up, thereby making herself look much younger than she actually was. Sara hated, loathed and feared her. The underlying anxiety related very much to the body-image distortions which she projected into this woman; she felt she did not know what was real and what was artificial about the other woman and that she distorted and changed her body in a confusing way. For instance, this older woman had had a plastic operation to improve her nose and had had a face-lift. It emerged that Sara is very confused about the masculinity and femininity of her own body. She is partly proud of her strength which she feels is that of a man's and is contemptuous of her breasts which she feels to be inadequate. Underlying this is a great confusion about her sense of gender identity and confusing relationships to both her mother and her father. She seems to have replaced the absent father by an intensely male identification with him as a soldier, turning herself into an amazon.

Another man whom she hates and fears is Eric, an older man who has certain borderline features himself. His speech is at times highly abstract and difficult to follow and she attacks him unmercifully for this. Lack of clarity frightens her; she has sharply to define everything about herself in order to protect herself from the threat of losing her self-definition and of merging and blurring with other persons. She projects a confused and blurred aspect of herself into Eric and tries to control it and attack it in him and fears any contact with him as if it would represent the return of the projection in a persecutory and retaliatory fashion.

At times, she can speak very clearly about her problem with her sense of self and self-boundaries. She says that anyone can get right inside her because she does not feel that she has boundaries; and because of this, anyone who separates from her drags part of herself away like flesh sticking to the end of darts. Another time she said that when someone leaves her it is as if her entrails burst out whereas if she does the leaving, the parting is clean.

One can understand these experiences and her defensive fury and hostility when one recognizes that within her internal world the self-image and the object-image are fused, rather than separate, and that there is an internal striving towards the repetition of these fusional relationships which, however, are experiences that are very threatening. The only relationship that she can allow herself is that with her lover, towards whom she has very intense demands for a permanent state of bonding. The underlying development fixation is to that stage of separation–individuation where there is a cognitive awareness of separateness but an intense underlying need still to feel part of the other and for the other to feel part of the self.

Though highly intelligent and aware of her need for a greater contact with her inner self, she constantly uses manic-type defences to avoid reflective thought and introspection. As long as she moves fast, she does not have to think and the more she can exaggerate her emotions and her responses the better, for thus the other person does not really get close to her and neither she nor the other person have any chance of finding out what lies behind her impulsive actions. One of the things which she is beginning to be able to use the group for is to slow down in the speed of responses and to diminish the intensity of her affects.

The pattern of her relationship is on the surface nearly always dyadic. She engages with one person at a time and cannot allow herself consciously to be involved in a triangular-type relationship. Thus, she was always pushing the third person out of any dialogue that she is having with another member of the group, and one of the developments that is taking place is the beginning of the capacity to allow triangular situations to exist between other persons without disrupting them and sometimes to be involved in such situations herself.

The therapist's role in relationship to her has been to allow her to continue to shelter next to him and to feel understood and protected by him even though this involves some idealization and the maintenance of a split between good and bad. At one time she said that the reason why she liked the therapist and admired him is that he allows people plenty of rein. She sometimes admires and values his interventions with other members of the group; and towards the members of the group whom she likes, she will sometimes encourage them to develop close relationships of trust and intimacy with the therapist.

The much more difficult problem is to monitor and to make acceptable the intensity of the negative transference and projective identifications that go on between her and other group members. It has been more useful to try to show the other members of the group how and why they are responding to her than for the moment to show her what she is projecting into them. For much of the time we have been concerned with elucidating what she is doing with other persons and how she is using them to externalize unwanted and feared aspects of the self; we have only just begun to explore why she behaves like this. For instance behind her great rage and hostility that she has for a member of the group who is a successful businessman there lies envy and competitiveness because he is in a field in which she would also very much like to be successful.

One incidental benefit of her presence in the group is that other members perceive the awesome depth of intensity of feeling that this particular person experiences. There is no comfort for her in neurotic defences of inhibition and shallowness. Everything hurts and almost everything is important.

### The containable regression

By contrast, I now turn to the description of another patient's borderline features, a much older woman, Cynthia. Cynthia is a musician, who has had over twenty years of personal analysis. She is married, has grown-up children and many years ago she made a very serious suicidal attempt. She also had an almost delusional transference to her first analyst and came to my group because she had certain feelings of idealization towards me and felt that perhaps I would be able after all these years to help her to find more peace of mind. She, too, experienced great problems with her sense of boundaries and her sense of self. She often feels that she 'loses' herself in the group, by which she means that she goes away with a terrible feeling of void, emptiness and despair, particularly if something that has been important to her has not been reflected and responded to empathically. For her mirroring is indeed crucial. When this fails, she feels tempted to leave the group and has to resort to obsessional mechanisms to try to regain her sense of stability. She can feel that she has descended deep into a pit in the course of the group and that there is no ladder with which to reascend, for the group is blurred, it has no clarity and there is too much going on for her. Very often, she sits in stony-faced silence and only towards the end of the session will she declare herself to be 'drowning'. Often she accuses the therapist of neglecting her and indeed she produces this neglect by the way in which she will silently withhold her thoughts and feelings. However, when she does feel understood by the therapist, this is a most important and gratifying experience for her. She evokes much sympathy and caring from other group members. They recognize her need for reflection and for mirroring and for being helped out of her state of despair, when she feels that she is drowning. The first patient whom I have described, Sara, somewhat idealizes Cynthia and sees in her a woman who has mastered enormous psychological problems and who therefore holds out some hope for her. Sara sees Cynthia as gradually thawing out in the group and once said that one of her pleasures is in coming to the group and seeing this happen. She feels that Cynthia, because she has been in a state of despair which led to attempting suicide, can understand her own deep anguish. Cynthia responds to Sara by keeping her distance and not wishing to be too closely involved with her as if recognizing Sara's and her own propensity for fusion and over-identification. She also greatly resents the therapist's protectiveness and interest in Sara, and clearly for Cynthia this evokes triangular situations, principally an intense jealousy of a younger sister in relationship to her father.

Though these two patients have similarities in their underlying developmental blocks – that is, both of them have intense needs and wishes for fusion and then have to defend themselves vigorously against this – their defences take very different forms. Sara uses rage and hostility to strengthen her self-boundaries and to maintain distance. She projects massively negative aspects of herself into other persons, attacks them there and then, fears reintrojection and being used by the persons for their own projections. She splits the group into attackers and defenders and evokes a great deal of hostility. Cynthia has a much more mature and better-adapted personality and the borderline aspects of her personality are confined to one sector. She is successful in her work and manages to handle a wide range of emotional relationships socially. Her wishes and fears for fusion do not invoke in her defensive aggression; she uses defences of withdrawal and isolation though she then experiences the despair of feeling abandoned. She has a great hunger for empathic mirroring and reflection, whereas Sara, though she desperately needs this at a very deep level, still feels that she will be overwhelmed and overpowered by sensitive empathy.

## SOME FURTHER FEATURES OF REGRESSION IN GROUP ANALYSIS

The fragile patient in the more regressed state of mind is caught in cycles of projective and introjective identification. For example, patient A feels that she carries away from the group all the pain, misery and suffering that other persons are denying and that she constantly suffers psychological torment for the other members of the group. She know that is probably not so, but that is what she feels. She says to John that in last week's session, when he spoke about his wish to live in a country like South Africa at the turn of the century, where people lived so far apart that it took three days' travelling by ox cart to go to a neighbour and that once they had arrived, they would sit together on the verandah for a whole day and not say anything and then just say goodbye, that she felt that he was hiding great pain and desolation, emptiness and loneliness in his life. John says promptly, clearly and quite forcibly to her that that is her way of responding to him and it was not at all what he meant. What he meant was that sometimes, it suits him, and is very important for him, to be able to take things very slowly and to be able to control his interaction with other people. Another member of the group links this to John's sexual impotence and his need to have a female partner who will take things very slowly with him and help him to regain his confidence and his potency. A is able to accept this and a useful piece of reality-testing and internalization of a psychic process at a higher level of integration possibly takes place.

## RESONANCE AND LEVELS OF PSYCHIC ORGANIZATION AND EXPERIENCE

It can be to the advantage of the group and to both the neurotic and the borderline patients that different levels of experience are brought together in the same situation (Hearst, 1988). This is not always the case and sometimes the level of regression of the borderline patient is very difficult for the other group members to respond to empathically and to contain the primitive affects and fantasies. In the same group session, the patient referred to above, John, who is impotent, and who also suffers a congenital or birth injury to his vision which has left him vulnerable to blindness, speaks about his response to a recent retinal haemorrhage. The group responded to him on the level of his psychological short-sightedness and blurry vision, that he does not see how other people see him and is not able therefore to change his own image of himself. The group play freely with mirror metaphors and imagery; John says that the group is a mirror to him where he can see himself but that his life lacks any other mirrors and that the mirror that he got from his parents did not provide him with a good image of himself. Responses are: that his mirror is fogged; that he needs to clean it up and really see how other people see him. The metaphor of the group as a mirror changes to the group as a psychic lavatory where what comes out of oneself can be accepted and that one can cease hiding inside a solitary psychological lavatory to which one retreats as an escape from outside interference but also to hide a feared bad aspect of the self from the other people in the world.

Earlier in the session, John talked about hiding his image of himself from other people and used as image that it's as if he was a Jew hiding from the SS by pretending to be a member of the SS. A's response to this was to say that she felt that she was like an SS disguised as a Jew. The group's attention was concentrated on other patients for the first hour of the session. Eventually, A broke in saying that for her the group was not a forum or psychological lavatory where it was safe to let things out. No one had responded to what she said about herself. A potentially healthy confrontation took place between her and Tom, who said that as far as he was concerned, it was a place where she could bring out whatever she felt: if she needed to scream and shout at him and be very angry with him, he was prepared for this, but she had to be prepared for his response and that she might really get some bad feelings back in reality instead of constantly fantasizing that what she was getting back were bad feelings. A grew progressively agitated and felt that no one in the group was understanding her and that the group was the cause of all her distress and she could no longer tolerate it and she suddenly rose and left the room.

Naturally there were feelings of concern and guilt towards her, also some projection into her of levels of distress and fantasy, with denial that other members of the group could understand those experiences, that they had ever been at that level themselves, or alternatively that they all did understand what it was like and therefore she was no different to them. The group members quite appropriately felt that the responsibility for handling a crisis like that belongs with the therapist who was able to tell them that he had an arrangement to see the patient individually the next morning.

## WORKING IN DEEP AND DARK AREAS

Foulkes shows that by sharing a common 'foundation matrix' members of a group are able to understand one another on quite deep levels as the group-analytic situation develops, aided by the therapist. But when we reach to the levels of borderline functioning and psychotic functioning the situation becomes much more threatening. For understanding and containment at this level, either the group analyst has to be the provider or fortuitously or fortunately there may be other group members who can do so because they can be in touch with such levels of experience but are more able to verbalize and to organize themselves than are the more disorganized and disturbed patients. When, however, this is not possible one patient can become isolated and vulnerable for scapegoating and for premature drop-out.

It is with the more disturbed borderline patients that the profoundest levels of primitive rage and destructiveness are encountered. Once the defences against exposing this rage are weakened or removed, patients become terrified by the intensity of the savagery, become frightened of the fantasied destructiveness and often appalled by the overwhelming sense of evil and destructiveness that they now experience as originating within the self. Desperate attempts to remove this inner threat by projection then ensue, leading to paranoid attitudes, a constant search for the weaknesses or flaws in the environment that will enable this projection to hold and, in line with the mechanism of projective identification, an attempt unconsciously and also partly consciously to manipulate the recipient of the projection into fitting the internal schema of persecution. The greatest intensity of this type of desperate rage is, in my experience, encountered more in individual therapy and becomes an extremely painful situation both for the patient and for the therapist. Therapists have to be able to contain the negative projections in which the patient attempts to envelop them. They have to experience, without retaliation and with a sensitive acceptance and understanding, the patients' overwhelming need to see them as evil and as the origin of all the pain. It is a great demand upon therapists' tact and sensitivity, and one which they cannot always be expected to demonstrate.

## TRANSFERENCE AND COUNTERTRANSFERENCE CONSIDERATIONS AT THE BORDERLINE

I will begin with countertransference, because with the borderline patient, the countertransference is often acute and difficult to manage. The patient uses primitive defence mechanisms, projective identification, splitting into ideal and persecutory part-object relations, and because the narcissistic defences of devaluation, arrogance and contempt are used, the therapist and the other patients in the group, if the group is one of both neurotic and borderline patients, are often in a situation of acute stress. As therapists, we try to maintain the capacity for relatively neutral yet empathic responses to our patients. We try to monitor our internal reactions, to think about them, try to use them in understanding the experience of the patient to form a basis either for interpretation or for some other appropriate response. One of the pleasures of effective psychotherapy is this capacity to understand another person and to see how well one's understanding of them is often received. Anxiety is reduced, the patient becomes more relaxed and more open when a well-timed empathic interpretation is given. One person has understood another person and they can become closer and less defensive. One of the diagnostic signs with the borderline patient is that this desirable and pleasant position for the therapist is rarely attained; the therapist and the other patients in the group, who might otherwise be able to function as co-therapists, feel themselves to be distanced and often bewildered. The patient maintains a prickly distance, remains isolated and yet will often subject the other members of the group to very powerful and intrusive comments. Rage, anger and contempt may suddenly erupt leaving the recipient of the attack shaken and alarmed and, of course, these attacks can be followed by counter-attacks and thus a vicious cycle of escalating conflict arises. When these phenomena occur, we know that we are in the presence of primitive projection and introjection processes.

Early on in his work, Foulkes saw that destructive forces in the group are consumed in attacking one another's resistances and that this allows the loving constructive forces in the group to predominate over the destructive ones. With borderline members, the destructive forces are not used to attack the other person's resistances because these members do not see or understand the need that other persons have for such defences. That another person needs sensitive handling, that we protect ourselves from conflict and psychic pain by defence mechanisms, is not understood by them. They wish to be gratified instantly by the other person's complete attention and to derive narcissistic nourishment from them. They are excessively gratified by hurting other persons and seek to be able to project unwanted aspects of the self into other persons, and in order to do so, need to manipulate others into a position to receive them. Thus, if I want to get rid of bits of myself that seem very bad, very destructive, very contemptible or frightening because they represent needs and greeds that are too primitive to know about, then I will not only seek to find someone who will take in these characteristics but try to induce them to behave in such a way that the projection and the other person's behaviour will fit. For instance, Sara, already featured above, was very frightened of her own sadism focused on the physical characteristics of a man in the group. This man was a rather quiet, inhibited man, very much the passive, weak partner in a marriage, whose voice was quiet and gentle and his sensitive understanding of other people was quite marked. All of this was meaningless to her. All that she related to in him was the fact that he had large hands. For her, these were the hands of a murderer or a butcher. The fact that the man was in a profession, where the sensitive and accurate use of his hands was called for, made no difference to her. For her, he was simply the brutal male to be kept at a distance by her attacks and who could also be the recipient for her own sadism. Thus she had a part-object relationship to the man and could easily incite him to respond to her aggressively. Much of the work of therapy with these patients is making sure that the response to the primitive attacks is not simply a reciprocal mirroring. It is only by the constant exposure to a more benign and a higher level of psychological responsiveness that a more benign cycle of projection and introjection can occur. This is what I have called 'trading' part-object for whole-object relationships. This has led me on to consider the transference of these patients to other members of the group, to the group-as-a-whole and to the therapist.

I return to a discussion of Sara, already mentioned above. By her activity in the group, Sara provoked a split of the group into factions, those who could tolerate her and those who disliked her. She provoked great hostility in those whom she disliked, and she was expert at derisive remarks and comments, particularly to people with whom she felt herself to be in competition. It was clear that she experienced her family situation as a very unfair one in which her father was an absent figure. She was sensitive to her fear of, and capacity for, fusion with others and she needed distancing in order to preserve her own sense of self. She needed to keep herself clearly defined and sharp, and used hostility as her main capacity to do this; she was either hostile or withdrawn. She was threatened by contact with other persons whose boundaries and outlines seemed to her to be blurred. This was shown in her response to an older member of the group whom she saw as always being vague and weak, and as usual there was a core of reality in her perceptions and responses.

She had a fear of being taken over and being rendered passive and becoming only a ventriloquist's dummy. However, she defended herself against a recognition that much of her behaviour was motivated through anxiety and fear. She was impulsive and used her rapidity of thought and speech evasively to avoid finding out what lies behind her actions and responses. The group gradually helped her to slow down and to be a little bit more reflective.

She evoked positive transference feelings in the therapist who felt quite protective towards her, aware that she was the most disturbed member of the group, bordering on a psychotic breakdown. However, his protectiveness of her aroused jealousy, particularly in other women. They also resented his enjoyment of her impulsiveness and verbal wit. What he approved of in her seem to be those aspects of herself of which approval was denied in the family.

Clearly she avoided allowing herself to get into any triangular situations and maintained one-to-one relationships in the group. She demanded that her egocentricity be accepted and had little capacity for empathy with the other members she attacked. However, she could be empathic with persons with whom she felt an identification through similarity of life situations or emotional problems.

Sara could manipulate other persons in the group into becoming receptacles for her contempt and for devaluation. One man, with whom she felt rivalrous, she tried to devalue, pouring scorn on all his achievements; another man she used as a receptacle for the disturbance of her body-image distortions. She was confused about whether she was male or female in body and outline, and she seized upon this man's body as something which she could try to distort. The vulnerability of her own boundaries was consciously recognized by her because she could say such things as 'anyone can get inside me and I cannot protect myself from invasion'. She had a very difficult relationship with a violent boyfriend, which seemed constantly to lead her sadistically to revenge herself upon the men in the group, thereby turning passive into active. She actually succeeded in getting one man to feel that she was a threat to his own positive self-evaluation, and that she seemed to get right inside him as a destructive bad object. In this way, she forced him to experience what she herself experienced in relationship to her boyfriend, who did not seem to value anything that she felt was good about herself.

Sara had very clear and definite ideas about each member of the group and had a different type of relationship with each of them. Let us first take the women: the oldest member of the group, who had great problems with a teenage daughter with whom she had very destructive and aggressive attacks and whom she could not value, Sara saw as being shallow, manipulative and essentially worthless. She had no compunction in attacking her ruthlessly and enjoyed the counter-attacks this produced. Sara and this other patient, in fact, reproduced the relationship the older woman had with her daughter. In contrast to this, Sara idealized Cynthia, an older woman in the group, and saw her as a person who had been able successfully to deal with her own rage and bad feelings. One of the reasons for her to continue to come to the group, she said, was because she could enjoy seeing how this older woman would unthaw from her frozen personality. She failed often to understand the depth of this person's unhappiness and how she aroused painful feelings in her; she was unaware of her sadism towards the woman whom she was idealizing. Towards a third woman, she had nothing but contempt, seeing her as dull and uninteresting, again accurately pinpointing an area of considerable concern in the other person. This is another characteristic of the borderline patient, a particular form of 'borderline empathy'. This is that the borderline patient is extremely empathic to particular and restricted sectors of the other person's personality, those which are necessary for these particular forms of externalization and protection to occur. The rest of the person is of no significance to them and can be thrown away like the pulp of an orange from which the juice has been extracted. Thus the borderline's relationships remain on a primitive part-object level and they are not in touch with the higher-level structures and functions of the other personalities.

Towards the men in the group Sara displayed equally selective perceptions. I have already mentioned the man with the large hands; another man, who was a successful entrepreneur, again aroused nothing but contempt. In fact he seemed to be a more successful version of herself, in that he, too, had a very ready wit, a very good command of language and could himself be very destructive. Towards a third man in the group, an older man who on the surface appeared rather weak, she was full of rage and contempt and accused him of being impotent and half dead. The fourth man in the group, a younger one, whom she could identify with in a more benign way, she was encouraging to.

In fact, at one time, she tried very hard to get this particular man, to whom she felt benign, to see that he ought to strive to improve his relationship with the therapist. To the therapist himself, she also preserved a benign relationship. It was very important to her that he was accepting and tolerant of her behaviour, and that he did not insist on analysing everything that she did and that he supported her right to behave in her own way until such time as she could begin to modify it.

In the course of several months, the intensity of her reactions began to diminish and she became more comfortable to be with. She became a very regular attendant at the group, apologized at times for her rude behaviour, began to give up her destructive sado-masochistic relationship with a very disturbed man and began to show some sadness and depression. The other members learnt more about her as a person, of her childhood, and there was the beginning of a capacity for mutual empathy between her and the other group members. She began to be supportive and caring and even minimally to allow herself to be cared for. For this to happen she had first of all to experience the therapist and the group entity as relatively benign, not overwhelming and invasive.

During the first months, when her behaviour was so provocative and difficult, the therapist was often accused by the group of being over protective to her, of making her a favourite and of enjoying her behaviour rather than being critical of it. He often had the feeling that he was the only person who cared for and could see anything positive about her and had hopes for her future, that she might benefit from the group and use it as a place for constructive change. He often had to act as a negotiator between her and the other group members, when quarrels took place, usually when she succeeded in provoking another member into a vicious counter-attack.

But, regrettably, in the end he had to ask Sara to leave the group. This was after an episode where another patient felt so abused by some racially coloured comments that physical violence broke out. Sara, though somewhat apologetic, was not able sufficiently to understand and therefore to repair the injury that she had caused and seemed relieved that she would not have to continue in the group, which would have meant altering her position in it. He heard a few months later that she had moved to another part of the country and was working and he has not heard from her since.

## NEGOTIATION AND MEDIATION

I believe that it is again characteristic of borderline patients that the therapist is often drawn into these intense and bitter strifes where he or she has to act as a negotiator or mediator (Pines, 1984). He or she has in a way to reconcile the two persons to one another and help them to see that the outcome of such quarrels can be constructive ones. The criteria for the constructive resolution of these quarrels is that each person shall recognize that they are partly right and partly wrong, that what the other person says about them has some validity, that this validity can be acknowledged but that it is accepted that this is not the complete truth. Each is a whole person and whatever is at issue only represents one aspect of the whole person. Furthermore whatever each one is accusing the other of is something which is an aspect of themselves.

Thus, in the destructiveness and in the attack upon the other, there is a hidden mutuality. It is the job of the therapist to bring out this hidden mutuality. In so doing the therapist, I believe, raises the level of the interaction from a destructive dyadic one to a constructive triadic one. In this, the therapist with his or her capacity for reflection and distancing from the destructive struggle, the capacity to remain relatively uninvolved, to reflect and to think about what is happening, the position as the relatively uninvolved third person in the situation, brings about triangulation. The level of triangulation is a higher level of psychological development than the level of dyadic confrontations. I am reminded here of the myth of Perseus and the Gorgon. Perseus could only be in the presence of the Gorgon and not be petrified by her by using a mirror which was derived from the armour of the goddess Pallas Athene. This goddess represents wisdom, the highest reflective level of psychic function and organization, symbolized by the mirror which enabled Perseus to catch the image of the Gorgon. Catching the image on the mirror represents the act of symbolization which is possible through the capacity for reflection.

I can only touch briefly upon the subject of mirroring, brought on to this by these clinical manifestations. Benign mirroring is a developmental process of the highest importance, as the work of Winnicott, Mahler and Abelin has clearly shown. Mirroring is a selective and empathic response which one person makes to another which enables one to feel understood, held, cared for, soothed and enhanced. Kohut popularized the notion when he talked about the mirror transferences of the narcissistic personality, where the patient simply wants the therapist to reflect back to them aspects of the wished for and needed grandiosity. *This is because at this stage the child is still dependent upon the other person, the self-object, to maintain a sense of cohesion of self.* Without it, the person is prone to narcissistic swings of loss of self-esteem which turns into rage at the self, with a sense of painful emptiness.

Winnicott has likened the psychotherapeutic process to the earliest relationship between mother and child when the mother, by the way she looks at the child, begins to give the child an idea of who he or she is. If the mother looks benignly at the child, lovingly and caringly, the child begins to experience itself as real and good. If the mother is angry or cold or distant, the child begins to experience itself as bad, as unpleasing. When things go well, there is a two-way process, a significant exchange with the world. What Winnicott says is that psychotherapy is not making clever and apt interpretations; by and large it is a long-term giving the patient back what the patient brings. It is a complex derivative of the act that reflects what is there to be seen. Dealing with a somewhat later stage of development, Mahler has shown that the mother is constantly selecting from the child's responses those that she herself will respond to benignly and thus begins to give the child a good image of itself. If she responds unpredictably, or selects those aspects of the child's behaviour for attention that she dislikes, the child is deeply imprinted with this as its own bad self-image. Time and time again, the patient will bring this image to therapy in order to have it disconfirmed and there seems to be no way in which we can escape being put into the position of the bad mother who only responds to the badness of the child or, as so often happens, we reverse roles and the patient becomes the destructive hostile parent, who subjects us to the feeling of humiliating childishness and helplessness. It is by survival of these attacks and the gradual acknowledgement by the patient of the reality of the person beyond the projection that benign cycles of introjection begin to replace the evacuative projections.

As for techniques: I have already mentioned negotiation and mediation as characterizing borderline phenomena. I have also already mentioned splitting and the intensity of the projections and the need to contain and not to retaliate with counter-projections. Patience, caring and above all fairness are needed. Stone and Gustafson (1982), Harwood (1992) and others have written about the technique with borderline patients along similar lines, asserting that much work is necessary before the patients can begin to recognize that their inner worlds are dominated by archaic needs, that they do not take into account others as separate and autonomous persons. For them to be able to realize this and to behave differently, they need to interact in non-interpretive modes with the therapist or other patients. The therapist must often try to show the other members of the group the meaning of the patient's behaviour before the patients themselves can begin to grasp the meaning. They make the point that the idealization by the patient of the group or of the therapist is a necessary state in accepting group membership. At this stage, idealization is not defensive and to interpret it as such is faulty technique and often leads to the patient leaving the group. Later on, the idealization may need to be interpreted as defence against the underlying negative feelings, but this can only be done when the patient is securely embedded in the group and held by the experience of support and understanding.

So to summarize: my recommendations are that we treat these patients in mixed groups, that we make sure that these patients do not predominate either qualitatively or quantitatively and that the group to which they belong has sufficient resources to withstand the regressive pulls of their primitive mechanisms. An understanding of the nature of their defences and an appreciation of their inner anguish and the great need that they have for help will sustain the therapist through the many difficult episodes which are bound to come his or her way.

## SOME BASIC POINTS

In conclusion, the characteristics of group-analytic therapy with the more disturbed patient can be summarized (cf. Pines, 1980) as follows:

1. The borderline patient will not behave as a relatively separate independent and autonomous person. Because of developmental arrests and faults, (s)he will inevitably in varying degrees seek to merge or to fuse with the therapist or, in a group, with other members or with the group-as-a-whole. Very intense feelings of need, and inevitably of deprivation, will be evoked and anger and rage are to be expected.

2. In a similar manner other persons involved with the patient are not treated as separate autonomous persons, centres of their own motivation and activity. They are mainly related to as 'need-unsatisfying objects'. The subjective response of the other persons range between hurt, bewilderment, anger, rejection or fascination and submission.

3. Great fluctuations and swings in mood, attitudes and relationships are to be expected. Typical cycles are those between closeness leading to threat of merger and consequent great distancing and aloofness.

4. The varying ego states are not integrated or acknowledged as belonging to a unitary personality. There is often a poorly established observing ego, little capacity to see that 'I feel this and that, I have more than one self and I know the difference between them and can see that at one time I feel this way and at other times I feel and behave that way, which is totally different'. The ego states are vigorously kept apart and the therapist's efforts to bring these contradictions to the patient's attention are strongly resisted. Often the warded-off contradictory part is experienced as being in some other person. That person will then be feared or attacked and have to be controlled.

5. There is a tenuous hold on psychic reality. What feels real is treated as if it were real. The patient will often treat fantasy as reality and act upon this. This will occur when affect has been raised or when some other aspects of psychic reality have to be warded off. Therapists or other patients will often find themselves caught up in the patient's fantasy world without knowing what is happening. The patient may be living a waking dream and other persons are often a part of it. It is often very difficult to understand what is happening between oneself and the patient. One feels lost and under pressure. The patient reacts to this loss of understanding catastrophically and the management of these catastrophes is the essence of the treatment. Treatment has to fail, to be annihilated and then to recover from this. The therapist or the group have to be reliable and caring when the patient is despairing and annihilating. They must respond to the patient as a whole person when the patient is feeling and behaving primitively and relating to other people not as whole persons.

6.  Relationships must be maintained when interpretation fails.

7.  The treatment is full of traumas. It will be long and the most primitive stages of human development will be reactivated.

8.  Don't expect the patients to care for you. By the time they are able to do so they are well on the way to recovery.


## REFERENCES

Foulkes, S.H. (1983) *Introduction to Group-Analytic Psychotherapy*, London: Karnac.

Harwood, I.H. (1992) 'Advances in group psychotherapy and self psychology: an intersubjective approach', *Group* 16 (4).

Hearst, L.E. (1988) 'The restoration of the impaired self in group psychoanalytic treatment', in N. Slavinska-Holy (ed.), *Borderline Conditions and Narcissistic Patients in Therapy*, Madison, CT: International Universities Press.

Kernberg, O. (1984) *Severe Personality Disorders*, New Haven: Yale University Press.

Kutter, P. (1982) *Basic Aspects of Psychoanalytic Group Therapy*, London: Routledge & Kegan Paul.

Loewald, H. (1980) *Papers on Psychoanalysis*, New Haven, CT: Yale University Press.

Nitsun, M. (1991) 'The anti-group', *Group Analysis* 24 (1).

Pines, M. (1980) 'What to expect in the psychotherapy of the borderline patient', *Group Analysis* 15 (3).

—— (1981) 'The frame of reference of group psychotherapy', *International Journal of Group Psychotherapy* 31 (3).

—— (1984) 'Reflections on mirroring', *International Review of Psycho-Analysis* 11 (27).

—— and Hutchinson, S. (1992) 'Group analysis', in A. Alonso and Hi Swiller (eds.), *Group Therapy in Clinical Practice*, Washington, DC: American Psychiatric Press.

Roberts, J. and Pines, M. (eds) (1992) *The Practice of Group Analysis*, London: Routledge.

Roth, B. (1990) 'The group that would not relate to itself', in B.E. Roth, W.N. Stone and H.D. Kibel (eds), *The Difficult Patient in Group*, Madison, CT: International Universities Press.

Stone, W.N. and Gustafson, J.P. (1982) 'Technique in the group psychotherapy of narcissistic and borderline patients', *International Journal of Group Psychotherapy* 27.

# 7 Group thanatropics

*Jeffrey Kauffman*

## EDITORS' INTRODUCTION

The relationship between groups and the mourning process has been addressed in the group therapy literature from two standpoints: (a) grief, separation and loss as central motifs in the development of all groups; and (b) the convening of specialized groups to work through issues of bereavement. In this chapter, Jeffrey Kauffman, a psychotherapist who specializes in bereavement therapy, discusses both aspects.

First, Kauffman revives and reworks Freud's contentions, articulated in *Beyond the Pleasure Principle*, about the centrality of death in human psychology. Kauffman posits radically that death is present as a motif, as a phenomenological background object, and as an imago in all groups. He relates this hypothesis to Freud's theory that group life began with the murder of the father (cf. *Totem and Taboo*, *Moses and Monotheism*). Kauffman compares his theory in some respects, to Melanie Klein's formulations of the depressive position. Citing Bion's writings, he postulates that an understanding of group relations from the standpoint of mourning allows for a radical new view of the group as a space (a 'cluse') for mystical experience and spiritual transformation.

Importantly, Kauffman connects the group dynamics of death, what he calls 'group thanatropics', to the new psychology of shame. Kauffman sees shame as a regulator of the intensity and nature of grief reactions in the group. He holds that shame and grief are regulating affects for group cohesion, norms, boundaries and development.

In the second part of this contribution, Kauffman provides a depiction of bereavement groups which should serve as a useful 'primer' for anyone considering convening such a group. This very practical segment can be read as a kind of introductory supervision session, independently of the theoretical discussion.

This chapter is divided into two sections. The first section, 'Thanotocentric phenomenology of the group-as-a-whole', focuses on the place of our human mortality and of the mourning process in group psychotherapy. A meta-psychological hypothesis is developed to support the position that death and mourning have a central place in the theory of group dynamics: death is the spark that ignites the Ring of Fire, and mourning is the developmental and therapeutic process of groups.

The second section of this chapter takes up a different set of issues. This section, 'Bereavement groups', addresses clinical and practical issues of the bereavement group. The bereavement group is a group set up solely for the purpose of facilitating the mourning in group members. In this section some basic topics of therapeutic process, countertransference, structuring of the group and selected bereavement theory concepts are addressed.

## THANOTOCENTRIC PHENOMENOLOGY OF THE GROUP-AS-A-WHOLE

### On the genesis of group

Freud gives an account of the origin of group in *Totem and Taboo* (1913). The question of origins has to do with defining the underlying characteristics of a topic (Bion, 1970). To know the origins of group is to know what sets its dynamic in motion. By Freud's account *group originates in murder*. The band of brothers, a primal horde, is the proto-group that is to become group through the act of murdering their father. The consequence of this group-founding, group-defining action is guilt.

This mythos of the origin of group in death and mourning articulates, in the prehistoric action that founds group, the underlying phantasy that constitutes group. What is instructive for our understanding of group dynamics about Freud's account is precisely that (a) it leaps to the mythic dimension and (b) it presents us with a myth about murder and mourning. The sphinx illuminated in the centre of the Ring of Fire is death and mourning.

Psychoanalytic theory has evolved beyond the oedipal patriarchal and phallocentric presupposition of Freud's theory. The thanotocentrics presented here likewise do not centre death and mourning on the experience of guilt. The thanatropic presence which compels the group to dream and which prompts the group need to mourn is an experience of loss (that is, grief), of which guilt is an ingredient. This group phenomenon of guilt – both secures the bond (identity/adhesion) of the members (murderers) and prompts the tension between members. It expresses a phantasy at the core of internalized group space. In Freud's patriarchal phantasy, death is contained by aggression and implodes as guilt. However, when this dynamic is recognized as a mourning scene, the context of understanding shifts. Aggression and guilt are signs of group mourning. They are loci of grief, indicators of specific mourning needs. The process which transforms the containment/implosion of death and the associated pathognomic dynamics of aggression and guilt is a group mourning process. Aggression and guilt are signs of the thanatropic presence at the core or origin of group. They are indicators of the underlying pull of death. The unconscious group phantasy about violent and intentional loss is a part of a primitive affective disturbance. Out of this, the group need to mourn as the basic trajectory of group development is generated.

A broad affective range associated with annihilation anxiety sets in motion group dynamic patterns. Basic-assumption states (Bion, 1959) are, for example, patterns of defensive manoeuvring for fending off thanatropic anxieties or phantasized annihilations that emerge from the group core.

In a group in which the expression of aggression was not sanctioned by group norms, a group member with strong masochistic traits functioned as a lightning rod for otherwise diffuse and threatening group aggressions. As attacks on the member flared up more frequently and his scapegoat role could no longer contain the fire, members assumed basic assumption states. When the scapegoated and shamed member, however, found a voice for anger that others could hear, there began some scattered, partial reintegration and owning of the devaluations that had been projected on to him. As these projections subsided in a couple of group members, a sadness began to develop in the group.

This triphasic process of (a) disturbing affect that is difficult to contain, followed by (b) a degree of containment, followed by (c) the manifestation of sadness is an enactment of a mourning process. Group mourning process recurs, like a musical theme and variations. Each time it repeats the group is metabolizing a derivative of the underlying thanatropic presence.

In this same group, as members came to be better able to experience and express their differences and to feel safe with confronting other members, the group member who had been in the scapegoat role began to recall and talk about childhood feelings of abandonment. He talked about a sense of loss and worthlessness that had always been present and affecting his sense of self and his behaviour, but had never before been crystallized in his consciousness. Other group members identified, expressing diverse loss experiences. Over the next several months, experiences of sexual abuse, loneliness, rejection and other losses were intensively focused.

On an individual level, the unresolved grief over these losses had been fuel for the fiery turmoil that had erupted in group. On the group level, the scapegoating, the basic-assumption states and the depression of the group evidence the evolution of the underlying thanatropic pull in group dynamics.

The concept of the thanatological origin of group dynamics posits that the inherent developmental trajectories and processes of group are both expressions and transformations of death. The pre-presence (always being beforehand) of death constitutes and compels the need to grieve. There is either grief or the avoidance of grief. Rather, there is usually grief *and* the avoidance of grief. Whether the group affective experience of pain is dissociated from death, mortality, murder, helplessness, being overwhelmed and out of control and associated core anxieties, or whether the group is swirling into and lost in basic assumptions – the dynamic is no less thanotocentric than when the group is relatively present with its pain and grief. Not any specific loss, but the constitutive condition of group (its origin), is the basis of a thanatocentric understanding and of the assertion that the therapeutic risks and possibilities of group are relative to the mourning process of group.

## Introduction to a thanotocentric phenomenology of the group-as-a-whole

Clinically, shame is the pivotal group process issue in facilitating the mourning process. When we speak of shame we usually mean an affective disturbance. It is only in recent history that this has been the primary meaning of shame. As recently as a hundred years ago shame was spoken of primarily as a virtue, as in modesty and humility (Schneider, 1977). Philosophers praised shame as the key to moral and spiritual development. The etymology of the word traces back to a pair of opposite meanings (Schneider, 1977). It means both *cover* and *exposure*. It is this dual meaning that enables us to understand shame as a regulative principle (Kauffman, 1988). Disregulative shame is either of the extremes of inhibiting experience (cover) or overwhelming experience (exposure). Normative protective shame enables self-experience and self-disclosure. If when a loss occurs the specific affect that needs to be experienced (guilt, helplessness, loss of control, and so on) is either inhibited or is overwhelming to a degree that it is not suffered, the loss (or some aspect of the loss) is not mourned. The shame-based denial of grief is a response to feeling exposed or overwhelmed in the very opening of deeply vulnerable parts of the self prompted in intense grief. The mourning process is a natural process; that is, there is an inherent flow from death/loss impact towards healing and growth. However, mourning never flows this course without considerable indirection, pain and disruption of ordinary reality, and the experience of the self and the object world being altered. Shame regulates mourning process and the experience of mourning, enabling or blocking the flow. Numbed, frightened, overwhelmed, awestruck experience initiates the process, leading to painful and disturbing affects and realizations that mark a flow of mourning that is characteristically turbulent.

Passage through the turbulence experienced in the wake of a loss is commonly thought of as the transient process of grief and healing. Mourning is constructed as a series of phases with a beginning, middle and end. Such conceptualization serves to help contain the affective reality of loss and death and compartmentalizes the disturbing affects and reality of grief into a circumscribed time frame. This is a falsification of the mourning process and of its significance in human existence. The tendency to dispel, so far as possible, the primitive affective experience and the pain is a part of our human nature. However, mourning after a great loss does not really come to an end. Preoccupation with the loss subsides, aspects resolve, integration occurs, but the underlying mourning process continues. It continues as a thread in the fabric of loss and mourning that constitutes our deep psychological being, and is at the core of the inner reality of subjective and group life. In the *Tibetan Book of the Dead* (Evans-Wentz, 1960; Frementle and Trungpa, 1987) man's spiritual and psychological development, his passage through the state between birth and death, is a process of facing (and avoiding) his/her fear of death. The thanotocentric understanding of group life proposed here is consistent with that view and seeks to articulate the central place of death and mourning in group. When group is evading, inhibiting or imploding loss experience and primitive object relations are enactments of abandonment, loss or annihilation anxiety/phantasy or murderous phantasy, thanotocentric therapeutics recognizes these disturbances as indicators of where things are in the group mourning process. In every kind of group, the progressive frame of group process is the transformation of death into the value of the group – for example, therapeutic (health), political (peace), existential (creative life force) and spiritual (transformative) group values.

When the pain of loss or death is present but not experienced, group denial is associated with underlying annihilation anxiety and depression. Grief that is not experienced has a peculiar status in the group. It is everywhere and nowhere; while it blocks the mourning process and the therapeutic development of the group, it may hardly leave a trace of the incipient loss and mourning; split-off losses and associated traumata form the undercurrent channels that subvert the task-orientated direction of group (Kouffman 1994b).

Discrete events in the life of a group, such as membership changes or issues that emerge from the group dynamic, may trigger the breakthrough of background thanatological anxiety.

In a group that had developed a pseudo-intimacy among members and had not been able to progress to a more genuine level of mutual openness and receptivity, the pseudo-intimacy heightened, accompanied by sporadic conflicts, when a membership change occurred in the group. A need to mourn that was dissociated from the underlying sense of exposure and abandonment (that was a ubiquitous undercurrent of group life) came into the conscious group experience around the group membership change.

Linking the (a) group anxiety that emerged with (b) individual developmental losses and with (c) anger, shame and fear in the group interaction helped the group dissolve the devaluation and group disintegration/separation anxiety that was experienced by the group in the departure of a member and projections on a new member.

Shame may inhibit the experience of loss and mourning in group through very subtle and implicitly enforced norms that prevent group members from getting in touch with an underlying grief. For group to increasingly contain shame-inhibited vulnerabilities, group norms need to securely and implicitly be receptive to the grief that is kept covered/inhibited in the group's experience. The therapeutic development of group-as-a-mourning-process is growth in the group norms of receptivity to inhibited and dissociated grief. The safer and more carefully secured the shame boundary of the group, the greater the group's capacity to facilitate the mourning process. The development of group mourning space is secured by mother-group (Scheidlinger, 1974) as a protective cover for the mortification that may erupt before a basic trust is established in group and at critical regressions when the group exposes or scapegoats in a shaming attack on an object in the group space.

Helplessness anxiety is a basic group-thanatropic manifestation. It may take many forms, for example:

In one group there was a period when the group was unfocused and scattered in a particularly striking way. The inability to focus was intensively present, as if the object of group attention had vacated the group. In the vacuum, there was neither pain nor anxiety, but rather, a dull emptiness. As the group came out of this state, it was more dependent, and seemed to be seeking refuge from an elusive sense of helplessness.

Helplessness and primitive omnipotence are two sides of the same phenomenon. Primitive omnipotence is the transformation of death into its opposite; and helplessness is the presence of death within omnipotence. The group-dynamic processing of helplessness-omnipotence is an underlying mourning process of group. The group disintegrative tension of helplessness-omnipotence becomes group developmental process through the mourning of primitive all-powerfulness and primitive helplessness. The container of this process in group is shame. Without protective shame, helplessness and omnipotence would flare out of control in a group disintegrative panic.

## The ubiquitous lost object of the group mourning process

The mourning process involves a hypercathected internalization of a lost object (Freud, 1917; Lindemann, 1944–5), which, in normal mourning process, is an object both specifically present and ubiquitous. This lost object is a focal point of mourning, representing the deceased, the bereaved's relationship with the deceased and death. Death, however, may not be sufficiently contained by the image of the deceased or may not be sufficiently integrated into self, and so will be ubiquitously present. In the process of mourning the death of the beloved, the internal object is transformed from being a living object to being a deceased object. The primitive affective surge at the death of a beloved infusing the bereaved with grief, tends to saturate the self and the internal object world. Grief is focused in a highly overdetermined and intensive preoccupation with the image of the deceased; the internal object of the deceased and the effect of the death is scattered about the internal object world of the bereaved – everywhere and nowhere death and the beloved and the primitive affective range of grief are present.

These disturbances are partially centred in the image of the deceased, *in which the deceased is not yet really dead*. This is the normal condition of the mourning process. The bereaved *knows* that the deceased is deceased but does not *know* it. Awareness of death is dissociatively scattered in consciousness so that as awareness and realization occur, denial splits off other regions of awareness (Kauffman 1994b).

A 14-year-old girl dreamt of her dead father. She dreamt that he came to her and said he was alive. She said to him, 'You're dead. Go away.' He said, 'That was just a joke. You didn't really believe that, did you?'

We can hear in this dream dialogue between her and her father a fairly straightforward internal dialogue. After a death, the relationship with the deceased continues in internal-object dialogues, and marks out the process of mourning. The continuing dialogue traces the course of the struggle to integrate specific aspects of the loss, and indicates that the mourning process is proceeding. Here, the denial, the belief he is not dead, is placed in the mouth of the deceased, all the more to prove he is alive. Being alive within her, his ghost, who was at that point always with her, spoke for itself in the dream. In her telling him, 'You're dead. Go away', two distinct trends of thought are evident: (a) realization that he is in fact dead; and (b) fear of him as dead. The task of mourning to integrate the fact of his death is impeded by the fear. The dialogue between the internal objects in the dream expresses the inner movement of the mourning process. If the fear were to be heeded and the dialogue broken off, the mourning process would be stuck there.

The mourning process splits off and subjectively imbeds unmetabolized parts of the internal-object representation of the deceased love object.

A woman whose sister had committed suicide several years earlier had not been able to allow herself any close relationships. At a time when relationships began to develop, she dreamt that she was in a maze and she had to find her way through it. The passageway narrowed and, embedded in the wall, was her sister's dead body. She was terrified and had a difficult time getting through the passage.

Associations to this expressed her anxiety about getting close (abandonment anxiety) and the intensity of her longing for warm human contact. While fear of her sister's dead body and related feelings of abandonment and coldness persisted, she also experienced her sister's 'presence' around her and this was a loving, living, protective sister. At this time in the mourning process, preoccupation with the death had subsided and she had internalized a strong sense of purpose – that she accomplish things for her sister and in her sister's honour. Partial identification with her sister had helped her identify long-disowned parts of herself and set her on a path of self-discovery. So, while she came a long way through her mourning and was no longer grieving as she had been for more than two years after her sister's death, the mourning process continued.

During the in-between or mourning state, the death that has already happened but has not yet been sufficiently realized to constitute a peaceful memorial object is *anticipated* (Winnicott, 1974). Whatever aspects of the loss are most affectively threatening and denied are lived as a future that is in danger of happening. The deceased is also scattered about in dream fragments representing continued internal object relations with the deceased (Kauffman, 1989).

Now, thanotocentric phenomenology of group-as-a-whole recognizes further that death has always already happened (Derrida, 1978), that the death that has always already happened in group experience constitutes (within internalized group space) an object presence of a lost object that is always ubiquitous. This ubiquitous lost object of normal group dynamics may appear as an elusive and haunting disturbance. 'In denial,' writes Grotstein, 'the object is sent into oblivion. Its ghost returns as nameless dread' (Grotstein, 1985, p. 171). In a thanotocentric phenomenology of the group-as-a-whole, the destructive power of death or group annihilation anxiety is recognized as the source of the ghosts that haunt the margins and shadows of group experience – and are far more central to the whole dynamic of group than their often peripheral status in the group experience may suggest. Undercurrents of death and mourning in group process may intensify group experience and seem to be erupting towards some action the group urges to take. The ubiquitous lost object of nameless group annihilation anxiety may surge into a tidal force in group process, possibly mysterious, possibly presenting as a specific affect/conflict or dynamic. Not unlike the slain patriarch in Freud's primal horde myth, this ubiquitous lost object is a primitive affective presence dissociated from its origin. The unmourned primitive guilt in which the slain patriarch is dissociatively present in group is not the core phenomenon; core grief involves guilt as part of a complex of object loss affects, bound up with the primitive narcissistic anxieties of helplessness, abandonment, being overwhelmed, loss of control and rage. We have learned from the Kleinians to understand primitive grief to be a reintrojection of annihilation phantasies. In my view of the anxiety and group-level phantasy present in group mourning processes, the primitive affect core of grief appears not to differentiate thanatophobia, human aggression and the reflexive omnipotence (guilt) of primitive grief. The boundary of the self experiencing itself as mortal (Kauffman, 1994a), through which these become differentiated, is the earliest *shame boundary* – developmentally nurtured in the dyadic experience of the maternal holding environment.

The possibility for loss is an existential condition of attachment. It is co-present with primary bonding and with the earliest incipient self. The possibility for loss – in other words, annihilation anxiety or abandonment anxiety – is co-determinate with the earliest conditions of psychic existence. As both self and primary object relation coalesce, primitive omnipotent and narcissistic fields are transformed into self- and object-representations. At each phase of the development of primitive omnipotence and narcissism into more cohesive psychic organization, the loss of the earlier omnipotence and narcissism is processed. Processing the loss of primitive omnipotence and narcissism is a critical feature of the development of self- and object-representational fields, that is, of inner reality. Mourning is usually understood to occur only if there are sufficiently stable objects to internalize. However, here we see the processing of loss to be a condition in establishing object constancy. The inner object world comes into being through processing loss. This proto-mourning process is not merely a precursor of mourning. The process of mitigating, releasing, integrating and transforming primitive omnipotence and narcissism is both developmentally prior to, and at the crux of, the mourning process proper.

Maternal nurture contains death in the valuations with which she, mother-group, holds her dyadic partner of the earliest group dependency phase. Valuation is the counter-valence of death. Devalued, shameful aspects of the group identity – split off, projected and hidden – need maternal nurturing and acceptance valuations. Mother-group, which Scheidlinger says to be symbolic, excludes death at her inception; yet, death remains or returns as a danger also associated with mother-group (Scheidlinger, 1974; Durkin, 1964; Durkin, 1989). Protector and threat, mother-group symbolizes the all-powerful presence of life and death, container and contained. Mother who contains death, the mother of mother-group-as-a-whole, is the same mother who prompts basic-assumption tropisms in group.

These virtually pre-ambivalent presences are only represented in primitive objects (*are only representable*) to the extent to which the mother-group, in the earliest sense of creator/destroyer of group, *is mourned*. The internalized object world of group develops out of and through mourning. The group represents mother-group in its primitive objects only in the process of mourning her as dead omnipotent mother. Only through losing mother-group as a primitive pre-object presence, is she constituted ambivalently in group-object space. The dead mother as a pre-ambivalent presence, however, persists in constituted group-object space as a ubiquitous presence. She is a ubiquitous presence to be mourned. André Green, writing about a phenomenon closely related to this says 'the dead mother complex is a revelation of the transference' (1986, p. 158). The elusive presence of the dead mother 'breaks into the open' in the transference of the group members to mother-group. It is not a specific or factual death, but the ontological origin of group that constitutes the mourning transference to the dead mother. Green writes,

> It does not concern the loss of a real object; the problem of a real separation with the object who would have abandoned the subject is not what is in question here. The fact may exist, but it is not this that constitutes the dead mother complex.
>
> (Green, 1986, p. 149)

The ubiquitous lost object of group experience is the dead mother real *and* originary or primary who constitutes, haunts, disturbs and bounds group-object space. As the affects of primitive object relations stir in group and the primitive aggressive fire heats, the ubiquitous dead mother haunts object-relational space. Mortal dread of her power and omnipotent yearning for her revivification compete for expression in group process. As a group moves through tense periods, dependency behaviours, projective identification of hostilities and members hiding from the affective inferno may be evidenced. With the capacity to mourn, to reintegrate aggression-and-helplessness derivatives of the loss of omnipotence and to recognize split-off parts of oneself in others (integration of the interactive field), the omnipotent threat of the ubiquitous lost object recedes again into the group dynamic background.

## Thanotocentric group process

In the regressions of early group and at nodal points in group history, we witness a stirring, sometimes a turbulence, of primitive anxieties. In these group events, the symbolic mother-group object is a pre-oedipal mother who is rejecting and overprotective (Durkin, 1964), omnipotent and helpless, compelling submission and opposition and representing a wish to annihilate and to bring back to life.

In Bennis and Shepard's (1956) barometric event the dependency group turns against the group therapist/leader in revolt. While Bennis and Shepard understood this as an oedipal rebellion and today we recognize in the upheaval pre-oedipal separation anxiety, thanotocentric group psychology recognizes the barometric event as a node in the cyclic return of death. Death returns both in the underlying anxiety and in the act. It is returned to the therapist who inevitably fails to mirror and protect, who abandons, who is separable and unavailable, who is worthless and powerless; *who is not omnipotent*. Death needs omnipotence as a boundary to secure group life. As the compelling need to mourn death returns as unconscious group process, it also defines the therapeutic task of groups; that is to say, the barometric event is therapeutic if the loss of omnipotence invested in the leader is *mourned*. If the group does not mourn the barometric event, it is without therapeutic consequence. Neither the symbolic, nor the group dynamic consequences of the barometric event is therapeutic. What is therapeutic is the mourning process. The power invested in the leader by the dependency group is mourned (reintegrated) into a greater independence of the group-as-a-whole, and a greater mutuality of the members. As a group develops, primitive annihilation and abandonment anxieties that are at an early deep level of the thanotocentric organization of group spur development towards individuation and mutuality. This occurs in a roughly triphasic movement: (a) loss anxieties, (b) avoidance of mourning, and (c) mourning. At each stage of group development, the specific issues of that group developmental stage focus the underlying thanatropic anxiety. Each of these parts of the thanotocentric movement tends to be simultaneously represented by different members. An example of this process is described by Ashbach and Schermer in their description of the emergence of the stage of development when the group begins to become cohesive. They write, 'A process of mourning is noticed in some members, but the group-as-a-whole avoids grieving by aggressivized or pseudo-sexual thrusts at each other or by magical re-fusion and loss of distinctiveness' (Ashbach and Schermer, 1987, p. 169). As the group moves from beginning of cohesion – with the upsurge of thanatropic anxiety and avoidance of mourning that this occasions – towards becoming more firmly cohesively bonded, aggressive and sexual defences and regressive fusion pulls are less prominent and more evidence of a mourning process emerges in the group.

The mourning work of group strengthens the capacity of the group as a container of anxieties that subvert mutual understanding, empathic communication, intimacy and safety. Growth of the group-as-a-whole as a container for loss anxiety, narcissistic injury and death strengthens the group's therapeutic efficacy. Group space is safer for experiencing and integrating deeper, more vulnerable aspects of the mortal self. The greater the capacity of the group to include the affective reality and meaning of thanatropic anxieties, such as the loss of omnipotence, the more secure the boundaries of the group-as-a-whole.

## Mourning as a transformation of container/contained: Bionian reflections

In her primitive aspect mother-group is container and contained; or, rather, container and contained are virtually undifferentiated. While this is a state of impossible instability (a radical conceptualization of group structural catastrophe), it defines the regressive horizon of the group container/ contained structure. Approaching this horizon, the very infrastructure of thinking about group tends to be relieved of its presuppositional underpinnings. As omnipotent mother-group is also helpless mother-group, container/contained indeterminacy defines the boundary instability of primitive mother-group dynamics. In the unstable dynamic processes and disintegrative volatility of early group and of regressive trends throughout group history, thanatropia energizes internal-object-space dynamics. Mourning is the process which integrates death and differentiates container and contained. Death and diverse losses are mourned and death is contained in being transformed into a more stable and bounded container, analogous to the Kleinian depressive position. Death is the mysterious, irreducible difference which prompts or requires the originary structure container/ contained. In the transformation of container and contained the originally

excluded, divided and ultimately uncontained significance of death transforms the group organization. In Bion the transformation of container and
contained is mystical achievement, 'perpetually breaking through the
barriers intended to control it and threatening to disrupt' group (Bion, 1970,
p. 116). The capacity to contain death – that is mourning – is a subtle,
disturbing and ongoing transformation of container/contained into a higher
level of differentiation. Mourning transforms this relationship by
assimilating and integrating excluded thanatropic fragments that required
the differentiation of container/contained (lest they precipitate a
disintegration and annihilation of group).

Bion sometimes spoke as a mystic. What a mystic has to say about death
may say everything about the mystic. Bion's comments on death are most
startlingly evident in his autobiography, where it is his own death that
addresses us. I wish to draw your attention to his final words: 'Happy
Doomsday!' (1979). What are we to do with this wry, disturbing farewell?
Is this a mystical opening upon the unknown, or does this express the
ultimate collapse of the mystical back into fear and hostility? Is there an
ironic twist in the transformative power of the catastrophic realization of
death? I do not know what Bion's intention is in this curious finale of his
autobiography. It seems to express a failure to transform the annihilating
significance of death into regenerative significance. 'Happy Doomsday!'
There is an ambiguity between reference to his own death and reference to a
more universal catastrophe. But perhaps this very ambiguity is the point. We
could cite this as the failure to differentiate personal self/personal death from
the destruction of humankind, or we might see this identification as a deep
connection to the meaning of death. When we try to learn from Bion on this
point, we are truly left uneasy and in the dark.

For Bion, the mystic is group anomalous: generative of, yet at odds with,
the ordering structure of group; a creative source of group truth, the mystic
and his/her truth is not containable by the group; the group is not hospitable
to the mystic's truth.

Death is mystical; it is the ultimate mystic; it is the locus of unknown,
uncontrollable and ultimate reality, whose appearance within known,
contained and ordinary reality is *disruptive*.

## The power of membership: cluses and membership boundaries

A cluse is a 'shut up place', such as an 'enclosure, a narrow passage, close,
a bond, a prison' (*Oxford English Dictionary*, 1971). On this list, the term
*bond* stands out as not fitting in the sequence the same as the others. *Passage*
and *prison* have variant drifts of meaning.

A cluse is a restriction of space in which a man may dwell. It is a bounding up of space or a bound space – *which constitutes internality*. The internal referencing of cluse includes the indwelling nature of what is bound up. An example of this is provided by the *OED*. A passage from a text by Claxton, written in 1481, reads:

> He hath bylded a cluse, theryn dwelleth he.

The cluse is bylded, constructed; the man made a place to live. A boundary is constructed, constituting in and out; inside he dwelleth. The cluse may also serve as a spatial representation and metaphor for the power of inclusion/exclusion, the group's membership boundary.

This group enclosure bond is secured by shame. To be *excluded* from the security and nurturance of the enclosure bond, exposed, cast out of the cluse – is to be shamed. The shame-bounded group membership boundary shelters those on the inside from thanatropic anxieties and threatens to scapegoat or annihilate a symbolic object representation. Group thanatropic anxieties persist within group as undercurrent dynamics. In the life of the group, securing and maintaining of membership boundaries (when a group starts or is experiencing a fear of ending, when a group takes in a new member or when one leaves, when changes in group are in the works, and other times) establishes a group identity and cohesive pull that is rooted in the necessity of the death-excluding boundary. The group-as-dwelling is the dwelling for the being who lives on the inside of a boundary against death, including the recluse; the common internal objects shared by group members inherit the power of death as the progenitor of a boundary between inside and outside.

## Summary

This thanotocentric phenomenology of group attempts to provide an account of human mortality as it is inscribed in the inner workings of group dynamics. While the metapsychological hypothesis that places death at the centre of the organization of group process is difficult, it is presented as an invitation to the reader to consider the fundamental simplicity of the thanotocentric hypothesis that the fear of death is the spark that ignites the Ring of Fire. The grounds for putting this hypothesis forward are (a) the observation that the mourning process is central to group developmental and therapeutic process, and that, accordingly, group theory should account for and reflect this centrality; (b) that a thanotocentric group theory provides a unitary organizing principle for very diverse phenomena; and (c) the awareness that human mortality is the key to understanding human nature, and that, accordingly, group theory that reflects this will come to more deeply illuminate the meaning of group dynamics and the mystery of death in everyday life.

## BEREAVEMENT GROUPS

Having laid out some of the issues and problems in the development of a thanotocentric theory of the group-as-a-whole, we will now shift our focus. In this section, we will set aside the metapsychological concerns about the foundation of group process. We will direct our attention to a specialized type of group, the bereavement group, and will take up some basic clinical and practical concerns of facilitating a bereavement group.

A serious disparity is evident between the deep need to process loss and the societal norms which govern the mourning process. Subjective, family and community empathic supports necessary to facilitate a mourning process tend to underestimate and unsanction the need, and abort the process. In the context of the insufficiency of normal social supports the bereavement group serves basic supportive as well as therapeutic functions.

Mourning is a normal psychological function. The disturbances experienced in mourning resemble pathology, and there is a risk that, as clinicians, we may pathologize a normal process. Normal, healthy mourning is disturbing and painful for the bereaved and for persons who come into contact with the bereaved. Bereavement groups provide safe passage through a normal disturbance. Recognizing disturbance as normal may challenge our presuppositions about normalcy.

### The mirroring function in bereavement groups

If we listen to what persons who join bereavement groups tell us about their needs and experiences in these groups, we find that the experienced therapeutic value of loss-processing groups is primarily in their mirroring function (Foulkes, 1948, 1965). These groups are supportive in the sense of group members leaning on one another. More basic, however, to the supportive and therapeutic efficacy of these groups is the mutuality and reciprocity of recognizing and being recognized in one's grief. This mirroring (subjectively and intersubjectively) sanctions grief. It facilitates the release and experiencing of grief. It provides the sense that one is known by another in the intimacy of pain. It provides the sense that thoughts abhorred, hidden and experienced as (pathological) disturbances are normal and known by another. It normalizes and facilitates admission to consciousness of hidden grief. Group members frequently discover their own feelings through recognizing the feeling in and through another. One group member, listening to another talk about her anger at her husband whose death she experienced as an abandonment, realized that she too had been angry at her deceased husband and had not allowed herself to realize this. While feelings of abandonment and anger at the deceased are normal parts of the phenomenology of grief, they are feelings that one may feel are 'wrong'. These are frequently disenfranchised (Kauffman, 1989).

When a need to mourn is not (socially) recognized this is called unsanctioned or disenfranchised grief. Kenneth Doka writes,

> Disenfranchised grief can be defined as the grief that persons experience when they incur a loss that cannot be openly acknowledged, publicly mourned or socially supported. The concept of disenfranchised grief recognizes that societies have set norms – in effect 'grieving rules' – that attempt to specify who, when, where, how long and for whom people should grieve.

> (Doka, 1989)

To this we may add that grieving rules also specify which affects and cognitions may be experienced, and how deeply one is permitted to grieve.

Bereavement group mirroring facilitates the sanctioning and release of inhibited grief and may foster the relinking of inhibited cognitions and affects with lost parts of a deceased love object that yet need to be mourned. Mirroring functions in groups to mitigate the sense of social isolation and the narcissistic injury associated with it. This constitutes a significant secondary injury. A secondary injury, an injury that is related to the death or to the mourning process, and that is secondary to the death injury, is disruptive to the flow of mourning. The bereaved are particularly prone to narcissistic injury. Exposure of deeply vulnerable, normally covered layers of the self – as mortal, helpless and abandoned, accompanied by the mobilization of the transient affects of bad self-object introjects – leave the self prone in bereavement to experience narcissistic injury. The mirroring function among bereavement group members functions to secure protective shame boundaries (Kaufman, 1985), helping to heal the narcissistic injury.

A new group member arrived feeling inhibited in the expression of her feelings and ashamed. She reported that friends and family had been saying to her that it had been long enough since her husband's death and she should be over her grieving. It was now eighteen months since her husband's death and she had been hearing this with an increasing sense of rejection of her and her grief, she reported, since three months after his death. Finding in the group several other group members who were struggling with intense grief reactions for as long as she and hearing many other group members describe their experience of family and friends spurning their grief helped her begin to normalize her grief. As she felt her grief to be all right in the eyes and experience of others in the group, she also began to accept it in herself and to express and ventilate in group disturbing affects. The narcissistic injury from the death of her husband that had been compounded by the narcissistic injury of having socially unacceptable feelings began to ease and the mourning/healing process could now flow.

The group's sanctioning of mourning soothes the narcissistic injury and allows the natural process to move along. In the terrible and often unfathomable aloneness, the whole object world may be transiently buried in the blackness of the absence of the beloved.

The realm awakened when the bereaved is submerged in the hyper-cathected internal object of the deceased is a threat to social order. The painful aloneness compelled by the presence of death within the internal object world is augmented by both subtle and gross social tendencies to exclude the bereaved. Social rules of mourning serve not only the function of recognizing individual and family grief and the social unit's grief, but of protecting the social or group order from the power of death present in the pain of the bereaved. Persons commonly feel it is socially correct to avoid their grief. In the recognition of the self through the others of the bereavement group, inner reality is affirmed, the pain of grief is validated and the permission to mourn is granted. Norms that sanction and facilitate the experience of the pain of loss need to be carefully cultivated and secured in the group process.

The internal object of the deceased, riddled with the pain of death and loss, is confusingly represented as both living and dead. Profoundly nuanced dissociative representations of the object as dead and alive underlie a prolonged process (the mourning process) in which the progressive trajectory is a gradual (if never complete) transformation of the internal object from being alive to being dead. Along with the sometimes tumultuous object-transformation process from living to dead, possibilities of one's mortality may be realized.

## A note on countertransference

Bereavement groups are implicitly and explicitly sanctioning places for the bereaved. Yet, the tendency to deny and close off the pain and disturbance of a loss may also be present in a bereavement group. Care for the group norms and group space in which the vulnerable and infectious affects of deep and disturbing grief can be safely experienced and expressed need to be secured by the group therapist. The establishment and maintenance of the therapeutic space of the bereavement group requires of the therapist (a) an openness to the pain of death within him- or herself cultivated by his/her own mourning process that nurtures a growthful tolerance of the reality of death and helplessness in their life, (b) a keen, sensitive attentiveness to the narcissistic vulnerability and the shame-hidden pain and anxieties of the bereaved, and (c) a knowledge of the phenomenology of mourning and group process.

In approaching the mourning process the group therapist needs to take his/her bearings by the pain of the bereaved. This may, however, not be so easy to abide. At the heart of the difficulty lies our relationship to death, our own death and the death of our love objects.

Freud wrote that our psychological relation to death is the least evolved aspect of our human nature (1915). The evidence of the presence of death in the mourning process is of an extraordinary and primitive power. In acute grief and its sequelae the affective intrusion of death visits upon the internal object world disturbing and uncanny powers of very great magnitude. The capacity of the self to contain the presence of death and the implosion of associated primitive affects is quite limited in normal psychological functioning. Group norms tend to be guided by the need to seek efficient closure. Denial is the most powerful common defence. The group excludes the presence of death and its vestiges as expeditiously as possible. In the idealized identity of a group there is no helplessness and no being overwhelmed by the primitive affects uncovered by death's presence. The tendency of workers in the field of death, dying and grief, and of the dying and bereaved, to seek religious or spiritual understanding of their experiences and of the reality of death has to do, in large measure, with the presence and significance of death as *awe-inspiring annihilating omnipotence*. The therapist working with bereavement needs to have the means of handling very unusual powers present in the mourning process. Denial as a defence against one's helplessness in the face of death, projected as the bereaved's need for closure, forecloses hospitable group space for suffering grief. The therapist's denial of helplessness or intolerance of the realization of death can mobilize (a) rescue fantasies (i.e., a wish to save the bereaved from the pain of the loss), (b) undervaluing the bereaved's need to suffer his/her helplessness and loss, and (c) compulsive defences that rid the group space of the threat of helplessness, loss and death.

My own tendency when oversaturated with the pain of grief is for dissociative thought processes to block my empathic attunement.

> Our yearning for closure, our subtle denials, our whispers of self-assurance, our urges to fly from the agonizing emptiness, our dread and numbness, our aching for release of tensions, and our passion to cure the *helplessness* of those we care for must be recognized as signals.
>
> (Kauffman, 1993)

It is not that issues in the grief history and *Todesangst* (death anxiety) of the group therapist may be touched in the group processing of grief. It is that they will inevitably be touched. The group therapist contains death by being receptive to grief in the group. Receptivity to the pain of death means that the primitive death anxieties in the therapist have undergone a transformation in functioning to become live containers of the group mourning processes. Containing grief in group is facilitating openness of members to one another's pain. This is conducted through the group therapist's receptivity.

## Tensions in bereavement groups

In bereavement groups the underlying fire of the therapy group appears to be, generally, less hot. Perhaps the intense subjective preoccupation of grief and the common bond of recognizing one's own pain in the other that tends to be so immediately present in these groups mediates, subdues and absorbs the underlying group process. However, the bereavement group does sometimes become a 'Ring of Fire'.

When primitive affect such as hatred (aimed at the deceased or at others) is expressed, the member expressing this may be shunned and outcast or the projective identification may trigger anxiety and conflict as other group members are threatened by their own split-off primitive hatred. This presents both a serious risk and an opportunity for deepened grief work in the group. The clinical management of this situation involves the dual task of actively supporting, validating and exploring these affects and acknowledging the scariness and unseemliness of such feelings, helping others in the group to identify similar feelings in themselves. The heated affects that may emerge are links to unrecognized grief in other group members. However, often group members will not be able to reclaim split-off primitive affects. If expression of primitive hatred recurs in a stereotypical way without modification over time, bereavement group may not be the appropriate treatment for that person. The safety and grief-processing integrity of the group may be compromised and the group member stuck in that primitive affect, not helped by the group.

Narcissistic vulnerability is heightened in the bereaved, and, while the bereavement group is a great protector of narcissistic exposure, group may also inflict an injury. Most often this leads to an inhibition of grief. When this occurs without any specific noticeable indication, other group members may vacate vulnerable places and the group enter into a manic flight mode. A dead or empty space may be felt in the group-as-a-whole. The injured party may hide his or her reaction, or he/she may strike out at another group member, triggering tensions and conflict. The therapeutic task is to acknowledge and process the injury inflicted and link it, for each party to the injury, to his/her mourning process.

The most complex and explosive issue that I have seen in bereavement groups has to do with feelings of revenge. This feeling may come up whenever there is perceived culpability in a death, but especially in a violent death. The upsurge of a powerful wish for vengeance can tear a bereavement group apart.

In a group for families of murder victims, one member's violent screams for revenge polarized the group into those who identified with her vengeance wishes and those, some of whom were no less vehement and filled with fear and rage, who gathered under the banner, ' "Vengeance is mine," sayeth the Lord'. While there were some on both sides who were calm, several members leaped to their feet. One member leaped up shouting that she wanted to kill her son's murderer and then collapsed to the floor.

Even now as I recount this event, my eyes well up and I gasp at the merciless anguish of the wish for revenge and the relentless injustice that can tear victims of violence apart and precipitate intense conflict in group. A basic wish for justice rarely yields to the healing of forgiveness in violent loss, though the intensity of the wish for revenge usually eases (but may not cease) over a period of years. The sense of injustice is only aggravated by well-intended or fearful expectations of forgiveness. While this conflict is extreme in loss with perceived culpability and especially in violent loss, feelings of unfairness and anger are normally present in bereavement.

## The principle of homogeneity

Membership grouping by the homogeneity of loss experiences is a basic principle of loss-processing groups. The principle is based on the mirroring function in which persons facing a loss have a need to recognize/be recognized in the likeness of the other person's experience. The bereavement group functions primarily to validate the invalidated grieving self, thus facilitating the natural flow of the process. Traumatic loss experiences tend to leave one feeling stigmatized, alienated and different. There may be a sense that one's internal world has been disrupted by an emptiness or strangeness, that a part of oneself has died. Dread, shame and fear prompt a dissociation of tender, intimate and vulnerable links to the object world. These disturbances may be present as adumbrations, may be ubiquitous, or may be manifestly present to consciousness.

The homogeneity of experience sought by bereavement group members is a wish to be with others who have an experience like their own (a) in all the disturbing or isolating aspects of the experience, (b) in aspects which define one's role relationship to the deceased (i.e., parent, spouse), or (c) in other aspects that define oneself and the experience, such as one's age. The homogeneous groupings of the bereaved for membership in bereavement groups is, so far as practical, defined by such factors as these.

We should note that in understanding the experience of the bereaved, attention to the circumstances of the death is crucial. In our awareness of the significance of object relations, we may be inclined to attend more to the relationship of the deceased than the death itself and the circumstances of the death in our understanding of the difficulties in the mourning process. Yet the trauma of the death, specific features of the circumstances of the death (for example, perceived preventability) or the events leading up to death (for example the anguish of intrusive medical technologies) are often the focus of affective disturbance in the mourning process. Circumstances after the death, such as reactions of family and friends or experience with the criminal justice system in a homicide, are also crucial factors in the mourning process.

So, we may organize groups according to the type of death (cancer, suicide), role relationship (spouse, parent) or other factors (an adolescent group, young widow/widower group, bereaved from a particular airplane crash, and so on).

In a homicide bereavement group, a woman whose husband was murdered, anxiously sought other women in the group (which was predominantly mothers of murdered children) whose husbands were murdered. The issues of spousal loneliness were sufficiently different from the aloneness experienced by others in the group that she was not able to find a satisfactory mirror of her experience in the group. While it was not practically possible to sort out this subgroup as a separate group, other subgroupings of the homicide bereavement group were possible. A separate group for persons for whom there was no arrest was set up. The specific anxieties and unsettledness of the unsolved criminal case, on the one hand, and the specific grief inflicted by the judicial system when arrest does occur were critical secondary injuries and focal themes that prompted the decision to divide into groups this way. Special need subgroups may be split off for part of a meeting. In open-ended bereavement groups the intense, acute pain of the newly bereaved requires special attention. This is especially so in widow and widower groups where long-time members have bonded as subgroups and have moved into a socialization/reintegration phase. Each situation is evaluated according to the principle of homogeneity (of key elements of grief experience) in order to maximize the mirroring experience for members.

## Structure in bereavement groups

Group therapists sometimes choose a model for bereavement groups in which structured experiences or educational programmes are included. Bereavement groups are thought of as special clinical situations in which group members need these structures to contain and facilitate the mourning process. However, these structurings of bereavement groups often serve the purpose of suppressing the pain of loss and death. In setting up a group, the therapist's opinion that structure may make members feel safer and less overwhelmed by the pain of grief may, however, be overprotective and express the wish of the therapist to avoid the pain of grief and reality of death. The hopes for the group with which the therapist approaches the pain of death that members bring to the group (and that foster group cohesion) deserve careful attention when planning a group and periodically (or ongoing) through the life of the group.

Being aware of one's own disposition towards the pain and meaning of death is a basic preparation process for doing a bereavement group. Accommodations for the group's grief within the internal object world of the therapist provides a group space for holding mourning, regardless of structural scaffolding otherwise used in constructing a therapeutic group space.

Yalom is a noted contributor to the literature on bereavement groups. He points out that the themes of growth, identity and responsibility for the future are 'themes that preoccupy bereaved spouses' (Yalom and Vinograder, 1988). In my experience these themes occur in widow and widower groups at a point in time when the bereaved is in the final stage of his or her active grief and are focal topics of a resocialization for the bereaved. Perhaps because participants were not self-referred to Yalom's group, and because of the norm-setting protocols used – for example he writes, 'We hoped that the group would focus primarily on the future' (Yalom and Vinograder, 1988, p. 444) – these themes appeared to be less prominent in the grief-processing groups I have worked with.

Yalom began his work with bereavement groups by using structured group exercises. He soon learned that 'The members welcomed a simple forum where they could talk openly and the imposition of structure was thus generally counterproductive' (Yalom and Vinograder, 1988, p. 426). We should follow Yalom's example of listening to and learning from group members. We need also to listen to our own fear/anxieties and denials of the pain and the impossibility of reversing death.

The hope that the group would focus primarily on the future supports the active and progressive trends of mourning. Empowering the active ego in the mourning process may be therapeutic. It should not displace or override the opening of passive suffering. Suffering and the need for progressive action require an appropriate balance. For example, a bereaved group member whose marriage was a highly dependent relationship got stuck in helplessness in the mourning process. She was unable to suffer the helplessness and find the developmental trajectory towards greater independence and autonomy. Recognizing and actively choosing independent, forward-looking behaviours functioned in the mourning process in tandem with suffering helplessness and working through the meaning of the anxiety associated with loss and dependency. While active and passive trends need a functional blend in the mourning process, the compassion that nurtures growth and a deepened source of hope is based primarily in the strength of the group to contain the pain and the diverse meanings of death and loss in the group.

The flow of grief is not regular. The process flows in fits and starts; there are delays and interruptions, unanticipated outbreaks of grief and shifts in focus. In open-ended groups I find that some members choose a short-term experience and, having had a positive therapeutic experience, leave group after six to fifteen sessions. However, others choose to stay and need to stay for up to a few years. Yalom advocates fairly short-term work with bereavement groups. The advantage of an ongoing group is that it can be available to diverse needs over time and see a person through the process, as needed. Once in a while someone will want to stay indefinitely in the group. This will need to be assessed and the person may need help through a separation process from group. With adolescent and children groups, six- to eight-week, time-limited, focused experience has seemed to me most suitable, though some will often attend for several six- to eight-week cycles. We cannot explore issues of the set-up of children and adolescent groups here.

The inclusion of educational objectives, especially about normal mourning, may be an appropriate and helpful part of the therapeutic design of a bereavement group. In conjunction with the therapeutic interaction of group, educational interventions (a) may be informative in ways that reassure and normalize and (b) may help focus and contain diffuse or marginally conscious grief. Whether the educational intervention is a speaker on a topic or addressing needs within the interactive group process the clinical concern is that it not violate the needs of group members to experience empathic attunement in group. Educational aims function within a clinical strategy designed to facilitate normalization and deeper ventilation of grief.

In a bereavement group where members seek a more structured educational format the request may be an avoidance of a painful issue in the group. The group requesting an educational structure may be seeking/avoiding the sanctioning of an unsanctioned mourning need. The group's wish for educational structure may be indicative of the group's, or the therapist's, thanatropic anxiety.

## Summary

Bereavement groups are specialized groups for persons with a common loss experience. They provide a social context to experience, validate, express and process the pain of a loss. A safe and sanctioning environment that compassionately holds the pain without the need to fix it is the heart of therapeutic benefit of bereavement groups. Members mirror one another's loss experiences and unsanctioned grief and facilitate the processing of grief. The therapist is faced with the special responsibility and opportunity to recognize his/her own death anxieties and maintain an open, empathic attunement with the terrible pain of death.

## REFERENCES

Ashbach, C. and Schermer, V. (1987) *Object Relations, the Self and the Group*, London: Routledge & Kegan Paul.

Bennis, W.G. and Shepard, H.A. (1956) 'A theory of group development', *Human Relations* 9: 415–37.

Bion, W.R. (1959) *Experiences in Groups*, New York: Basic Books.

—— (1970) 'Container/contained transformed', in *Attention and Interpretation*, London: Tavistock.

—— (1979) *A Memoir of the Future*, vol. 3, *The Dawn of Oblivion*, Strath Tay, Perthshire: Clunie Press.

Bowlby, J. (1961) 'Process of mourning', *The International Journal of Psycho-Analysis* 42.

Derrida, J. (1978) 'Freud and the scene of writing', in *Writing and Difference* (transl. A. Bass), Chicago, IL: University of Chicago Press.

Deutsch, H. (1937) 'Absence of grief', *The Psychoanalytic Quarterly* 6.

Doka, K. (1989) 'Disenfranchised grief', in K. Doka (ed.), *Disenfranchised Grief*, Lexington, MA: Lexington Books.

Durkin, H. (1964) *The Group in Depth*, New York: International Universities Press, 1972.

Durkin, J.E. (1989) 'Mothergroup-as-a-whole formation and systemic boundarying events', *Group* 13 (3 and 4): 198–211.

Evans-Wentz, N.Y. (1960) *Tibetan Book of the Dead*, London: Oxford University Press.

Foulkes, S.H. (1948) *Introduction to Group-Analytic Psychotherapy*, London: Karnac.

—— (1965) *Therapeutic Group Analysis*, New York: International Universities Press, 1965.

Frementle, F. and Trungpa, C. (1987) *Tibetan Book of the Dead*, Boston, MA: Shambahala.

Freud, S. (1913) *Totem and Taboo, Standard Edition* vol. 13.
—— (1915) 'Thoughts for the times on war and death', *Collected Papers*, vol. IV, New York: Basic Books, 1959.
—— (1917) *Mourning and melancholia, Standard Edition* 14: 67–104.
Gorer, G. (1965) *Death, Grief and Mourning*, London: Cresset Press.
Green, A. (1986) 'The dead mother', in *On Private Madness*, Madison, CT: International Universities Press.
Grotstein, J. (1985) *Splitting and Projective Identification*, New York: Jason Aronson.
Kastenbaum, R. and Aisenberg, R. (1976) *The Psychology of Death*, New York: Springer.
Kauffman, J. (1988) 'On shame and grief: introduction to the psychological regulation of grief', in the newsletter of *The Study Group for Contemporary Psychoanalytic Process*, 2 (1).
—— (1989) 'Intrapsychic dimensions of disenfranchised grief', in K. Doka (ed.), *Disenfranchised Grief*, Lexington, MA: Lexington Books.
—— (1993) 'Spiritual dimensions of suffering the pain of death', in K. Doka (ed.), *Spirituality and Death*, Amityville, NY: Baywood Press.
—— (1994a) 'Blinkings: a thanotocentric theory of consciousness', in J. Kauffman (ed.), *Awareness of Mortality*, Amityville, NY: Baywood Press.
—— (1994b) 'Dissociative functions in the normal mourning process', *OMEGA – Journal of Death and Dying* 28 (1): 31–8.
Kaufman, G. (1985) *Shame*, Rochester, VT: Shenkman Books.
Lindemann, E. (1944–5) 'Symptomatology and management of acute grief', *American Journal of Psychiatry* 101.
Parkes, C.M. (1970) 'The first year of bereavement', *Psychiatry* XXXIII.
Rando, T.A. (1984) *Grief, Dying and Death*, Champaign, IL: Research Press.
Raphael, B. (1983) *The Anatomy of Bereavement*, New York: Basic Books.
Scheidlinger, S. (1974) 'On the concept of the "mother group"', *International Journal of Group Psychotherapy* 24: 417–28.
Schneider, C.D. (1977) *Shame, Exposure and Privacy*, Boston, MA: Beacon Press.
Winnicott, D.W. (1974) 'Fear of breakdown', *International Review of Psycho-Analysis* 1: 103–7.
Yalom, I.D. and Vinograder, S. (1988) 'Bereavement groups: techniques and themes', *International Journal of Group Psychotherapy* 38 (4): 619–46.

# 8  Therapeutic responses to the expression of aggression by members in groups

*Saul Tuttman*

## EDITORS' INTRODUCTION

If there is an ultimate challenge to the group therapist, it is the potential for violence and rage in the group. In what follows, Saul Tuttman offers a measured and well-considered approach to aggression in groups, which allows for the members' healthy expression of hostility yet with the kinds of therapist interpretations and interventions which allow the anger to be worked through and integrated into the mature ego.

The conceptual framework which Tuttman calls upon for the task of mastering member aggression is a pragmatic – and perhaps typically American – blend of ego psychology with borrowings from the object-relations perspectives of Melanie Klein on splitting and projective identification, D.W. Winnicott on holding and on 'hate in the countertransference' and Otto Kernberg on the ego states, defences and affects of borderline patients.

In addition, Tuttman utilizes Scheidlinger's important work on group identifications and on the positive, supportive features of the group as a transference object. Using Margaret Mahler's perspective, Tuttman regards the therapy group as a 'second chance' to rework the deficiencies and defects of the symbiosis/separation–individuation process. Tuttman also discusses (with a human quality that is tantamount to bravery) the hate induced in the therapist's countertransference by the group's projective identifications.

## INTRODUCTION

The title of this volume, *Ring of Fire*, arouses many associations, among them: the intensity of emotion and impulse manifested in the interaction of certain volatile group members within the psychotherapy circle. My focus in this chapter is on the problem of those members of the group whose rage and resentment can erupt in the course of group treatment. I am concerned about the welfare of such angry individuals and of the other group members and the group leaders who might be caught in the crossfire. All can be engaged in a conflagration of fury which has the potential to spread, and overwhelm. The group leader may also become victim, or (under some circumstances) even a perpetrator (Main, 1957) of assaultiveness, abuse, rage and dangerous acting out. Leader and members may find involved in themselves toxic reactions and emotions which can also lead to further incendiary developments – a negative spiral may ensue.

Although all of this focuses on one pole of the (love/hate) group atmosphere continuum, this chapter emphasizes that pole which is potentially most dangerous to the survival of any group and its therapeutic matrix. Such situations require understanding along with sensitive and helpful responses from the group leader. These have been insufficiently addressed in the group literature. In other presentations (Tuttman, 1986, 1991), I have emphasized the nurturing matrix qualities of therapy groups which are vitally important in promoting a therapeutic milieu and a 'holding environment'. The problems of rage and the breakdown or absence of controls need special attention for at least two reasons: first, a deeper understanding of the potential for angry eruptions may help us cope with such impulses and affects within ourselves as well as in the responses of others; and second, since conducive, 'facilitating' group participation can be therapeutically invaluable, such an atmosphere needs to be protected from the potential disruption which can often happen when anger erupts in groups.

This chapter explores such difficult problems and important issues by examining some applicable psychodynamic formulations of possible mechanisms at work in the personalities of so-called 'dangerous patients'. It is important to consider that there are various types of potentially enraged patients. Sometimes circumstances provoke otherwise peaceful and relatively emotionally healthy individuals, but the likelihood of uncontrolled outbursts is more likely in those suffering from psychotic states, severe borderline and narcissistic conditions or low-level character disorders.

## SOME PSYCHODYNAMIC FORMULATIONS APPLICABLE TO THOSE INCLINED TOWARDS VIOLENCE IN THE GROUP

What are some prevalent psychological characteristics and mechanisms present in the personalities of those who sometimes become dangerous patients? Such individuals are often potentially harmful to themselves, their groups and their therapists (in both group and dyadic treatment). What are the applicable psychodynamic formulations which can help us appreciate those patients most likely to become enraged, if not violent? It is important to recognize that such group members are often as afraid of their dangerous impulses as are their peers or the group leader! Sometimes these patients also dread the very punitive response they sense that they may invoke in others. Having worked with such individuals for many years, I can discern factors in their histories and personalities which have contributed to their potential for violent behaviour. For one thing, in the course of early life, some 'acting-out' violent patients have identified with sadistic, bullying caretakers. As a result, such patients may develop an aggressive and belligerent attitude towards those for whom they are assigned to care. Sometimes pressures from aggressive parents impel their youngsters to develop a 'false-self' (Winnicott, 1960) conformity. This may result in great frustration and a damming up of underlying resentment and tension which can add to an eruptive potential which may be triggered and which can erupt under stressful conditions when the group member feels frustrated or provoked.

Among other factors operant in such patients are: the lack of a clearly delineated sense of 'self', on one hand; and a concomitant lack of awareness of the qualities, drives and affects of 'object', on the other hand. In Federn's (1952) terms, such problems often reflect unstable and insufficiently cathected psychological boundaries. Related developmental difficulties occur sometimes when caretakers were not able to provide clear and stable objects for internalization. This absence interferes with the acquisition of inner psychic structures which are needed to maintain firm boundaries and control over impulses, affects and ideas. The brittle super-ego signs we sometimes see (in patients more inclined to violent 'acting out') are also often related to their poorly maintained and delineated borders and poor impulse or affect controls. Ego pathology (Kernberg, 1975) in these patients include stereotyped, naive views and the use of pathological psychological mechanisms (that is, splitting and projective identification).

In some cases the patients we consider potentially violent are those who have problems involving poor reality-testing and paranoid reactions. Frequently in their histories, such individuals have had psychological difficulties along the symbiosis/separation–individuation developmental line (Mahler *et al.*, 1975). Such problems interfere with youngsters growing psychologically towards self–object differentiation and a sense of identity with concomitant mature ego and super-ego functions. Those who have been impeded during the symbiosis–individuation process are inclined to specific narcissistic and 'borderline' problems described by Kernberg (1975).

I have summarized these personality problems in previous writings and most recently in the first chapter (Tuttman, 1990) of *The Difficult Patient in Group* (Roth *et al.*, 1990). In the same volume, Pines (1990) similarly noted that such patients have not successfully evolved through separation and individuation stages. Consequently, they suffer a structural deficit. They do not have an adequate 'capacity for self containment, for stability in time and space'. Pines's image of the borderline patient is that of 'a ship without bulwarks, without water-tight compartments, so as to keep the vessel buoyant, even when one compartment is breached and flooded . . . the entire vessel is quickly flooded and goes under. There is the danger also of internal catastrophe: an explosion or fire will spread rapidly through the vessel and destroy it' (Pines, 1990, p. 36). Often, in such patients, there is an ongoing threat of low self-esteem which can be overwhelming for a personality which does not have the capacity to soothe the self or control damaging 'acting out'.

## PARTICULAR VALUE OF GROUP TREATMENT AS A MODALITY FOR SUCH PATIENTS

The group modality has value for patients who have personality disorders disposed to rageful and uncontrolled behaviour. The deficiency in development which most of these patients have suffered has been described above as a lost opportunity in early life to have 'worked through' the separation–individuation phase. When young children do not experience good-enough caretaking, they suffer the consequences of inadequate mirroring and empathy. They do not have the advantages of experience with a beneficial blend of constructive discipline and separateness along with intimacy and acceptance. Parents who have effectively harnessed and can utilize both aggressive and loving responses in a context of good reality-testing and available – neutral – ego energy help their children feel safe and secure enough to make use of anger and love constructively in their relationships. In such ways, 'good-enough' caretakers facilitate in their children the development of solid boundaries, realistic ego functioning, healthy identifications and good self-esteem regulation. The dependent child needs to have experiences with a caretaker whose attitudes and reactions help facilitate that child's potential to feel cohesive and a sense of separate selfhood. The 'holding environment', as Winnicott (1960) called it, or the 'container', as Bion (1959) stated it, is vitally important in helping individuals to harness and channel their aggressive and other impulses – often, this can be achieved in a manner which helps them to integrate further. Out of an early life, archaic and fragmented state, there can develop a cohesive personality with cognitive capacities and self-regulatory mechanisms so important in order to organize, initiate and, when necessary, postpone behaviour. All of this can help group members work towards goals which are meaningful for each evolving member.

The group often becomes a 'second chance' for those who have not had good-enough providers who could respond, intuitively, at crucial times, with appropriate combinations of love and discipline. Constructive identificatory processes are often catalysed and facilitated in groups (Scheidlinger, 1955).

An imbalanced developmental history (where there was insufficient opportunity to experience and internalize reliable and realistic objects) often leads to a 'psychological deficiency' state. There are good reasons to consider the dynamic group as a milieu which offers effective therapeutic engagement and opportunities for productive relatedness. Healthier identifications can grow within the group matrix. Therein a safe support atmosphere and a facilitating regressive reworking situation is possible such that thwarted or blocked potential psychological growth is again possible (Scheidlinger, 1982; Tuttman, 1979).

In other words, the group, along with reactivating a potentially archaic primitive state in its members (Bion, 1959), also can provide emotional support and reality reinforcement, as described by Scheidlinger (1974) in his paper on the mother-group. Such groups offer therapeutic opportunities for mirroring, for trial-and-error behaviour, for feedback, for multiple sources of identification, for group cohesion, for a sense of separateness as well as a sense of togetherness. Both Greenacre (1971) and Jacobson (1964) pointed out that an opportunity to perceive both differences and similarities between ourselves and others offers each of us the chance to become clearer about our own identity.

## GROUP TREATMENT FOR SUCH PATIENTS

What are some relevant group psychodynamic concepts which can be meaningfully applied to the treatment of the types of patients under study in this chapter?

Freud (1921) described how group experiences evoke intense emotional bonds and how the very interaction in the group in some way seems to bring out manifestations of previously repressed, archaic patterns. This characteristic contagion, although originally used to describe behaviours of a mob or crowd, also applies to the psychotherapy group where feelings are sometimes primitive, and greatly exaggerated. Freud (1921) appreciated that in the very process of group formation, members identify with one another and develop a sense of group cohesiveness. He hypothesized that often such members externalize their rage and need the leader to replace individual ego-ideals. Wilfred Bion (1959) was the first psychoanalyst who offered a group-psychodynamic theory particularly applicable to treating more disturbed patients wherein the group leader can become catalytic in facilitating a working through of the unconscious basic assumptions dealing with fight and flight as well as with pairing and dependency needs. Bion believed (consistent with Kleinian theory) that essentially all humans deep down are frightened of their own primitive part-object fantasy remnants that persist unconsciously in the memory bank left over from the distortions of early life. Mental representations related to these archaic perceptions remain deeply buried in the human psyche and this can be most anxiety-provoking. He said, 'This does not mean I consider my descriptions apply only to sick groups. On the contrary, I doubt if any real therapy could result unless psychotic patterns were laid bare with no matter what group' (Bion, 1959, p. 144). We have also learned from the views of other analysts how mechanisms of projective identification and splitting are so all pervasive. To experience, analyse and attempt to understand these psychodynamics at work provides an opportunity for patients and leaders to join in observing and feeling a profound working through of underlying personality patterns connected with archaic basic assumptions. This reality work gives rise to the hope of perspective, of constructive and therapeutic resolution.

In 1980, Kernberg proposed that whereas individual treatment tends to activate 'higher-level' object relations involving transference neuroses, group interaction probably elicits aggressive and sexual fantasies on a primitive regressed level. Although this is frequently true, the group also offers a treatment modality which provides support, encouragement and reality-orientated feedback which can be conducive to growth by creating a safe atmosphere in which to explore and harness the potentially violent eruptions. The group situation can offer in a constructive working therapeutic situation the possibility of both regressive and progressive movement. If the group leader and other members succeed in encouraging adequate observing egos to develop in patients who have both an inclination towards archaic regressive pulls but also towards progressive potential; the group matrix, with its transitional opportunities, with its trial-and-error emotional play characteristics, with the availability of empathic resonance and realistic feedback, with exposure to the clash of inner worlds and confrontations in a safe and structured atmosphere – then progress may ensue! Scheidlinger (1982) in his papers on identification in groups and regression in group therapy has written about such matters. He described two levels of group interaction: the contemporary dynamic and the genetic regressive levels. Many of these ideas fit in with Winnicott's (1951) object-relations concepts about the function of transitional objects. Several psychoanalytic group therapists have written about this aspect of the therapeutic group situation (Kosseff, 1975; Tuttman, 1980; James, 1982; Schlachet, 1986). A recent article about principles of analytic group therapy applied to the treatment of seriously disturbed borderline and narcissistic patients described the benefits of analytic group treatment in dealing with the intensity of the split-off rage in borderline and narcissistic patients which when ventilated in dyadic treatment alone often leads to negative therapeutic reactions (Tuttman, 1984).

The perceptions that make up early-life mental representations are contaminated by the primitive and naive nature of archaic impressions which were probably embanked in primitive psychic layers. Along with those concepts that fall within the object-relations framework, there are overlapping concepts which have an emphasis on what we might call psychoanalytic developmental ego-psychological ideas. The recent work of Dan Stern (1984) and others who have studied young infants, along with the understanding of developmental issue described in the work of Spitz, A. Freud, Jacobson, Greenacre – all of this has provided a framework which sensitizes us to the probable early pathways of psychic development. The therapeutic dyad in individual treatment often involves a transferential recapitulation of infant–caretaker interaction. Implicit is the opportunity to work through many unresolved issues in the course of first acting out and then understanding the history of these problems and issues in treatment. In recent years the group therapy psychodynamic literature (Tuttman, 1980, 1990) refers to the way ego-developmental and object-relations concepts have influenced group-dynamic theory. For example, in addition to Mahler's perspective (Mahler *et al.*, 1975), Winnicott's (1951) concept of the transitional experience and the transitional object can be applied to the group which can be experienced developmentally as a caretaker–infant unit or matrix, out of which emerges the individuality of more mature and related individuals. The group is capable of serving the function of a 'container' or as a facilitating atmosphere or 'matrix' (Foulkes, 1948, 1973) out of which emerges individuality. Winnicott (1971) stressed not only the good-enough mother and the facilitating environment but also the importance of play, trial-and-error learning, and the gradual acquisition of a capacity to use objects. In the group, we see a cluster of objects with qualities of their own as well as space for play and experimentation of individual members' fantasies and projections. In the group, we have a possible externalization of the inner repertoire of mental representations within each group member's psyche. Examples below will show how these often acted-out scenarios can be worked through in group treatment. Group interaction encourages: 'me/not-me' recognizing which a member can experience in the group; being both part of and being apart from the group; observing qualities of the group members at large; and providing feedback and perspective for individuals in the group. These are among the rich repertoire of possibilities available within the group for the group member to experience.

Some of these concepts will be illustrated in the examples from individual cases and groups in which individuals are overwhelmed with frustration and rage and the group leader and the group must deal with and help channel and contain provocative and dangerous rage reactions.

I have sketched out and summarized some of the theory and the therapeutic means that the dynamic group therapist and the group members have available to help cope with the frequently occurring dramatic, emergency issues that confront the group when there are very angry patients involved. A series of relevant vignettes will be presented which offer examples of the problems of rage and violence in patients in group therapy as well as some manifestations of these problems in trainees, therapists and supervisors.

## CLINICAL EXAMPLES

Recently, a psychiatric resident/supervisee discussed one of his patients with me.[1] This patient is a tough, angry truck driver, a single male in his thirties who lives alone in an apartment one floor above his widowed mother's home. He spends his time alone aside from an occasional date with a woman with whom he has a sexual relationship but no real intimacy. He drinks with a few buddies on weekends, and during the hunting season they go into the woods and hunt together. He came into treatment with the following complaint:

> I'm angry at the fucking police. I rarely visit my old mother downstairs. I don't get along with her. I don't enjoy her. And when she telephoned the other day in a panic and asked me to come see her because she was feeling sick, I did go down and found her sprawled out on the carpet. The room stunk. She shit on the rug. I was so enraged, I felt like . . . killing her. I went upstairs to get my pistols and then, realizing what I was about to do, instead I called the police. A radio car came to the house, the cops handcuffed me and took me off for psychiatric observation. The judge had them take away my guns and finally I was released. I've never in my life hurt anybody, although I often feel like it. I knew I felt like killing my mother when I found her downstairs on the carpet, but I understood that this feeling of mine was dangerous, and I decided to call the police instead. To take away my pistols makes me feel helpless and queer. These guns are what give me a feeling of power and strength. This helps me feel safe in this unreliable world. What will I tell the few buddies I have when they want us to go hunting together, that I no longer have guns, my guns?

The patient elaborated how much security, safety and comfort he feels by having his weapons at his disposal. He reiterated how he was absolutely confident that under no circumstances would he ever assault anyone; yet he himself in a state of panic, aware of the danger, had called for help to protect himself and others from his own impulses. Therefore he called the police and asked them to help him. Here is an example of an individual who has partial insight and partial awareness into some aspects of the danger of his vengeful, rageful urges. I believe that the assigned psychiatric resident can treat his patient effectively although I recommended that, at first, this man should be treated in individual psychodynamically orientated therapy, and later, in group therapy as well.

Now that the resident has completed his initial diagnostic 'work-up' and has established a relationship with this patient, we (the resident and supervisor) explore together the vital factors involved in treating this angry man. We must appreciate the patient's rigidity, limited ego resources in terms of insight, fear of tenderness, dread of closeness; yet, we appreciate how he tries to protect himself and others from his violent propensity which he both recognizes and denies. He requires a cautious, consistent relationship which responds to his need for therapeutic alliance in a non-intrusive space. Although this patient is not confident enough to tolerate group interaction at this time, and since he needs the therapist to be an available object, group would probably be premature. As soon as possible, I believe, group participation will prove catalytic in his therapy. For one thing, it will probably diffuse the intensity of his needs and intense reactions increasingly directed towards his therapist as his transference increases. Further, it will diffuse his rage directed at the therapist alone, when frustrating realities are voiced by group members who will also become available for support as well as confrontation.

There are individuals we encounter as clinicians in which rageful anger may be split off in a manner which is unknown to the patient. For example many years ago when it was my responsibility to evaluate the murderers in a psychiatric hospital of a county diagnostic centre and report to the court with the hope of helping the judge evaluate the specifics of each situation, one of the subjects for study was a woman in her fifties who had 'chopped' her husband with a hatchet into many small pieces. Upon examination, I found this middle-aged woman to be, characterwise, one of the most quiet and gentle people I had ever met. And not only was this indicated by her clinical manner at the time of evaluation, but all reports of neighbours and relatives about how she had conducted her entire life indicated that she was generally a very meek, discreet, deeply religious, kind person who at no time had ever hurt any living creature until the dramatic incident involving her husband. When investigating the specifics of this extreme act, she mentioned that her husband beat her physically quite often, especially when he had been drinking heavily. Each week she was a church volunteer who spent many days visiting parishioners, comforting others and collecting funds for local charities. One evening upon returning home she found her husband very drunk and more abusive than ever. In his stupor, he mocked and beat her many times until he fell into a deep sleep. The injustice of his assaultiveness, she explained, and the physical pain and the mental torment he inflicted upon her so many times had reached a peak of endurance. In a state of utter numbness and indignation, she picked up an axe and performed this murderous act mechanically and repeatedly. Although I consider insight therapy of probably limited value for this patient, support and guidance may prove helpful. Her brittle ego functioning and her circumstances and limited abilities contra-indicate insight therapy, in all likelihood.

There are perhaps less dramatic 'little murders' we often witness as members and leaders of therapy groups. One of my patients in the course of a group therapy session one night expressed intense rage when he believed that members of the group were laughing at him.

Melvin listened carefully as another group member, Jim, described his early and his ongoing struggle ever since his father had disappeared before Jim's birth. Melvin found the material about Jim of great interest. Later, he acknowledged some parallels in his own background. But this was the first time Mel felt inclined to speak about himself in the group. He had been in individual psychotherapy with the group leader over a period of two years. For the past few months, at his therapist's suggestion, he joined the group, but thus far seemed disinclined to participate openly. Somehow Jim's description of a somewhat parallel history encouraged Melvin, and so he began to share his own painful memories about his own father. He acknowledged that he wished that his father had also disappeared, because he attributed much of his unhappiness throughout his childhood to the presence of his belligerent, sadistic father who seemed to enjoy tormenting him. His father owned a grocery store in a tenement neighbourhood. It was Melvin's job, after school, to carry heavy crates from the basement to the store. He had been a small and sickly youngster, and he did not have enough strength to comply with his father's demands. Whenever he could not follow his father's instructions, the 'old man' would become impatient. At such times, he would offer his leather belt to his son. 'Hit me as hard as you can', the father said. By this time Melvin was quite familiar with the sadistic games. He sensed that once again he was trapped. It would be dangerous to comply, but it would be equally hazardous to resist. It was, as a result of such forced choices, that Melvin learned to try to avoid crises by acting foolish, silly and a bit seductive. He tried to tease and distract his father (by making weird facial gestures and laughing strangely), but this did not succeed. He took the belt and struck his father, as instructed, and the inevitable occurred: father mocked his son's weakness and proceeded to demonstrate his own superior power by grabbing the belt and striking Mel with full fury! Although Mel was not successful in dealing with this kind of sadistic game, he somehow learned to succeed with his schoolmates and others in the neighbourhood by becoming a clown. In that way, he assuaged the street bullies. Although these tough, older kids were often amused, sometimes Melvin found himself initiating trouble, inadvertently provoking them through his jesting and grinning. Although he basically wanted to ward off attacks, his own anger and frustration sometimes resulted in his sending excessive and provocative jesting signals. In one group session, Melvin remembered an incident from childhood which he had never before recalled. In his public school, all the boys were supposed to bathe in the public shower room after gym. In the behaviour which had become a tradition of teasing and taunting 'Melvin the clown', the boys in the shower encircled him and urinated on him. He told the story with great embarrassment; nevertheless, he was experimenting with talking to an understanding group in which it looked safe – for the first time – to open up painful and disturbing emotions and memories.

In my experience, on several occasions, group members have brought up from repression memories of earlier traumatic group events which somehow found their way to consciousness in the context of an accepting and constructive group situation. I have known several patients in individual sessions who do not always recall such group traumas of earlier life. Perhaps it is in the context of group treatment, when the group situation parallels earlier life group experience and when a leader's role facilitates an exploratory and open approach, perhaps it is then that such memories are more inclined to return to consciousness. When the group first heard the story of the shower-room humiliation, out of anxiety and surprise some group members began to laugh. Melvin misunderstood this laughter. He reacted with indignation and rage. He felt that it was very difficult for him to talk about painful matters and the group's response upset and enraged him. Immediately, members of the group clarified that they were not laughing at him, rather they were anxiously distressed that as a vulnerable kid, he had experienced such abuse. Gradually, it became clearer that Melvin had developed a self-defeating masochistic style as a way of coping with his rage in response to father's and the neighbourhood bullies' mistreatment. It was also clear that he was in the process of liberating himself from that repetition compulsion. As a teenager he had sought individual therapy. In the cause of working on his problems, he moved away from his family, went to a public college, worked in his spare time to earn money for treatment as well as for living expenses. His self-negating and provocative manner dramatically diminished, and over time he continued working in both group and individual treatment.

While still at college, Melvin joined the National Guard. At that time, it was an alternative to being drafted into the military. Each summer, he was committed to spend several weeks at a military camp. One year, while he was on manoeuvres, I received an unsigned letter containing words which were scribbled impulsively: 'You are a no good son of a bitch.' The only clue as to who had sent it was the envelope postal mark of some unfamiliar village in rural New York. A glance at a map led to the conclusion that the area from which the letter came was in the vicinity of the military camp! Clearly, this required a therapeutic response (preferably unencumbered by counter-transference).

As group leader, it was my responsibility to ascertain, in the course of the following group session, whether Melvin could tolerate exploration of this potentially humiliating and embarrassing matter. The quality of his ego functioning, his resistances, the strength of our therapeutic alliance and the capacity of both this patient and the group to tolerate stress and anger were considered. I decided quietly to mention that his letter had arrived! Although he looked quite flustered, he described to the group what he had written. Again, some group members laughed. Other members inquired rather sensitively as to his feelings and thoughts when he wrote this note. He said, 'This year, I was scared about going back to the army camp. It had become a tradition for the other soldiers to amuse themselves by teasing me, year after year. But I have been changing, and I was not willing to be the butt of the barrack joke. I do not wish to continue this painful way of coping by clowning and being victimized. I now know how to avoid being teased.' But not having been with these soldiers for a year, he was clearly frightened and worried at the thought that they would certainly press for the old rituals which they enjoyed at his expense. How angry they would become if he did not play the old game! Indeed, he was correct. As usual, the soldiers began teasing. At a moment of frightening confrontation, Melvin glanced at his watch and saw it was time for the mail to go out. He said he had to write a letter urgently, and he ran off, grabbed a paper and envelope, scribbled the message hastily, addressed the envelope, and sealed in his rage and frustration while thinking about our group and myself. He knew he had found enhanced self-esteem and the beginning of a sense of poise, and he wanted to connect with his group and therapist at this painful moment since he was not yet ready to handle the situation safely to his advantage. At the same time, he was quite angry with us. He bitterly resented this new-found danger he was confronting (which he recognized had resulted, ironically, from his 'growth') as he dropped the letter into the mail sack.

He described all this to the group. Everyone in the room was moved. They spoke of the meaningfulness and the sense of irony in all that Melvin had recounted. We all appreciated how awesome, how frightening, how dangerous groups of people can be to one another. We also felt the healing power and the changes in each of us which the group relationships have catalysed. This incident reminded us how confusing and yet reassuring changing can be. It reflects both the tenacity and pressure of past mental representation and the consequences of the leader's role, the power of the group, and the wish to strive towards greater health and reality mastery, even though there can be considerable pain and danger in the course of the process.

Rage manifests itself in various ways. Melvin's grimace, his laughter and his grin were expressions of great anger towards his sadistic father and towards me, transferentially, when we began to work together. The note, 'You are a no good son of a bitch', also reflected great anger but somehow, as I got to understand the communication, it was a kind of love note, too.

There are times in the course of my practice (especially when dealing with very angry patients) that I find myself responding to a patient with anger. One night, in group, Margaret, a rather heavy woman, over six feet tall, instead of sitting in her usual chair, sat on my glass-topped desk. As she sat down, everyone heard a loud cracking sound. The glass had shattered under the impact of her weight! She was mortified. It was a night when I was not feeling well physically but decided to 'carry on' and hold the group session none the less. It was clear to all that I was annoyed, irritated at the 'event' involving Margaret. She had been in the group for years – a person struggling with deeply repressed rage, having been brought up in a small New England town by her home economics teacher mother and her minister father. Both took pride in their civilized, good manners and their lofty positions in a very conventional neighbourhood. Margaret had been taught to be a compliant and dutiful child. Recently she told the group how, when a young child, she visited her relatives in another city. A cousin her own age, sensing Margaret's gullibility and naïvety, took her into the street, gave her a stone from the gutter and told her to scratch the paint off each car door and body on the block. Margaret complied, having great fun, reassured by her cousin that the act would do no harm since everyone had a special remover which would polish off the scratches! To her surprise, her cousin had lied and then blamed Margaret when neighbours complained about the damage. Margaret was punished and embarrassed by the adults when her cousin 'confessed' that Margaret was the culprit. In treatment, over the years, Margaret had learned that, under her controlled exterior, she harboured resentment and anger which she could only vent when she was overwhelmed by frustration and righteous indignation. Such feelings were only expressed when the rage reached bursting point.

The night of the desk-top glass breaking, the group members who had been previously the target of her assaults were pleased to see her 'get the business' from the leader, of all people! Some identified with her humiliation, exposure and poor judgement. Some empathized with her embarrassment and fear. Some sympathized with the 'victim' leader. Some were angered and/or frightened by the leader's apparent loss of control! The image of a 'bull in the china shop' was applicable to all of us and helpful. Margaret was delicate and vulnerable, so was the glass, so was the leader.

Margaret was tough and yet quite sensitive, so was the leader. But we had enough of a working alliance and soon, a new desk top and healed wounds. We went to the next interaction with sufficient observing, comparing, experiencing and interpreting to learn so many rich dimensions about our experiences. I usually do not feel good when I lose control of my feelings; quite the contrary, I feel sorry and guilty, especially when conducting treatment. And yet something authentic is happening. Sometimes to express such reactions takes courage. I must avoid a self-justifying rationalization, a tendency to provide a moralistic bulwark against my personal potential for anger or defensiveness after just 'losing it'. Sometimes anger is simply human responsiveness. I have many ideas about such expressiveness in group, as patient or therapist. I will refer to some aspects of 'therapist anger' later (see pp. 191–6). It is often difficult 'to know' for sure what is involved. The inevitable ambiguities remind me of Theodor Reik's (1948) comments about the analyst's 'courage not to understand'. To distinguish when it is therapeutic for the group therapist to verbalize to the group rather than to struggle internally, to strive privately to understand one's inner reaction, is an important issue – especially when rage is a factor in treatment (as it often is).

When Susan first entered the therapy group, she reluctantly told of the events of her life which involved overwhelming pain and considerable tragedy. Her first husband had been murdered at about the same time their child was stillborn. Later, when she married again, she gave birth to a son who had severe congenital defects and who has required special care. Her mother, having disapproved of Susan and her husband, expressed bitter disappointment at the fates of her grandchildren and expressed in Italian, 'from shit comes shit'. For years, her mother expressed great disappointment with her own husband and mother-in-law as well as with Susan (all of whom lived with mother who supported the entire family financially) while contending 'You, your father and his mother all smell bad!' Only Zelda, Susan's older married sister, was considered wonderful by Mama. Most members of the group felt very supportive of Susan and expressed appreciation of her suffering and ongoing courage, especially admiring her success in graduating from night college and attending graduate school. Finally, she left her office job and worked as a professional, achieving status and salary increases. Nevertheless, she told the group of her unhappiness in the second marriage. Whereas the first husband was reckless and of questionable morals, the second mate was a shallow, compulsive laboratory technician who was meek and emotionally isolated. Susan described all of this to the group and eventually told them she wanted a divorce. At this time, she developed a deep feeling for Al, an older member of the group who was well to do, professional and devoted to her. When Al suddenly died of a heart attack, Susan felt devastated, once again. All the group members were shocked and tried to console her except for Jim. Her expression of anguish and disappointment enraged him. Most group members and the leader were not surprised that Jim criticized Susan endlessly. We all knew him to be a 40-year-old gay man who usually attacked 'suffering women', especially those who reminded him of his mother (who had abandoned him at an early age and who has suffered and pleaded with him for forgiveness whenever Jim and she met subsequently). Details of his history and group experience have been reported (Tuttman, 1992). Although Jim has developed social skills and a greater capacity for warmth and concern, somehow he found Susan particularly upsetting. He accused her of condemning his homosexuality. He accused her of a mocking, patronizing, hypocritical attitude of concern when she was really completely without appreciation for his predicament that she was giving him a hard time devoid of understanding so much like the sadistic nuns in the orphanage where his mother 'dumped' him at the age of two. Susan felt devastated, especially when he added in his bitter sarcasm:

> You put me down and sabotage my efforts to have more warmth and love in my life. Look at you. You're an old bag who has chosen one lousy guy after another out of your desperation. You've suffered endlessly because of these lousy choices and hypocritical compromises. Now you're old and ugly, and you still can't find anyone worthwhile with whom to connect. But instead of working on that you have to put me down.

It was true that Susan's first husband was a psychopathic character to whom she 'hooked' herself in a desperate effort to be 'rescued' from her mother's home. He was completely unable to appreciate the need of anyone else and did not do a good job of taking care of anyone, given his own self destructiveness and his need to manipulate the world.

Husband number two represented for Susan an effort to find respectability as she was attempting to move on from a secretarial job to become formally educated now that her self-esteem was improving. She did not want to end up disrespected by her mother and herself, and she wanted the dignity of a professional achievement, and so she struggled at night to go through college and graduate school. Her second husband was a compulsive worker. His schizoid isolation and his lack of attention and his shallow focus on living was very shocking and disappointing to her.

All that remained was the deformed son of her first marriage, a youngster who had brain damage as well as cardiac problems. His wish to become more independent led to great pressures on Susan as he grew older and he moved to a sheltered community.

Finally, Susan married husband number three, a man who had been profoundly wounded emotionally in early life, although he was quite gifted and intelligent. He did much better when he kept himself in isolation because of his exquisite hypersensitivity and the degree to which he could be hurt and disappointed in relationships. He was very needy and he wanted Susan to nurture and protect him. She resented this since she needed exactly the same thing herself and it became a kind of 'wrestling match' as to who would be entitled to receive more care and nurturance. Despite a deteriorating marriage, her husband refused to move out of the house, so they had a cold truce and things went on unhappily. The group was a source of some solace and some hope of being accepted.

Most people in the group were accustomed to Jim's assaultiveness when he felt injured. They were accustomed to his vengeful attack when anyone, especially a woman, challenged or objected to what he said. The group and group leader pointed this out to Susan and offered her some support. But Jim insisted that Susan's opportunism and bad choices regarding men reminded him of his mother. The group and leader sensed the 'connections' when Jim mercilessly attacks a woman (the same age his mother was when she abandoned him). This type of reaction is an old pattern of his; however, he has been choosing more available male partners while continuing his disdain towards women like Susan.

Jim was so belligerent, so critical and so harsh that he probably reminded Susan of her own mother and of her fear of her mother. One day he spoke about his new relationship with a young man, something he tried desperately to develop (most of his relationships had been so incomplete, so filled with alienation). This time, he proudly talked about his efforts to go further in getting close to another human being. Susan, enraged at him for his criticism of her, minimized his efforts to grow. He concluded that she was rejecting him because of his homosexuality. The group reminded Jim of a parallel reaction he had with another divorced group member, Abigail (see Tuttman, 1985, pp. 26–7).

But neither Susan nor Jim could relinquish the bitter, enraged reaction to the other – although all of us in the group clearly saw their respective unconscious mental representations and the rage at work in each.

The leader began to wonder if Susan might be looking for justification to get away from the group, as if she wanted to give up this one hope for achieving a good relationship which also had its share of disappointments and pain. Events had convinced her that she could never really solve her problems. Susan appeared to 'use' her experience in the group with Jim as more rejection. This justified withdrawing from the group, and she stormed out leaving one soliloquy behind: 'I will not take any further assault or abuse. I have had enough rejections. I do not deserve to be chastised and attacked and criticized whenever I try to express myself and struggle to work out my problems and my relationships.' As leader of the group, I noted with distress that Susan allowed herself this one-sided summary. Perhaps I felt a narcissistic injury, perhaps it was my distress that after we had worked so hard together and, in a way, had achieved so much, now she threatened to leave. I believed she was much closer to a better manner of conducting her life. She none the less felt she did not wish to remain in the group.

In retrospect, it appeared likely that she experienced Jim as the group leader's 'favourite child' and saw herself as the unwanted child. As group leader, I do not believe I felt a favouring attitude for Jim, but in her transference, so true to the history of her life, Susan did experience it that way and for the first time in all the years I knew her, she withdrew from working on problems.

I may have miscalculated in one regard: in retrospect, I believe Susan's rage at rejection from mother, husbands numbers one, two and three, her child, Jim and finally an unexpected rejecting event at her job – all of this proved so devastating that she shifted from her usual role of the abandoned victim to the abandoning, angry aggressor.

Why did Susan walk out manifesting such indignation and rejection because in the group I did not, on this one occasion, openly side with her when another patient in the group verbally attacked her? She did say quite emotionally, 'My mother attacked me and no one offered any help or support. Now you [referring to the therapist], you let this creepy bastard [Jim] assault me with disgusting, nasty words?' She expressed anguish and great rage. Perhaps the greatest pain came from Jim's suggestion, that she was an 'old bag' who had worn herself out by choosing nasty inadequate husbands who abandoned her or whom she dumped over the years. I understood how she felt, but by this time, she had considerable experience with Jim, the other group members and myself. Time and time again she demonstrated her capacity to understand his pathology and his assets. Why did she need to make an 'end point' of treatment at this moment? Although I do not fully understand her reaction, I appreciate that many factors contributed to an overdetermined acting out. Her mother favoured her older sister which mortified Susan. She believed her mother's contention that she was not lovable (both she and her father 'smelled bad' according to the mother). Now, in her mind's eye, I was 'favouring' Jim and protecting him while she was wounded by him. Her father never protected her against her mother. Now I am experienced as failing her. She expected me to rescue her, to nurture her, to love her! We had been through this before, but now it was all the more painful as she was becoming older. She has had so many disappointments: most recently marriage number three down the drain!

The group therapist, when working with enraged, acting-out patients, sometimes experiences the situation as close to impossible, especially when each member needs (and demands) support and acceptance and seeks 'leader collusion' (in the form of a wished-for 'self-object'). The leader attempts to encourage the observing egos as well as the experiential aspect of each member, and to utilize the group 'matrix' and contribute to group stability by offering a 'holding' and empathic stance. When the leader can tolerate the desperation and rage of the group-as-a-whole or of individual members and has good countertransference control, usually all gets worked out. But in 'real life', this is not always the outcome!

In her final private visit, Susan told me how her old boss, who had valued her so much that he gave her prestigious assignments, had deeply hurt her recently. He had promised for years that she would become administrative chief upon his retirement. Now she discovered that he was retiring and was giving the job to a male co-worker of hers. Her mentally defective son was successfully separating from her in his adjustment to a residence centre and no longer needed her as much! True, nowadays, she said, she has good reason to feel adequate and worthy of respect and acknowledgement. This was hard won and how angry it made her when she believed that others (such as Jim) still showed signs of disrespect for her!

Patient rage can be helpful or harmful. Can therapist 'rage' be therapeutic, or is it always pathological and anti-treatment? Often patients react with absolute shock if not indignation: how can you, a therapist, be so emotional and so out of control? There are, at least, two ways of looking at this. If the leader feels strongly and passionately and is deeply involved, the spontaneity of the reaction may reflect confidence in one's self and in one's patients and one's group, and such a group therapist might simply 'let it hang out'. On the other hand, a certain amount of therapist self-control, leaving space for patients to manifest their ventilations, is perhaps wiser and therapeutically indicated. Yet if the therapist is to serve as a source for more effective identifications and internalizations (perhaps demonstrating that he or she can be comfortable enough to be spontaneous, having enough trust in self and object to simply express what he or she feels), might not this reflect an extraordinarily helpful attitude? Much depends upon how comfortable or uncomfortable the therapist is with hostility and how much the particular members of the group can tolerate such spontaneity. Disclosure and ventilation by the therapist is double-edged; it may be therapeutic or it may interfere with the therapeutic atmosphere – depending upon the cast of characters and the needs and problems of the particular group. Have therapists and patients glorified (and thereby constricted) the therapist's role as having to be so reasonable, so constructive, so facilitating, so holding, so neutral, so interpretive, so insightful, so perfect? Is it humanly possible always to provide just this kind of perfect balance and nurturance? Pressure to live up to such an 'ideal' role can induce resentment and other countertransference reactions, especially in the treatment of patients inclined to act out provocative, vengeful fantasies towards their therapist leaders – authorities symbolically experienced as parents.

The pull of projective identifications is frequently part of the relationships of therapists with borderline patients in both group and dyadic treatment (Kernberg, 1975). Can one humanly avoid 'Hate in the Countertransference' (Winnicott, 1947)? I remember the lullaby, as did Winnicott (1947, 1971), 'Rockabye Baby, in the Tree Top'. It seems to me that for the singer to soothe the baby by suggesting that it might fall out of the cradle in the tree, may inform us of something important: sometimes (maybe often) babies are needy and demanding; they wake up, burst into tears, or require ongoing care. The singer/caretaker may want to soothe the baby, but the singer/caretaker may need soothing too and may be resentful of the demanding infant. Could it be that the sadistic 'When the bough breaks, the cradle will fall, and down will come baby, cradle and all' relates to the frustration and anger of those who feel pressured to cater to the needs of helpless ones in their care? Yes, often there is hate in the countertransference (Winnicott, 1947); in fact, do not all relationships impose frustrations and involve demands, and therefore sometimes evoke ambivalent or angry reactions? The question is: does therapy advance more effectively when therapists so control and contain their resentment that they discourage such material from permeating the treatment? Or does the treatment advance in a more authentic way when there is a place for the range of emotions that are generated in the relationship to have some expression in the course of the interaction? Is it possible that anyone can have deeply harmonious feelings that are never encumbered by negative ones? What policy could determine the most effective therapist attitude? It does not help reality-relationship potential of therapist or patient if therapist and members of the treatment group suppress rage. To have no connection with strong, underlying emotions or impulses can impede therapy. No one who is very angry will end up feeling comfortable unless rage is somehow acknowledged or contained within the treatment. Therefore, I consider it essential that group therapists work on this anger potential so as to become more comfortable with anger within themselves in order to harness and channel it effectively. This mastery is a prerequisite for doing meaningful and useful group therapy, in my opinion. That does not mean this must always be shared with patients. That is a matter for evaluation and policy-making in each situation. When the therapist feels comfortable enough with rage so that it can be appropriately experienced and verbalized to enhance his/her self-awareness, this gives the group a better chance for therapeutic engagement and constructive working through of emotions which can be crucial in some group situations.

Some time ago, one of my patients, in both individual and group therapy, expressed great hostility and was extremely critical of me and some group members. I concluded that her fear of intimacy and her perfectionism was underlying her verbal, haughty assaults. Although there was some therapeutic alliance, both she and I had serious problems which interfered with treatment. Overcoming the developmental issues underlying her difficulty could only occur if we both faced our respective problems. I came to recognize that my need to be appreciated for my efforts on her behalf was met by her degrading and rejecting me. This aroused great indignation and resentment in me and had to be worked through before I could be of further help to her – regardless of her problems and her contributions. True, we had achieved some serious success in the treatment because of her need to get well and my wish to help; but, we each had limitations obstructing further progress in group or individual therapy.

Did I need 'too much' acceptance from her before I could, again, work on healing myself and improving the relationship? I cannot possibly help her if I subject myself to too much of her abnegation. Although I haven't the right to expect my patients to 'cure' me, I may need my patients to play an active role in my growth. This can sometimes help me to do a better job.

Often group therapists do understand very much! But, does this mean that we can always maintain a balance in ourselves, our groups and our patients? Can we learn to leave space for our own limitations and accept the disappointment and rejection of others in ourselves? Perhaps most difficult of all, for the group leader and the group as well as the enraged, attacking member, is what happens when we and the group simply do not have enough perspective to help a member to go on, to continue? Believing that Susan (see pp. 187–91) has the potential to regain perspective in her situation and yet to watch her persist in 'throwing it all away' is painful, upsetting and also enraging. Her tantrum, her angry assertion and her determination to handle it her way (by righteous withdrawal) arouses frustration and anger in the other group members and in the leader.

There may be parallels in the manner in which children thrive and do best when brought up by parents who are able to integrate aggression and libido in a balanced manner. Things work best when parents, therapist and group members have sufficient neutralized energy and are able to express affection and anger in their interactions realistically, as part of a constructive interplay in life. In this context, it can prove helpful when the therapist has the capacity to feel comfortable enough with both anger and affection. Of course, a therapist does not and should not take the liberties of a parent in personal relationships. For one thing, the therapist's task is to provide an atmosphere which is sufficiently neutral and 'containing' as to serve and help patients and groups deal with a morass of responses in a context where there is a 'space' for the patient which is not contaminated by the needs and feelings of the therapist. The primary function of the treatment is to serve the interests and emotions of the patient, not of the therapist.

Treatment involves a process of reparative internalizations so needed by our patient population. Opportunities for healthy internalization were not available, developmentally, all too often. When parents were not healthy enough to experience a broad enough repertoire of feelings and impulses, they do not serve as 'good enough' sources for their children's healthy identification. Under such conditions, it is sometimes vitally important that the group leader and the individual therapist serve as a reservoir of human qualities so needed for internalization and positive mental representations. Thus, it is very important that the therapist 'knows' aggression and can cope with it when it originates inside and outside the therapist's self. It is part of the therapist's task to make the environment a safer place in which all present (including the therapist) can function with confidence in being true to all the qualities that people experience and manifest, while at the same time providing a safe enough, comfortable enough and secure enough atmosphere in which containment is possible and available. The skill of the therapist in understanding how to deal with a patient's rage is in some way connected with that therapist's capacity to cope with the reservoir of primitive rage within the therapist's self. There are times when control, structure and the use of aggression to contain another person's aggression is essential. There are times when a quiet acquiescence, functioning as a witness who can tolerate what is happening without excessive anxiety and without excessive countermanding behaviour, is what is necessary.

One of my patients, Joel, told our group one night about a prior group experience he had in the army some years before: Joel appeared to be a good-natured, calm and affable man in his twenties. He was playing cards with his army barrack friends. Suddenly, there was an argument, and someone felt badly wronged. This individual impulsively pulled out a knife and started gesturing towards the person he considered the source of injustice and mistreatment. Joel had such a reservoir of rage, which he had managed to control – neither he nor others were aware of it. He found himself so stirred with anxiety and dread that a loss of control would result in bloodshed, that with his bare fists, he jumped impulsively towards the knife-wielder and forced him down to the floor, removed the knife from his hand, and only then began to calm down. In the session I had with Joel, it became increasingly clear that the only thing that had caused him to come close to losing control and thereby manifesting rage was his dread that anyone could lose control of their anger and commit irreversible, dangerous acts; a fear he probably had in regard to his own impulses which caused him to intervene when someone else looked to be close to losing control.

Had he been a therapist, such acting out might have proven most helpful to him since he would have had an opportunity to experience the dread of his own rage. Hopefully, through awareness, he could then work on his need to deal with rage, by feeling it more calmly, rather than by means of an impulsive, angry reaction such as occurred in the course of the card game. A group therapist needs to be familiar with his own emotions and potential reactions and, in an ongoing way, continually strive to know about and master inner impulses. All of this is part of a therapist's struggle; no matter whether the therapist responds calmly, sometimes firmly, sometimes passively to the assertions of group members, there is a greater opportunity for the members to identify with the therapist and thereby to strive towards mastery.

To recapitulate, sometimes a therapist in a spontaneous way simply feels and shows anger. Often patients react with absolute shock if not indignation: 'How can you, a therapist, be so emotional and so out of control?' There are at least two ways of looking at this: if one feels strongly and passionately and one is deeply involved, the spontaneity of the reaction may reflect a healthy confidence in oneself, in one's emotions, in one's patients and one's group; in such a situation, one's feelings may 'hang out'. On the other hand, a certain amount of control and restraint on the group leader's part is necessary so as to leave space for patients to manifest their ventilations. Clearly, some balance is therapeutically indicated. Yet if the therapist is to serve as a source for more effective identifications and internalizations, perhaps seeing that the therapist can be comfortable enough to be spontaneous, and 'let it happen', having enough trust in self and others simply to express what is felt – this indeed could be an extraordinarily helpful attitude. Much depends upon how comfortable, personally, the therapist is with hostility and how much the particular members of the group can tolerate such spontaneity. This can be therapeutic or can interfere with a therapeutic atmosphere, depending upon the cast of characters and the needs and attitudes that are expressed. Part of the art of working with potentially violent patients relates to the need to experience and accept the spectrum of reactions and to sense what would be most appropriate and therapeutic.

I have offered several examples of group interaction of angry group members whose peer responses involve regression, repression and rage reactions in a context of reactivated primitive unconscious object relations. The projection (of troublesome mental representations, projective identifications and intrapsychic super-ego conflicts) on to other group members and the leader leads to confusion which requires working through, appreciating and understanding each participant's unconscious conflicts and patterns. The group and leader can focus on sorting out the underlying needs and motivations. The function of the group leader in helping the group to utilize safely the acting-out inclination, when primitive and archaic impulses erupt, has been discussed. A cohesive group atmosphere is crucial if members are not to be overwhelmed by the intensity of rageful and competitive emotions and feelings which are often triggered by projections on to other members or the therapist of unconscious, archaic mental representations of a sado-masochistic nature.

Group members learn, in the case of group interaction, to observe, experience and communicate. We all become active participants who can contribute to enhancing a facilitating matrix. When safe, we can 'dare' become more autonomous psychological units (separate, individualistic entities), increasingly effective at harnessing and utilizing the full spectrum of human drives and feelings in groups, dyads and intra-psychic relationships.

## NOTE

1 All group examples in this chapter are taken from material collected over the years and are composites of several groups and patients. The details are accurate, although the names have been changed and features that might have been identifiable have been modified so as to assure confidentiality. For purposes of convenience to readers and to the author, the same clinical material has been employed for illustrative purposes in several papers (Tuttman, 1980, 1985, 1992), although the material has been utilized in various contexts and the purpose and mode of presentations have been different.

## REFERENCES

Bion, W. (1959) *Experiences in Groups*, New York: Basic Books.

Federn, P. (1952) *Ego Psychology and the Psychoses*, New York: Basic Books.

Foulkes, S.H. (1948) *Introduction to Group-Analytic Psychotherapy*, London: Heinemann.

—— (1973) 'The group as the matrix of the individual's mental health', in L.R. Wolberg and E.K. Schwartz (eds), *Group Therapy*, New York: Stratton.

Freud, S. (1921) *Group Psychology and the Analysis of the Ego*, Standard Edition 18.

Greenacre, P. (1971) *Emotional Growth*, New York: International Universities Press.

Jacobson, E. (1964) *The Self and the Object World*, New York: International Universities Press.

James, D.C. (1982) 'Transitional phenomena and the matrix in group psychotherapy', in M. Pines and L. Rafaelson (eds), *The Individual and the Group*, vol. 1, New York: Penguin Books.

Kernberg, O.F. (1975) *Borderline Conditions and Pathological Narcissism*, New York: Jason Aronson.

—— (1980) *Internal World and External Reality: Object Relations Theory Applied*, New York: Jason Aronson.

Kosseff, J.W. (1975) 'The leader object using object-relations theory', in A. Liff (ed.) *The Leader in the Group*, New York: Jason Aronson.

Mahler, M.S., Pine, F. and Bergman, A. (1975) *The Psychological Birth of the Human Infant*, New York: Basic Books.

Main, T. (1957) 'The ailment', *British Journal of Medical Psychology* 30 (part 3).

Pines, M. (1990) 'Group analytic psychotherapy and the borderline patient', in B.E. Roth, W.N. Stone and H.D Kibel (eds), *The Difficult Patient in Group*, Madison, CT: International Universities Press.

Reik, T. (1948) *Listening with the Third Ear: The Inner Experiences of a Psychoanalyst*, New York: Farrar, Straus.

Roth, B.E., Stone, W.N. and Kibel, H.D. (1990) (eds) *The Difficult Patient in Group*, Madison, CT: International Universities Press.

Scheidlinger, S. (1955) 'The concept of identification in group psychotherapy', *American Journal of Psychotherapy* 9.

—— (1974) 'On the concept of the "mother group" ', *International Journal of Group Psychotherapy* 24 (4).

—— (1982) *Focus on Group Psychotherapy: Clinical Essays*, New York: International Universities Press.

Schlachet, P. (1986) 'The concept of group space', *International Journal of Group Psychotherapy* (36) 4.

Stern, D. (1984) *The Interpersonal World of the Infant*, New York: Basic Books.

Tuttman, S. (1979) 'Regression: is it necessary or desirable?', *Journal of the American Academy of Psychoanalysis* 7.

—— (1980) 'The question of group therapy from a psychoanalytic viewpoint', *Journal of the American Academy of Psychoanalysis* 8.

—— (1984) 'Applications of object relations theory and self-psychology on current group therapy', *Group* 8 (4).

—— (1985) 'The unique opportunities offered by group psychotherapy', Group Therapy Monograph no. 12, Washington Square Institute.

—— (1986) 'Theoretical and technical elements which characterize the American approaches to psychoanalytic group psychotherapy', *International Journal of Group Psychotherapy* 36 (4).

—— (1990) 'Principles of psychoanalytic group therapy applied to the treatment of borderline and narcissistic disorders', in B.E. Roth, W.N. Stone and H.D. Kibel (eds), *The Difficult Patient in Group*, Madison, CT: International Universities Press.

—— (1991) *Psychoanalytic Group Theory and Therapy*, Madison, CT: International Universities Press.

—— (1992) 'The role of the group therapist from an object relations perspective', in R.H. Klein, H.S. Bernard and D.L. Singer (eds), *Handbook of Contemporary Psychotherapy: Contributions in Object Relations, Self Psychology, and Social Systems Theory*, Madison, CT: International Universities Press.

Winnicott, D.W. (1947) 'Hate in the countertransference', in *Through Pediatrics to Psychoanalysis*, New York: Basic Books, 1958.

—— (1951) 'Transitional objects and transitional phenomena', in *Through Pediatrics to Psychoanalysis*, New York: Basic Books, 1958.

—— (1960) 'Ego distortion in terms of true and false self', in *The Maturational Processes and the Facilitating Environment*, New York: International Universities Press, 1965.

—— (1971) 'The use of an object and relating through identifications', in *Playing and Reality*, New York: International Universities Press.

# 9 Utilizing co-therapy in the group treatment of borderline and narcissistic patients

*Robert H. Klein and Harold S. Bernard*

## EDITORS' INTRODUCTION

The co-therapy dyad conveys in graphic form one of the fundamental dynamics of group relations: the relationship between the couple and the group, whether it be Romeo and Juliet in the context of their feuding families, Oedipus and Jocasta in Thebes, the couple in the pairing basic assumption, the mother–infant dyad, the analyst/analysand partnership, or lovers differentiating from the masses. In what follows, Klein and Bernard view the co-therapist pair as a subsystem of both the therapy group and the institutional/societal context.

Klein and Bernard join the ongoing debate on the usefulness of co-therapy with borderlines by offering a combined systems and developmental model to understand what happens between co-therapists and borderline/narcissistic patients in group. They utilize the 'totalistic' model of countertransference, in which the therapists' feelings and reactions are 'grist for the mill', a source of information about themselves, their relationship, the patients and the group-as-a-whole.

The authors' meticulous attention to countertransference demonstrates how reactions which are often 'invisible' when the 'singleton' therapist works alone in the group become 'visible' in the intimate 'I–thou' cauldron of co-therapy. Such exposure of therapists to one another has the potential to evoke either shame and anxiety or insight and mastery.

---

In this chapter we will explore the use of co-therapy as a way to treat borderline and narcissistic patients in groups. We shall begin by selectively reviewing the literature on both co-therapy and the generic treatment of borderline and narcissistic patients. A theoretical schema that incorporates both systems theory and developmental theory will then be presented; it is this schema that will inform our perspective throughout the chapter. We shall subsequently discuss countertransference issues in some detail, focusing on patient, staff, group and context variables and offering many clinical examples throughout. Finally, we shall describe our point of view concerning the utility of the co-therapy format for dealing with these challenging patients in groups.

## LITERATURE REVIEW

Although there has been a great deal written about co-therapy in group treatment, much of the literature does not explicitly address co-therapy with the most difficult-to-treat outpatients: borderline and narcissistically disordered patients. A review of the literature suggests that, in general, co-therapy is a widely endorsed and highly valued treatment format among psychiatric residents (Friedman, 1972), therapists in university counselling and student health centres (Berman *et al.*, 1972), and members of the American Group Psychotherapy Association (Fidler and Waxenberg, 1971; Rabin, 1967).

Despite the above, we know of no rigorous experimental study that has compared outcome measures of single therapist versus co-therapist models. Such research would be extremely difficult to conduct given the variables involved (for example patient type, group composition, training and expertise of therapists, the co-therapy relationship, and so on). Nevertheless, most authors extol the virtues of the co-therapy arrangement. It is widely believed that co-therapy can decrease therapist anxiety, particularly for novices; co-therapists can supplement and complement one another in terms of understanding of patients, techniques and therapeutic styles; and co-therapists can provide one another with support and relief from the isolation of the therapist role and with invaluable feedback about their work. At a practical level, co-therapy allows for continuity of treatment, and the collaboration can be stimulating and refreshing. Therapists working together can assume a greater range and variety of roles in conducting a group, can provide a broader range of stimuli to elicit patients' transference reactions, and can help one another, and their patients, to tolerate and explore intense transference and countertransference phenomena.

Particularly in the case of male–female pairings, the co-therapy structure constitutes a re-creation of the primary family constellation which may permit a 'corrective emotional experience' (Davis and Lohr, 1971). Mixed-gender pairings provide a same-sex therapist for patient identification, and for exploration of any gender-related difficulties. Regardless of gender, co-therapists who work well together provide a model of an effective, differentiated, collaborative relationship, which can help patients work through the residue of dysfunctional family systems.

While many of the advantages cited are generic, some pertain specifically to the treatment of severely disturbed patients. Thus, it has been suggested that co-therapy can provide needed cognitive and emotional support, increased capacity for limit-setting, more freedom and flexibility for handling disruptive or otherwise demanding patients, and an ongoing mechanism for reality-testing (Davis and Lohr, 1971; Dick *et al.*, 1980; Greenblum and Pinney, 1982; Klein *et al.*, 1986; Klein *et al.*, 1991). The few contributions that directly address the treatment of severely disturbed outpatients by co-therapists tend to view the group as a holding environment wherein the inevitable splitting that occurs can be most effectively examined when one therapist is experienced as the 'bad' one, but the other can be heard. In addition, they emphasize that assaults upon the therapists' ego boundaries and self-esteem can best be counteracted by having a colleague available for collaboration and support.

There is, however, considerable difference of opinion concerning the impact of co-leadership on transference and countertransference phenomena. Predictably, severely disturbed patients tend to split co-therapists, reflecting childhood experiences and subsequent development of character structure and defences (Cooper, 1976). Advocates of co-therapy with these patients believe that co-therapists can lend objectivity to the understanding of complicated transference and countertransference phenomena. From this perspective, the therapist who is out of the immediate line of projective fire can provide a more reality-based and less distorted assessment of what is taking place in the group at the moment. Those who argue against co-therapy with severely disturbed patients claim that it complicates, rather than clarifies, transference and countertransference phenomena, and therefore makes it more difficult to make use of such material to therapeutic advantage.[1] While we plan to address these and related issues in greater detail in the material to follow, there are, unfortunately, no empirical data reported in the literature that can help to resolve this age-old debate.

However, the value of co-therapy for training purposes, and the legitimacy of providing emotional support for therapists, have been questioned. MacLennan (1965) argues that co-therapists are not interchangeable, and that co-therapy should only be used for special purposes, preferably by experienced clinicians. McGee and Schuman (1970) contend that co-therapy tends to confound transference and countertransference phenomena, and emphasize the importance of 'carefully balancing' co-therapy dyads. No matter how well chosen the particular team, patients can find the co-therapy arrangement confusing when the therapists' roles are not clearly defined or when transference reactions are counter-intuitive (for example, when the male therapist of a male–female dyad is experienced as the more maternal figure). Some argue that co-therapy promotes dependency in therapists and interferes with therapists assuming full clinical responsibility for their patients. Others point to the inefficiency of two therapists doing what one could do alone (for example MacLennan, 1965). Furthermore, co-therapy can increase the likelihood that special forms of resistance will manifest themselves, such as when one therapist is 'played off' against the other (Anderson *et al.*, 1972).

Some efforts have been made to identify the characteristics that distinguish successful from unsuccessful co-therapy teams. In one of the few empirical studies in the area, Piper *et al.* (1979) cite data to support the notion that *consistency* is the most important characteristic of a successful co-therapy pair. Interestingly, *dissimilar* teams produced better outcomes on at least one of their outcome measures than did similar teams, as long as their contributions to the work of the group were consistent. Paulson *et al.* (1976) found three primary areas that determine the success of co-therapy pairings: similarity of theoretical orientation, how problems between co-therapists (primarily of style and skill) are resolved, and feelings about one another's quality and quantity of participation. Much of the rest of this literature focuses on the quality of the relationship between the co-therapists. Specifically, different authors emphasize the crucial importance of such factors as open communication, trust, mutual respect, commitment of time, and so on (Heilfron, 1969; Davis and Lohr, 1971).

Stages of development of the co-therapy relationship have also received some attention (Winter, 1976; Dick *et al.*, 1980; McMahon and Links, 1984). In general, such stages are thought to be linked to, but not to parallel precisely, the developmental stages of the group itself, but they, too, have not been validated by any empirical evidence.

The most compelling and persuasive rationale for the use of group therapy in the treatment of borderline patients has been provided by Horwitz (1971, 1977, 1980). He views the primary task of the group as facilitating the integration of the split between good and bad internalized self and object representations. In successful group treatment of these patients, the group becomes a positive holding environment. Horwitz notes that groups can be activating for withdrawn patients, can bolster self-esteem and gratify dependency needs, can attenuate abrasive maladaptive behaviours, and can diminish patients' fear of hostility when they see it expressed by others without destructive consequences. In addition, the group setting allows for a more controlled therapeutic regression. By introducing a reality matrix that includes the presence of others, patients' unrealistic expectations and tendencies towards idealization and devaluation can be counteracted. Groups dampen intense narcissistic expectations and erotization of the transference, expose patients to multiple objects for identification, provide opportunities for detachment and disengagement when needed, and render therapists less prone to loss of their therapeutic stance. Macaskill (1982) adapts Winnicott's phrase in describing the group as a 'transitional object'. The group contains the primitive rage, fear and feelings of fragmentation that patients bring to it; and when patients remain undamaged by such potentially destructive phenomena, they emerge as more intact and better integrated individuals.

The traditional view is that transference responses are diluted in the group setting because of the presence of other patients and multiple therapists. Most clinicians would agree that unwanted regressive reactions, more likely to occur in the one-to-one therapeutic relationship, can be attenuated, However, Horwitz (1977) argues con- vincingly that there are tendencies towards *both* intensification and dilution of transference reactions in groups, and that skilled therapists can exploit one or the other as the clinical situation warrants at a particular point in time. This perspective seems to us to capture the reality that, how groups unfold and what psychic phenomena are elicited in group members, depends very much upon how the therapists work. For instance, do they work to open up the exploration of preconscious and unconscious material, thereby encouraging regression, or do they focus on conscious material, thereby discouraging regression? How experience-near versus experience-distant a stance do the therapists take? How active are the therapists at different stages of the treatment process? These are only some of the many variables that influence how intensive a group experience may become for its members (and therapists).

The value of concomitant individual and group treatment remains open to question. Horwitz (1971) believes that competitive feelings aroused in group are likely to be dampened when patients have concomitant individual sessions, which encourage patients to feel they have a special relationship with the therapist. He also feels that concomitant individual sessions may inadvertently suggest that the group has limited purposes and utility. However, Wong (1980) asserts that individual treatment provides an opportunity for distancing and emotional refuelling after the repeated injuries that narcissistic patients suffer in group interactions. Some therapists believe that concomitant individual therapy can be supportively orientated and soothing, permitting patients to consolidate and integrate what they learn from the group, which can function in a more confrontive, insight-orientated fashion.

Depending upon whether one maintains the view that the underlying psychopathology is based upon a deficit or a conflict model (Roth *et al.*, 1990; Klein *et al.*, 1992), specific techniques have been emphasized in working with borderline and narcissistic patients. Stone and Gustafson (1982), for example, represent a self psychological approach to treatment. They argue that the establishment of a therapeutic alliance with these patients, clearly no easy task, is a goal of the treatment process, not a means to an end. Their focus is on empathy as the therapist's major tool.

Similarly, Horwitz (1977) advocates increased activity, warmth, transparency and empathy by therapists, and the active encouragement of socialization among group members. Kibel (1978, 1981), maintaining an object-relations perspective, has emphasized the value of the 'clarifying interpretation' in short-term inpatient groups for borderline patients. Wong (1980) suggests an early emphasis on empathy to build a therapeutic alliance and a later focus on interpretation of both positive and negative transference manifestations.

Finally, it is important to note the controversy regarding homogeneous versus heterogeneous grouping of severely disturbed patients. Most authors advocate homogeneous grouping (for example Slavinska-Holy, 1983). Roth (1980) focuses on the need of such patients to be soothed rather than understood when they enter a group, and implies that this is best accomplished when all group members begin with comparable needs. Morrison (1981) describes the borderline patients' severe aggressive response to people who have seemingly attained the satisfactory peer relations that have always eluded them, and concludes that homogeneous grouping is necessary for patients with severe deficits in peer relations. Cooper (1978) suggests that severely disturbed patients do poorly in groups with healthier patients because it takes so long for them to genuinely engage with one another. In contrast, Wong (1979) argues that when primitive affects (such as envy, rage, idealization and devaluation) are experienced in a group, it can be overwhelming and intolerable. Thus, he advocates heterogeneous group composition.

However, there are many questions in this area that have not been sufficiently addressed in the literature. For instance, can a severely disturbed patient benefit from being in a group in which all the other patients are higher functioning, or do such patients require at least one or more fellow-patients in their functional range for effective treatment? In the absence of empirical data, therapists will continue to air contradictory opinions based upon only anecdotal evidence.

## A SYSTEMS/DEVELOPMENTAL PERSPECTIVE

We conceive of the co-therapy dyad and the work of psychotherapy in both systems and developmental terms (Klein *et al.*, 1992). Let us briefly explicate how we see these theoretical schemas contributing to an understanding of the work of co-therapists with borderline and narcissistic patients.

We start with the notion that groups need to be understood as social systems with delineated parts that are separated by 'boundaries'. One such boundary is that between the co-therapists and the patients who constitute the group. Another is between the group and the larger context in which the group is being conducted. In private practice this boundary is not particularly salient, but in institutions, where co-therapy is most frequently utilized, it most certainly is. Thus the co-therapy dyad can be thought of as working on the boundary between the group members and the larger context in which the group exists.

Before a group begins, co-therapists must negotiate two kinds of contracts: an 'outside' contract and a set of 'inside' contracts (Klein, 1977; Singer *et al.*, 1975; Rice and Rutan, 1981). The outside contract involves negotiations with representatives of the institution within which the group will be conducted. It consists of structural issues like where and when the group will be held, administrative matters like record-keeping requirements, clinical issues associated with such matters as leader qualifications, responsibilities and authority, and training issues such as supervision.

Some aspects of the outside contract can be complicated, and can have profound implications for how the group unfolds. For instance, when the group is one aspect of a multi-faceted treatment programme, there is the question of how high a priority is attached to it. This is not a matter of being told that group is important, which is an easy thing to say. It has to do with such things as the circumstances under which group patients will be asked or told to do something other than to attend the group: for instance, to see their individual therapist, go to X-ray, attend recreational therapy, or to see a vocational counsellor. Such intrusions into the sanctity of the group communicate a message to therapists and patients alike concerning the importance that is attached to the group experience.

Another important issue is the extent to which the therapists can make decisions about who will be taken into their group. Arrangements vary from therapists having total control over the membership boundary to having no control at all: that is, a team assigns a patient to a particular group and the therapists are obliged to try to work with whomever is sent their way. This latter arrangement can easily result in therapists feeling their group is not theirs at all; when this is their feeling, unfortunate forms of counter-transferential acting out often result.

Yet another complicated and important matter is that of confidentiality. In a private-practice setting it is much simpler to establish criteria concerning what material will be shared with others under what circumstances, though even then it is not simple: for instance, if some or all of the patients are in individual treatment with other therapists, it is not a simple matter to delineate what will and will not be said to them. However, it is even more complicated in institutional settings in which contact with other treating therapists is usually frequent, and in which there may be expectations concerning communication between and among staff members. It is crucial that these matters be made as clear as possible during the pre-group phase.

Once the outside contract has been negotiated, the therapists are ready to begin negotiating a set of understandings with prospective patients. This task is much easier when the therapists are comfortable with the terms of the outside contract, but in any case it must be done. Central to this set of negotiations is the delineation of therapeutic tasks, the group format and participant roles: what is expected of the group members, what can they expect from the therapists, and how will the work be pursued? The goals for the treatment experience need to be clarified, as well as the methodology that will be employed. Since many authors have written about the preparatory phase in group treatment (for example Klein, 1977, 1983a, 1983b, 1983c; Yalom, 1985; Bernard, 1989), we shall not delineate all of the issues that are ideally reviewed before treatment begins.

Thinking about the co-therapy dyad as a subsystem within a larger system sheds light on whether therapists are a part of the group or are somehow outside of and separate from it. Using the language of systems theory, the answer to this question is clear: co-therapists are both a group within a group and are also a part of their groups, but in a differentiated role. The group would not be whole or the same without them, but their roles, tasks and responsibilities are fundamentally different from those of patients. This is not to say there is no overlap between the tasks and roles of therapist (or co-therapist) and patient. For instance, both participant roles might involve some self-disclosure. But whereas patients engage in self-disclosure to become known and to explicate the issues on which they are working, therapists, whose primary responsibilities are different, selectively utilize self-disclosure when, in their judgement, it will facilitate the psychological work of an individual, a subgroup or the group-as-a-whole.

Once the outside and inside contracts are negotiated, the therapeutic work is ready to begin. The work of the co-therapists can be construed as involving the monitoring of a number of boundaries: between affect, cognition and action; the amount of anxiety being experienced by individuals within the group as well as the group-as-a-whole; between the amount of conscious vs preconscious vs unconscious material introduced into the group by its members; and so on (Klein, 1979). Of course, the monitoring of such boundaries constitutes the work of all group therapists. What is important to note is that the stakes are extremely high when working with borderline and narcissistic patients. If the various boundaries are not well monitored, the viability of the treatment enterprise may be seriously compromised, if not destroyed. Severely characterologically disturbed patients have a strong propensity to act out their feelings in ways that can be treatment-destructive, so that inculcating the norm that feelings, no matter how powerful, must be talked about rather than acted upon, is particularly crucial. Similarly, the premature disclosure of material a group is not yet ready to hear and work on, and/or an individual is not yet ready to have others know about, can easily lead to the experience of overwhelming shame within the patient and/or derision from the rest of the group, which can often lead in turn to premature terminations which leave both the individual who has fled, and the group s/he has left behind, feeling damaged. While such outcomes can never be completely eliminated, they can be minimized by careful attention to the many boundaries that need to be monitored.

This brings us to the way in which we think about therapeutic work with severely disturbed patients as developmental in nature (Klein, 1983b; Klein *et al.*, 1986, 1990; Klein *et al.*, 1991). The co-therapist subsystem begins by maintaining (carrying) the executive decision-making responsibility by themselves. They negotiate the outside contract and deal with ingress–egress (membership) and other boundary issues by discussing such matters and trying to reach a united front, which they present to the members of the group. Similarly, the creation of an optimal affective climate is a responsibility that co-therapists think of as theirs during the initial phases of a group's life. Specifically, co-therapists do what they can to create a safe holding environment which can contain the powerful affects that simmer within the patients we are discussing in this chapter.

Our view is that in the successful treatment of these patients, the responsibilities at first carried exclusively by the co-therapists are gradually assumed by the patients themselves (Klein *et al.*, 1990). This does not mean that the therapists ever stop monitoring the various boundaries we have already discussed, as well as others we have not specifically delineated; rather, the patients come to join the therapists and in effect become collaborators who also bear some responsibility for the group becoming a therapeutic agent. The assumption of such responsibility is an excellent measure of successful therapeutic outcome. In our opinion, it is essential for these patients, whose internal boundaries are often poorly articulated and maintained, gradually to internalize boundary-regulating, self-sustaining and soothing functions that are initially provided by the therapists.

Let us hasten to add that we are well aware that the treatment of such challenging patients often does not reach such a felicitous end point. Work with these patients is often aborted by one or more of the following factors: patients act out feelings within them (whether generated by the treatment experience or not) which undermine the treatment enterprise; they introduce material which is more than can be handled and which results in their being extruded from the group for one reason or other; trainees finish their rotations and move on; or insurance runs out and treatment must be terminated. Nevertheless, we believe it is desirable to have a model of hoped-for progression in treatment, because it informs our strategy at each step along the way as long as the treatment experience continues.

Let us now move to an exploration of how countertransference manifestations can influence the group treatment experience.

## COUNTERTRANSFERENCE

### Definition

To begin with, some definition of countertransference appears to be in order. Two theoretical positions have been identified within the psychodynamic framework: the classical position, which defines countertransference as the largely unconscious reaction of the therapist to the patient's transference; and the totalistic position, which views countertransference as the total emotional reaction of the therapist to the patient in the treatment situation (Kernberg, 1975b).

We subscribe to the totalistic position. From this perspective, countertransference is not simply and pejoratively regarded as a pathological process rooted in the psychopathology of the therapist, that is, something that impedes treatment and must be overcome for effective care to be provided (Book, 1987). Rather, countertransference reactions are an inevitable and ubiquitous aspect of clinical work that can be thought of as having both 'subjective' (neurotic) and 'objective' components (Winnicott, 1947). The latter can be elicited in the therapist on a relatively universal basis in response to the extreme manifestations of patients' behaviour towards the therapist(s).

### Importance of countertransference

Depending on how they are explored and utilized, we believe that such countertransference reactions can either facilitate or hinder the treatment process. More specifically, they can inform the therapeutic work by providing important clues regarding the nature of patients' pathological internal object relations and their characteristic ways of relating to others in the world around them. The transference–countertransference interaction can be thought of as a special form of communication on an emotional level of primarily unconscious preverbal data that the patient cannot necessarily put into words and that, therefore, might otherwise remain inaccessible (Klein *et al.*, 1990; Klein *et al.*, 1991).

Racker (1968), writing about individual psychotherapy, introduced a schema involving two patterns of countertransference – concordant and complementary identifications – that is useful in explaining how countertransference can promote a deeper emotional understanding of the patient's experiences of himself or herself and significant others. A concordant response occurs when the therapist is identifying with the patient's experience of him- or herself; a complementary response occurs when the therapist is identifying with the significant other as experienced yet rejected, dissociated or projected by the patient. Concordant identification permits the development of finely tuned empathy for the patient, but also runs the risk of over-identification with consequent loss of objectivity. In contrast, complementary identification may enable the therapist to gain increased understanding of the patient's significant others, at the risk of becoming less empathic with the patient's experience of him- or herself.

Since such a large proportion of the therapeutic work with borderline and narcissistic patients involves dealing with pre-oedipal material, the careful exploration of countertransference reactions is especially important. To make effective use of countertransference as a clinical tool requires that one first become aware of it, put it into words, and inhibit the tendency to enact it. Next one needs to try to identify its source – that is, what is the origin of the reaction? What dynamic features might be contributing to its emergence at this time in the treatment process? And so on. One is then in a position of being able to explore whether, when, and how one can convey this additional understanding to the patients in the group (Kernberg *et al.*, 1989). Ormont (1991) has recently suggested a five-step method for clarifying subjective countertransference that begins with introspection and then involves the therapist turning to the group for vital information to shed light upon his/her reactions.

### Sources of countertransference

From our point of view, the sources of countertransference reactions are multiple in nature. Here we are not referring simply to those therapist needs, desires, cravings, and so on, that give rise to particular positive and negative subjective countertransference responses. Rather, on a conceptual level, we are referring to our belief that countertransference can be thought of as arising or as being induced in response to four interacting sets of variables: (1) patient variables, (2) staff variables, (3) group variables and (4) context variables.[2] In much of the classical literature on countertransference it is only staff variables that are given any consideration. However, from a totalistic view of countertransference, as well as from a systems perspective, in order to arrive at a more comprehensive understanding of countertransference phenomena, it is important to examine the impact upon the therapist of these four interacting levels of the group as an enterprise that functions in a particular environmental context. At each level therapists may experience both subjective and objective countertransference reactions.

Since our purpose here is to address those aspects of countertransference that are most relevant for the work of co-therapists in groups, we shall only briefly outline how group and context variables serve to shape countertransference. The role of patient and staff variables, particularly the implications of adopting a co-therapy format, will be given more detailed consideration.

## Forms of countertransference

### The role of patient variables

Although the particular countertransference reactions experienced by co-therapists working with borderline and narcissistically disturbed patients may not be altogether unique in nature, their primarily pre-oedipal content and especially intense quality often threatens to disrupt therapy. To a significant extent, this results from borderline patients' capacity to arouse feelings and behaviours in therapists that make management unusually difficult (Kernberg *et al.*, 1989). Suffused by severely pathological relationships from the past, the transference with borderline patients is likely to be highly unstable; only a weak working alliance typically develops. Rapidly shifting levels of psychological functioning, intermittent affective storms, protracted struggles for control, bouts of destructive acting out, and an inconsistent commitment to treatment are commonplace as developmentally primitive relationships are continuously re-enacted. In many instances the treatment process itself becomes quite confused, with the meaning and purpose of therapy, and the therapist's intent, subject to severe distortion (Klein, 1983b; Klein *et al.*, 1991).

In addition, these patients are uncanny in their ability to elicit the unconsciously desired or feared counter-attitudes in others, including therapists. Because borderline patients defensively rely upon splitting and forceful projective processes, therapists may find themselves sometimes being dragged reluctantly into collusively playing out the necessary part to sustain the patient's internal drama. Under these circumstances it can become extremely difficult to accept the aggression of these patients, serve as a container for their destructive negative projections, and yet preserve reality-testing and maintain one's own differentiation (Klein, 1983b; Klein *et al.*, 1991).

The following clinical vignette demonstrates some of the difficulties associated with maintaining a solid working alliance with a patient who experiences shifting levels of ego functioning, problems with affect regulation and expression, inconsistent reality-testing, and a tendency to resort to primitive modes of defence:

Deborah, a 20-year-old single black woman, was a member of a long-term inpatient group for late adolescents and young adults. She was diagnosed as having a borderline personality disorder and presented with a history of having grown up abroad as an only child in a dysfunctional family that was racked with dissension and despair. Her parents had divorced when she was 3 years old and she had little contact with her father thereafter. Her mother, whom the patient experienced as cold, self-centred and belittling, was a multilingual interpreter whose career frequently took her from one country to another. Deborah felt dragged along on each successive move, an unwanted encumbrance who only made travel and relocation more difficult. Although generally regarded by others as a beautiful, particularly striking young woman, she harboured enduring serious concerns about her weight and eating behaviour, and had a history of self-abuse involving cutting her arms. During periods of heightened stress, she became intermittently delusional about the size and shape of her nose which she insisted required surgical correction.

As a member of the group, Deborah was perceived by her peers as vain, ill-tempered, conceited and unconcerned about the needs of others. She frequently became embroiled in caustic arguments with other members. Especially frustrating for others was her reluctance to consider the feedback they offered regarding the effects of her behaviour upon them. Following one particularly upsetting visit from her mother, the group attempted to confront her about her offensive behaviour towards other group members. During the course of several heated exchanges, she apparently felt unprotected by the therapists and began to attack the senior male co-therapist. She accused him of being insensitive, incompetent, lacking sufficient training, and as totally unfit, both as a therapist and as a person. As her scathing indictment continued, unabated and undeflected by input from other group members, the co-therapist commented that she showed little concern for the impact of her rage upon him. He stated that she was treating him as if he had no feelings, as if he were simply a piece of furniture. She looked him squarely in the eye, and after a dramatic pause, said with dripping sarcasm, 'Don't flatter yourself!'

The next afternoon the co-therapist was seated alone at a large round table in the deserted cafeteria quietly eating a bowl of soup some time after the commotion of the lunch hour had subsided. Deborah unexpectedly entered the cafeteria, and seeing the co-therapist, sat down a few seats away from him at the same table. The co-therapist greeted her non-verbally, but said nothing. He simply continued to eat his soup. As they sat together in silence Deborah began to muse in an offhand way about how she was beginning to understand why others found her so difficult to deal with and unpleasant to be around. Because there was so much on her mind, she stated that she found it difficult to listen to the concerns expressed by others. She noted that she became easily frustrated and impatient, was prone to be extremely moody and unpredictable, and that she frequently lost her temper and lashed out at others.

As she continued to speak, she did not connect any of these accurate and apparently painful observations about her behaviour and her relationships to her encounter with the co-therapist in the group the previous day. The co-therapist remained silent but attentive, impressed and pleased by her introspective work. Just at that moment, two female psychology trainees entered the cafeteria engaged in an animated conversation punctuated by shared laughter. Immediately upon seeing them Deborah sprang to her feet, sending chairs and soup flying, and screamed at the co-therapist, 'Why have you been telling them about my treatment?!' When the co-therapist asked her what made her think that he had been doing so, she screamed in exasperation, 'That's it, try to make me think I'm crazy!', and stormed out.

Stunned by the intensity of her reactions to him and her rapidly shifting and unpredictable level of functioning, the co-therapist sought out his co-leader to share and examine these experiences. This was clearly a situation in which two heads were better than one. They attempted to sort out the effects of the patient's use of forceful projective mechanisms, especially projective identi-fication, and the co-therapist's countertransference responses. By working together they were not only able to begin to make better sense of what had happened, but also were able to contain and diffuse the emotionally charged responses of both the patient and the co-therapist. In addition, they were able to begin to formulate a strategy for therapeutically utilizing the co-therapist's reactions. Thus, in subsequent work with this young woman the co-therapist was able to make good use of these experiences to convey his understanding of what it felt like for her to be treated as a damaged, devalued, non-person by her unpredictably hostile mother, whom she felt she could never trust.

The dynamics of acting out and splitting – often related in their mani-festations – are a compelling aspect of clinical work with borderline patients and others in whom there is a prominent personality disorder (Klein *et al.*, 1991). Such patients operate at pre-oedipal levels of functioning, demonstrate inconsistent reality-testing and rely upon primitive defences – for example splitting, projective identification and denial (Roth *et al.*, 1990). Dominated by intense (frequently aggressive) affect with little capacity to tolerate anxiety, borderline patients often manifest an absence of stable internal ego structures that results in extreme difficulties with limits, boundaries and impulse control (Klein, 1983b). Action, not words, becomes the primary mode of expression (Klein *et al.*, 1991). Some acting-out behaviours are more obvious and dangerous, leading, for example, to self-inflicted physical mutilation, antagonizing and provoking others, persistently placing oneself in high-risk situations; while others are more subtle but nevertheless troubling for the treaters, for example, violations of the group contract by coming late, unexplained absences, demands for individual contacts, refusal to disclose extra-group contacts, and so on.

Whatever the particular form the acting out may take, it is often precisely at these moments during the course of treatment that therapists need to provide patients' missing ego functions. Setting appropriate limits and insuring appropriate boundary maintenance to preserve the safety and sanctity of the therapeutic enterprise without simultaneously depriving, punishing, overgratifying or abandoning such patients often proves to be quite difficult to accomplish. Misuse of both support and confrontation are not uncommon as the therapist's capacity to preserve empathic concern is severely tested (Adler and Buie, 1972; Hannah, 1984; Roth, 1980).

A senior group therapist shared the following clinical example which involved a breakthrough of angry countertransference feelings surrounding the setting of limits in response to extreme patient behaviour:

The group which she was co-leading had been meeting on a weekly basis for about one year in the outpatient clinic of a community mental health centre. Membership had remained stable for some time, except for the recent addition of an unmarried 32-year-old woman, Linda, who entered the group with a diagnosis of narcissistic personality disorder. Her presenting problems centred around an abusive relationship with her live-in boyfriend. Two weeks after Linda had joined, the group was shocked to learn that the teenage son of another group member, Alice, had been shot and killed. Alice had not attended the group that week and had just returned in the session to be described. The group began with other members turning to Alice and encouraging her in a sympathetic and concerned fashion to talk about this tragic event in her life. As she started to describe the violent episode that led to her son's death and to share some of her exquisitely painful reactions, Linda interrupted her to state that she, too, knew about violence and the destructive consequences it could have for relationships. She then proceeded to launch into an angry, rambling monologue about her boyfriend who had been physically abusive the night before, and whom she regarded as a self-centred 'asshole'. Group members sat in stunned silence, unable to respond. The senior female co-therapist simply leaned forward in her chair and said, firmly and with obvious irritation, 'Lin, cool it!'

Other members, including Alice, then began to chime in, expressing their collective sense of disbelief and outrage that Linda could behave in such an insensitive and self-centred manner. Like her boyfriend, they felt furious at Linda for having very little regard for the needs of others. The group then returned to an exploration of Alice's reactions to her son's death. There was no examination of the impact of the co-therapist's response. Later in the session, however, Linda informed the group that, much to her chagrin, this was not a new experience for her. She tearfully acknowledged that in similar situations outside of the group she often responded in exactly this way. Usually others had become so enraged with her that she wound up feeling unfairly criticized and that her needs were being overlooked. In contrast, the group worked constructively with her during the remainder of the session to understand how and why Linda managed to get herself into these situations, and to explore the consequences of her behaviour.

At the conclusion of the session the co-therapists met to review what had taken place. The junior co-therapist stated that he felt surprised but pleased by his partner's intervention with Linda. He noted that the intervention had seemed out of character and unusual for her to make since she typically focused on the group-as-a-whole and encouraged the group to deal with the disruptive behaviour of individual members. He indicated, too, that she sounded angry when she addressed Linda. Subsequent discussion with the co-therapist revealed that, indeed, she had felt angry at Linda. She also realized that the group was initially paralysed and felt that they needed some sort of help to proceed. She noted, however, that her response to Linda was not formulated after any conscious careful assessment, but came out of a similar recent experience with her own daughter, who also happened to be named Linda! (In fact, she even addressed her with the more familiar and affectionate reference, 'Lin', which she used with her daughter.)

Thus, it appeared that, caught up in a complementary identification, the co-therapist's response served to relieve and gratify the anger that she, her co-therapist and the other group members had been experiencing towards Linda. Input from her co-therapist had proved extremely helpful in clarifying her reactions. While we might agree that this constituted a piece of countertransference acting out, it worked well for this group at this time. In the case of a less experienced group therapist such an intervention might be thought of as psychotherapy from the spinal cord, not the cortex. That is, in general, relatively little conscious thought goes into the formulation of such a response; rather, it is made more or less in a reflexive fashion. With a more experienced therapist, it is difficult to know how much she had already successfully processed about the patients and the group prior to making what at first glance may appear to be an impulsive response. Furthermore, this response certainly had important elements of genuineness, directness and immediacy, all of which might have aided in its therapeutic efficacy. In any case, there are many instances in the course of working with narcissistic and borderline patients when experienced co-therapists feel propelled into making emotionally impactful interventions, some of which may prove to be helpful while others do not.

To complicate matters further, many borderline and narcissistic patients, especially those treated in the public sector, are also active substance abusers. Effective treatment of these dually diagnosed patients poses complex therapeutic and management issues for outpatient clinicians. Particularly intense countertransference reactions are likely to be aroused in the course of working with such patients who often deny substance abuse problems or avoid treatment, but whose already impulse-ridden behaviour is further disinhibited as a result of their abuse.

One borderline woman recently arrived for her group therapy session intoxicated. The co-therapists assessed her clinical state and directed her home. Indignant about their decision, her departing communication was to urinate on the stairs of the clinic. The meaning of this act was not lost upon the group as the other members, as well as the therapists, felt degraded, devalued and outraged. When one member stated 'Well, piss on her, too!', there were cheers in the group, followed by widespread acknowledgement of the fact that all were feeling 'pissed'.

Another patient, prior to beginning treatment with the group to which she had been assigned, reported that, while intoxicated, she had quarrelled with her boyfriend and that she 'may have stabbed him'. Subsequent investigation with the aid of concerned family members confirmed this behaviour. Her co-therapists strongly recommended hospitalization, but the patient refused. Since she was no longer intoxicated and denied any homicidal or suicidal ideas or intent, involuntary hospitalization was not feasible. It was only after the patient, who claimed she could not speak openly to the female co-therapist whom she perceived to be 'fragile', was able to meet individually with the male co-therapist and seductively elicit from him that he 'wanted' her to go into the hospital, that she agreed to do so.

These patients display propensities for acting out anxiety and aggression, and sophisticated abilities to split clinicians and systems. They manifest intensely conflicted dependency needs, desires for special attention, and a pervasive inability to abide by the rules of treatment. As a result, they often pose recurrent dangers to themselves and others, both inside and outside the therapy group. They also express intense demands, during repeated crises, for clinicians to make active, extensive interventions which can have profound implications, for example hospitalizing a patient. Hence, the usual boundary between therapy (in which therapists take a more traditional neutral psychotherapeutic stance) and management (in which therapists take a more active directive role that involves social control and has consequences in reality) cannot be conveniently maintained (Klein *et al.*, 1991).

## The role of staff variables

Group therapists working with borderline and narcissistic patients are prone to experience countertransference issues that are often deeply disturbing, prolonged and not subject to easy resolution. Because so many of these issues are pre-oedipal in nature, they are difficult to verbalize and to admit into consciousness. Although the variations are infinite, Klein *et al.* (1990) have summarized the most common pre-oedipal countertransference themes evident among therapists engaged in long-term inpatient work with severely disturbed borderline and narcissistic patients:

1  fears of being attacked, injured or killed by a patient or a group of patients, or (as a result of their use of forceful projective modes of defence or the collapse of one's own defensive resolutions) wishes and fears regarding the expression or enactment of an unacceptable level of aggression towards a patient;
2  fears that one will become the object of patients' intense oral needs and in the process be drained, devoured and eventually discarded;
3  fears that one will succumb to patients' madness and primitive modes of defence, resulting in the loss of one's boundaries, allegiance to reality, adaptive function, and personal and professional identity;
4  fears that the patients' situation is utterly hopeless or, conversely, wishes that although parents and other mental health professionals have repeatedly failed, one will none the less succeed in understanding, rescuing and even curing the patient, and that one will gain the recognition and gratitude one so richly deserves.

These authors note that these themes are clearly related to the major dynamic issues mobilized in both patients and staff during the intensive treatment process: enormous rage, intense struggles for control, primitive orality, fears of attachment and closeness, threats to boundary maintenance and self-preservation, and narcissistic needs for omnipotence, omniscience and fame.

Our purpose here, however, is not to provide an exhaustive catalogue of frequently experienced countertransference reactions and the defences used to cope with them. Many commendable efforts have already appeared in the literature with regard to working with borderline and narcissistic patients (for example Kernberg, 1975b; Kernberg *et al.*, 1989; Roth, 1980; Meissner, 1984). Instead we wish to focus on those staff-related factors that are most likely to exert a powerful, but often overlooked effect upon the countertransference responses of co-therapists working with these patients.

To begin with, just as co-therapists experience both objective and subjective countertransference responses to patients, they also experience a variety of such responses to one another. In fact, it is likely that staff-related countertransference issues are at work prior to the time that the therapists begin to co-lead their group. A case can be made for the fact that such countertransference responses are present from the moment that the therapists consider a co-therapy format. In exploring early countertransference responses found among co-therapists, for example, experienced supervisors often begin by examining what factors influenced the therapists to adopt a co-therapy model, and how and why they selected one another to work with or were thrown together, as it were, by others within the institution. Important clues about countertransference fears, wishes and areas of vulnerability frequently become apparent in the course of such an inquiry.

Not only do co-therapists react to one another as individuals, they also respond to one another as partners or members of a pair. The conscious and unconscious meaning this has for each therapist is activated. Together the co-therapists form the group, or more properly, the subgroup within the group. Furthermore, patients react to the pair, as well as to the individual co-therapists. Indeed, our clinical experience with more severely disturbed patients serves to confirm the traditional theoretical view that the leadership pair structure, especially when it is male–female, along with the presence of peers, powerfully augments the development of family transference patterns among group patients. With borderline and narcissistic patients in particular, the re-enactment of family-based part-object relationships is promoted and stimulated by the ready availability of this structural analogue to the primary family.

One of the most crucial distinctions that needs to be drawn in relation to co-therapy teams is whether the two therapists are equal or unequal in status. While status differences can conceivably be hidden from patients, they are usually obvious. The two most frequent circumstances under which co-therapy is utilized are when a supervisor and supervisee pair up to conduct a group together, and when two supervisees are paired as part of their training experience. In the former, there are usually significant differences in age and appearance, as well as evident confidence and clinical experience, that make the differential status of the therapists quite obvious. In the latter, the co-therapists are usually (but by no means always) relatively similar in age and manifest clinical competence and experience.

Some authors believe that when two therapists of unequal status conduct a group together, the relationship cannot truly be thought of as 'cotherapy'

(Roller and Nelson, 1991). Their view, apparently, is that the term implies an equality between the two members of the dyad (Anderson *et al.*, 1972). Our view is different: we believe that any two individuals who jointly take on responsibility for conducting a treatment are co-therapists. However, we are in concurrence with the view that when therapists are of unequal status the experience is enormously different from when they are of equal status, so much so that the two arrangements can be seen as more different than similar.

When therapists are of unequal status, their respective roles are often quite different, though this is not always made explicit, either between themselves or to the members of the group in question. As Anderson *et al.* (1972) construe it, both therapists have dual roles: the junior therapist is a trainee as well as a co-therapist, while the senior therapist is often responsible for the leadership of the group as well as training the junior therapist. It must be noted that the senior therapist does not necessarily have to take primary responsibility for the leadership of the group; in fact, one set of authors argues that it is crucial for the senior therapist to hold back in order for the trainee co-therapist to have the opportunity to learn by doing and not just by modelling (Bernard *et al.*, 1980). However, in fact the senior therapist most typically does take the lead, for a number of reasons:

1 senior therapists are often in fact better equipped to deal with the complexity of the group therapist role, and so feel that the responsibility to provide optimal patient care dictates that they take the lead much of the time;

2 senior therapists convince themselves (and there is merit in their view) that the best way they can teach is by modelling effective therapeutic work; and

3 junior therapists often adopt a passive stance when working with senior co-therapists, deferring to their experience and expertise, and hoping to learn what they can by observing.

Of course personality characteristics of both senior therapists and junior therapists come into play as well, but the role distinction between senior (supervisor) and junior (supervisee) typically carries great weight.

When co-therapists are of equal status, role distinctions emerge as well, but they are a matter of demographics, personality and therapeutic style rather than status disparity. One of the dimensions on which therapists differ enormously is activity level: one therapist is often much more active than the other even when the two are of equal status. Other distinctions are typically perceived as well: confrontative vs supportive, warm vs cold, and so on. Sometimes these distinctions are quite real, but at other times these perceptions seem (to the therapists) to be mostly distorted. Why does this occur?

The best single explanation is that there is a natural propensity to see pairs of people in contrasting, either–or ways. This tendency towards 'splitting' responses is certainly most pronounced in severely disturbed people, but in more modified form it is a universal human tendency. Thus, both equal and unequal co-therapy teams engender splitting responses. Ultimately, the split is experienced as between 'good' and 'bad', though the more high-functioning the individual in question, the more layers of distinctions there are to explore.

With unequal teams, senior therapists are construed as the repository of power regardless of what posture they assume in conducting the group – that is even if they remain quite laid back. As a result, many of the feelings group members develop towards the senior therapist are displaced on to the junior therapist (Solomon and Solomon, 1963). Thus junior therapists are required to contain a lot, as such displacements often take quite some time to be appropriately redirected. Often the senior therapist is idealized while the junior therapist is denigrated; this is typically not easy for junior therapists, especially because they are often dealing with their own feelings of self-denigration as they compare themselves unfavourably to the seemingly all-knowing senior therapist.

The tendency to denigrate one or the other therapist often emerges even when the therapists are equal in status. As the differences between the therapists become manifest, one often comes to be viewed more favourably than the other; a polarization into 'good' and 'bad' therapist is more the rule than the exception. This puts strain on the co-therapy relationship, and demands a great deal of skill from both parties. Favoured therapists must avoid being seduced by the group's view, which is particularly difficult if they secretly concur with the group's evaluation of their colleague. The denigrated therapist must be supported but not patronized, and patients must be encouraged to explore their splitting responses.

Those who argue that co-therapy arrangements can be facilitative of treatment, even with severely disturbed patients whose pre-existing tendency towards splitting responses is well known, believe that the tendency to idealize one co-therapist and denigrate the other provides useful grist for the mill if it can be worked with effectively. This view is based on the notion that the denigration of one of the members of the co-therapy dyad is first and foremost a projection of patients' feelings of self-denigration: the denigrated therapist comes to represent the feelings of inadequacy and worthlessness that so many patients (especially the severely disturbed) harbour. The job of the therapists is to make sure these projections do not become projective identifications: that is, denigrated therapists must be in a position, both within themselves and in their relationships with their co-therapists and supervisor, to avoid identifying with the feelings being projected on to them. Only then will they be in a position to do the hard work required to help patients 'take back' their projections and, ultimately, rid themselves of the self-hatred that generated their perceptions in the first place.

Of course, any leadership pairing does not emerge full blown from the head of Zeus. It is neither fully formed initially, nor static and unchanging; it is a process that undergoes a developmental sequence, as does the group itself. Moreover, these two evolving systems, the leadership pair and the group, reciprocally influence each other's development. What the group, for example, needs, wishes and fears at a particular point in time, and the developmental tasks with which it is struggling, affect the nature of the co-therapy pair's development and capacity to function, and vice versa. It is not sufficient to focus simply on how co-therapists are meshing with one another; one must also be aware of how the co-therapy pair is meshing with the group. Thus, as a function of these parallel, interactive, reciprocally influential developing systems, the countertransference patterns found among co-therapists frequently appear to be phase-specific in nature. Winter (1976) has outlined such a parallel developmental sequence and has suggested that the task of co-leaders in each phase is to solve as a two-person group the particular problem which the group is simultaneously confronting, while demonstrating that the group's deepest fears about that phase are unwarranted.

When viewed from a systems perspective, it is not surprising to discover in supervision that these two systems often demonstrate parallel processes, and that problems that originate in one system may be incorrectly attributed to the other. Thus, for example, an unresolved issue from the co-therapy relationship is sometimes perceived by the therapists as a problem or roadblock that is emerging spontaneously within the patients. If the source of the difficulty cannot be properly located, the appropriate solution can be even harder to discover. While the presence of an unsettled issue between the co-therapists may indeed incapacitate the group, especially when it, too, is struggling with dynamically similar issues, in order to work through the problem with the group the co-therapists must first resolve it themselves.

Differences between co-therapists

Let us now turn to the matter of differences between co-therapists, and how these are implicated in group therapy with borderline and narcissistic patients. To begin with, differences are inevitable. Davis and Lohr (1971) divide the personality factors involved in co-therapy interaction into three categories ranging from most to least observable, accessible and conscious: (1) extrinsic factors – age, sex, race, physical appearance, discipline, and so on; (2) characterologic factors – activity, passivity, affect, timing of interventions, cognitive style, and so on; and (3) dynamic factors – defensive patterns, competitive strivings, self-esteem operations. While the extrinsic observable differences provide a framework for the development of initial transference and countertransference reactions, their importance diminishes over time. Characterologic and dynamic factors, those which are less available to consciousness and therefore potentially more harmful in their effects, gradually assume more importance in influencing transference and countertransference reactions.

It is important to note here that not only do patients react to each member of the co-therapy pair and compare the two members of the pair, but that therapists, too, react to one another and compare themselves. Most therapists, particularly neophytes, are keenly aware of how they are functioning relative to their partners. Differences in discipline, status, experience, pay, and so on, may all provide an initial basis for staff-induced countertransference responses. Furthermore, co-therapists are busily comparing and evaluating one another in terms of activity, goodness and potency as therapists, and as collaborators/partners. When working with more severely disturbed borderline and narcissistic patients, these comparisons often extend to our capacities to be effective surrogate parents as well. For many therapists, the issues of competition are the most difficult to openly acknowledge, perhaps as a result of personality organization as well as the ego-ideals that are nurtured and encouraged during our training programmes. Nevertheless, it is not unusual to find co-therapists unconsciously competing with one another, for example, to be the brighter, more intuitive and more empathic therapist, the more dependable, non-defensive and supportive partner, or the warmer, more cherished good mother.

When co-therapists are not competing with one another for some preferred role or status, they may be unconsciously defending against such urges, especially through the use of reaction formation and conscious efforts to hold back so as not to dominate, intimidate or antagonize their partners. Considerable attention must often be devoted to clarifying and finding workable solutions to these problems in order for the co-therapy pair to function effectively as a team.

These and other similar issues are well known to those of us who have worked as co-therapists or have supervised such pairs. They are not issues which are unique to working as co-therapists with borderline and narcissistic patients. What is special in clinical work with these patients, however, is how the inevitable differences and competition between the therapists are perceived and responded to during the treatment process. More specifically, our experience indicates that such matters are exaggerated, distorted and projectively endowed with meaning that serves patients' unconscious needs. In large part this results from the fact that these patients tend to rely upon splitting and projective processes, and that the co-therapy format provides a ready-made, conveniently available structural template for the deployment of these defences. Thus, part-object relationships can be enacted by patients who are able to recognize and, in a sense, capitalize upon the differences which exist between co-therapists. Of course, even in circumstances where the co-therapists are able to function in an integrated fashion without any significant differences coming between them, such patients can nevertheless attribute important differences to them.

Thus, in the course of creating a safe holding environment for the group to do its work, containing patients' aggression and other potentially disruptive reactions, preserving necessary limits and boundaries, untangling patients' projective processes and assisting them to begin to recover the split off parts of the self, and so on, differences between the co-therapy pair are bound to become apparent. Because the co-therapy pair structure provides a ready-made template for the use of splitting as well as for the selective deployment of forceful projective processes, even minor differences between therapists are likely to be invested with elaborate meaning. Patients' differentiated reactions and behaviour towards each member of the pair then serve to promote and encourage the forcible maintenance of splits between the therapists, as each therapist is drawn into the re-enactment of pathological part-object relationships.

Over time, each of the therapists will have an opportunity to learn on an emotional level about aspects of the patients' preverbal world of self and object relationships, bits and pieces of which will be re-enacted in the transference/countertransference interaction. In contrast to treatment with a single therapist where part-object relationships are enacted sequentially with the same therapist, these relationships, which typically involve the expression of intense, extreme and seemingly incompatible reactions, may be simultaneously enacted with co-therapists. But, like the blind men and the elephant, each therapist gains an impression based upon partial, incomplete data, for example a specific part-object relationship. The efforts of the co-therapists must then be directed to getting all the pieces of the puzzle on the table, and open for examination, so that the patients' recovery of disowned parts of the self can proceed and so that splits can be integrated and healed. Only by working collaboratively can the therapists pool their respective experiences so as to gain a fuller, richer, more complete and detailed view of patients' inner worlds and how these are expressed at a behavioural level. To accomplish this, each therapist must be able to resist the temptation to conclude, usually because of unresolved narcissistic and competitive needs which can be augmented by being cast into the role of the 'good object', that he or she somehow has the inside track with the patient, that only he or she really knows the patient, or that he or she has an exclusive view of the 'truth' about the patient.

Careful examination of the roles therapists are cast into by the patients is essential not only to avoid unconscious collusion with an ego-syntonic preferred role that one is being invited and at times cajoled to assume by patients, but also to remain aware of the impact this may be having upon one's co-therapist. Thus, patients exaggerate and distort therapist character-istics and magnify any differences between them. The process of transforming therapists into stereotypes based upon the patients' fragmented and distorted intrapsychic representations of significant others is constricting, inhibiting and distressing for therapists. Through projective identification, therapists are repeatedly invited to play into patient dramas, thereby reinforcing this view of themselves and forfeiting a fuller role in the treatment process.

The following example (cited in Klein *et al.*, 1991) illustrates how the absence of one co-therapist may be dramatically used to split the co-therapy team:

One weekly dual diagnosis group for borderline and narcissistic patients was co-led by a male–female pair. When the male therapist, CS, went on vacation for two weeks, the female therapist conducted the group by herself. In his absence, one group member became explosively angry during the group session. She began to yell and scream, throwing furniture around the room, having a full-fledged temper tantrum. When the female therapist actively intervened to restore order, the patient turned to her and said, 'This would never have happened if CS had been here!'

In this situation, with her co-therapist on vacation, the female therapist was faced with behaviour that was so extreme and dangerous that it demanded uncompromising limit-setting, the imposition of external controls, and the exercise of consistent, firm authority. In contrast, when the female therapist was away on vacation, the largely female group expressed a litany of complaints about her to the male co-therapist. This not only placed him in an understanding, caretaking and privileged role in relation to the patients, it also separated and distanced him from his co-therapist.

Discussion in supervision of this and other episodes revealed that the female therapist in this particular group was frequently 'set up' by her partner to play the 'bad therapist' role. It was she who was responsible for setting disliked limits and boundaries and confronting patients about violations, rendering her a convenient target for considerable anger, and making it difficult for her to provide support and empathy for patients. She was restrictively perceived and responded to by the group members as withholding, harsh, critical and exploitative. The male therapist, who assumed the role of 'good object', was able to remain supportive and empathic while carefully avoiding any potentially angry encounters with patients. He was seen as giving, nurturing, understanding, accepting, and caring. Thus, he also functioned in a constricted role in that he was less able to set needed limits and to assist in providing structure and containment. Demonstration of the use of splitting ranged from one patient's steadfast refusal to speak to the female therapist when the patient was allegedly in crisis, to another patient's vicious personal attack upon the female co-therapist when her partner was not present.

As one might well predict, tension arose between the co-therapists relegated to these part-object roles. For each, their range of potential interventions was limited, and their therapeutic effectiveness as a team was reduced. Furthermore, it became clear that a parallel process was getting enacted in supervision, with the co-therapists playing out their rigid and stereotyped roles.

With support the female therapist was able to acknowledge her discomfort and dissatisfaction with this negatively valued part-object status. Once this was identified and confronted the pattern began to change. As noted by Klein *et al.* (1991), to be cast as the bad object and to unconsciously collude with the maintenance of such a role can be demoralizing and damaging to self-esteem. This can not only undermine the work of treatment, it can result in therapists' feeling that they cannot trust or count on one another for needed support, objectivity and collaboration.

As noted earlier, a major area of countertransference that is related primarily to the interaction between patient and staff variables has to do with setting limits. Assaulted by patients' peremptory, often insatiable demands, their difficulties dealing with people in authority, and their perceptions of themselves as entitled victims who have been abused and deprived by others, co-therapists can easily get caught up in desperate struggles for control with patients as they attempt to maintain appropriate boundaries. Many co-therapy teams, of course, intellectually recognize the importance of setting reasonable and consistent limits in order to protect the patients and to insure the viability of the treatment. However, they are sometimes unable to do so because they are intimidated by patients' ragefulness and capacity to act out destructively when frustrated.

Outpatient co-therapists often report experiencing a sense of helplessness and imminent danger because of the severity of patients' psychopathology, the often tenuous therapeutic alliance, and the lack of external structures and controls more typically available in inpatient settings. The risks escalate dramatically when the co-therapists are dealing with dual diagnosis patients maintained on psychotropic medications who may then have the means available – provided by us – for lethal action (Klein *et al.*, 1991). The presence of an emotionally neutral co-therapist who is out of the immediate line of projective fire can not only help support and reinforce limits and boundaries, but can offer invaluable assistance in realistically assessing the risks and dangers involved, and in placing such potential struggles into some therapeutic perspective.

Although most of the core treatment issues with these patients are pre-oedipal in nature, the transference may become highly eroticized, resulting in intense, disturbing and sometimes immobilizing countertransference reactions (Klein *et al.*, 1991). One female co-therapist, for example, received an extremely amorous poem from a male group member, another was approached for a date, and a third was seductively engaged by a male patient during a chance encounter in a local supermarket. Similarly, a female group member informed her male co-therapist about her graphic sexual fantasies, another recounted the details of the underwear she was wearing, and a third telephoned her male co-therapist 'to warn him' about her surging sexual interest in him. As noted by Klein *et al.* (1991), countertransference responses in these situations range from fear, loathing and disgust to interest, excitement and guilt. The presence and availability of a co-therapist often enables therapists to explore their needs to deny, rationalize and flee from their own emotional responses and fantasies, to understand the meanings of such communications, and to determine how best to respond.

Effective limit-setting, coupled with the capacity to maintain an integrated therapeutic stance is essential, too, with regard to the extreme practical, managerial and emotional demands posed by groups of borderline and narcissistic patients. Many such patients telephone their therapists virtually every day; case-management tasks abound; frequent crises, incidents and hospitalizations arise; individual meetings with group members are often necessary; enormous amounts of paperwork are generated; numerous meetings may be required with the psychiatric back-up, other treaters involved with the patients, the group supervisor, and so on.

We believe that co-therapy can be very efficacious in dealing with these demands, as well as with the many ways in which limit setting is necessary in dealing with these very challenging patients.

*The role of group variables*

Not only do individual patient characteristics serve to stimulate and to evoke countertransference responses; so too do characteristics of the group-as-a-whole. For example, it is not unusual for therapists to look forward to conducting certain groups while dreading others. One psychology trainee working as a co-therapist with a severely personality disordered group of patients revealed that she routinely experienced a vague sense of apprehension and mild panic symptoms associated with impending disaster as she prepared herself to face the group. Another, hearing the weather forecast about an approaching snowstorm, admitted that she was reluctant to cancel the meeting scheduled for her 'higher-functioning' group, but eager to postpone the 'Axis II' group session! The opportunities provided for supportive discussions with a concerned co-therapist often enable therapists to resist acting on such feelings and impulses.

Several aspects of working with borderline and narcissistic patients in a group appear to be implicated in such responses. Here we wish to underscore the importance of group size and composition, on the one hand, and group developmental stage and rate of growth, on the other.

To begin with, the old adage well applies: the whole is greater than the sum of its parts. Therapists who have few qualms about meeting individually with a borderline patient often feel uneasy at the prospect of dealing with such patients in a group. Their sheer number is, for some, intimidating. In part, this results from the fact that the full range of concerns of individual members is often amplified and augmented in the emotionally contagious atmosphere of the group. Surrounded by their peers, patients are likely to feel stimulated and provoked by others. Stark emotional reactions, that under ordinary one-to-one circumstances might be dampened down in amplitude and might take a much longer time to emerge, seem to be encouraged and enabled by the power of the group (Klein, 1983b). Buffeted by intense poorly modulated affect, the deployment of primitive defences and the continuous re-enactment of pathological object relations, patients may be disinhibited and emboldened to act out their concerns. Forceful challenges to the structure of the group and to the authority of the group therapist(s) are likely, as are lapses in control. Klein *et al.* (1990), discussing inpatient groups for such patients, emphasize the unpredictable nature of the group and the frightening prospect of facing angry, needy patients without adequate support from the rest of the staff. Under such circumstances, fantasies about Christians and lions are not uncommon among staff members at various levels of experience. Once again, the emotional support offered through the presence and availability of a co-therapist can serve to quiet such fears.

Furthermore, the group's developmental stage and rate of growth reflect the severity of individual members' pathology. Groups for lower-functioning borderline and narcissistic patients frequently seem to be stuck at an early level of development. There is little recognition or tolerance for the rights and concerns of others, grave reluctance to share the hated, feared but needed therapist(s), and enormous difficulty abiding by the rules and boundaries of the group contract. Parallel play, not mutual, goal-directed, cohesive interaction, is likely to be the rule rather than the exception. Transient regressive shifts, unpredictable alterations in adaptive level of functioning, and a host of 'pre-group' phenomena (Cooper, 1978), complicate an already flawed development. Consequently, development of the group and the establishment of constructive norms proceed very slowly. The situation on most inpatient units where the group composition is constantly changing and the group seems to be forever beginning anew is that much more challenging, requiring alterations in therapist strategies and techniques. Therapists in need of emotional gratification and affirmation of their skills and competence are likely to feel impatient, discouraged and hopeless. Starved for affection and recognition, staff members on inpatient units, in particular, are often left to wonder whether anything they are doing in the group is beneficial or has any meaning at all for many of the patients whose capacity for change and willingness to give much back emotionally is extremely limited (Klein *et al.*, 1990). A successful co-therapy pairing, in which the partners share a sense of being in this together, can often assist therapists to maintain a realistic perspective about what they are likely to accomplish, and can provide needed relief from feeling so emotionally drained and deprived.

*The role of context variables*

All groups function in contexts or settings. To a significant extent, these contexts serve to colour the attitudes, impulses, wishes and feelings that we experience in relation to the groups we lead within them. How important and useful is our group therapy work perceived to be within our setting? Is this work recognized, appreciated and suitably rewarded? What qualifications does one need to become a group leader? Is training and supervision provided? Is group therapy regarded simply as a sophisticated form of babysitting, a convenient way to generate revenue, an ancillary portion of an unrelated research protocol, or is it viewed as a primary treatment modality? Obviously, the answers to these and other equally important issues about the place of group therapy and the clinicians who conduct it in a particular context have a powerful bearing on the experience of those in the role of group therapist.

Clearly, in order to consider the role of context variables in countertransference reactions, it is necessary to maintain a systems perspective. Elsewhere (Klein *et al.*, 1992) we have reviewed the evolution of this point of view and its impact upon contemporary group psychotherapy. It may be sufficient here simply to note that, consistent with the contributions of von Bertalanffy (1968), Miller and Rice (1967), Kernberg (1975a), Durkin (1981), Ganzarain (1989) and others, we believe that it is important to view any therapy group as itself a subsystem embedded within a series of larger hierarchically integrated supra-systems. That is, the therapy group can be thought of as a subsystem or a part of the clinical services provided by an outpatient department or an inpatient unit, which in turn operates as a subsystem within a broader system, for example a university department or a psychiatry service, which in turn operates as a subsystem within an even broader system, such as a medical school or a hospital, and so on. Every part or subsystem influences and is influenced by every other part within the larger system, and bears the stamp of the overall enterprise. Furthermore, within every complex living system there are numerous reciprocally influential transactions that occur across boundaries at various levels in order for the overall system to remain viable and productive. Regulating transactions at the boundary involves the exercise of authority. These features require that we remain aware, as co-therapists, of the overall system in which our group is being conducted, our relationships with various components of the broader system, our own and other's authority, and the ways in which we are affected by the context in which we work.

Elsewhere we also have explored in greater detail how role strain and role conflict affect the functioning of staff members working in a tertiary care inpatient setting where they are providing long-term intensive group treatment for severely disturbed narcissistic and borderline patients and their families (Klein *et al.*, 1990). Consider, for example, that issues of role strain in the form of conflicted internalized values among staff are readily apparent within the context of most university hospitals (for example Kernberg, 1975a; Klein, 1977). Such complex organizations pursue multiple and at times incompatible tasks, including clinical care, teaching, research and the generation of income. At different times, as various leaders cope with changing external contingencies, one or more of these tasks may be endorsed as having the highest priority. Individual members of the institution must adapt to these changes while preserving their own sense of self-esteem and their commitment to their work.

Furthermore, individual staff members may simultaneously occupy several different roles connected with each of these various task systems. Role strain often arises from the ways in which different roles, and the values associated with them, are socially endorsed and maintained (Brown and Klein, 1985). In an effort to cope with conflicting internal values and discrepant role expectations, individuals adopt various strategies to reduce their levels of experienced distress. Procrastination in taking action, conventionalization of behaviour and role segmentation are among the more commonly observed manoeuvres (Merton, 1968).

From a systems perspective, the influence of context variables is readily apparent with regard to the conduct of both inpatient and outpatient group psychotherapy. In inpatient work, for example, it is clear that the social system of the ward with its norms, expectations and values plays an important role in determining patients' behaviour in group meetings and has a significant impact on the therapeutic process. Defined ways of thinking, feeling and behaving that are preferred by the community, and the community's values, are effectively communicated to new members entering the community. Borderline and narcissistically disturbed patients who require hospitalization are subject to rapid acculturation even on short-term units and in groups with a fluid census. As a result of the social isolation of the newly admitted patient, the inherent dependency and ambiguity of the patient role, and the process of decompensation accompanied by significant impairment of self–object differentiation and overdependence on external objects, the patient entering the ward is powerfully influenced by the prevailing norms and cultures (Kibel, 1978; Klein, 1977, 1983b).

These background contextual factors influence not only the patient conduct during all types of group meetings on the ward, but profoundly affect the experiences of group leaders as well. Neither the patients nor those who treat them are immune from influence by the world around them. In examining the dynamics in any psychotherapy group, it is not sufficient to search for explanations exclusively on an intrapersonal or intrapsychic level, while failing to take into account interpersonal and group level processes. In the case of the inpatient group it is essential to consider all of these, plus the role of extra-group context variables. Therefore, it is necessary to examine three dynamic levels of experience: the intrapsychic level of the patient, the processes of interaction (interpersonal and group levels) within the therapy group and the corresponding relationships to the dynamics of the total milieu.

As noted earlier, from a systems point of view the small therapy group can be regarded as a subgroup of the larger psychiatric unit. Since the membership of the small group, both patients and staff, represents the total membership of the entire unit, all the interactions involving all the staff and all the patients are mirrored in the transactions of the small therapy group (Klein and Kugel, 1981). A study of an inpatient group can provide a biopsy of the unit of which it is a part (Levine, 1980). The unresolved issues and tensions within the total unit as a system find their way into the small group, and thereby impinge upon and shape some of the therapists' countertranference responses.

On a more immediate concrete level, the psychiatric unit itself, or the larger supra-system of which it is a part, controls who, how and when patients are admitted and discharged from the unit and often from specific small therapy groups as well, whether group therapy will be provided and by whom, how patients will be prepared and selected for group therapy, how groups will be composed, the nature of the training and supervision offered to the co-therapists, and so on. These aspects of the context not only have an impact upon the nature, quality and dynamics of the group, they also affect the co-therapists' sense of autonomy, the degree to which they become emotionally invested in the group and in working with one another, their sense of value and pride in the service they are providing, and so on. Thus, these contextual variables can set the stage for the emergence of a variety of countertransference issues.

The potential impact of context variables upon countertransference is also apparent with regard to outpatient group therapy. Consider, for example, that the outpatient clinic, too, as one level in a hierarchically organized context of supra-systems, may be charged with determining who is eligible for treatment, by which clinicians, using what therapeutic modalities, and so on. On a practical level, outpatient group therapists are often most aware of the role of context variables with regard to two issues: (1) the referral process, that is, not only who is referred for group therapy but why and how that is accomplished, and (2) the nature of the current institutional pressures demands regarding staff performance.

With regard to the referral process, Klein and Carroll (1986) studied over 700 referrals for group therapy within a large university hospital setting. They found that such services were primarily provided for moderately to severely disturbed patients, many of whom were socio-economically disadvantaged, unemployed, poorly educated minority group members. Nearly 41 per cent of the patients initially referred never actually attended a therapy group. Of those who did begin group therapy, drop-outs occurred most frequently during the first three sessions, and more than half the patients were seen for a total of twelve or fewer sessions. Many of the patients referred were considered inappropriate for group treatment by clinic staff, and many were not interested in group treatment. Data were interpreted as highlighting the importance of implementing careful referral and preparation procedures, and as underscoring the necessity for developing short-term group therapy approaches for this patient population.

It is clear that clinicians on the front lines (often the least clinically experienced) who must make rapid referral decisions are influenced not only by their own personal psychodynamic factors, but each decision represents and is influenced by the institution, with its shared biases, misconceptions and prejudices about group therapy. Patients may well emerge from an initial clinical evaluation with the idea that group therapy is the low-priced spread as compared with individual therapy; that their problems are not sufficiently important to merit individual treatment; and that they are being discriminated against and offered a shabby second-rate treatment.

To the extent that group therapy is perceived by the institution, its clinical staff and the population it serves as a dumping ground for unmotivated, unimportant, unattactive or otherwise unsuitable or undesirable patients, the group co-therapists who receive these referrals clearly face an uphill battle! Closely related to this unfortunate state of affairs is the often institutionally supported belief that the 'best' training cases, or those patients who have the most potential for doing insight-orientated psychotherapeutic work, should be saved for individual treatment. The corollary to this, of course, is that many of the senior supervisors are themselves expert in individual treatment and are not adequately trained in group therapy, and thus tend to encourage such decisions.

In terms of institutional pressures and demands upon the clinical staff, it is not unusual for people to feel that they 'must get their numbers up', that is, see more patients so as to insure the viability of the clinic and protect their own jobs. Seeing more patients in groups holds for some the prospect of an economical solution to this pressure. At times clinicians face more specific demands such as the need to 'fill the group programme', or to provide a necessary transfusion of new members for an endangered small group that is limping along, on the brink of dissolving. At other moments, opposite kinds of pressures may exist within a given clinical system, such as the dictum not to treat patients simultaneously in more than one modality (resource conservation), no matter what might be clinically indicated. Most often, however, co-therapists who have openings in their groups and are actively soliciting referrals encounter difficulties in getting appropriate patients referred. Recently, during a seminar on group therapy, a staff member stated in exasperation, 'How come I have had only four patients referred for my dual diagnosis group when this clinic [located in the midst of an inner-city, drug-infested area] sees over 600 patients each month?!' Apart from their attitudes towards group therapy per se, fellow staff members may be reluctant to give up a patient they have been treating, knowing full well that another new patient will quickly be added to their caseload. For the group therapists there may also be vexing questions about what to do with the inappropriate referral. Quite often group therapists are concerned about cultivating and not inadvertently turning off referral sources. Furthermore, if the therapists are eager to start a new group and are experiencing some institutional pressure to 'get going' without being 'too finicky' about whom they accept, the stage is set for the intrusion of countertransference reactions.

The following is another example of how disruptive a borderline patient can be in a group:

Dr B. was a third-year psychiatric resident, and Ms C. was a pre-doctoral clinical psychology intern. They were co-leading an outpatient group in the clinic to which both of them were assigned as part of their clinical training, and they were being supervised by a senior faculty member. The group had been going on for three years, and passed down from generation to generation of group therapy trainees. They had been working together for about two months when Leslie was referred to them.

The group consisted of only four patients (three men and one woman) at the time Leslie was referred. The group had been geared to high-functioning patients since its inception, and the present composition was no exception. At the time Leslie was referred, all four patients were relatively successful professionally. All were between 27 and 35 years old, at the beginning of their careers, and basically pleased with their current work situations. Most of their concerns centred around romantic relationships (or the lack thereof) in their lives. Three of the four remained significantly involved with their nuclear families, so familial issues involving separation–individuation and autonomy received a great deal of attention during group sessions. Since all the patients were single, there was also a great deal of attention paid to dating relationships, the concomitant concern of two of the patients, whose social lives were not as busy as they would have liked. Though the severity of pathology differed somewhat among the four group members, they were all seen as manifesting neurotic and/or mild characterologic psychopathology.

The therapists were concerned about the fact that their census had fallen to four, and they were being pressured by their supervisor to generate more referrals, particularly of women, at the time Leslie was referred. As a result, they were vulnerable to making a mistake when they began considering her as a possible addition to the group.

Leslie presented a variety of concerns that suggested she would be appropriate for the group in question. She was a college graduate who had not quite found her way vocationally. She was interested in having more successful relationships with both male and female peers. She was struggling with conflictual relationships with both her siblings and at least one of her parents.

At the same time there were some indications that Leslie was more disturbed than the other members of the group. Her floundering was not a recent phenomenon, but rather a lifelong pattern. She seemed to be remote from everyone in her life, and this was reflected in the elusive way she related to the therapists during their screening interview. Leslie said she took pride in being 'unusual'; she said she sensed she did not fit in, but this acknowledgement was not accompanied by the troubled affect one would have expected.

It was difficult for the therapists to distinguish clearly between what they realized about Leslie at the time they screened her and what they came to understand about her after she entered the group. At least in retrospect, it seemed clear to them that she met the DSM III-R criteria for Borderline Personality Disorder.

However, at the time she was screened the therapists disagreed about whether to take Leslie into the group. Dr B. expressed some reservations, and at least wanted to see her again before making a decision. Ms C. was prepared to take Leslie on the spot. She was heavily influenced by the input of the supervisor, who was urging them to do all they could to find new members. The trainees reviewed their respective positions during their next supervisory hour and, with their supervisor's encouragement, decided to take Leslie into the group for a four-week trial period without seeing her again.

In Leslie's first group session, she mumbled a great deal. When other members asked her to repeat herself, she became obviously annoyed. Her efforts to respond to others were superficial at best; there were many indications that she was too self-absorbed to be able to listen and respond to others' concerns without projecting her own feelings and biases on to others in a transparent way.

At the outset of Leslie's second session, she announced that she had found a new career that was the answer to her longstanding problems. She went on to inform the group that she had met a new man and was planning to start a new business venture with him. The other members listened for a while and then began to raise questions and express reservations about what they were hearing. It was noteworthy that Leslie seemed completely unaffected by others' responses to her.

A few days before her third session, Leslie informed the therapists that her father had died. Though the therapists did not expect her, she came to the next session but did not say a word about the loss of her father. Another patient in the group talked about a lump that had been discovered in his neck that he was very frightened about. The patient in question was an openly practising homosexual, so that the fear that he might have AIDS pervaded the group, though it was not expressly articulated. In this context Leslie talked about an obviously minor pain in her chest, and compared it to the lump that was being discussed. This seemed so insensitive and cavalier that it aroused enormous rage in the other members, though it was barely expressed at the time and emerged only in subsequent sessions.

At this juncture the therapists were convinced they had made a major blunder in bringing Leslie into the group. After discussing it with their supervisor, they decided to remove her from the group immediately. They called her and met with her together, having decided to recommend individual treatment with Ms C., with whom she seemed marginally better connected, as an alternative. True to form, Leslie manifested no emotional response whatsoever to being told she could not continue in the group. She opted to work with Ms C., though it was not clear that this mattered very much to her either. She saw Ms C. twice a week for about two months (though she threatened to quit many times) until she terminated, citing dissatisfaction with the results of the treatment.

This is an excellent example of the intrusion of countertransference into clinical decision-making. The need for an adequate number of patients is a reality-based consideration at one level, but at another level it often gives rise to countertransference that can easily intrude upon clinical decisions that should be based on who patients are and what they need. These therapists, and their supervisor, felt the number of patients in their group was marginal and had a need to keep the group viable if at all possible. Furthermore, the co-therapists seemed to want to please their supervisor. What would happen if they were to not take Leslie into the group? While it is impossible to be certain how much these factors influenced their decision to bring Leslie into the group, and whether they would have decided to do so under different circumstances, it seems likely that these factors had at least some influence on their thinking and decision-making. While situations such as this do not always lead to bad decisions, often they do. All therapists, no matter how experienced and savvy, are subject to such errors. Not only are these types of patients difficult to evaluate and most challenging with respect to eliciting difficult countertransference reactions, but other considerations external to the group may also adversely affect our judgement, sometimes resulting in clinical blunders. However, the presence of a supportive co-therapist, as in the abuse example, may provide the treaters with sufficient reassurance and courage to confront rather than to deny such errors.

Thus, the ways in which the institution defines its tasks and priorities, identifies the populations to be served, develops its organizational structures and leadership, deploys its resources and so on, affects every individual member within it. Countertransference reactions may develop in response to these contextual features, as well as to patient, staff, and group variables. The mutual support that co-therapy can provide for examining and clarifying the impact of these features on therapist functioning is often invaluable.

## CONCLUSION

Though we have not made this assertion explicit up until this point, it seems propitious to do so now: we believe that a well-functioning co-therapy team can provide the optimal group treatment experience for borderline and narcissistic patients. Let us explain why we believe this is so.

First, as we have elaborated, these patients are enormously challenging and burdensome. They challenge the therapist's resources in every conceivable way. When a co-therapy dyad is well matched and has worked out ways to collaborate effectively, they can share the burden of working with such patients in a way that is (partially) relieving to both. At one level this involves making sense of the clinical data and formulating strategies for working with such patients; at another level it involves sharing the task of managing these patients, which can be formidable.

Second, the co-therapy format can be helpful in responding to the vagaries of the transference reactions these patients experience in the treatment situation. Such transference reactions are often quite intense. The co-therapy arrangement can be helpful in two complementary ways. First, patients are confronted with two (hopefully stable) objects who are giving evidence of their stability by productively collaborating with one another; this serves as a counter-balance to whatever malevolent projections and fantasies these patients might be generating about one or both therapists. Second, because one therapist is usually the primary object of enmity at any moment in time, the second therapist can attempt to work with the transference material in the context of an at least partially positive therapeutic alliance.

Third, a healthy co-therapy partnership can help immeasurably with the complex countertransference responses these patients invariably elicit. Co-therapists must be quite comfortable with one another to be able to acknowledge such feelings, which are often contrary to how we are 'supposed' to feel about those with whom we work, as well as to be able to give one another feedback about how these responses may be affecting the way each therapist is viewing, and responding to, the patient(s) in question. When such a comfort level exists, it can be very useful to have a colleague with whom to sort out our countertransferences, and with whom to consider how we can use them most effectively in our efforts to help patients heal.

Finally, the co-therapy arrangement constitutes a structural analogue to the family constellation in which so many borderline and narcissistic patients were damaged. Even when the co-therapists are both men or both women, almost all patients, regardless of diagnostic category, tend to experience one therapist as more harsh and demanding (the paternal figure) and the other as more warm and nourishing (the maternal figure). As such, the co-therapy treatment situation provides an opportunity to re-experience the primary family constellation. When the new 'family' works in the benign way for the betterment of the patients being treated, the experience can result in a working through of some of the trauma of the original family experience. In fact, this can occur whether this aspect of the treatment experience is explicitly discussed or not. We believe this can be one of the most powerful curative factors in a successful treatment conducted by co-therapists.

It is important to note that we have qualified all the potential benefits we have cited by referring to 'healthy' or 'well-functioning' co-therapy relationships. When a co-therapy team is not functioning in a collaborative way, it can get in the way of realizing some, and at times even all, of the benefits that are potentially available when co-therapists work together in treating borderline and narcissistic patients. While it is beyond the purview of this chapter to delineate all that is involved in a co-therapy relationship being successful, it certainly includes the following: genuine mutual respect; an ability to acknowledge and discuss feelings of competition and other dynamics that often emerge when mental health professionals collaborate, particularly when working with patients who are difficult to treat; an ability to give one another honest feedback; and a commitment to working on the feelings that get elicited in themselves and their co-therapist as the treatment process unfolds.

Even when the co-therapist relationship begins with all these characteristics, it can deteriorate once it is subjected to the pulls and swirls of working with borderline and narcissistic patients. This is why the availability of high-quality supervision is so important. Such supervision must focus on the exploration of countertransference, the provision of support, the maintenance of an appropriate clinical stance, and the enhancement of technical skills. Supervision can promote discussion of therapists' feelings, thoughts and fantasies, making this a legitimate focus of attention and an important source of clinical data. Both subjective and objective countertransference can be explored from a totalistic position that considers the multiple levels and sources of such responses. Establishing and sustaining a functional collaborative clinical team; maintaining limit-setting, reality-testing and perspective; and integrating part-object relationship data can all be enhanced through access to supervision. Furthermore, since powerful parallel processes exist whereby co-therapists replicate in supervision the dilemmas they are experiencing in running their groups, the supervisory process itself can be examined as a means for elucidating how the therapists relate and work with one another, as well as how they function as a therapeutic team with their patients.

Thus, armed with a good working relationship between them, a high-quality clinical supervisor, and a commitment to examine the complicated data presented by their patients as well as arising within and between themselves in an ongoing way, co-therapists are optimally prepared to enter the cauldron that invariably characterizes the group treatment of borderline and narcissistic patients. While it is never smooth or easy, we have seen some of these patients benefit enormously from a co-led group psychotherapy experience. When this occurs, it is extremely gratifying for the clinicians who have worked so hard to bring about such an outcome.

## NOTE

1 For example, consider what happens to transference–countertransference phenomena when one adds a second therapist to a group of seven patients and one therapist. Before the addition of a second therapist, these phenomena can occur at various levels: patient to patient (21), patient to therapist (7), patient to group (7) and group to therapist (1). Mathematically this can produce 36 different forms of such phenomena, without considering subgroup phenomena. The addition of a second therapist adds 8 more [patients to therapist (7) and group to therapist (1)] plus it introduces several other levels of such phenomena: therapist to therapist (1), patient to co-therapist dyad (7), group to co-therapist dyad (1). Thus the total increases to 53 different forms of such phenomena.

2 This model for understanding the sources of countertransference was introduced by Klein (1985). Since that time, it has been the basis for numerous presentations and workshops he has conducted, both alone and with Dr Bernard, but it has not previously been published.

## REFERENCES

Adler, G. and Buie, D.H. (1972) 'The misuses of confrontation with borderline patients', *International Journal of Psychoanalytic Psychotherapy* 1: 109–19.

Anderson, B.N., Pine, I. and Mee-Lee, D. (1972) 'Resident training in co-therapy groups', *International Journal of Group Psychotherapy* 22: 192–8.

Berman, A., Messersmith, C. and Muller, B. (1972) 'Profile of group therapy practice in university counseling centers', *Journal of Counseling Psychology* 19: 353–4.

Bernard, H.S. (1989) 'Guidelines for minimizing premature terminations', *International Journal of Group Psychotherapy* 39: 523–9.

Bernard, H.S., Babineau, G.R. and Schwartz, A.J. (1980) 'Supervision-trainee co-therapy as a method for psychotherapy training', *Psychiatry* 43: 138–45.

Bertalanffy, L. von (1968) *General System Theory: Foundations, Development, Applications*, New York: Braziller.

Book, H.E. (1987) 'The resident's countertransference – approaching an avoided topic', *American Journal of Psychotherapy* 41: 555–62.

Brown, S.L. and Klein, R.H. (1985) 'Role boundary dilemmas: special problems for women', *Journal of the American Medical Women's Association* 40: 181–5.

Cooper, E.J. (1978) 'The pre-group: the narcissistic phase of group development with the severely disturbed patient', in L.R. Wolberg and M.L. Aronson (eds), *Group Therapy*, New York: Stratton Intercontinental.

Cooper, L. (1976) 'Co-therapy relationships in groups', *Small Group Behavior* 7: 473–98.

Davis, F.B. and Lohr, N.E. (1971) 'Special problems with the use of co-therapists in group psychotherapy', *International Journal of Group Psychotherapy* 21: 143–58.

Dick, B., Lessler, K. and Whiteside, J. (1980) 'A developmental framework for co-therapy', *International Journal of Group Psychotherapy* 30: 273–85.

Durkin, J.E. (ed.) (1981) *Living Groups: Group Psychotherapy and General Systems Theory*, New York: Brunner/Mazel.

Fidler, J.W. and Waxenberg, S.E. (1971) 'A profile of group psychotherapy practice among AGPA members', *International Journal of Psychotherapy* 21: 34–43.

Friedman, B. (1972) 'Cotherapy: A behavioural and attitudinal survey of third year psychiatric residents', *International Journal of Group Psychotherapy* 22: 228–34.

Ganzarain, R. (1989) *Object Relations Group Psychotherapy*, Madison, CT: International Universities Press.

Greenblum, D.N. and Pinney, E.L. (1982) 'Some comments on the role of co-therapists in group psychotherapy with borderline patients', *Group* 6: 41–7.

Gunderson, J.G. and Kolb, J.E. (1978) 'Discriminating features of borderline patients', *American Journal of Psychiatry* 135: 792–6.

Hannah, S. (1984) 'Countertransference in inpatient group psychotherapy: implications for technique', *International Journal of Group Psychotherapy* 34: 257–72.

Heilfron, M. (1969) 'Co-therapy: the relationship between therapists', *International Journal of Group Psychotherapy* 19: 366–81.

Horwitz, L. (1971) 'Group-centered interventions in therapy groups', *Comparative Group Studies* 2: 311–31.

—— (1977) 'Group psychotherapy of the borderline patient', in P. Hartocollis (ed.), *Borderline Personality Disorders*, New York: International Universities Press, pp. 399–422.

—— (1980) 'Group psychotherapy for borderline and narcissistic patients', *Bulletin of the Menninger Clinic* 4: 181–200.

Kernberg, O.F. (1973) 'Psychoanalytic object-relations theory, group processes, and administration: toward an integrated theory of hospital treatment', *Annals of Psychoanalysis* 1: 363–88.

—— (1975a) 'A systems approach to priority setting of interventions in groups', *International Journal of Group Psychotherapy* 25: 251–75.

—— (1975b) *Borderline Conditions and Pathological Narcissism*, New York: Jason Aronson.

Kernberg, O.F., Selzer, M.A., Koenigsberg, H.W., Carr, A.C. and Appelbaum, A.H. (1989) *Psychodynamic Psychotherapy of Borderline Patients*, New York: Basic Books.

Kibel, H.D. (1978) 'The rationale for the use of group psychotherapy for borderline patients in a short-term unit', *International Journal of Group Psychotherapy* 28: 339–58.

—— (1981) 'A conceptual model for short-term inpatient group psychotherapy', *American Journal of Psychiatry* 138 (1): 74–80.

Klein, R.H. (1977) 'Inpatient group psychotherapy: practical considerations and special problems', *International Journal of Group Psychotherapy* 27: 201–14.

—— (1979) 'A model for distinguishing supportive from insight-oriented psychotherapy groups', in W.G. Lawrence (ed.), *Exploring Individual and Organizational Boundaries*, New York: Wiley, pp. 135–51.

—— (1983a) 'Some problems of patient referral for outpatient group psychotherapy', *International Journal of Group Psychotherapy* 33: 210–19.

—— (1983b) 'A therapy group for adult inpatients on a psychiatry ward', in R.A. Rosenbaum (ed.), *Handbook of Short-Term Therapy Groups*, New York: McGraw-Hill.

—— (1983c) 'Group psychotherapy', in M. Hersen, A.E. Kazdin and A.S. Bellack (eds), *The Clinical Psychology Handbook*, New York: Pergamon Press.

Klein, R.H. and Carroll, R. (1986) 'Patient sociodemographic characteristics and attendance patterns in outpatient group therapy', *International Journal of Group Psychotherapy* 36: 115–32.

Klein, R.H., Hunter, D.E.K. and Brown, S.L. (1986) 'Long-term inpatient group psychotherapy: the ward group', *International Journal of Group Psychotherapy* 36 (3): 361–80.

—— (1990) 'Long-term inpatient group psychotherapy', in B.E Roth, W.N. Stone and H.D. Kibel (eds), *The Difficult Patient in Group*, Madison, CT: International Universities Press.

Klein, R.H., Orleans, J.F. and Soulé, C.R. (1991) 'The Axis II group: treating severely characterologically disturbed patients', *International Journal of Group Psychotherapy* 41 (1): 97–116.

Klein, R.H., Bernard, H.S. and Singer, D.L. (1992) *Handbook of Contemporary Group Psychotherapy*, Madison, CT: International Universities Press.

Klein, R.H. and Kugel, B. (1981) 'Inpatient group psychotherapy from a systems perspective: reflections through a glass darkly', *International Journal of Group Psychotherapy* 31: 311–28.

Levine, H.B. (1980) 'Milieu biopsy: the place of the therapy group on the inpatient ward', *International Journal of Group Psychotherapy* 30: 77–93.

Macaskill, N.D. (1982) 'Therapeutic factors in group therapy with borderline patients', *International Journal of Group Psychotherapy* 32: 61–73.

McGee, T.F. and Schuman, B.N. (1970) 'The nature of the therapy relationship', *International Journal of Group Psychotherapy* 20: 25–36.

MacLennan, B.W. (1965) 'Co-therapy', *International Journal of Group Psychotherapy* 15: 154–66.

McMahon, N. and Links, P.S. (1984) 'Cotherapy: the need for positive pairing', *Canadian Journal of Psychiatry* 29: 385–9.

Masterson, J.F. (1976) *Psychotherapy of the Borderline Adult*, New York: Brunner/Mazel.

Meissner, W.W. (1984) *The Borderline Spectrum: Differential Diagnosis and Developmental Issues*, New York: Aronson.

Merton, R.K. (1968) *Social Theory and Social Structure*, New York: The Free Press.

Miller, E.J. and Rice, A.K. (1967) *Systems of Organization*, London: Tavistock Publications.

Morrison, A.P. (1981) 'Peer theory, dyadic primary, and destruction of the group: the borderline patient and group interaction', *Group* 5: 33–42.

Ormont, L. (1991) 'Use of the group in resolving the subjective counter-transference', *International Journal of Group Psychotherapy* 41 (4): 433–48.

Paulson, I., Burroughs, J.C. and Gelb, C.D. (1976) 'Co-therapy: what is the crux of the relationship?', *International Journal of Group Psychotherapy* 26: 213–24.

Piper, W.E., Edwards, E.M., Doan, B.D. and Jones, B.D. (1979) 'Co-therapy behavior, group therapy process, and treatment outcome', *Journal of Consulting and Clinical Psychology* 47: 1081–9.

Rabin, H.M. (1967) 'How does co-therapy compare with regular group therapy?', *American Journal of Psychotherapy* 21: 244–55.

Racker, H. (1968) *Transference and Countertransference*, New York: International Universities Press.

Rice, C.A. and Rutan, J.S. (1981) 'Boundary maintenance in inpatient therapy groups', *International Journal of Group Psychotherapy* 31: 297–309.

Roller, B. and Nelson, V. (1991) *The Art of Co-Therapy*, New York: Guilford.

Roth, B.E. (1980) 'Understanding the development of a homogeneous, identity-impaired group through countertransference phenomena', *International Journal of Group Psychotherapy* 30: 405–26.

Roth, B.E., Stone, W.N. and Kibel, H.D. (1990) *The Difficult Patient in Group*, Madison, CT: International Universities Press.

Singer, D.L., Astrachan, B.M., Gould, L.J. and Klein, E.B. (1975) 'Boundary management in psychological work with groups', *Journal of Applied Behavioural Science* 11: 137–76.

Slavinska-Holy, N. (1983) 'Combining individual and homogeneous group psychotherapies for borderline conditions', *International Journal of Group Psychotherapy* 33: 297–312.

Solomon, J.C. and Solomon, G.F. (1963) 'Group psychotherapy with father and son as co-therapists: some dynamic considerations', *International Journal of Group Psychotherapy* 13: 133–40.

Stone, W.N. and Gustafson, J.P. (1982) 'Technique in group psychotherapy of narcissistic and borderline patients', *International Journal of Group Psychotherapy* 32: 29–47.

Winnicott, D.W. (1947) 'Hate in the countertransference', in *Collected Papers*, New York: Basic Books.

Winter, S.K. (1976) 'Developmental stages in the roles and concerns of group co-leaders', *Small Group Behavior* 7: 349–62.

Wong, N. (1979) 'Clinical considerations in group treatment of narcissistic disorders', *International Journal of Group Psychotherapy* 29: 325–45.

—— (1980) 'Combined group and individual treatment of borderline and narcissistic patients: heterogeneous vs. homogeneous groups', *International Journal of Group Psychotherapy* 30: 389–404.

Yalom, I.D. (1985) *The Theory and Practice of Group Psychotherapy* (3rd edn), New York: Basic Books.

# 10 Intensive group and social systems treatment of psychotic and borderline patients

*Marvin R. Skolnick*

## EDITORS' INTRODUCTION

Skolnick's contribution is unique in this volume in addressing the social and political issues which influence treatment modalities. All groups are indeed part of the 'body politic'. This consciousness is consistent with Skolnick's emphasis on community and the role of institutions and intergroup relations deriving from his long involvement with the A.K. Rice Institute. One can also see Skolnick's deep commitment to healing and providing care to the mentally ill while at the same time recognizing their deep layers of genuineness and their implicit critique of the normative social 'madness'. In that respect, he has formulated an important new way of looking at therapeutic community, synthesizing social psychology, Miller and Rice's 'Systems of Organization' and the Winnicottian and Bionian concepts of a holding and containing environment.

What follows is rich with clinically relevant theoretical perspectives as well as detailed case examples of how the small- and large-group processes of the therapeutic community facilitate constructive dialogue and emotional development in the face of the powerful conflicts and dilemmas attendant on treating severe psychopathology.

---

Wagner's *Ring* cycle can be understood as a mythic drama of human development (Donington, 1979). In these operas, the supreme god Odin orders Brunhilda to be put into a death-like sleep and surrounded by a ring of fire as punishment for a differentiating act that defies the established order of the gods. Sigfried reaches Brunhilda by braving the ring of fire and brings her back to life, revitalizing the developmental process. One might think of the sleeping Brunhilda as any individual whose efforts at growth and differentiation have misfired into catastrophic states of breakdown incurring social quarantine. Interventions, as seen with the seriously mentally ill, usually focus on attempts to quiet the bizarre and unsettling aspects of these states, missing their potential for illumination and transformation. A 'therapeutic' blend of soporific medication and social control dampen the fire, and may seal off the disruptive but vital catalytic parts of the patient's self required for development. Bion (1977) has used the term 'catastrophic change' in an ambiguous way. On the one hand, catastrophic change for an individual can culminate in disastrous disintegration; while on the other hand, when it occurs in the presence of a containing other or group, it becomes a requisite part of developmental growth.

There are a multiplicity of meanings embedded in processes that culminate in breakdown, whether the breakdown is categorized as major depression, bipolar disorder, addiction, borderline disorder or schizophrenia. Meaning, relevant for the self of the patient, the family and the larger social system is buried when the field of inquiry and action is reduced to the study and treatment of the patient's diseased or 'chemically imbalanced brain'. When individuals identified as mental patients don't respond to treatment and remain in states considered diseased or socially disruptive, they tend to become dismissed as mad and are stripped of a meaningful voice in the human community.

The advent of psychoactive substances which ameliorate symptoms and an explosion of neurobiological research have generated promising theories about predisposing and/or patho-physiological factors in these disorders. However, the mysteries of brain, mind and social interaction continue to defy scientific mastery. The promising but inchoate material scientific findings on genetics and brain chemistry are often portrayed as the 'facts' that explain madness, and are often invoked as a way to dismiss the relevance of grappling with the human experience of breakdown and its implications for psychosocial development of the individual, the group and the society.

While individuals prone to breakdown and psychosis may be handicapped in their struggle for identity by biologically or psychologically determined impairments, many also have a canny sensitivity to destructive forces, conflicts and contradictions in the self, family or the prevailing culture that are denied, split off, and defended against by 'healthy others'. Foucault (1965) has posited that the process of creating medical classifications such as schizophrenia and their 'treatments' is part of western modernity's scientific project to silence a meaningful dialogue – not just with the vulnerable suffering individual whose madness is breaking out of acceptable norms, but also with the madness inherent in each human being and the covert madness in the social order. The reduction of madness to illness is to deprive it of its relevance and vitality. Disturbed individuals become cases that are studied and, one hopes, rehabilitated, but not heeded.

For example June entered our day-treatment community ten years ago with a paranoid psychosis. She felt that she had been poisoned by invisible gases at work and that she was being pursued by a sinister and powerful cult determined to slowly destroy the world. While June through her work in the community was able to discover that the feared cult was primarily persecutors of her inner world, it also emerged in the course of time that many of her concerns about the deteriorating environment were validated by the ecology movement. In addition, the Environmental Protection Agency found that the building where she had worked met the criteria for the sick building syndrome.

Like Sigfried with Brunhilda, those who enter intersubjective relationships with the mad not only stir the sleeping self within the patients, but ignite primal forces in themselves. Engagement with the phantasmagoric world of the mad with an openness to discover meaning rather than meaninglessness disturbs repressive barriers. Intense affects are stirred that threaten to overwhelm our everyday assumptions. Provocative questions are raised not only about what the insane are projecting but also what has been split off by 'normals' and projected into the insane.

## MADNESS, THE INDIVIDUAL, THE GROUP AND THE SOCIETY

Madness is defined by Foucault 'as that constantly changing region of human experience which defies any regulating intentionality; which speaks in the language of the fantastic and the passionate; which dwells not merely in historical time but also in a violent, timeless stream of subversion, flooding the secure banks of all that is positively known about the order of the self and world' (Bernauer, 1987, p. 349). This definition implies that whether madness is seen as an individual or group phenomenon, an illness or a creative endeavour, depends on the perspective and the eye of the beholder. The treatment and management of a segment of a society defined as mad cannot be fully understood without understanding the social, political and economic context in which these practices take place. Just as an individual life cannot be understood outside its historical context, psychiatric science cannot be taken as an objective given without an appreciation of the interactive dynamics and power relations between patients and those entrusted with their care and management. While the mad are dissected, deconstructed and reconstructed with abandon, there exists a paucity of interest in a comparable analysis of the psychological, economic and political motives of the authorities that speak authoritatively about the mad.

Individuals suffering from severe chronic mental illness can be seen as victims of madness gone awry. When attempts to create a unique identity out of the biological and social givens that permit negotiation between the conflicting demands of the inner world and outer world collapse catastrophically, they cast the potential psychotic adrift into the psychological equivalent of a black hole (Grotstein, 1989). Severe mental illness or psychosis thus can be understood as domination by a psychotic core of the personality that alleviates the nameless dread and fills the black hole with an inner world of phantasmagorical victims, persecutors, omnipotent saviours and demons, thus bringing some order, coherence and meaning from out of the ruins. In order to avert further catastrophe the psychotically defended individual projects much of this inner world into the external world and then retreats from relations with real others who might challenge its validity. The horror of non-being is transformed to the horror of being with others. Some individuals are so profoundly in pain and bereft of inner and outer resources that they defensively launch an attack on their own mental apparatus needed for experience which culminates in its fragmentation and projective evacuation (Bion, 1967). These individuals, who are left with an impoverished inner world and emotionally are inert, may have a veneer of health, are not disruptive socially, but are hard to reach (Ogden, 1982). Individuals captured by the psychotic part of their personality must eventually be helped to come to terms with aspects of the projections which profoundly interfere with thinking and warp relations with others, if they are to re-enter a social discourse.

However, no matter how withdrawn or bizarre these individuals may seem, or how much they try to destroy links with others, often there remain disguised pleas for help and attempts to communicate about the agonies of becoming and relating. For example, a chronic patient who communicated mostly in word salad had defeated the efforts of a number of therapists to establish a dialogue. While a consultant was interviewing him during rounds, he leaned over to the consultant, interrupting his word salad for the first time in weeks and whispered, 'Tell them to keep trying.'

On the other hand the 'sane' have a not so firm hold on sanity. To maintain a sense of being sane and a coherent identity the individual must contend with continual challenges from both inside and out. From Melanie Klein's (1959) perspective the individual never fully outgrows the phantasmagoric paranoid-schizoid inner world laid down in infancy. In this view, thought is born out of this madness and is never completely divorced from it. Within the most elegant reason, irrationality lurks. Bion (1967) posits that a psychotic component to the personality is universal. Winnicott (1969) suggests that behind the neurosis often lurks a hidden psychosis.

While the clinically psychotic patient may be experienced as dangerous because his psychotic language is often sprinkled with graphic references to violence, sadism, victimization and persecution, the destructiveness of the clinically psychotic patient pales in comparison to the destructive forces at work in *Realpolitik*. Perhaps the blatant madness of the insane is to some degree an introjection of the covert madness of the sane, leading the sane to recoil from the insane as one might from a frightening mirror.

Bion (1959) extended Klein's insights to the group aspects of life. He considered that human beings, because of their dependence on the group, resonate with the covert irrational forces that pervade group life. The capacity to maintain personal boundaries and differentiate between self and other that is often considered an important dividing line between the sane and the insane is compromised in the group even for the 'healthiest individuals'. Bion identified collective group defences – basic assumptions – in which individuals unconsciously collaborate through blurring of boundaries, splitting and projective identification to protect against psychotic anxieties generated in groups.

Jaques (1974), Menzies (1975), Miller and Rice (1967) and others at Tavistock in their study of organizations showed how extensively structure, leadership and boundary management are unconsciously shaped by social defences which are reactions to psychotic anxieties rather than rational work considerations. Goffman (1961) and Stanton and Schwartz (1954) looking at the mental hospital from a socio-anthropological perspective have identified processes that detract from the effective treatment of patients. They have examined how mental patients are vulnerable to exploitation and enmeshment when treatment systems are more driven by irrational institutional dynamics and defences rather than patient needs. Main (1975) observed how often psychiatric hospitals gravitate to an illusion that patients embody what is psychopathological and staff embody what is mentally healthy. Under these conditions relations and dialogue become as sterile as they would between two different species.

Modern man faces formidable threats to identity and sanity. Campbell (1968), Lichtenstein (1977), May (1991), Kafka (1989) and others have observed that in the modern world reason, science, technology and the capitalistic imperatives of production and consumption have not lived up to their promise to deliver us into a secure relationship with ourselves or to the cosmos. The dilution of the mythic and the spiritual dimensions of culture that helped humanity stay anchored to past and future have left us denuded with a precarious hold on meaning.

However, these dimensions of experience that the psychotic wrestles with openly are for the most part, in technocratic western society, relegated nervously to the shadows. When significant others and those entrusted with treatment of the psychotic project their own split-off madness and ontological trepidations into the psychotic and then dismiss the communication and experience of the psychotic as meaningless, social ostracism results. The ostracism is now less geographical than when these patients were sequestered in containers called asylums and state hospitals. It occurs now more through a process of objectification as if the patient is transformed from subject to an 'it' – a commodity in a mental health industry (Breggin, 1991). When the psychotic's retreat is responded to by a reciprocal retreat through objectification, a 'vicious cycle on non-recognition takes over' leading towards consignment of the patient to solitary confinement – a step towards chronicity and banishment from a meaningful and valued place in the community (Kovel, 1987, p. 342). The frightened, injured, enraged self of the patient with its unique story that needs telling tends to seal over when the patient is met with too much medication and stereotypic responses that may fit DSM categorizations but miss the person.

Bollas (1989) draws a relevant distinction between developmental implications of destiny and fate. Living out one's destiny represents the potential for becoming – the living out of the idiom of the individual which is a unique blend of endowment, opportunity and creative will. Being subject to fate on the other hand implies a predetermined future imposed on the self from forces divorced from the individual's creative will and striving. Whenever the emotionally overwhelmed individual is related to either as a biologically disordered machine or as a captive of environmental influences, the result is to foster passivity. To convey to individuals in psychotic turmoil that their experience has no meaning except as an epiphenomenon of a chemical imbalance is tantamount to a non-recognition of the striving and responsible self.

Symptoms, misidentifications and impersonal generalizations too often become false identities that are embraced in the systems that are designed to hold and treat the mad. Comparable false self-identities are fostered in those entrusted with the care and treatment of the mad by too strict adherence to stereotypic roles derived from bureaucratic specifications and psychiatric science. Thus patients are further estranged from authentic social discourse.

Kovel (1987) suggests that in technocratic cultures like the United States in which there are few spaces and little tolerance for integration of the irrational or ontological struggles, it is in the psychotherapy hours that less disturbed neurotic patients find their healing and developmental sanctuaries. However, for those identified as mad who have sustained global damage, a few hours of psychotherapy per week is usually insufficient to restore the psychotic to the human community. The proliferation of 'psychosocial' programmes has been a community response to the exodus of psychiatric patients from the old asylums and the influx of the new generation of the persistently mentally ill patients in the past decade. However, most of these programmes are inadequately staffed and funded and rely heavily on biological and behavioural approaches which stress conformity and neglect the inner life. While a blend of medication and education and social control can restore some patients to a semblance of productivity, stability or at least minimal nuisance, it leaves most patients estranged and developmentally frozen. More complete healing requires an immersion in a social environment that is not only supportive and affirming but one in which there are others who are not intimidated by madness and can participate in its shared meaning.

## P STREET INTENSIVE DAY-TREATMENT PROGRAM

The P Street Intensive Day Group Treatment programme was conceived twenty years ago to provide psychiatric patients who were assessed to be either chronically mentally ill or at risk of chronicity with an opportunity for more complete healing and restoration of developmental processes. The patients who have participated in this programme have reflected the diversity of a large eastern US city in terms of socio-economic class, gender and race. They have shared a diagnosis of a major psychiatric disorder such as schizophrenia, severe affective disorders or borderline personality, and most had logged several admissions to psychiatric inpatient hospitals. They also have shared a common social role as psychiatric patient, and this has dominated their relations with themselves and others, tending to foreclose development of other roles and potentials in their personalities. Most have had disturbed family histories and have failed to establish viable group relations outside their family of origin except in the constricted role of chronic psychiatric patient.

The programme began in 1971 as a component of a developing Community Mental Health Center in Washington, DC, when the community mental health movement was at its zenith. It was born out of the treatment optimism prevalent at the time that even the most severe psychiatric disorders would be responsive to a corrective blend of enlightened psychosocial and biological therapies.

The programme started inauspiciously by bussing both patients and staff from a closed psychiatric ward in a city hospital to a refurbished abandoned school building where a community mental health centre was being born. The psychiatric director's belief in the desirability of an open treatment system (unlocked doors, voluntary membership) was not shared by line staff or patients. Chaos ensued. While patients and staff who participated in the experiment ostensibly subscribed to the principles of open treatment, patients were frequently seen escaping from their freedom, dashing out of the building with staff in hot pursuit. Mirrors disappeared from the bathrooms, knives and other sharp items from the kitchen, open doors were locked, and the school building began to take on the appearance and ambience of a secure inpatient facility.

It is interesting that, on the whole, the patients survived the trauma of abrupt transition from the closed ward better than did the staff. Resignations and transfers plus the importing of staff congenial to less controlling and more psychologically informed ways of relating, gradually occurred. A social system with new assumptions and values began to develop, in part out of the necessity of finding ways to work and hold patients in a setting where customary means of social control such as locked doors, seclusion rooms and physically overpowering nursing assistants were not available.

Despite numerous intrusions from the larger institution to radically change or obliterate the programme, the basic frame of the programme has remained relatively stable over twenty years.The core therapy occurs in a variety of groups with different tasks and size within an overall frame of a therapeutic community. Each patient has a one-to-one relationship with a staff treatment co-ordinator with whom he or she meets once a week regularly. The six-hour day, five-day weekly schedule for twenty to twenty-five patients includes large-group community meetings, smaller team meetings, small-group psychotherapy, psychodrama, art therapy, medication group, patient government, patient–staff committee meetings, informal day-room socializing, multiple family groups, staff group meetings, vocational groups and other activity and enrichment groups. The programme meets four days a week from 9:00 a.m. to 4:00 p.m. and one day a week from 1:00 to 9:00 p.m. to allow for a family dinner and evening family therapy. There is a core multidisciplinary staff of four. The psychiatrist and nurse who started the programme remained a work pair for fifteen years until the nurse retired. The original psychiatrist remains on the staff and other core staff have turned over relatively slowly. This programme differs from most day-treatment programmes, which function as a time-limited alternative to hospitalization for acute episodes, or as a time-limited transitional way station between hospitalization and outpatient treatment, or as day care.The P Street programme is designed to provide an open-ended time frame that aspires like a functional family to be geared to the developmental needs of the patients. The modal length of stay for patients is three to five years, with a cluster of patients staying a few months and a few remaining connected to the programme (with varying degrees of involvement) for as long as seventeen years. The majority of patients who have stayed longer than a year appear to have made developmental progress, improved their quality of life, and have broken the cycle of revolving hospitalizations to inpatient units. There has not been a systematic or controlled study of outcomes.

# P STREET AS A HOLDING CONTAINING SOCIAL SYSTEM

The programme is conceptualized as a social system designed to promote healing and human growth. It utilizes the analytic systems framework developed at the Tavistock Institute by Miller and Rice (1967). Winnicott's (1965) concept of the holding environment and Bion's (1977) concept of the container and the contained which address the requisite conditions and process of the mother–infant developmental relationship are used as guiding principles at the core of this social system. The primary task, the group and intergroup process, the distribution of authority and the delineation and management of boundaries are fundamental defining dimensions of the system from a Tavistock perspective.

According to Bion (1977), the mother, through her reverie, serves as a container for her infant by taking in, metabolizing and responding to painful experience of 'absence' that the infant is not able to process or hold inside without calamity. It is through this process that the infant internalizes the mother's capacity to process emotional pain rather than evacuate it and comes to feel that experience growing out of frustration is worth enduring, has validity and can be a building-block for thought and meaning. This process of passing emotional experience from one human being to another and then back again in modified form through projective identification and introjection forms the bridge between intrapsychic phantasy and interpersonal transaction and is fundamental in its healthy form to intersubjective communication, empathy and emotional nurture. In its pathological form, when the container is absent or fails to function adequately, vicious cycles prevail leading to estrangement and pathological relations. Bion (1967) believed that individuals dominated by the psychotic part of their personality have not developed an adequate internal container or an apparatus for thinking to deal with frustration. The psychotic personality when confronted with 'absence' or the frustration of living is flooded by the painful emotions of rage, greed and envy. Rather than the patient being held and growing from the experience of 'absence', representations of the self, the other and parts of the mental apparatus itself are attacked, fragmented and forcefully expelled through the phantasy operation of a malignant projective identification, producing what Bion terms bizarre objects.

As Tustin (1986) and Ogden (1982) have noted, another alternative to the failure to come to terms with the pain and terror of this predicament is entrenchment in an autistic contiguous mode of being, resulting in a closed fortress-like state of non-experience that is too often reinforced by impersonal dispensing of numbing medication. Too often, treatment systems discourage patients from working with their experience by failing to function as adequate containers for emotional pain. It is imperative that a social system committed to human development encourage patients to be open to the frustration, the richness and learning potential of experience without having to face the calamity of unbearable psychic pain alone.

Winnicott (1965) also spoke to the process of human development in terms of a mother who provides a 'holding environment' that protects the child from unbearable anxiety and disintegration of 'the-going-on-being' experience. While literal holding and psychical care are involved, Winnicott's contribution also addresses the delineation of the psychological holding that is established through the mother's capacity empathically to interpret and contain the child's sexuality and aggression. She also serves a mediating or facilitating function between the child and the physical and social environment of others. This holding environment becomes a context in which the child experiences that his or her rage can be survived, that he/she can be known, know himself or herself and join the human community.

Grotstein (1986) has suggested that all dynamic psychotherapy proceeds simultaneously on at least two tracks. One track is related to the emergence and analysis of transference and countertransference object relations. However, deeper, analytic work, particularly when related to pre-oedipal pathology, cannot proceed unless it is supported by a holding, containing, facilitating context. Many patients like these under discussion have sealed off vital parts of their personality in efforts to preserve the self. Islands of inchoate capacities to think, feel and love, are concealed behind walls of paranoid rage or autistic capsules. Until these patients believe that they are safe enough from threats of disintegration or threats to their 'going on being', these capacities will remain inaccessible or hidden. Too often, these patients in acute episodes have been responded to by the mental health system with numbing doses of neuroleptics and management from a distance that tends to confirm their deeply held conviction that schizoid retreat, states of non-experience (Ogden, 1982) or encapsulation (Tustin, 1986) are the only hope for survival. It is the holding, containing facilitating environment that can reverse this despair by allowing real engagement – the linking of the patient's emotional experience, no matter how primitive or intense, with other human beings rather than imploding or being lost in infinite space.

The programme is usually referred to by patients and staff as the 'Community', as though it were a living entity distinct from patients, staff or institution. While a patient at any particular moment may be attacked by other patients, or misunderstood by staff members, or even scapegoated by the capriciousness of the group-as-a-whole, there remains the sense of being held, accepted and affirmed by a transcendent community which stands in contrast to previous experience of being invalidated by the societal community. For these difficult patients it is this community that can provide the holding, containing environment in ways that even the most dedicated individual therapist could not. In order to provide what very disturbed patients require for treatment, the community must be pleomorphic – firm, soft and flexible. It must be able to be like a surface that at times is firm, so that patients can adhere to it as they might to an inanimate object acting as a shield, and at other times is soft and inviting like a mother's body. This potential is critical for patients who are walled off from themselves and others because of a terror of disintegration.The adherence to something outside the self may be for some patients analogous to the newborn's adherence to the mother when she was more of a surface than a person, providing a boundedness to counteract the anxiety of draining into infinite space inherent in the process of adjustment to life outside the womb. Bick (1968) has termed this 'adhesive identification', a first step beyond an autistic capsule towards relatedness. The rhythmicity and regularity of meetings starting and stopping on time, the presence of bodies, the places to sit with bodies (aloneness in the presence of the other), a reliable temperature range, food available on a regular basis, community rituals, comfortable furniture, the respect for personal space, and protection from being coerced or intruded upon before one is ready – these are some of the characteristics that patients who present in a walled-off defensive state of non-experience seem to require for initial engagement.

As the patients thaw from the freeze of their autistic-like condition and move more into a paranoid-schizoid position, the community must be enough of a container that the patients experience that their destructive passions and forceful projections do not disappear into space, destroy others or rebound to destroy them. As patients become free to own and think about their experience in terms of their own authority and relations with others, then the community must offer a space for complex and symbolic object relations in work and play. Patient government, psychodrama, art therapy, picnics, projects, vocational opportunities, and small-group psychotherapy are some of the sectors of the programme that are best suited to this realm of experience that might be thought of as work from the depressive position.

Ogden (1989) has recently described the 'autistic contiguous mode of mental organization' that precedes the paranoid-schizoid position and the depressive position originally defined by Melanie Klein. This mode of experience relates to the original rupture between the mother and infant that occurs at birth and addresses the need to sustain a 'going on being' feeling in the face of this rupture. Ogden emphasizes the dialectical relationship between these three modes of experience. This view stands in contrast to a sequential developmental perspective originally delineated by Klein who held that these positions are lived and mastered sequentially. On the other hand, a dialectic view holds that these become modes of experience in dynamic interaction with one another, each making possible the other, as night makes day possible throughout life. Each enables the individual to contend with opportunities and threats inherent in the human condition, but each poses potential pitfalls. For example, the autistic contiguous mode makes possible the experience of boundedness and self-containment, but stasis in this mode leads to estrangement from others. The paranoid-schizoid mode protects the individual from internal destruction and generates aggressive energy to act upon the external world, but stasis in this mode can lead to perpetual belligerence and persecutory anxiety. The depressive mode of experience allows for wholeness and integration in object relations, but stasis in this position can lead to sterility and the action-paralysis secondary of obsessive guilt. Ogden suggests that pathology is evident not only in terms of the anxieties and conflicts of each position but in the lack of capacity to move with fluidity from one mode of organization to another as dictated by internal and external circumstances.

For the group or community to provide meaningful engagement and developmental opportunities for patients contending with the fear of disintegration, primitive rage, dependency, greed, fear, and guilt about sexuality, the community must have the plasticity to provide support in all three modes of experience. There must be room to permit self-containment and private inner space, the capacity to contain the repercussions of projection, splitting and expression of primal affects, and shared space allowing for the opportunity to work symbolically and towards integration of self and other. In many programmes for very disturbed patients the therapy is organized to operate in only one or two modes while excluding the others. For example in programmes emphasizing medication and support often both the paranoid and depressive mode of experience get very short shrift, while in programmes that emphasize analytic understanding and insight often the autistic contiguous and paranoid-schizoid modes are neglected.

The building of a holding containing therapeutic community for a group of borderline and psychotic patients in an outpatient setting that preserves space for play and symbolic work is a challenging task. Winnicott (1965) has described the subtle aspects of 'holding' by the mother and the therapist as the 'details of management'. Essential details of management that determine the quality of a therapeutic social system include the delineation and monitoring of the primary task, roles, authority distribution and boundaries.

## THE PRIMARY TASK

Miller and Rice (1967) define the primary task as what the organization was designed to do and what it needs to do to survive. The primary task of the P Street programme is promotion of healing and psychosocial development of psychiatric patients in the least restrictive environment. Bion (1959) has asserted that it is the shared task that transforms a collection of individuals into a group and satisfies the basic human need to be linked in meaningful ways with other human beings. This primary construct is the starting point for developing a lens through which to view every aspect of the system and to assess whether it facilitates the work or impedes it.

While the primary task might seem to be primarily a pragmatic construct, as it has evolved in the Tavistock tradition it also implies a commitment to values inherent in the task. When a group is engaging in work that promotes its survival but the survival activity conflicts with the values and objectives of the primary task, dissonance results which erodes the integrity of the work. For example, while many treatment systems claim that treating patients is their primary task, in actuality this task is relegated to a low priority in favour of training, profit-making, research, political agendas, employment of staff or social control. If one is sold a quality car by a salesman who misrepresents the process, the quality of the purchase is not affected as long as the price is good. However, in psychotherapeutic activities the integrity and authenticity of the staff is at the heart of the development of basic trust without which real treatment cannot proceed.

A matrix of authorizations legitimizes the work of the P Street programme. As a result of a class-action suit brought by hospitalized patients, the courts have mandated that the city shall provide non-restrictive psychosocial treatment of chronic psychiatric patients in the community. The city Mental Health Commission, the programme director and the staff become accountable for work on this task by accepting their organizational positions. Another vital set of authorizations comes from the patients themselves who are not taken into the programme until they have an opportunity to make an informed decision about joining. Candidates for the programme, no matter how psychotic they seem, are given the opportunity to meet with staff and patients currently in the programme both individually and in an open weekly orientation group. This procedure gives the prospective patient and family an informed basis to decide about joining. Pressures from family, referring therapists or institutions to admit a patient are resisted until the patient has an opportunity for a real choice. While the patient needs a holding and containing environment for treatment to proceed, it is also essential that the patient's autonomy is respected. This gives the patient an opportunity to work from the true self rather than being subordinated as a part object, subject to the dictates of a controlling 'total institution' (Goffman, 1961). To underscore the prerogatives of the patient, he/she is helped to discover and determine his/her own treatment goals even though this may require months and years of painstaking work. A negotiated treatment plan to achieve these goals becomes a basis for collaborative work.

Bion has underscored the difficulties as well as the potential of developmental group work. The dread of development that requires learning from experience is expressed by all groups and all individuals in the collaborative irrational defences which Bion (1959) called 'basic assumptions'. Pressures to subvert the development come from all directions – staff, patients, families, institutions and society as a whole. The primary task becomes an indispensable frame of reference to sort through irrational pressures generated by psychotic patients, confused staff and a treatment system that is embedded in a larger bureaucracy with many covert and competing agendas. Over the twenty-year span of the programme, threats to the community both from inside and out have mobilized patient and staff work leaders to call on the righting influence of their primary task to preserve the community and its purpose.

## BOUNDARIES

Boundaries and development are inextricably linked. It was out of the primordial soup that distinct entities arose with boundaries differentiating one entity from another. From a systems perspective, a boundary in a living system is a zone that is always permeable to varying degrees where critical choices are made about what is included and what excluded, what is taken in and what is exported. Too little importation or too much exportation leads to depletion and death; too much importation or too little exportation tends to overwhelm internal organization and coherence

As Pines (1990) has emphasized, one important way to understand the affliction of the borderline and psychotic-prone patient is his/her difficulty in establishing and managing boundaries between internal and external reality, between self and other, between self and group, between conscious and unconscious, between role and person, and between past and present. Very disturbed patients can be thought of as having boundaries that are either too permeable – leading to chaos – or too rigid – leading to depletion and failure to thrive. Ganzarain (1977) describes the boundary-decider subsystem of the troubled individual or the troubled group as archaic: choices are often made non-reflectively, based on past experience and anxiety rather than on judgements about current reality. Family studies also strongly suggest that schizophrenic, borderline and other chronically ill patients' self–other boundary development is stunted by regression in family boundary regulation. As the identified patient, they are loaded with split-off family pathology through projective identification (Shapiro, 1985). There is growing evidence that the borderline syndrome may arise from profound boundary disturbances in families manifested by traumatic violation of personal boundaries such as physical and sexual abuse. As chronic mental patients, they are vulnerable once again to use as split-off part objects carrying disowned irrationality of the institution or the society at large.

A treatment community which is subject to the regressive pressures inherent in the treatment process must pay close attention to the delineation, dynamics and management of boundaries. Attention to boundaries is critical in maintaining the integrity of the community as a container for its members as the mother was container for her infant. As Frieda Fromm-Reichman (1950) pointed out, the schizophrenic patient is in some respects undeveloped like the infant and is in desperate need of care and support, but is also at the same time an adult who needs respect for his/her autonomy and space for the evolution of being and the emergence of a true self. Individual therapists or traditionally structured hospitals attempt to supply auxiliary ego functions in ways that often unwittingly undermine the patient's autonomous healthy ego. Careful structuring of the system with sophisticated management of the system boundaries rather than direct control over the patient's boundaries provides more space for acting in and the play vital for learning and change through experience. Management of the system, rather than the patient, reduces the probability that the collaborative symbiosis required for growth will deteriorate into willful power struggles and parasitic dependency rather than generative interdependency.

Managing the boundary between therapeutic community and external environment is crucial in developing a therapeutic space without which no treatment could be coherent. Looking outward from the therapeutic community one encounters society at large, the urban mental health bureaucracy in which the programme is embedded, the patients' families, and the aspects of patients' lives in which they function as consumers and citizens. The priorities and values of society, the bureaucracy and the families are frequently at odds with the priorities and values of the therapeutic system. Often it seems that the psychotherapy group, to be therapeutic, must deviate from prevailing societal norms and values. It must resist pressures from outside groups to relinquish its identity and values, while at the same time interact collaboratively with these same groups which supply vital resources and authorization to work. The oversimplified dividing line between the sane and the mad is challenged as one wrestles with the interaction of the therapeutic community with irrationality of families and the outside world.

Often the most direct assaults on the therapeutic community come from the larger mental health bureaucracy. In the large, hierarchically structured bureaucracy in which this programme is embedded, managers making decisions that impinge on the treatment systems are often insulated from the impact of their decisions on actual patients or clinical staff. Decisions are often based on political power and expediency, avoidance of anxiety and bottom-line cost, reflecting prevailing values of the culture rather than values inherent in therapeutic work. The hierarchial impersonal and non-participatory management system is the antithesis of the participatory personal system of the therapeutic community. Administrative directives and memorandums emanating from a removed hierarchy often seem like Trojan horses that insinuate controlling forces that undermine the autonomy of patients. For example, the administration reacted to a patient newsletter as though it were a subversive document rather than an exercise of patient resourcefulness and organization. An administrator demanded that it be submitted for censorship before it could be published. In frantic and short-sighted efforts to secure endorsement from an accrediting body, attempts to impose policies applicable to inpatient units were inappropriately mandated for outpatient programmes, undermining efforts to help patients become more independent. An administrative directive, for instance, ordered staff not to allow patients to sit in rooms without staff present. Directives to ensure that each patient in the programme had qualified for the maximum entitlement possible ignored the issue of dependency versus autonomy for individual patients. Ignoring physical environmental problems such as lack of ventilation, lead in water fountains and asbestos in ceiling tiles results not only in threats to physical health but communicates indifference and validates paranoia. Efforts to transfer staff to other duties without considering the importance of continuity of care or calling staff away from clinical meetings without adequate notice delivers undermining messages to patients about the value of relationships and their reliability. These processes are often not reported in evaluations of success or failure of treatment programmes but they exert a quiet though often profound effect on the treatment, much as a contaminated operating field would affect the outcome of surgery.

These assaults on the primary task, when faced openly, can become grist for the therapeutic mill as the community struggles to deal with problems from outside its boundaries. For example, on hearing that the tried-and-trusted psychodramatist was being terminated and replaced as an outcome of a power struggle within the larger system, many patients began informally to drift away from meetings in a passive protest. As this passive protest became an active effort of both patients and staff to overturn the firing, the joint effort seemed to restore the holding power of the community. Even though it did not succeed, it served as an antidote to the inertia of therapeutic despair.

At other times patients are able to exercise more clout than staff in protecting the community. A small plot of land that was being used by patients as their garden was put up for sale by the city. This garden not only provided opportunities to work together on a project but symbolized their investment in growth. The patients were able to mount a campaign in the neighbourhood, the city council and through the newspapers to retain the garden. When the impact of the external environment on the community is neglected, often the integrity and the credibility of the therapeutic process is severely undermined. However, it is also important to appreciate that at times focus on external events and the 'common enemy' can be a diversion from addressing internal conflicts.

## INTERNAL BOUNDARIES

Internal boundaries that require management and understanding include boundaries between patients and staff, between inclusion and exclusion from the programme, between acceptable behaviour and unacceptable behaviour, between different modalities of therapy, and between patient government and the management responsibilities of the staff. Real engagement between patients and staff sets off escalating projective, introjective and splitting processes characteristic of the paranoid-schizoid mode of experience, with inevitable blurring of boundaries as a fusion and confusion of the inner worlds of both patients and staff are played out on the community stage.

To understand these processes in terms of discrete transferences and countertransferences between individuals becomes mind boggling, as the permutations are almost infinite. Understanding Bion's (1959) group basic assumptions (predicated on an unconscious symphony of projective and introjective processes in the paranoid-schizoid mode of experience) allows for a grip on these complex phenomena. The group basic assumptions of dependency, fight/flight and pairing can be seen as a group-level crystallization of this transference/countertransference matrix and a collaborative defensive effort against the primal anxieties generated by the task of growth and development.

An appreciation of the prevailing basic assumption at any particular moment is often a useful starting place for a sorting process. Covert primal emotions, needs, frightening impulses and shame are often crystallized out of the group process as individuals personify these shared but painful threatening dimensions of the human repertoire. The potential for abuse of vulnerable individuals as scapegoats is great, but if appreciation of the complex and unconscious ways individuals are used by the group process is maintained, all members can be eventually enriched by the opportunity to confront as in a mirror what in themselves had remained potent but in the shadows. What emotional role each member of the community plays in the basic-assumption life of the community can be understood as a function of each person's unique history, inner world and projective and introjective tendencies – or of what Bion (1959) terms *övalenceò* and what the group attributes to the individual by virtue of his or her work role or visible characteristics.

As group members come into emotional contact with one another, passions are stirred and projections fly, leading to blurring of boundaries and modes of experience characteristic of paranoid-schizoid organization. As the group sorts through its experience, projections are reowned and integrated at a higher level characteristic of a more depressive organization. With continued work more blurring occurs, needing more sorting. The dialectic between blurring and sorting process can be conceptualized in terms of the dialectic between the paranoid-schizoid and the depressive organization, and between the basic-assumption group and the work group. Appreciation of the interaction and mirroring between the patient group and the staff group serves as an antidote to the basic assumption that therapists often hold that all distorting pathology resides in the patients and that it is primarily the patients who fuel the problematic dynamics of the social system. Clear delineation of group tasks, work roles and boundaries provide an invaluable frame of reference to make the sorting through possible.

In this model the internal experience of the patient in role is valued not just as revealed pathology that is to be interpreted by the expert, but also as a meaningful contribution to the understanding of the whole. Often the mad in their metaphors speak most eloquently to painful but hidden dimensions of truth although it may escape their own notice. Lear when mad spoke eloquently to the corruption of his kingdom that in his sanity he had missed. The internal experience of staff members in role is not just a product of a rational processing of the patients' irrationality; it is also a reflection of the shared covert and irrational forces in the group-as-a-whole. It is the commitment by both patients and staff to a shared task – the developmental project – that provides a context for negotiated interpretation of the varying experiences of individuals which together form the larger mosaic or picture of the whole. This interpretive activity requires the imaginative use of irrational experience. When this works well the estranged patients are linked once more to the community and the staff are linked to their split-off irrationality.

## CLINICAL EXAMPLE OF LONG-TERM TREATMENT OF A PATIENT

Dan has been a patient in the programme for fifteen years. His clinical course illustrates the three modes of experience and how each has been prominent in different phases of his treatment.

Dan had eight acute psychotic episodes in six years beginning at the age of 18, at a time that he was attempting to make a transition from life in his family of origin to the wider world. These episodes were explosions of paranoid rage and grandiosity that propelled him into belligerent provocative collisions with authority figures, including the police. These episodes culminated in hospitalizations and treatment with high doses of neuroleptics and lithium with rapid resolution of acute psychotic symptoms. Since the treatment of these episodes was primarily aimed at resolution of symptoms rather than exploration of meaning, their psychodynamic developmental implications remained sealed off. Between episodes Dan remained on relatively high doses of neuroleptics and a therapeutic dose of lithium. He lived quietly at a halfway house, spending most of his time sleeping, meditating or attending Eastern religious ceremonies. In contrast to his volatile psychotic states, he remained almost inert and his primary interaction with others was to sermonize occasionally on the virtues of love and peace. He began to appear more and more the chronic mental patient. These states, in which he caused no trouble, were punctuated by acute psychotic disruptions which seemed unrelated to life events and were resolved with hospitalization and higher doses of neuroleptics. He entered our programme after his fifth acute episode. Medication was lowered but he spent the first three years sleeping on the day-room couch, more adhered to the programme like a new born infant lying quietly enfolded in his mother's arms than interpersonally involved. He attended meetings very irregularly – just enough to qualify as a community member, but did not participate actively. During his second year in the programme he suffered an acute psychotic episode that required brief hospitalization due to his dangerously provocative behaviour. As he gradually became more involved in the programme after returning from the hospital, his withdrawal suggested passive aggression rather than autistic retreat. This passive aggressivity provoked exasperation in other patients and impulses in staff to discharge him. However, the aggression that he projected and stirred in others was contained therapeutically through interpretative work and relatively empathic confrontations.

As Dan felt more deeply accepted and held by the community, he gradually began to awaken and explode with affects of rage and terror that heretofore had been only expressed during acute psychotic episodes. His most vivid memory of childhood was being stung by a bee at the age of 3. He recounted that when he went in pain and terror to his mother who was playing majong, she told him that she was busy and to come back later. His loving but repressive and obsessive father was also portrayed as impossible to reach, and frightening. This experience of being stung suggests a screen-memory standing for many experiences that taught him that there was no reliable container outside himself, and that to survive he needed to avoid emotional linking with others human beings to escape overwhelming pain. Dan was able to recall with rage the innumerable times that his mother had characterized him in the presence of others as 'such a nice boy who never gets angry'. Gradually he learned that it was possible to feel and express anger and a range of other feelings that apparently had not been unacceptable in his family. (His 'healthy' sister who shunned Dan and family therapy after his psychotic episodes, committed suicide three years ago, suggesting that she also sealed off until she imploded.) As he encountered the intensity of his ambivalence towards authority figures, he became aware of both murderous rage and a yearning for merger. His defensive pseudo-self-image as the loving, peaceful, independent Buddha-like figure – which to some degree functioned as a capsule sealing off vital but explosive parts of his personality – shattered. He became acutely psychotic but this time the psychotic symptoms could be linked to meaning and developmental processes and were contained in the community without requiring hospitalization. Following this last episode, Dan dreamed that he floated away from the Buddha inside a bubble past other Buddhas that were smaller and smaller until the bubble broke and he found himself in a community meeting where the members gave him directions on how to live outside the bubble. The shift from concretely believing that he was Buddha to using Buddha as a symbol in a dream seemed profoundly significant to Dan and many other members of the community. During this phase of his work he relived the bee-sting incident with his actual mother in a family psychodrama. Although his mother loved him and intellectually understood the problem, she required several 'takes' in the psychodrama before she could respond in a different way to her 'little boy' who came to her in terror and pain.

In the next phase of therapy, Dan took on part-time employment in a nursing home and emerged in the community as a leader, demonstrating an impressive capacity to understand and reach other patients. He participated for several years in intensive small-group psychotherapy dealing with a complex array of transferences to other patients and staff, as well as ongoing family psychotherapy dealing with the interplay of his internal world and the reality of family relationships. His sheltered employment evolved into a competitive full-time job. He enrolled in college, eventually obtaining a degree in mathematics near the top of his class, while he used his connection with the therapeutic community as a surrogate family. He had a brief psychotic episode after graduation from college as he struggled with anxieties about the loss of his patient identity and terror of being in the world without support; this seemed to be a revisiting of disintegration anxieties of the autistic contiguous mode of experience. He bounced back quickly from this episode and was again able to link the episode into a contextual meaning about his development as a person instead of sealing over issues. He now has a part-time job in his profession and is in the process of seeking full-time employment. In therapy he is focusing on his sexual feelings and the complexities of moving from a more secret auto-erotic sex life to the development of sexual and committed relationships.

Dan's change has been dramatic, but it did not occur quickly. The experience of being adequately held, accepted and understood – treated by a clock that works on developmental time rather than arbitrary imposed time limits – is probably the most crucial factor in Dan's transformation. His clinical story has the quality of natural unfolding. Today, it is very difficult to find treatment time frames or environments that are responsive to patients' needs for development. When severely disturbed patients are thrust into treatments that are driven by insurance time, institutional time or government time, it is not surprising that most do not form the bonds necessary for real treatment. Patients' awareness, conscious or unconscious, that they may be dropped in mid-course contributes significantly to the superficiality and as/if quality of many programmes. It has been striking that if patients, even those who seem well on their way to deteriorating chronicity, can form a meaningful bond to the community, they will then reveal surprising strengths for their own treatment and contribute to the therapeutic holding and containing power of the community.

## EXAMPLE OF THE DAY-TREATMENT GROUP AND INTERGROUP PROCESS

A description of a week at P Street Intensive Day-Treatment Program which revolved around the suspension and reinstatement of an individual patient illustrates the therapeutic community from a process perspective showing the systemic interplay of intrapsychic, interpersonal, intragroup and intergroup dynamics and their therapeutic implications.

At a weekly patient government meeting chaired by the patient president, the priority item on the agenda was consideration of Jim's suspension from the programme and whether the committee should recommend to the staff that Jim be reinstated in the programme. The suspension had been imposed five days earlier after Jim smashed a window in a violent outburst during his small-group psychotherapy. Most of the patients including Jim were present at the patient government meeting, as well as a staff consultant.

### History of the suspension

For months, Jim and Carol, another patient, had been carrying on a vendetta against one another which often challenged the containing capacity of the community. They sparred frequently in community meetings, team meetings, art therapy and other meetings but the vehemence of their fight was often greatest in their small-group psychotherapy. They treated one another with scorn, each representing for the other a bad object. Both believed in the law of the talion and tended to retaliate when injured. Jim had originally attempted to enlist Carol as one of his admirers (like his attempts to enlist mother, who throughout his childhood was depressed and emotionally inaccessible), but Carol persistently expressed a strong distaste for him, remarking that not only wasn't she attracted to him, but that his attempts to monopolize the attention of the therapist were 'sickening'. She furthermore charged that his hateful prejudices towards homosexuality, overweight females and Jews were intolerable to her. Jim often retaliated by attacking her bisexuality, her obesity, and her Jewishness. Carol had a long track record of provoking violence in males who had characteristics similar to her drug-addicted but seductive, narcissistic father, which would end in manic or depressive episodes requiring her hospitalization. Jim too had been hospitalized numerous times. Disappointments at work or rejection by a woman usually preceded psychotic episodes that revolved around a woman whom he both idealized and whom he felt was trying to seduce and manipulate him (this seemed to be an externalization of an internal object composed of a fused representation of the unresponsive mother and the attractive favoured sister). Other group members had identified similarities in the perseverative fight of Jim and Carol with their own struggles with exciting bad objects. At times, other group members tried valiantly to persuade Jim and Carol to empathize with one another as a step towards facing what they had projectively identified in one another. At other times, group members used Jim and Carol's fighting as a channel to vicariously express their own rage or as a smoke-screen behind which to hide when other painful issues were confronting the group. During a week preceding the small-group meeting in which Jim broke the window, the group was grappling with the imminent departure of the female co-therapist who was pregnant. Behind a cloak of well-wishing joy for her and the baby simmered rage about abandonment, envy, and murderous rage towards the unborn baby, and fantasies about the therapists as a sexual couple. As an alternative to experiencing and expressing these feelings directly with the risk of stirring guilt, shame and painful memories of oedipal defeats, the other members provoked the provocateurs, Jim and Carol, as a way to vicariously discharge their collective hurt and anger. The therapists' efforts to interpret, to empathize or to calm were not successful. Insults escalated. After Jim invoked the authority of his father to denigrate Carol, Carol called Jim's father 'a silly old jerk'. Jim's face reddened, and he lurched towards Carol in a rage. When the male therapist put up his hand to motion Jim away from Carol, Jim changed directions, threw a coke can at the wall and then deliberately strode to the door and thrust his hand and arm through the frosted glass panel of the door. His arm reddened with blood as he remained almost expressionless. It seemed to the therapist at that moment that Jim was reliving a variation of a repetitive nightmare in which he rushed into the family home that was engulfed in flames to save his family and redeem his lost pride in a final dramatic sacrifice.

Jim, appearing dazed and confused, was given first aid by the psychiatrist. This seemed to have a calming and orientating effect. An emergency community meeting was convened in which the incident was explored. Regaining his composure, Jim argued that he should not be suspended for violating the 'no violence' rule and in fact should be commended for not acting on his impulse to punch Carol. The community agreed that Jim should be suspended because his behaviour had been physically menacing and someone might well have been injured by the flying glass. Jim was at first irate and on the way towards a psychotic escalation. However, with encouragement from other patients and the staff he began to struggle to contain his rage. By the end of the meeting Jim had resolved to work through the suspension procedure in order to be reinstated in the programme. Meetings with his treatment co-ordinator, the patient government and the community were scheduled to take place during the suspension period over the next ten days. Jim was accompanied to the emergency room in order to mend his injuries. In a significant variation from his accustomed pattern he returned to his apartment that night instead of provoking a commitment to a hospital.

The suspension procedure is designed to establish a boundary between acceptable and unacceptable behaviour in order to limit behaviour that could be destructive and have a chilling effect on the therapeutic process. However, the suspension procedure is also structured so that the suspended patient can choose, as they usually do, to stay in a modified status in the programme while the incident is understood and worked through. The patient has the task of making a credible case that he/she accepts responsibility for his/her behaviour, will make reparative efforts, and will strive towards developing more acceptable means to deal with destructive impulses and feelings. The community has the task of reaching an understanding of what impelled the patient's action and the conscious and unconscious contribution of the group and other individuals in the incident. Through this process the social contract is re-established. Even the most psychotic patients have been able to mobilize constructive and non-psychotic aspects of their personality in this effort when there is sufficient meaning in the relationships to fuel their desire to do so. Holding patients accountable, even when psychotic, seems to have a more calming and stabilizing effect than if one tries to impose external controls.

During the initial days of the suspension period prior to the patient government meeting, Jim attended meetings with his treatment co-ordinator, and one community meeting to discuss the suspension. In this meeting patients focused on Jim and their anxiety about his volatility. He acknowledged the validity of their concerns and his propensity to retaliate almost reflexively when insulted. He did not invoke his diagnosis and chemical imbalance to exonerate himself from responsibility as he had done on many previous occasions, but rather seemed to more thoughtfully own the problem. There were attempts to explore Carol's role in provoking Jim and the possibility that she was acting out her own violent impulses through Jim. Carol rather belligerently discouraged pursuit of this possibility by accusing others of blaming the victim. There was some speculation that the incident may have been linked to a shared anger at the staff.

Jim appeared, looking confident, at the patient government meeting on the following day, the fourth day of his suspension, and other patients seemed ready to welcome him back into the fold. He smiled coyly as he volunteered that smashing the glass pane was a way to try to get rid of the pain, but that he was resolved to deal with the pain differently in the future. He agreed to be responsible for replacing the pane of glass. At this point the meeting took an unexpected turn.

The patients were preparing to take a vote on a recommendation that the staff lift the suspension, with the stipulation that Jim be responsible for replacing the window, when Lori spoke up. Lori, an attractive young woman with a penchant for wrist-cutting and rageful outbursts, had become a prominent voice in the community after being in the programme for just a few months. Lori pointed out that this was the second time that this pane of glass had been broken by an angry patient. 'This was not Jim's fault,' she continued. 'It is the staff who should be held responsible. Will another patient have to smash the window before they realize that the whole door should be replaced by a solid door? This door invites smashing.' Lori had been outraged by what she considered invasions across her personal boundaries by questions from staff or patients. She had put people on notice through piercing screams that her boundaries needed to be heavily guarded. She wanted to express her feelings to empathic listeners but unwanted questions were too much like the sexual abuse she had suffered as a child. Any pressure from others made her feel destroyed as a person because she felt forced to comply like a puppet. Lori's personal boundaries seemed both paper-thin and made of concrete. 'Furthermore,' she added, 'if they don't put in a solid door, I may smash the glass and then sue the staff for negligence. Does it take three strikes to awaken these jerks?' Several patients echoed Lori's rallying cry. Dan (described earlier in the chapter), a veteran patient moving towards full-time professional employment, bucked the growing tide when he reflected that a solid door would not solve the problem because there were windows to break, knives in the kitchen and destructive implements all over the city. 'The staff could try to turn this place into a hospital but would it make us safer?' The staff consultant at this point made his only comment. 'The work we are doing together is often painful and triggers intense anger – the trick is to work with these intense feelings and keep a dialogue going while not being destructive.' Another patient rejoined that the door of the small psychotherapy group room should be more solid to give patients a feeling of security and privacy so that they could deal with frightening intense feelings more safely. A thoughtful discussion ensued about different ways to contend with anger other than violence, such as taking time out or talking about the impulse rather than acting it out.

Later that day in the staff meeting, the staff discussed the request from the patients for a solid door. At first it led to some ventilation about the nastiness of some borderline patients. This prompted a lecture from the white male psychiatrist about borderline dynamics, which seemed to induce sleep. The black male programme manager interrupted the lecture to announce that he and other staff would be required again to miss clinical meetings in the next week to attend administrative meetings designed to prepare for an imminent site visit by an accreditation body. The psychiatrist complained that patient meetings should not be cancelled without notice, particularly when the reason was cosmetic while actual patient care suffered. The psychiatrist continued that the patients were already reacting to a sense of being abandoned by the staff. The programme manager responded that the psychiatrist never seemed to understand that if the administration was alienated, there would not be a programme to fight about. The dispute between the programme manager and the psychiatrist escalated as they sparred like a marital pair. The sense that racial tensions were implicated in the dispute seemed to hang in the air unspoken. Each rattled off a laundry list of longstanding differences and grievances as other staff quietly aligned themselves on one side or the other. Issues such as the degree of patient input into administrative decisions about the programme, and the excessive tightness or excessive looseness of boundaries which may have contributed to the smashing of the door were rehashed. Each regaled the others with examples of other incidents through the years to fortify their respective positions. The female social worker questioned whether the male psychiatrist had a countertransference issue with Carol related to sexism and had in fact favoured Jim, thereby fuelling the escalation between the patients. The psychiatrist, feeling that the social worker was aligning herself with the programme manager, responded with a heavy-handed comment to silence her. The programme manager complained that the psychiatrist was sabotaging the family-night dinner by not attending. The psychiatrist responded that the programme manager was sabotaging patient responsibility by fixing the dinner himself. Angry that other staff and the programme manager seemed oblivious to the underlying dynamics and the proper priorities, the psychiatrist exclaimed that clinical issues were being trampled on by heavy-handed administration and that as senior clinician he needed more authority. Enraged, the programme manager stalked out of the room, perhaps as an alternative to smashing the glass pane in the door – or the psychiatrist. The meeting ended and staff retreated to their respective offices.

In the next community meeting, five days after the suspension, patients reported on the success of their government meeting but complained that the staff were unresponsive to the need to have a solid door. David interrupted to say that he had heard enough about the door (he had smashed it previously). 'I am not going to be superman today,' he said. 'I am really scared. My birthday is coming up and I'm remembering my mother trying to kill me and how she deserted me.' David recounted the horrors of his early life, but people seemed unmoved by his story, which they had heard often before. David desperately tried to capture his audience with an implied suicide threat: 'I don't know if I can stand another birthday.' Carol reacted, 'David, I am glad you are not doing your superman routine, but what do you want from us?' David then began to boast about his power and invulnerability, that he was employed both by the CIA and the Mafia and despite his small size could tear limb from limb anyone who gave him a hard time. He punctuated these claims by hurling insults at Carol and the group. Jim sat smiling quietly, apparently appreciating the shift of focus. As David interrupted everyone who tried to speak, rage filled the room; patients looked at the staff imploringly to do something. The psychiatrist, feeling pressure to both silence and protect David, began to wonder what role David was playing for the group. Ruth declared the meeting a travesty as David was clearly out of chemical balance. The psychiatrist suggested to the group that David might be thrown off balance by the difficulty of feeling that his needs were not being met by the group – something others might feel also. As the psychiatrist pondered the possibility that David was serving as a target for displaced rage at the staff, Carol began to complain that staff were hard to find recently and that they seemed to be always out to lunch or fighting with one another. Another young female patient, Mary, got up from her chair abruptly and exclaimed, 'The demons want to tear me to pieces. They want to make me a worthless piece of shit. Someone needs to lock me in a seclusion room to keep them away. I just want a reality check. Is that so?' She walked out but returned a few minutes later. Another patient, Margie, then accused the programme manager and the psychiatrist as being just like her parents who were more interested in beating up one another than in taking care of the children. Jim revealed that he had heard staff fighting in the staff meeting yesterday and wondered whether staff members should be suspended. Elaine, an older female patient, stood up waving her arms dramatically and exclaimed that the psychiatrist was 'the right and true one – the one that keeps me from suicide! He is the connection with the Universal Intelligence. The programme manager is a civil serpent – always spouting about rules – always hiding behind his administrative branch.' Carol interjected that the psychiatrist was no better. 'He has a big fat ego and he cares more about having his way than he cares for us. We aren't here to make him feel good.' Like a Greek chorus, several other patients joined in to prod the staff to 'get your act together'. The meeting ended on an acrimonious note, despite attempts on the part of the staff to make soothing interpretations.

After the meeting the somewhat shaken psychiatrist and the programme manager agreed that they needed to meet with one another. After an hour of trading 'interpretations' about the other's countertransference problems, they finally settled down to listen to one another's point of view.

The next evening the psychiatrist swallowed some of his pride and joined the patients for the family-night dinner, eating the food prepared by the programme manager.

The following day in the community psychodrama, patients and staff reversed roles. The patients were uncannily able to recreate a typical staff meeting, capturing the idiosyncrasies of each staff member with good-natured humour. The psychodrama ended on a note of harmony. In the staff meeting that followed the links between patient acting out and staff unavailability, conflict and countertransference were explored. In the small psychotherapy group later that day Jim and Carol listened to one another, perhaps for the first time, and began to consider how they might be using and abusing one another. Friday seemed to be a day of resolution as patients left for the weekend

On Monday, new troubles began, of course, with a revised cast of characters.

## DISCUSSION

The small intensive psychotherapy groups that meet twice a week admit members of the community who have moved beyond the state of relative non-experience or paranoid-delusional fixation. Small-group members have developed emotional links with the community and people in it and are at least ambivalently interested in exploring the problems that arise in relationships. Some patients begin small-group therapy shortly after admission to the programme, while others develop interest and readiness after months and sometimes years. In the above clinical example the small psychotherapy group is contending with a complex matrix of projective identifications that is focused principally on the relationship between Jim and Carol. On the one hand, members are attempting to help Jim and Carol identify what they have projected into the other as exciting and bad objects; on the other hand, they are using Jim and Carol as a fight pair to hold the group's disowned rage and envy (intensified by the pregnancy and imminent departure of one of the therapists). The members are not able to contain the unleashed affect within the boundaries of the group, illustrated by Jim's smashing his fist through the door. The explosion through the container of the group, however, does not end in a permanent casualty or rupture of the work. The explosion is absorbed in other sectors of the programme and reinternalized by the small group and Jim after it has been processed by the community. The patient's inadequate internal container and capacity for boundary regulation is supplemented by the holding, containing, and regulating capacities of the community, obviating the necessity of using force to control Jim's behaviour. The more subtle holding and containing of the community preserve the space for Jim to mobilize his own ego resources instead of having to expend his energies in a self-preserving paranoid power struggle.

Many times in the past Jim had reacted to narcissistic injury with rage, fragmentation and psychosis culminating in hospitalization followed by a sealing-over until the next episode. The suspension procedure can be understood as an extension of the container that confronts patients with a meaningful boundary between acceptable and unacceptable violent behaviour but decreases the likelihood of a splitting-off and a sealing-over that so often occurs when treatment continuity is lost through over-sedation or hospitalization. Because Jim is not separated from the interpersonal and group context of his violence, he has the opportunity to move from explosive paranoia towards a more reflective depressive mode of experience by appreciating the ways in which he was affected by the projections of others, experiencing appropriate guilt for his actions and making reparation. The process also enables other members of the community to reown their projections, an opportunity that might have been lost if Jim, as the embodiment of rage, had been exported. At first, Jim was the focus of the process, but later, through a complex intergroup process, intense affects filtered through many sectors and levels of the programme including the staff group.

The patient government meeting that considered Jim's suspension grappled with boundary issues pertaining to differences and similarities between patient and staff roles. A regressive basic-assumption dependency process led by Lori attempted to deplete the patients' role of real authority or responsibility. The patients' threat of calculated destructive behaviour seemed designed to mobilize coercive responses in the staff as part of an unconscious plan to locate all responsibility for behaviour management into the staff. The shared experience that psychiatric disorder did not exonerate Jim from accountability to the community for his actions stirred depressive anxieties in many patients about the burden of being responsible for their own actions and impulses. This development then propelled the pendulum back in the direction of a paranoid-schizoid mode of organization.

Dan, described earlier, is a patient who has developed internal structures that enable him to manage depressive anxieties without massive projection. He was able to lead the patients back to a responsible work mode by underscoring crucial reality considerations about the impossibility of the staff's providing a totally safe environment. Following Dan's leadership most patients were able to replenish their egos that had been depleted by massive projection and use their strengths to address the shared problem of how to make the environment safe enough. By establishing meaningful participation in the management of the community through patient government, patients are restored to fuller membership in the community. They are able to further develop the healthy part of their personalities through the exercise of real authority towards a common purpose. Experienced patients like Dan provide invaluable role models for patients like Lori who early in their course are preoccupied with testing the safety and reliability of the holding environment. Jim, by personifying the problem of explosive rage, enables many other patients to work through their own impulsivity vicariously. The movement back and forth between the belief that staff are persecutors and patients are victims and the assumption of shared guilt and responsibility can be understood as part of the dialectic between the paranoid and depressive modes of organization which provides an opportunity for insight into and modification of powerful but often covert object-relations pathology.

## The staff role in the process

The staff has a complex set of tasks and roles. The staff is primarily responsible for the development and the maintenance of the structure of the programme and for the management of the boundary between the programme and the larger system. Staff also act as individual, group and family therapists, while at the same time they are interactive members of the community. Perhaps their greatest challenge, however, is to manage their own irrationality. Kernberg (1973) has emphasized that an important role for the hospital staff involves utilizing its experience and internal conflicts as data about the inner worlds of patients. For example, when a doctor and a social worker are fighting about the treatment of a patient, analysis of what the staff are experiencing and what the patient did to instigate this fight can provide glimpses into the split inner world of the patient that cannot be obtained from merely taking a history. The conflict between the social worker and the psychiatrist that surfaced in the meeting around Carol and Jim was multi-determined, but an aspect of it was related to a re-enactment of old scripts involving Carol with her mother, father and brother.

However, the staff are more than receptive containers for the pathology of patients. The psychotic aspects of staff members' personalities that are ordinarily hidden under repressive barriers are stirred and resonate with the patients' pathologies. The murderous feelings that came to the surface between the white male psychiatrist and the black male programme manager could not be explained as just a consequence of patient 'splitting'. The pervasive social madness about race and gender that festers just under the surface exists with or without the added ingredient of patient pathology. One is often hard pressed to determine whether splitting of patients engenders splitting in the staff or splitting in the staff engenders or exacerbates splitting in the patient group. Latent splits in the staff always seem to be present, organized around tensions between disciplines, gender, race roles, personalities and treatment philosophies. The patients' pathology and pressure to split cannot be blamed as the only culprit. Intrusions from the larger system also stir anxiety and conflict within the staff as contradictory clinical and administrative priorities frequently clash.

A vital capacity of the staff is to be able to function as a container of its own experience rather than project it into patients unmetabolized. It may be that many therapeutic communities founder when staffs are seduced by basic-assumption defences to deny or neglect this aspect of their role. The staff must be able to experience and own primal emotional upheavals of comparable intensity to that of the borderline and psychotic patient. The nature of the relationship between the treated and the treater creates a strong suction to reproject what has been projected by the patients into the staff back into the patients, together with activated unintegrated parts of staff pathology. Patients looking for a container in the staff may well be confronted with their rage, envy and destructiveness returning to them with increased force and malignancy. This reprojection can occur quietly and insidiously through management at arm's length, through excessive use of medication, aggressive non-empathic 'interpretations' and controlling interventions such as seclusion, restraints or inappropriate discharge. The surface manifestation of this undermining process may look like the staff and patients routinely relating to one another as though they are different species, one healthy the other sick, as described by Main (1975). In the clinical example, the staff deny their own troubles and splits while intellectualizing about the primitiveness of their patients. When painful unacknowledged and unworked passions of the staff threaten to break into the open (as they later did in the staff meeting), this may be averted by training the focus on the 'common enemy' the patients. Under these circumstances a compelling urge to treat can lead to excessively medicating patients like Lori who, despite her paranoia, was also communicating a painful but important message to the staff. Staff are at risk of colluding with one another to ignore the truth in patients' projections or transference and present a united front locating all the pathology in the patients, thus reinforcing their negative identity and deepening despair about relations with the 'helping other'.

In addition to the fact that Jim, Carol and Lori were revealing their deep-seated pathology, they were also holding up a mirror to the staff. While the patient demand for a solid door was in part a magical denial of their own need to acknowledge destructive impulses and take responsibility for containing them, it also conveyed both concrete and metaphorical truth. The sense of the group room as a reliable structure would probably be enhanced by a more substantial door. The patients also called attention to the staff's failures to contain its own anxieties and to regulate its own boundaries, as reflected in excessive absences and the cancelling of clinical meetings without adequate notice. Kafka (1989) has suggested a revision of the Bateson double-bind hypothesis about the family's role in the aetiology of schizophrenia. He proposes that the central family pathogen in schizophrenia is concrete reductionism and the intolerance of living with multiple conflicting realities that are inherent in human existence. The capacity of a therapeutic community to acknowledge and work with multiple, often conflicting levels of reality is crucial in determining whether a community is therapeutic or is likely to recapitulate previous invalidating experience.

Despite theoretical agreement in the staff to work from experience and help one another find the kernel or boulder of truth in the patients' 'transference', in practice most staff meetings tend to gravitate to a dissection of the patients or the bureaucracy. This serves to defend staff against suffering its own pain. The staff in these instances attempt to export psychologically into either patients or administrators of the larger system what it should be processing internally.

If the staff allows itself to reflect more deeply on its experience, new complications arise, as in the explosive staff meeting where envy, rivalry and hate came to the surface. Individual staff members defending against painful truths about self, manoeuvred one another through projective identification into personifying what felt shameful or painful. The psychiatrist and programme director at first appeared to be carrying on their own personal fight, with other staff as detached spectators; however it emerged that all staff had a personal stake in the confrontation. A major pitfall for staff in attempting to work at this level is the risk of becoming so embroiled with its own process that the reason for being there – work with patients – slips out of mind. Unchecked this can then lead to escalation of splitting and paranoid processes that fragment the holding and containing power of the staff and culminate in patient casualties.

In order for staff to be effective in their roles they must be able to move from the paranoid mode into a depressive mode of experience in which the pain and suffering of the work is not avoided and projected into one another, the patients, their families or absent bureaucrats. Staff members must come to terms with their limitations to resolve guilt about imagined or real injuries inflicted on past or present objects and the failure to cure others or themselves of all emotional disturbance. If this limitation is not confronted and mourned, staff become susceptible to the endless manipulations of patients, who cast them in starring roles – particularly basic-assumption dependency – in basic-assumption groups. In other words, staff often have to suffer what the patients are at first unable to suffer. The staff demonstration that it is able to contain and suffer can serve as implicit model for patients to emulate. It frequently seems that painful staff work is often followed by effective work in the patient group. The psychiatrist and the programme manager moving painfully from a paranoid relationship to a more depressive whole person relationship perhaps paved the way for Carol and Jim to experience one another less as bad part objects and more as whole persons who could listen and empathize with one another's pain. The psychiatrist learned something in his fight with the programme manager that had eluded him despite many years of analysis. He realized that his sometimes gratuitously judgemental and provocative way of relating to his staff colleagues, coupled with solicitousness towards patients, in part derived from his unconsciously equating the patients with his psychotically depressed father and the staff with his mother, whom he perceived as castrating his father rather than helping him.

## THE THERAPEUTIC POTENTIAL OF LARGE-GROUP PROCESS

In the community meeting David's desperate attempt to hold himself together by exacting caring and exclusive attention could be seen not just as an individual's struggle but also as an embodiment of the community's struggle to maintain cohesion in the face of disruption of the holding and containing functions of the staff. The community often is able to respond empathically to needy, overtly psychotic and monopolizing patients like David much like a good self-object. However, in the community meeting described, the group projectively identified the shared oral rage, greed and fears of madness and disintegration, which were too threatening and shameful to own collectively, into David. The group seemed to be operating on the unconscious assumption that if David could be manoeuvred to embody oral greed, madness and rage, then these disruptive affects could be controlled by sacrificing David. David, on the other hand, was easily manoeuvred since the group attack fed his narcissistic grandiosity and insulated him from painful vulnerability and insatiable neotenies. The community is seldom if ever without members who have the valence to personify what feels too shameful, dangerous or painful to face directly.

In the treatment of psychotic and borderline patients, exploratory community meetings without fixed agendas designed to increase awareness of irrational group processes have been criticized as regressive and fragmenting. The emergence of the basic-assumption group can be also viewed not just as regressive in a negative way but also as an opportunity. The stars of the basic-assumption group become personifications of what yet cannot be acknowledged or integrated by other members. Underdeveloped and psychotic parts of the personalities of group members that have remained overtly silent while covertly exerting undermining effects are in this sense crystallized in the basic assumption and become more accessible for work. The community meeting that is often immersed in basic assumptions can enable individuals to experience these deep-seated disturbances in an emotional context with other human beings rather than to project them more autistically into space. In the ideal therapeutic group sequence, what is split off and denied is first experienced in an individual or subgroup charged with a hostile or rejecting affect; the hostility through psychological work is transformed into empathic understanding; then members reinternalize in a more accepting form what had been projectively identified. Emotional growth results. While this seldom happens in neat steps, over time, with many repetitions, the process tends to move in this direction when the community can function as an adequate container and avoid extrusion as a solution. For example, in the community meeting described, June, a very experienced patient, suggested to Carol that she reconsider her determination to rid the community of David. June revealed that she used to feel hate and contempt for David but that a miraculous thing happened to her: 'I looked at David in a new way and my hate turned to understanding.'

Staff members are clearly not immune from the suction of basic-assumption life particularly in the large group, but the capacity of at least some staff at any particular moment to stand between the experience of primitive affects and destructive behaviour is critical. Staff need to demonstrate that hatred, destructive rage and envy that come to the surface in many of these meetings do not have to destroy capacities for feeling and thinking. In this way the staff at times serves as containers and models for thinking that can be internalized by the group in a process similar to that between mother and child described by Bion. In this clinical situation the strict Bion-like group-process interpretation often is not sufficient or called for. An understanding of the group process seems essential but a versatility and empathic understanding of what can be heard at a particular moment seems as critical as the understanding of the process. The use of playful humour, sharing of personal experience, linking members with one another and the group, empathic reflections, reframing and protection of patients at risk of becoming causalities are just some of the categories of intervention that have proved to be helpful in protecting the group from calamity. For example, in another community meeting in which rage threatened to fragment the community and result in a casualty, the psychiatrist made a long and involved interpretation about the group process. The rage and sense of crisis seemed to abate. A patient who seemed to speak for the group exclaimed, 'I didn't understand a word you said but I sure like the way you said it.' The importance of staff not colluding in scapegoating cannot be stressed too much. Although it interferes with a defence and can arouse increased rage, each patient has had some experience of being scapegoated and if this can be tapped, the strength of the community to have room for all its members can be reaffirmed. In this belonging the healing begins.

# REFERENCES

Bernaeur, J. (1987) 'Oedipus, Freud, Foucault: fragments of an archaeology of psychoanalysis', in D.M. Levin (ed.), *Pathologies of the Modern Self*, New York: New York University Press.

Bick, E. (1968) 'The experience of the skin in early object relations', *International Journal of Psycho-Analysis* 49: 484–6.

Bion, W.R. (1959) *Experiences in Groups*, London: Tavistock.

—— (1967) *Second Thoughts*, London: Heinemann.

—— (1977) *Seven Servants*, New York: Jason Aronson.

Bollas, C. (1989) *Forces of Destiny*, London: Free Association Books.

Breggin, P. (1991) *Toxic Psychiatry*, New York: St Martin's Press.

Campbell, J. (1968) *Creative Mythology*, New York: Penguin.

Donington, R. (1979) *Wagner's 'Ring' and its Symbols*, Boston, MA: Faber & Faber.

Foucault, M. (1965) *Madness and Civilization*, New York: Pantheon.

Fromm-Reichman, F. (1950) *Principles of Intensive Psychotherapy*, Chicago, IL: University of Chicago Press.

Ganzarain, R. (1977) 'General systems and object relations theories: their usefulness in group psychotherapy', *International Journal of Group Psychotherapy* 27: 441–56.

Goffman, E. (1961) *Asylums*, New York: Anchor Books.

Grotstein, J. (1986) *Splitting and Projective Identification*, New York: Jason Aronson.

—— (1989) 'Chaos, meaninglessness and the black hole: a new psychoanalytic paradigm for psychosis', paper presented at Sheppard Pratt 26th Annual Scientific Day, Baltimore, MD, April.

Jaques, E. (1974) 'Social systems as a defense against persecutory and depressive anxiety', in G.S. Gibbard, J.J. Hartmann and R.D. Mann (eds), *Analysis of Groups*. San Francisco, CA: Jossey-Bass.

Kafka, J.S. (1989) *Multiple Realities in Clinical Practice*, New Haven, CT: Yale University Press.

Kernberg, O. (1973) 'Psychoanalytic object-relations theory, group processes, and administration: toward an integrative theory of hospital treatment', *Annual of Psychoanalysis* 1: 363–88.

Klein, M. (1959) 'Our adult world and its roots in infancy', *Human Relations* 12: 291–303.

Kovel, J. (1987) 'Schizophrenic being and technocratic society', in D.M. Levin (ed.), *Pathologies of the Modern Self*, New York: New York University Press.

Lichtenstein, H. (1977) *The Dilemma of Human Identity*, New York: Jason Aronson.

Main, T.F. (1975) 'Some psychodynamics of large groups', in L. Kreeger (ed.), *The Large Group: Dynamics and Therapy*, London: Constable.

May, R. (1991) *The Cry for Myth*, New York: Norton.

Menzies, I. (1975) 'A case study in the functioning of social systems as a defense against anxiety', in A.D. Coleman and W. Bexton (eds), *Group Relations Reader* I, Washington, DC: A.K. Rice Institute.

Miller, E.J. and Rice, A.K. (1967) *Systems of Organization: Control of Task and Sentient Boundaries*, London: Tavistock.

Ogden, T. (1982) *Projective Identification and Psychotherapuetic Technique*, New York: Jason Aronson.

—— (1989) *The Primitive Edge of Experience*, London: Jason Aronson.

Pines, M. (1990) 'Group analytic psychotherapy and the borderline patient', in B. Roth, W. Stone and H. Kibel (eds), *The Difficult Patient in Group*, Madison, CT: International Universities Press.

Shapiro, R. (1985) 'An analytic group-interpretative approach to family therapy', in A. Coleman and M. Geller (eds), *Group Relations Reader* II, Washington, DC: A.K. Rice Institute.

Stanton, A. and Schwartz, M. (1954) *The Mental Hospital*, New York: Basic Books.

Tustin, F. (1986) *Autistic Barriers in Neurotic Patients*, New Haven, CT: Yale University Press.

Winnicott, D.W. (1965) *The Maturational Processes and the Facilitating Environment*, New York: International Universities Press.

—— (1969) 'The use of an object and relating through identifications', *International Journal of Psycho-Analysis* 50: 711–16.

# 11 Glacial times in psychotic regression

*Salomon Resnik*

## EDITORS' INTRODUCTION

As is suggested by the title's transformation of the 'fire' motif into its 'glacial' opposite, Salomon Resnik's work exemplifies with clinical sensitivity the Freudian and Kleinian emphasis on unconscious phantasy in the life of the individual and the group. Influenced by intellectual currents in France emphasizing a 'return to Freud', Resnik goes back to the 'master' for rich insights into mental and group processes. Yet there is a contemporary flavour to this chapter which derives in part from Resnik's application of Bion's writings, evident in the author's astute understanding of the group-as-a-whole and the sophisticated use of Bion's concepts in comprehending the fragmentation of the psychotic's inner life.

Many group therapists will find Resnik's contribution controversial. They will be concerned that he is treating psychotic patients using a depth psychological approach, in contrast to the current stress on psychoactive medications and group/milieu caregiving and structure. It is important, however, to note Resnik's sensitive attunement to the ego states and transference of the patients. Remember, too, that Resnik conducted this group in an inpatient setting with staff and team supports.

The in-depth interpretation of unconscious phantasy is in some danger of becoming a lost art within group psychotherapy. In this chapter, the reader can look forward to discovering the work of one of the true artists of depth interpretation. Judiciously used and properly attuned to the patients' needs, the grasp of the phantasy life and of internalized object relations is a powerful group therapy tool.

_____

Emptiness, silence, heat, whiteness, wait, the light goes down, all grows dark together, ground, wall, vault, bodies, say twenty seconds, all the greys, the light goes out, all vanished. At the same time the temperature

goes down, to reach its minimum, say freezing point, at the same instant
that the black is reached, which may seem strange.

(Samuel Beckett, 'Imagination Dead Imagine')

In August 1988, I was invited to give a seminar on psychosis for a group of
psychologists and psychiatrists working in the Santa Giuliana Mental
Hospital in Verona, Italy.

The director of the hospital, Professor Ferlini, gave me the opportunity of
choosing my teaching method. Due to the fact that I have been working for
many years in institutions, with individuals and with groups, I suggested that
we should see patients together, and thereby we would be able to share the
same field experience. The idea was to see the patients in a special room with
a one-sided mirror. Professor Ferlini was to be with me as a silent observer
and the rest of the doctors were to be in the next room behind the mirror, as
'invisible' witnesses. (The members of the group had been informed about
the 'particular presence' of the medical staff 'through the looking glass'.)

I shall try to describe the first meeting, which became the starting point
both for our clinical research and for a group therapeutic experience which
has lasted three years and is still continuing.

It was a mixed group composed of patients aged between 20 and 35. Most
of the members, about ten individuals, were diagnosed as suffering from
schizophrenia, and a couple of them were suffering from deluded hypo-
chondrias and hallucinations.

It is very difficult for patients such as these to tolerate panic or psychotic
anxiety. They cannot cope with life and as a result they become blocked and
cold. In other words, they become indifferent and apathetic. Perhaps what is
upsetting for any human being is being confronted with someone who is
apparently incapable of feeling and who is unresponsive like a reified object
or a dead body. Devereux in *De l'angoisse à la méthode dans les sciences
du comportement* explains, 'Man's reaction is one of panic when faced with
the lack of reactivity or unresponsiveness of matter', and he then adds, 'The
need to deny this fact and to control his panic pushes him to interpret any
physical event in an animistic way, and to attribute meanings to them that
they do not in fact have, in order to be able to experience them as "answers".'
One of the dangers, as in every psychoanalysis, is to remain monolithically
silent, unresponsive, or to give a quick, sudden interpretation in order to get
rid of countertransference anxiety (as a psychopathological dynamic aspect
of transference and countertransference). The destination of the verbal and
non-verbal communication between the patient and the psychotherapist or
psychoanalyst, the same in an institution between patients and staff, depends
on their capacity for maternal *rêverie* (Bion) – therefore, their capacity to
contain and to deal correctly with anxiety.

Our aim was to teach, while exploring a group of patients in the presence of part of the institutional staff, in order to share the field experience of observing the patients' gestures, words and behaviour and to gauge the atmosphere, which was, in fact, very difficult to do from the other side of the mirror.

A group discussion ensued after the second session with the members or the hospital staff (of course in the absence of the patients) in order to exchange our views and feelings concerning this experience as a working group. Bion said that the ideas of task and co-operation in a group were very important in the mental life of a working group (Bion, 1984). However, this group was constantly perturbed by influences coming from other complex group phenomena (Bion, 1961, p. 129). By further expanding upon Bion's explanation, one could say that the cycle of empathy within the mother–child relationship is a model, in which the child's unbearable anxiety is being received, contained and accepted, and transformed into a bearable one by the Other.

Freud, in his *Group Psychology and the Analysis of the Ego*, points to the relationship between individual and group psychopathology (Freud, 1921). Using the concept of inner world suggested by Freud and later on in Melanie Klein, one can conceive of a multiple world of instinctual drives and objects (internal objects) cohabitating either in peace or at war. According to Bion, 'The individual is a group animal at war, not only with the group, but also with himself for being a group animal and with those aspects of his personality which constitute his "groupishness" (Bion, 1961, p. 131).

I should like to turn now to our first meeting and thus to the beginning of this history. During the first session, a young schizophrenic patient called Natasha (her father had given her this name out of admiration for Tolstoy's heroine in *War and Peace*) was sitting on a chair, and like the rest of the group was very detached. Her face was very tense, inexpressive and rigid. Beside her was sitting Loredana, a young, very detached, hebephrenic patient. She had great difficulty in thinking for herself. She was like a hopeless, empty-headed doll; she was, therefore, very dependent on the minds of others. From her expression and her eyes alone one could tell that she was either confused or distracted.

Next to her was sitting Silvia, a very unusual, beautiful girl, who seemed very cold and flat reminiscent of a Florentine Madonna of Renaissance times. Sometimes her apathy changed into an enigmatic Mona Lisa smile. Rossana sat next to her – a young girl, who looked, however, very old and resembled an elderly melancholic woman. She sometimes resembled an angry-sad witch by hanging her head and allowing her hair to fall forward hiding her face. This patient wrote three different diaries, which she has been keeping for three years. Two of them she felt able to give to the staff, and thus indirectly to me. The third diary remained inaccessible, like a sort of intimate, sacred temple (an idealized, private part of herself). Although she was not usually able to talk in the group, she was experiencing and expressing her feelings in an indirect way through her behaviour in the clinic and through her writings.

Next to her was Sylvano, a very sad, young boy, who was not in touch with either himself or other people, but only with his legs or, to be more precise, with his right leg. His usual attitude was characterized by continuous complaints of heaviness and tiredness in his leg. With a fixed look and a pained expression he would say: 'My leg is sad and crushed. My legs are weak and cannot support my body.' He was in this way splitting off the mind into the leg – from the upper to the lower part of the body – all the suffering that he was unable to accept mentally. Curiously enough, this boy who complained about his legs had worked in a sock factory prior to being hospitalized. This hypochondriac anxiety, delusional in its nature, was a sign of his pathetic state, and was revealed in his physiognomy by a pained and touching grimace.

The next patient was Marco – a young man of 27 who was obese and seriously ill with a schizophrenic process. His schizophrenia began at the age of 18, when his mother, not yet separated from his father (who later died), had introduced him to her boyfriend. His mother had asked him to go out for a drive for a few hours so that she could be alone with her 'boyfriend–lover'. It was at that moment that he was overcome by an attack of delusional agitation and deep regression, for which he had been hospitalized. I had previously seen him alone a few times. He would talk in his delusional way about the 'sun' which was sometimes his friend and sometimes his enemy. He would ask me to close the window because he was frightened of the sun's powerful rays. He used to talk about his stomach being a cemetery where his father and uncle were buried with awful monsters. He also spoke about us in terms of Buffalo Bill, which was me, and Sitting Bull, with whom he identified. He had also claimed a space for himself and his starving tribe of the living-dead. As he was very attached to his mother in a strong, symbiotic and erotic way, I advised that he should be hospitalized again in the Santa Giuliana hospital in order to see him separately as well as with the group.

His voice was like that of a small child during the first session when he referred to the Virgin Mary, which he called 'the Madonna and her child'. From time to time he would adopt a fatherly tone, which was both persecuting and violent. He used this tone in order to frighten the rest of the group, thereby ridding himself of his own fear through projection into the others, namely by imposing his frightening, paternal super-ego on them.

Next to him was Alberto, an intelligent, slim, young boy who was very maniacal. He often spoke about his girlfriend, who in reality had died in a car accident. However, he was convinced that her death was entirely his fault as he claimed that she had died as a result of a football match when Verona's team, his favourite team, had defeated Turin's team, his girlfriend's favourite team.

Lastly there was Maximo, a very fat boy, who was always monolithically mute, cold and detached. Sometimes he would show his presence by expressing his need for some space of his own in his parents' house. He used to say: 'At home I don't have a proper room for myself, everything is full.' From this I understood that in his big body, there was no room for himself, for his own 'ego' since other things were occupying the space – filling up his emptiness. He felt always enclosed, immobile and paralysed in a little 'corridor' in his 'body-house'; or else he felt far away, out of himself, scattered in many distant places. Sometimes he would hug himself, suggesting a sort of symbiotic condensation of mother and child: a centaur-like *rêverie*.

In the first minutes of the initial session the silence was very tense and dense. The feelings of defiance, persecution and at moments sadness, were a contrast to the desperate and panicked looks which sought help. Initially, all eyes were upon me and the director of the hospital. It seemed that the patients were seeking support from us as a helpful parental couple and at the same time, as representatives of the institution, the bearers of the solutions to their preoccupations and deepest feelings.

As I saw that Sylvano was still looking at his sad leg, and Rossana was still hiding behind her witch-hair looking at her feet, I interpreted that these two individuals expressed the group's depressed feelings of falling into pieces – a catastrophic depression. In response to this downward attitude, Alberto proposed that the group should imagine themselves climbing a mountain. Alberto did not waste any time; he used the image of the mountain to suggest seeking help from above – a mystical approach. He said that it was necessary to reach the top of the mountain where he knew there was a cross. I imagined Rossana personifying the depressed part of the group flying off into the air with her broomstick. She believed in magic and was convinced of being responsible for her mother's death as it coincided with her hospitalization. Between depressive descent (of feelings) and manic ascent, between despair and hope, the idea of God appeared in the group unconscious fantasy. The official leader of the group, the therapist, became the ideal ego of the group. They were expecting maternal and paternal help.

I felt that the depressing group feelings were expecting me to be a sort of paternal, 'divine' puppet-master. A powerful demiurge able to pull them up or to hold them. Marco addressed the group suggesting that they should all participate in a challenging sport (defying mental pain and hopelessness with action). One person proposed basketball and Alberto mentioned football.

After an attentive silence a climatic change took place in the group.

In psychotic experiences, matter and feelings of the environmental atmosphere of transference often become passive and inert. I have discussed this subject in my book *L'esperienza psicotica* (Resnik, 1986). We also know that one of the reactions of the self is to stop motion and e-motion from entering into the experiences of daily life. There emerges a coagulation of repressed or denied feelings which are transformed into a dense, pressurized and polluted atmosphere. By allowing the possibility of change in the group climate or in the atmospheric matter, a sort of dead substance can change into a living one. The vacuum becomes a living void and subsequently, a piece of matter is capable of moving in a pulsating, oscillating rhythm – be it constructive or destructive movement. That is what was happening during this silent, pregnant pause. It was as if Eros and Thanatos as living forces or drives were colluding together ('collude' from Latin *colludere*, to play *con*, together) in a way that could be understood as a substantial union of forces. I use the idea of matter in psychic phenomenon to convey an existing experience in which a particular mental state changes. Changing from a static model into a moving and vibrating one, introduces movement and, therefore, life in the form of a substantial force. This force can still be pathological in its nature, but it nevertheless provides a sort of vital expansion of crushed life. Elias Canetti in *Das Geheimherz der Uhr* (*The Secret Heart of the Clock*) says, 'What interests me is the substance of life – this takes up all my time' (Canetti, 1991).

Marco, resembling a large inflated ball or balloon, personified the group's infantile, greedy and foolish demands. The term 'folly' derives from the Latin *follis* – a windbag full of air. A fool or a deluded mind is a sort of windbag-ball full of air (megalomaniac feelings or ideas), which can be destructively overflated until it bursts or else it can be catastrophically deflated. This definition of folly helped me to develop my ideas on narcissistic depression, and also on the idea of inflation and deflation of the ego-ideal in psychosis.

Marco with his fat or inflated face insisted upon his oral-erotic demands and tried to impose his will on the group as a personification of his incestuous mother. I pointed out to him that his favourite inflated, exciting ball was his mother's breast, and his 'favourite sport' was to play his exciting endogamic game with his mother's body, to which he was affectively and sexually attached. This attachement became still more symbiotic and erotic when a doctor advised the mother to be tactilely affectionate with him. Such misunderstandings, in which affection becomes confused with erotic feelings, plays a very important role in pathological child development and therefore in psychosis.

At one point Marco looked at a cross that was fixed on the wall and spoke once more of the Virgin Mary and the Christ-child or, in other words, of his idealized mythical relationship with his mother. This relationship was, in fact, part of a triad, whose third element was the missing father; the figure of Joseph the carpenter often appeared to him as the victim in the triad. (I should mention that this hospital is a religious institution and part of the administration are religious sisters.) One day Marco spoke about three teeth being part of the same mouth: one he called the Virgin Mary, the other the Christ-child, and the other Joseph. At this time, he referred to the figure of Joseph as 'Peter', which is the name of his mother's boyfriend. One day he asked me, 'Who is that man called the Holy Spirit?' The group was conceived by him as a big mouth – a very greedy, incestuous one, who was trying to chew and digest this complicated triad.

Ten years ago, when the mother's boyfriend appeared, Marco entered into a state of psychomotor confusion and agitation. He began having delusions about Jesus Christ, the Virgin Mary and Joseph whom he saw as being betrayed. He often spoke about Christ's nails and his own nails in his head and stomach. This punished and idealized son bore a part of Christ. Marco, in his delusion, had transformed the nail in his stomach into an anchor penetrating the ground and through which he felt fixed to the floor. Without this nail/anchor, Marco, who felt empty and light like a levitating foolish balloon (an inflated stomach), was frightened that he would fly out into the cosmos unable to fix himself into the earth.

This symbol of the foolish balloon appeared in the group in the form of a 'sports' competition between the members. The group enacted a community of battling brothers and sisters – each one seeking their ideal point of attachment to their God, who was at once their cross and their anchor (the anchor when upside down becomes a cross).

Rossana, the witch-like, melancholic girl whose long hair covered her face, smoked in an avid and desperate fashion. 'In this place you die,' she said, kicking the air with her right foot as if aiming a sort of ball-bomb at the corner of the room where there was a basin of water. Something (a folly-bubble) was about to explode in her stomach. The bubble's hallucinatory voice was telling her to leave the room before a catastrophe occurred. She listened to the voice and left the room. Thereupon, Alberto left his chair to sit on Rossana's newly vacated one. With a cigarette between his lips and raising his head, Alberto said, 'I'm putting the voice that says "In this place you die" into my cigarette; and I'm going to turn it into smoke and send it up to paradise.'

It was in this way that the group acted out the confrontation between life and death. The accumulated time, which appears as a state of 'chronicity' (which comes from the word *chronos*), was in the process of awakening and transforming like a time-bomb about to explode. The time-bomb – the potential acute breakdown, as a chronic expectation, was following the group's sporting itinerary. Rossana had kicked the inflated bubble-balloon or ball-bomb into the corner near the wash-basin – perhaps the firemen would attend to it; the alternative was Alberto's alchemic proposition or salvation formula. His suggestion was to incorporate (introject) the bomb by projecting it up, and transform it into smoke whereby it would be sent skywards and vanish. It was a sort of divine sublimation of the magic witch-mother, which Alberto was personifying (an archaic Kleinian mother).

Rossana had recognized the voice coming from her stomach as being her mother's voice. This hallucinated voice was telling her to run away on her broom with all her might. Faced with such an individualistic and egocentric decision taken by Rossana in conjunction with her dead mother's voice and appearance, Alberto took it upon himself to play the charismatic and Messianic role of saving everybody. He was aided in his shamanistic function by the time-bomb, which had been transformed into a divine smoke-cloud, symbolizing the magic bridge between earth and sky or the bond between the mother – Gaia (the earth) – and the ideal father – a condensation of Chronos and Zeus, who were situated up above in the cosmos. Their mountain expedition became a procession to heaven where the cross stood like a divine nail anchored in the sky. Confronted with the depressive feeling of being down or falling down into the mother earth, an ideology of 'levitation' or of ascension towards the supreme father was instituted in reaction.

In the group transference it seemed obvious to me that my role was to personify a shaman or idealized father whose mystical 'idealized smoke' was intended to save the group. Thus a charismatic model of object relationships based on delusions of salvation was established as the group's – patients' and staff's – ideology.

A very dense and pregnant silence ensued, full of anxiety but also abounding in unpolluted life. Alberto, who was dramatizing through identification my role of shaman-psychoanalyst, proceeded as this personified, omnipotent figure towards the basin in the corner to ascertain whether he had succeeded in alchemically transforming the ball-bomb, or whether it was still there. Alberto washed his hands and looked at himself in the mirror. Several patients would alternately look at themselves in this mirror and in the one-sided mirror. Perhaps this was their way of trying to identify themselves with the public by splitting off the parts of themselves which were projected as their inner, auto-observers. The ego-observer of the group's mind was able to look at himself and down into his own inner world. The patients were therefore dramatizing the way of gaining some insight into themselves and discovering or liberating their mental space.

Alberto drank a glass of water and gave a speech dramatization through histrionic gestures about the end of the world and its subsequent rebirth. He spoke of a river flowing around the earth, and delivered a cosmological and cosmogonical discourse to the group, via which he addressed the whole of humanity, explaining the cataclysms which have been wrought upon our planet from the time of the universal catastrophe. He said prophetically, 'The sky was torn in two; everything on the earth became cold following the catastrophe.' I understood that he was speaking about regression to glacial times. Another member of the group asserted that 'it was the atomic bomb and the resurrection which took place', thereby describing an apocalyptic time. This kind of group metaphysical atmosphere conveyed a state of anxiety and deep regression in the transference, which acted as both an escape from and an aesthetic solution to their mental suffering by means of flight to the frozen past.[1] At the same time in the apocalypse of the divine ideal of a divine ideal ego, the Messiah, who was represented by the paternal super-ego, judged the good from the bad, pure from that which was contaminated by the sin of humanity – incestuous and murdering fantasies. It was the father's function within the group to judge and help discriminate during crises between the value systems inside the mother-world. The function of this paternal super-ego role was both to repair and to structure this world.

At this point, I wish to differentiate between Bion's maternal *rêverie* and what I call paternal *rêverie*. The concept of paternal *rêverie* was introduced by Dr Flavio Nose, who was my assistant and one of the witnesses present behind the mirror. Maternal *rêverie* means containing the nameless dread of the child or of the psychotic regressed patient, and sending back (reprojection) in its place bearable feelings. On the other hand, the paternal *rêverie* has to do with organizing and helping to give structure in space and time and to help accumulated or chronic time to become fresh and lively. In this way, among the prosecuting and depressive phenomena, the world's group space endeavours to recapture 'life', and thereby attain a certain emotional harmony.

The 'group stomach' was not yet capable of digesting this experience of the end and rebirth of the world. Marco, the fat schizophrenic boy, began to speak about the toughness of experience and about his stomach being full of prehistoric animals and important past and present figures from his life, who were beginning to wake up from a nightmarish hell. Christ's nail in Marco's personal, mythical delusion was hurting his stomach. However, this pain was also a symptom of his newfound attachment to life. Marco would speak of his stomach as being the holy place – the cemetery where his father and maternal uncle were buried. His father was an animal lover and was especially fond of horses (Marco sometimes described himself as a small horse dearly loved by his father). His uncle, whom he had admired, had been a photographer, and had collaborated with Fellini, the prominent film director. Marco often confused the name of Professor Ferlini with that of Fellini. This phonetic equation conveyed the presence of an admired father and idealized uncle super-ego figure in the group transference. The image of the father was at times devalued and at other times so excessively inflated and idealized that it represented either God or the cross itself (or the nails in the cross), upon which the sacrifice of the victimized son took place. The group as a global entity took on the role of the mother and sometimes that of the Virgin Mary holding the Messiah (the Christ-child) in her arms. A symbolic relationship was established between the nailed Christ and Marco's stomach.

The group's regression to glacial times resembles Freud's archaeological hypothesis on human evolution concerning early ontological anxiety. 'Übersicht der Übertragungsneurosen' discusses the notion of *Realangst* (anxiety in the face of a real danger), which is like the notion of *ängstlich* (anxious). *Realangst* is an emotional reaction when individuals are confronted with their own *Angst* (anguish) about unexpected or new occurrences. *Realangst* is manifested when daily life is altered and unanticipated incidents invade a programmed routine. In other words, the security of a monotonous life is subject to the unexpected. One may thus understand the tendency to follow repetition in delusional thought and in routine life as a security system against intrusions.

Infantile anxiety, as anxiety of the real when faced with what is strange, pathologically justifies regression to the dispositional point either of neurosis or of psychosis.[2] Confronted with the reality principle, it is intolerable for the fragile ego and 'hard' for the omnipotent and stubborn child.

At this point I would like to mention R.E. Money-Kyrle's paper on cognitive development (Money-Kyrle, 1978). He suggests that mental illness is the result of unconscious moral conflict. He also speaks about the fact that patients, whether clinically ill or not, can suffer from unconscious miscon- ceptions and delusions. To this I would like to add that psychotic patients are people who have not had the chance to clarify their misconceptions. Therefore, if a misunderstanding of a chronic psychotic patient is left unresolved, it can become a very strong conviction, which results in the inability to deal with doubt, ambiguity and ambivalent feelings, all of which is a part of normal life. A 'chronic conviction', a petrified ideology, or a frozen system of ideas, therefore, becomes part of a deluded mental construction.

In the above-mentioned essay, Freud speaks about regression and makes observations about phylogenesis and ontogenesis. According to him, the anguished state of reality (*Realangst*) determines the awakening of an archaic fear destined to be frozen. In this light, Freud talks of a regression to glacial times and 'geographical' spaces, where the anxieties or anguish of the child (and the child who inhabits the adult) are treated as the equivalent of a present, exterior danger. A group that has been petrified, frozen or inanimate will rebel against the dangerous feeling of a catastrophic reintegration into actual life. According to Bion (1970), the notion of a catastrophic change is a painful and disturbing 'turning point' in present life – a critical moment, which can give rise to an archaeological opening into the present transference situation of old buried fragments of the self. With the advent of a catastrophic change, there is a mixture of ghostly fear and positive feelings of hope in the geographical context of present history.

In another session, the group started out with a paralysis of the mind related to a somato-psychic kind of feeling. The inability to make associations and to recall or continue the story was disturbing in contrast to the lively and anxious part of the group personified by Alberto.

Alberto was looking at the carpet, where he discovered a bit of thread attached to the carpet's label on which there was a picture of a goose. 'Geese have no soul, they have no intelligence, they are stupid', said Alberto. In saying this he defined himself as leader of the group whose members were handicapped, stupid, incapable of making associations – and thus, incapable of thinking. Silvia, the girl of Renaissance beauty, smiled, as if the bit of thread had become a very important find. The group did, in fact, resume the 'thread of thoughts' and the 'thread of speech'.

It was Silvia, the first to take up the thread of speech, who, with emotion, spoke of her interior void. 'I have a void of memories . . . I cannot remember things, and that makes me angry with myself.' The association that she made seemed to confirm her feeling of despair and rage whether against her illness or against life or against all help, depending on the particular moment. She then said, 'The thread can also be a rope to hang yourself with.'

At that moment, looking at Rossana, who was the one that had taken away the bomb, she seemed to react to Silvia's statement on the rope, and I said, 'The voice that says "In this place you die" is challenging life and transforms the thread of rediscovered thoughts into a rope which kills life.' This game of oppositions, this war between the urge for life and the urge for death (life instinct and death instinct), creates a state of crisis.

The lost thread, which had been rediscovered, had transformed the empty and useless group mind or 'the stupid goose' into an intelligent, living 'animal' network. The members of the group became spinners and were able once more to think. Through my help and the parts of the ego, which were left out (projected also into the staff), they were able to continue spinning the 'pensum' of that day in the context of our daily institutional life as a working group entity.

Thread is an important concept for such a group. The thread is a nexus between one thought and another – an articulate bridge, a sort of spinal cord of the mental apparatus, which is able to tolerate and link feelings and thoughts and to give them shape and sense. The psychic spinal cord stands for the introjected phallic institutional function of the father, which helps as a repairing axis. Its mission is to conceive a vertebrate within the containing mother function of the individual mind, the group mind, or the clinic as a whole institution in order to create order or incoherence.

The state of glaciation leads to the phantasy of a catastrophic deglaciation, an experience of an unstoppable flood. This is sometimes equated to a flood of blood or psychic bleeding. In my previous work 'The space of madness' (Resnik, 1992), I discussed a group of older and more seriously psychotic patients. During one of our sessions, one of the members showed me an old scar on his finger and said: 'This is the scar from an old wound. Before awakening an old wound, you doctors ought to know the coagulation time of the patient.' I thus learned, thanks to the patient's reminder, that one must be most prudent when dealing with an individual patient's regressive phenomena or with a group's massive regression because of the danger of a psychic bleeding crisis.

Crisis denotes a critical point between the choice of life and death. The word crisis is derived from the Greek verb *krino*, which implies an idea of separation or differentiation, or even the idea of difficult judgement at a critical point whose decision will lead to a decisive transformation. In man's social and individual history one speaks of periods of crisis or of 'moments of truth'.

My long experience with psychotic and non-psychotic patients has confirmed my hypothesis that, for better or for worse, crisis is always a decisive moment of lucidity (Resnik, 1985; 1986, p. 167).

When the group considers themselves in such terms as being backward, 'stupid as a goose', but also as being able to think again, and therefore being intelligent, this indicates that they are faced with ambivalent feelings as well as at certain moments with ambiguous feelings concerning their own existence and mental apparatus. If the group ego cannot deal with ambivalence, a splitting mechanism takes place and a regression into the paranoid-schizo position reappears. At that point some extremist attitudes of self-overestimation or devaluation or deep disillusion with themselves occurs.

Bion first speaks of the Messiah or of the mystic image, as being the ideal charismatic child, to whom the holy couple give birth in a pairing group (Bion, 1961). The charismatic child, like Christ (produced by the couple – the Virgin Mary and the Holy Spirit), personifies the hope and the beliefs of the group. Producing a Messiah (a person, an idea or a utopia) corresponds to the capacity and the need to materialize, to give shape to the ideal ego of the group self. The danger, of course, is the 'disillusion or deflation' of the idealized image and the feeling.

In his article 'The mystic and the group', Bion (1970) examines this subject and develops the Messiah fantasy as a mystic and charismatic ideal of the group.

Alberto, after having found the thread in the group's magic carpet, examined the label and remarked that the drawing of the goose 'looks like the map of Poland – the country next to Russia'. The 'free' associations of the group with my Slavic name – Resnik, which was probably Russian or Polish for them – connected me with that of a country. They felt the need to place me in the geography of their history.

Simultaneously, on the other side of the mirror, the group of doctors discussed the importance of sensations and feelings. When a psychotic patient seems paralysed or frozen emotionally, what attitude should one take? How does one feel when this occurs? First, aspects of the institutional transference between the patient and the members of the team were opened up for discussion. What is the emotional attitude of the psychiatrist, psychologist or nurse who feels emotionally involved in the therapeutic process? One staff member remarked, 'Yesterday, watching the group, I felt confused and I didn't understand what was happening; I had the impression that the patients were saying something important, but in an inarticulate and apparently disjointed way.' Another spoke of the depressive feeling of the group, which had particularly touched him. Another mentioned the anxiety and fear that the group members had of everything from outside, including the other patients, and myself. They commented that the group climate had been glacial except when Rossana's hostility excited the room when the group thermometer manifested extremely high temperatures like those of an atomic mushroom. It was like the bursting of the ego from paralysis. Some team members were sensitive to the persecuting aspects, while others were aware of the relaxed and serene atmosphere.

These climatic variations in the group of patients seemed to me to be a succession of glacial space–time, with interglacial periods or pauses. These pauses I imagined were cracks through which the affective heat made its way. The intense regressive state appeared temporally in the group's history of humanity manifesting itself in the transference as actual reality or as actual neurosis.

Another member of the team felt a battle of opposing emotions had been transpiring in the session. I suggested that this battle was a fight between the life instinct and the death instinct and was the continuous tension between split tendencies. The observers were impressed by the striking way in which the patients were capable of rapidly dramatizing shattering and profound situations.

Marco manifested the split tendencies by alternating between depressed and violent intonations depending on whether or not he was identifying with his paternal, critical and dominant super-ego.

After Rossana had compulsively and aggressively left the group, Rossana's own psychiatrist, who was a member of the staff, had to ask her what had happened. She replied, 'My father and my mother are dead; and these two dead people are in the process of waking up . . .' 'Even if this feeling is disturbing, you should explain it to the group', said the doctor.

Another colleague remarked that Natasha, who was usually devoid of feelings, had a sad, emotional expression on her face after Rossana returned; as if the affectivity or painful reality had entered the room and was reintrojected by her. Rossana's momentary absence had certainly been experienced by the rest of the group as an opportunity for them to liberate themselves from intolerable fantasies, experiences or objects which had been too greatly persecuting for them. The group body-mind had split off these feelings and attached them to Rossana's mobile flying body thereby using her as a sort of hermetic-witch-carrier of painful or persecuting feelings, which the group was not able to digest by themselves. They were able to reaccept these feelings from the leader-mediator during these times when the *rêverie* group and institutional process was effectively taking place. However, more often than not, their reintrojection of these feeling was sometimes too painful and terrible for the group's psychic apparatus.

Another of Rossana's functions was to transport outside the dead people or dead aspects of each one or of the group-as-a-whole like the Greek ferryman, Charon, in the underworld of Hades. She transferred the lifeless aspects or dangerous internal objects of the group's mind-baggage out into the corridor like the river of the lower world. This river could represent a vein into which the group was projecting or expelling aspects of themselves into the institutional circulatory system.

There were life and death drives in the group and also warm or painfully burning feelings, of which they tried to get rid, in contrast with cold and frozen ones. The frozen or glacial objects posed the problem of the inter-glacial states – in other words, the catastrophic phase of deglaciation and the fear of a thaw-flood. The glacial times of the group ego were therefore always present as a ghost, a worrying shadow lurking in wait.

The group's deathless experience and void of feelings were often personified by Rossana and sometimes by Natasha. The fear was that the scapegoat or the carrier of everything that the group needed to expel would return. This was part of a potential nightmare in which the return (dreadful reintrojection) will be a painful and catastrophic one. On the other hand, feelings of grief and the mourning process (Rossana's dead mother) will appear symbolically in the form of a shadow of the living dead.

Rossana had indicated to a nurse her fear that if she stopped hallucinating, her mother's voice would disappear for ever. The hallucinations were a way for Rossana to keep her interior cemetery alive and loquacious, and thus to fill the void of intolerable or persecuting absences.

Freud examines this preoccupation, which Rossana was experiencing in terms of the loss of the hallucinatory voice, as the presence of the shadow of the lost object falling back into the ego in his paper *Mourning and Melancholia* (Freud, 1917). Freud speaks of psychosis and its related problem with the serious melancholic void.

Concerning mourning and the shadow of the absent object, Freud explains that in the case of psychotics, this shadow often acquires the character of a ghost or a vampire, as I have just suggested, who claims the blood of those alive. This reminded me of the shadow of Nosferatus projected on to a wall in Murnau's film *Nosferatus*.

In the discussion seminar, Rossana's doctor told us that after the first session Rossana had gone to visit her brothers and sisters at Bolzano and also to see the psychiatrist who had sent her to the clinic at Verona. Rossana told him that she was afraid of getting better, if it meant awakening her corpses and bearing the responsibility for her own life. The colleague in Bolzano had recounted this episode to us, and I made use of it later to stress the indirect method of communication that Rossana, like all psychotics, needs in order to express certain experiences that were intolerable to convey directly.

In my book *Personne et psychose* (Resnik, 1973), I develop this idea of the phobia of proximity in psychotics and their need to communicate at a distance often through transitional spaces, elements, objects or people such as doctors, nurses or other patients. The Bolzano psychiatrist, in Rossana's case, acting as spokesperson, communicated to us something that could not have been otherwise transmitted. The patients in the group knew that we were being observed through the mirror by the staff. At the same time the mirror served as a means to communicate transitively through a crystal-like wall that was at once transparent and opaque. The problem of a direct or indirect mode of communication presented itself to the staff and the group psychoanalyst – myself in this case. One must be careful to differentiate between a direct and careful interpretation with one that is aggressively direct, which would overwhelm a fragile self. A psychotic patient often experiences a direct approach as an intrusion into his or her personal world. Being direct and straightforward, if possible, basically means aiming at the patients' conflicting 'node' without intruding into their private world. One should be careful and straightforward so as to determine the optimum, non-hurtful distance of approaching them. I am convinced that there is always an optimum point in the transference, a focal point, like in optics, from which we can reach the patient's world with sensitivity and respect.

In as much as the patient is more regressive and more sensitive to all exterior influences, the confrontation with the reality of the meeting must be carefully handled.

Rossana, as mythical spokesperson for the most regressive part of the group, personified regression at the fixation point or an archaic dispositional point, where there is not always a differentiation, as Freud pointed out, between the preconscious and the unconscious – at that stage there is neither speech nor censorship (cf. Freud's most recently discovered paper on metapsychology, Freud, 1915). The concept of the dispositional point was developed by Freud in *Three Essays on the Theory of Sexuality* (Freud, 1905) and in the case history of Schreber (Freud, 1911). At the time of the *Three Essays*, Freud was already concerned with the innate variety of sexual constitutions and the concept of regression. Freud uses the concept of the point of fixation – the point to where the regressive phenomenon may be traced back, as well as the concept of the choice of neurosis, which he had suggested in 'The neuro-psychoses of defence' (1896a), and later developed in his paper on the aetiology of neurosis (1896b). Freud made some corrections concerning 'infantile sexual traumas', and speaks of unconscious fantasies in childhood which could play a role in regression, and in the unconscious choice of the type of psychoneurosis.

In the case of Rossana, the fact that her hospitalization coincided with the illness and sudden death of her mother increased her magic belief in the traumatic situation, and in her own responsibility. Her admittance to the hospital and the death of her mother were thus equated and related in a causal way.

Maybe one could add, from a Kleinian viewpoint, that censorship corresponds to an archaic and heavily persecuting super-ego. One must not forget that Klein speaks of the death instinct corresponding to a first persecuting image or object of the primitive, persecuting figure and a tyrannical super-ego.

In the transference experience one is both a witness to and responsible for the fact that certain patients cannot tolerate their own basic ontological solitude. In regards to their own ego, phobic patients strive to enter different spaces. The phenomenon of projective, spatializing and invading identification corresponds in this case to the fantasy of leaving one's own mental space and entering into the Other's mental space.

In my book on the psychotic experience (Resnik, 1986), I described the meaning of psychosis as metempsychosis,[3] that is, to escape from one's own unbearable body in order to animate other existing natures. Often this leap of projective identification into the Other, through the abyss, becomes a catastrophic experience of confusion and huge anxiety. Kurt Goldstein, in *Human Nature in the Light of Psychopathology*, describes what he calls a catastrophic situation or condition, as being the expression of a great disorder, either psychic or in the organism itself, which stems from a serious breakdown (Goldstein, 1951). This author also uses the term 'catastrophic reaction', to which it may perhaps be necessary to include the concept of catastrophic anxiety, which is defined by the onset of panic. I find that when a sudden and violent terror appears in psychotic patients, they are afraid to express this feeling. Panic terror is etymologically linked to the demigod Pan who disturbs and frightens all the animals and monsters of the forest when he abruptly wakes up in a rage. Theodore Thass Thienemann (1967) speaks of panic (from the Greek *panikos*) as a sort of terrifying fear. He uses the expression 'groundless fear' to mean that Pan cries out in a terrifying, uncontrolled voice from inside a 'mouth-tomb' or grotto. For the psychotic, panic anxiety becomes the equivalent of a sudden attack. Patients cannot control the feeling of imminent danger exuded by a place, which is bound to their own body. Rossana spoke of a terrifying voice that came from inside her, and sometimes this voice came from Marco's stomach. Later she was to express this feeling and her sense of apprehension in one of her diaries.

Sylvano, the boy who complained about his leg and who was very often panicky, told his doctor that the previous night he had been disturbed and could not sleep but was able to think.

One of the working hypotheses of the post-group seminar was to retrace the thread of our discourse, as Alberto had done in the group. To find the link between the patient's group, the seminar and the institutional network was one of the aims of the linking/thinking process of my teaching or our learning laboratory group. Seeking a link in the complex and essential network in the labyrinthine life of the institutional unconscious, is 'macroscopically' complementary to what happens microscopically in the group in question.

As the sessions continued, new patients joined the group (Ornella, Sandra, Ludovico, Christian, Alice, and others).

Ornella, one of the new patients, personified the classic, difficult, borderline patient that Malcolm Pines describes in his paper, 'Group analytic psychotherapy of the borderline patient' (Pines, 1990). Ornella used to be a primary school teacher, and being very narcissistic, she used to experience the group or the whole institution as being her children or pupils. In this way she was able to split off her regressive, infantile and devalued self into the others. She was thus able to remain an omnipotent ego-ideal and also the ideal ego for the others, able to control and to manipulate fragments of her own reality that she could not accept as being part of herself. When she was not able to split and control people, she became aggressive and violent, blaming and placing guilt on the staff. Devaluing other people, mainly members of the staff, was part of her destructive, demanding and critical personality. There were days when she felt better and quieter; but these periods did not last long. She was unable to express recognition and gratitude. Her narcissistic wounds, when she was helped, provoked feelings of revenge. She became very attached to Loredana, the unexpressive, hebephrenic patient I mentioned earlier. In one of the sessions, Loredana, looking out of the window, said, 'How nice the garden is! And how nice the bird song.' After a pause she said, 'I would like to leave the clinic. I would like to walk through the garden, to stop a car in the street, and ask them to take me home. I like hitch-hiking.' In Italian hitch-hiking is called *auto-stop*, which some of the patients in fact associated with stopping life, or committing suicide. In fact both Loredana and Ornella, who were very close, became an alternating suicidal couple: sometimes it was Loredana who wanted to stop her life, and sometimes Ornella. Later on, in conversations with members of the staff, I learned that both of them had attempted suicide several times.

As the group would often speak about Christ and the Crucifixion, I understood that they were associating Ornella's attacks on links with the crucifixion of any sort of thread or *filum* in the group matrix. The attacks on linking stood also for a murderous, envious attack against an archaic, phallic or paternal function, which consisted of 'bridging' thoughts, or fertile newborn ideas.

At the end of the first year, Sylvano, the hypochondriac boy who suffered 'only' from his legs, spoke of an important change that had taken place within him. He said, 'Yesterday evening it was not my legs but my ego that had bad diarrhoea. Today my hands are sweating profusely, I don't know why. Is it water leaking from my intestines and out through my hands?' While he was speaking, Giovanni, who was sitting next to him looked sadly from me to Sylvano. There was a depressive atmosphere and the group was revealing its heaviness, presenting itself as a 'huge leg' that was weary and sad. Sylvano's leg, the symbol of the group's feeling, corresponded to the experience of not withstanding the strain on the great fragility of a body-group ego. The group's psychic ego, touched emotionally, was beginning to thaw and to express itself in a depressed fashion – 'crying' through the medium of Sylvano's intestines and hands.

I interpreted for the group that their sad state of mind and their search for 'good maternal arms' and the organizing strength of a father was a way to protect themselves and to allow them to express anxiety (paranoid and depressive anxieties) as well as a method to integrate themselves and fulfil their 'needs'. While watching Giovanni's and Sylvano's eyes become sadder, I commented that the group cried through their hands and intestines because of their inability to cry through their eyes. Suddenly Giovanni, as Sylvano's *Doppelgänger* (the double of himself) or shadow, started crying. The thawing of the glacial times was transformed by the group into tears; a situation which expressed the capacity of the group's psychic ego to be back in touch with its bodily ego.

Moreover, Sylvano's leg, in which he had deposited his 'mourning and melancholia', symbolized the group's splitting hypochondriac mechanism or phenomenon, which ascended progressively from the leg to the intestines (inside) to the 'sad' weeping hands and finally reached the head, the mental pain, which had previously been resisted could finally be manifested. Giovanni personified the ability to think and to mourn the loss of the object. On the other hand, the loss of an object is a relational phenomenon, that implies the loss of part of the ego (the part linked to the object) such that a fragment of the ego separates leaving a hole – a wound in the psychic body.

In normal mourning process, says Melanie Klein (1975), the subject is able to assume pain and suffering but tries to bring back the living memory of the object as good souvenirs – 'to reinstate the loved object inside themselves'. But in pathological mourning the subject feels incapable of saving and securely reinstating the good aspects of the lost object. Instead of the object, there is a bleeding wound. After some time, the unbearable feelings of loss are substituted by a lack of affectivity and an a-motion of vacuity – as if emptiness or apathy replaces the painful loss. This is what we are confronting in this group of young chronic patients.

Delusional thinking is one of the fundamental phenomenon in the psychopathology of psychotic patients. The term delusion (*Wahn* in German) designs a complex of thoughts more or less organized (*Wahnideen*) but out of the normal flow of the formal way of thinking and experiencing daily reality. It is a pathologic solution but a 'necessary one', if a better one cannot be found. If delusion is a pathological illusion, the disillusion and dissolution of the delusional megalomanic world appears as a new cata-strophic experience. The idealization not only of the lost object or the persecuting one but also the idealized part of the ego (ego-ideal) feels the danger that the reality principle will teach them that delusion thinking is part of a great misunderstanding. This can be extremely painful for the ego, which experiences the loss of the ego-ideal (the idealized part of oneself) as an unbearable, narcissistic disappointment. I call this phenomenon *narcissistic depression* and it can stimulate suicidal attempts, if the patient feels that after the deflation of the delusional ego there is nothing 'good' left.

The principle of unreality (but real for the patient), which dominates his or her delusional construction, feels crushed by the reality principle. Psychotic patients have their own principles of reality – and therefore, they do not easily accept what comes from the norm – the cultural norm. The Other – the psychiatrist or the analyst, representing the norm – does not correspond to the patient's expectations of 'reality'. Narcissistic depression implies not only the loss of an important object but mainly the loss of an over-valued part of the deluded ego-ideal (Resnik, 1980, p. 373). The awareness of delusion for this group of psychotics was accompanied by the feeling of being depossessed not only of an object and idealized power, but also of the most precious part of their personality.

Freud, in his famous essay 'On narcissism: an introduction', stressed the fact that the pathological, narcissistic attitude, according to my interpretation, is accompanied by an expansionist tendency to appropriate space and objects from the surrounding world (Freud, 1914, p. 67). The egocentric delusional structures transform and deform the nature of all the elements involved in their movement of expansion. The starting up of time that has been blocked, or a regression to glacial times is often conveyed by a frenetic, incoherent movement of the alienated ego which greedily attempts to envelop, swallow and 'transform' the matter and form of any existing object that is part of an inner and outer world and whose landscape is not in harmony with the delusional group ideology. The system of delusional thoughts, which are part of a psychotic ideology, tends not to negotiate with formal, environmental reality principles. The deluded ego tends to impose its views and to convert religiously any other belief which questions its own convictions. But in any group of psychotics there is also a potential struggle between neurotic and psychotic beliefs. The difference is that the neurotic part of the personality is aware of the existence of different views concerning categories of life; but the psychotic part of the personality does not like to discuss its principles and tends to expand and impose its views on others. This psychotic part believes that the other should modify its views and mould itself to the delusional beliefs and outlook.

In this way Professor Ferlini and myself experienced the sensation of being swallowed up by the group chaotic mouth (*caos* – chaos is akin to Greek *khaos*, *khasma*, signifying a gaping abyss, a vast cleft in the earth or a catastrophic swallowing yawn). The observers, as well, hidden behind the mirror, also seemed to be greedily swallowed by the group, a large, mythical, open mouth.

Marco's symbiotic, erotic, delusional relationship with his mother often manifested itself in the group transference. A strange mixture of desperate and erotic sensations and feelings appeared on the horizon of our visual and mental perspectives like a confused and disturbing amalgamation of substances or different states of matter (solid, liquid or gas), which eventually filled the space and time of the meeting. One often had the impression of witnessing deep states of regression in the transference; as if one were observing the birth of language, and the origins of thought. The climate of the session was conveyed by a nebulous atmosphere, in which anyone might start crying, and once started might never stop. It was a sort of contained storm, which when once broken forth or exploded would make way for a restrained state of primordial anxiety – persecuting or depressive in its nature, accompanied by an unbearable sense of grief. The vulgar Latin word *dolus*, implies the idea of being in pain, normally closely linked with the mourning process. There are traces of memories linked to the ego's archaic biography, which the body is unable to contain or re-create.

Sandra, a patient who joined the group later, had hallucinated a monster during the session and described herself as suffering from what she called a 'heterotopic delusion', which I understood as an unusual, different (hetero-) sort of delusion. When I asked her what this meant for her, she replied, 'When my head is aching badly I need to submerge my brain in a recipient head full of ether, and that makes my delusion ethero-topic.' A short time afterwards, she felt 'deflated', deprived of her delusional ether, and therefore at the mercy of her internal persecutors and of her intolerable, depressive suffering. She expressed her panic in a hallucinatory way, seeing a monster on the ceiling of the room. This monster was represented by a chimera: a spider-mother or archaic, Medusa-like figure with a dog's head who by her gestures and facial expression succeeded in terrifying and fascinating us. Sandra's Medusa became a warring and hallucinatory image for the group. She petrified the group who felt worried and almost in a hallucinatory state. Sandra's Medusa knew that she was mortal, as in the myth. But she was not able to differentiate in time a helping Perseus from a murdering one. In fact Perseus' shield was a mirror with which he was going to confront Medusa with her own image – and therefore, to help her 'therapeutically' understand who she was (my own mythical fantasy).

In the seminar after the session, we discussed the danger of being disappointed or disillusioned, not by the Other, but rather by oneself. The phenomenon of narcissistic depression or of the swelling of the ideal ego appears then, as I mentioned above, as a deeply disappointing feeling, when the subject discovers his own mirror image. One of the functions of the ego-observer in Freud's conception is to acquire the right outlook and inlook about one's self. For the group, Professor Ferlini was the institutional mirror through which the patients were able to face themselves by an understanding of the therapeutic process within the hospital framework. Professor Ferlini mentioned during this seminar that Sandra had associated the hallucinated monster (the chimera with a dog's head), which she projected on to the ceiling of the room, with an empty packet of cigarettes, which her father had twisted and deformed into a monstrous shape and then left behind. As she also associated the monster with a spider-mother or an archaic mother, I understood that this frightening object ejected on to the ceiling stood for a frightening, persecuting image of a probably upsetting primal scene, in which her parents became a confusing bizarre, condensed and dangerous object. Nameless fear was being aroused in her along with her capacity to experience feelings again when repression became ineffective. The anaesthesia, the 'useful ether' of the heterotopic experience protecting her from intolerable pain, had lost its power, and this was very difficult for her to withstand.

This was overwhelming for such a fragile and sensitive ego and provoked the need to expel this unbearable, persecuting object out of herself. The monster fell 'upwards' into the group mind (upper part of the body-group), changing the group-body scheme into a frightening chimera. On the one hand, if the group became the father's cigarette packet, the containing mother or group mother, into which she evacuated her monster, would become a contaminated entity that she would need to avoid. On the other hand, she herself, like many psychotic patients, could not stand 'her own body', a painfully deformed packet of cigarettes. In other words, Sandra through pathological projective identification felt squashed inside the monster-like packet.

Sandra wanted to get rid of the monster or to kill her own monstrous containing father. The exciting, incestuous subsidiary body was equated unconsciously to Dr Ferlini, the formal father-figure of the hospital. She wanted, on the one hand, to live inside her paternal super ego, and to be seen in an exhibitionist and omnipotent way by the group, through hallucination. I experienced, together with the rest of the group, the stressful experience of actually 'perceiving' the monster in collusion with the patient. On the other hand, she wanted to kill that relationship, and I felt that the group was using her in order to get rid of a distressing monster-like inner psychotic experience. Sandra, like some other patients in the group, had made several attempts at suicide. When she started to experience feelings again and to return to her own body, she underwent great psychic pains (also reduced ether). However, she was inspired by the feelings and wrote poems full of warmth, which were much appreciated by the other patients and by the staff. Unfortunately, during the weekend, despite the clinic's care, she once more attempted suicide, and this time succeeded.

Sandra's death inspired feelings of deep mourning in the group and in all of us at the institution. However, her suicide was admired as it demonstrated 'courage' in defying life and feelings. But it was too much for her; mental pain and strong persecuting fantasies were awoken in her. This narcissistic, defiant investment in death was a very difficult moment for the staff as well as for the group. Destructive narcissism (Herbert Rosenfeld) and negative therapeutic reaction become more pronounced when the omnipotent, narcissistic ego of the psychotic patient is wounded. It is the combination of unbearable pain with a wounded pride or pathological arrogance, which characterized such a painful and hopeless situation.

In a session that preceded Sandra's suicide, Marco appeared wearing a shirt with a picture of a sailing boat. The sail, which the group fantasized as being black, appeared as a flag which both symbolized the group's mourning but was also seen as a sign of triumph.

One of the phenomena studied by Herbert Rosenfeld (1965, 1987) concerned the psychotic's destructive narcissism and, in the case of negative therapeutic reaction, often appears, as I pointed out, in the analysis of psychotic patients when they on the one hand improve but cannot deal with the new situation or with the catastrophic change (Bion).

In the same session, several members of the group began to dramatize a pathetic procession by identifying themselves with different parts of the group boat on Marco's shirt. While Giovanni chose to be the air or wind, and someone else the water and its waves, Marco chose to be the tiller and was, therefore, the captain or charismatic leader of the mad boat in its state of distress and suffering. Rossana, the melancholic witch-like girl, who was characteristically hunched over and silently hiding behind her long hair, said unexpectedly, 'I am the boat's anchor.' Rossana was fulfilling a very important leading role for the mad and suicidal boat of being the melancholic anchor of its rebellious past.

The depressive part of the group was thus anchored in the frozen waters of the 'glacial times' through regression and petrification. It is important here to differentiate the psychotic's cold and often glacial or frozen depression from the neurotic's anxious and 'heated' depression. In this boat scene, the two levels of psychotic and neurotic states of being were becoming fused and confused. One may also understand that each time the hallucinatory voice of Rossana's mother told her to leave the group – for example when she compulsively fled into the corridor – the boat would lose its anchor and would begin to navigate in an incoherent, unbridled and uncoordinated fashion. The group's anchor in this way became a fixing or reference point that was important for the group's stability. It was as if between life and death, between affective anaesthesia and painful hyperaesthesia, or else between reconciliation and paranoid claims, we were trying to find the mediation of a possibility of negotiating opposite discordant feelings.

Thus between Eros and Thanatos, positive and negative transference, between challenge and recognition, a complex and difficult confrontation/ exchange took place among antinomic feelings within the group.[4] It was as if different drives were trying to achieve reconciliation in the group-boat. This image reminds me of Bosch's painting *The Ship of Fools* in the Louvre in Paris. The struggle stands for an inner living motion or continuous state of transformation among primordial, metaphysical elements – air, water, heat (fire) and earth. This state corresponds to an awakening of energy and feelings which were frozen for a long time.

Speaking of these four primordial elements, which are part of the natural and cosmic world, it is interesting to note that in the history of ceramics, which is a combination of all these elements mentioned above, one of the first objects conceived by prehistoric man was the funeral urn. It seems as though primitive people (*Homo sapiens* and *Homo habilis*) was aware of the need of an object to contain the unbearable and inconceivable idea of death. They therefore needed to create through ceramics an object able to contain that which the living mind could not. Freud points out several times that the unconscious can neither conceive of nor contain the idea of death. This is why primitive man felt the need for a subsidiary body, a maternal containing object, such as the urn which was capable of carrying and conserving the insupportable *rêverie* of death.

To return to the group, I would like to emphasize that in such a hopeless state, in which a group of psychotics can gain awareness through 'living regression', the idea of mourning and reparation of the lost object can become intolerable. This implies the presence of the awakening of a nameless distress and experience of death, which cannot be contained. Therefore, they need a subsidiary complementary body. The subsidiary body can be any member of the group, the staff or the institution as a mother figure. The overlapping dimensions of a terrible pain related to Sandra's death was manifested in the group as dramatized by the ritualistic boat funeral. This situation teaches us how the group is using or personifying a dying or dead part of themselves and how frightening can be the awakening of painful, old, frozen feelings. Perhaps the whole group needed to submerge the group brain into a recipient plane of ether, therefore becoming an etherotopic delusional experience. This was also a way of commemorating Sandra's delusion. The process of deglaciation could be experienced as a panicking transformation of an anaesthetic death state into life. The fear – the necessary nightmare – was the danger of an overwhelming flood. The transformation of Okeanos – the enveloping river-sea – into a stormy deluge became both crazy and painful. Substantial changes in the group nature imply both risk and hope.

During the course of the three years, some of the patients left both the institution and the group; others left just the institution but continued to attend the group session as outpatients. Giovanni became less deluded, more lively and warmer; and thus, he was able to accept a technical job in television. From a group dynamic point of view, one could witness periods of mental dismembering or dismantling (in Meltzer's use of the word) of the group, and mental 're-membering' or 're-mantling'. The group was able in this way to recall and to experience nostalgic thoughts, and hence the idea of warm times. They could thus confront delusional and non-delusional feelings and thoughts. During the psychoanalytic, therapeutic process of the group, one could differentiate neurotic from psychotic moments of experience, but more often they were combined or muddled together. In general, the regressive phenomenon became less cold and subsequently, more vital and warmer. But the menace was always present as a catastrophic deglaciation, a sort of unstoppable mental bleeding equated to physical bleeding.

One of the problems in psychosis, as shown by Paul Federn (1953), is the loss of ego boundaries during the state of crisis, and therefore the lack of distinction between inner and outer space. Freud pointed out the loss both of reality-testing and feelings of reality in psychosis, which was further examined by Federn. Sometimes the group was able to re-establish its boundaries or to repair its frame. In those cases, the group ego was able to become a useful body-ego able to contain the flood, the frameless feelings.

In a dream, Silvia, the beautiful Renaissance Madonna, spoke of an art gallery in which she or her mother were lying on the floor, wearing a white shirt with BIRMANIA written on it in big letters (Birmania is Burma in Italian). The associations of Silvia and also some of the group members helped us to understand that the group mental apparatus, or group mind, could enter or put on her shirt-skin or bodily ego. Therefore, they were unable to become a living global unity – a well-tempered psychic musical instrument. Not being able to live inside its own boundaries, where it was too painful to be oneself, allows the ego or pieces of a broken or dismantled ego to 'escape' and occupy other spaces. I was able to understand from this that these wandering, suffering entities, called ego fragments ventured away into unexplored, mysterious and 'extravagant', exciting places, such as Burma.

On other occasions, this same dream was taken up in situations where Silvia or other group members became maniacal and dissociated – a split between depressive and maniacal feelings or between hot and cold sensations.

In another session, I felt that the group image was that of a Madonna rediscovering her maternal, seductive body and her real life and who was re-establishing contact with wandering and extravagant fragments of its broken psychic apparatus. The reintrojection of long-distant projective identifications in space or in time (as far as Burma or even further into other galaxies of the mind) seemed, in contrast, like a glacial 'brr' – a 'Brr-mania' – which was unbearable for an ego that was just beginning to warm up, and experience real sensations of being alive, and thus, to have feelings.

Sometimes a need to flee, not only outwardly to Burma, but also inwardly in the group's visceral and labyrinthine life is imperative. Introjection of this labyrinthine aspect could be experienced as the intestines of the group body-ego, where projective fantasies were conceived. This kind of 'hypochondriac body image' of the group enabled me to understand the flight from mental space or mentalization into the body – an upsetting part that is split off from the mind into a 'hypochondriac body'. Monica, a patient with very serious hypochondriacal delusions, would often say, 'There is something in my mind that drives me crazy, which I need to throw with anger into my body'. This was often the way in which the group was using Monica as an organ such that the group as an organism was splitting off upsetting feelings, which were difficult to 'mentalize'. Monica symbolized the 'soma-psychotic' defensive mechanism, which the group could not always resolve mentally. In other words, they were unable, in general, to integrate antinomies or contradictions of the mind and body (Eros and Thanatos).

I should now like to discuss the meaning of depression itself. I have described the phenomenon of narcissistic depression (Resnik, 1980) which takes place in every patient during the psychoanalytic process – and this is especially true of psychotic patients at a turning point, when they become aware that their narcissistic beliefs are just inflated, 'heterotopic' delusions. In other words, an enormous capital of energy and sometimes intelligence and culture (as in the *Case history of Schreber*) has been invested in delusions of hope in order to expel hopeless, painful feelings of despair. Delusions of grandeur become the expression of ambitious hope and hyper-idealized wishes of becoming or building up a 'real', famous figure – a messianic ego-ideal. Therefore when deflation and disillusion take place through a psychoanalytic confrontation with reality, the feeling of disappointment is so painful that psychotics tend to develop both a tremendous hatred of themselves and a desire for revenge upon themselves, which sometimes leads them to commit suicide. Thus, it is imperative to provide intensive institutional care for both hospitalized and outpatients who are in this state. This point of view of depression concerning the loss of an idealized and privileged part of the ego (pathological ego-ideal), and disillusion of the ideal ego, is developed in more detail in my paper on narcissistic depression.

A real mental space is always a three-dimensional entity where the addition of time as a rhythmically vibrating, temporal force produces a four-dimensional world. Psychotics, in order to avoid mental pain and anxiety, often tend to transform the three-dimensional inner space into a bi-dimensional inner space; likewise they fill up mental space with smoke (as in the group's meeting room), or with any other material such as words, in order to transform emotion into 'a-motion'. Subsequently, the space is no longer a conducive place for thinking and feelings and a condition of accumulating of lifeless experiences results. In chronic psychosis, non-emotion or 'a-motion' becomes an ideological, delusional belief – an affirmation, in which being almost dead, or surrounding oneself with ether or not experiencing life, is a paradoxical way of dealing with existence.

Bion, in his 'Development of schizophrenic thought' (1956), speaks about psychotic and delusional transference, and mentions Herbert Rosenfeld's views (1965, 1987) concerning projective identification, with the analyst as an object – a method of escaping from painful, confusing states. Bion suggests that psychotic anxiety triggers off in patients a hatred of their own mental apparatus, because it has put them in touch with a very painful inner and outer reality. As a result of this attack, the apparatus is split into minute fragments – fragments which are being expelled through projective identification from the self. The 'success' of this destruction appears as a mutilation of the mental apparatus. Bion explains that the expelling of particles of the ego will lead to an independent and uncontrolled existence outside the personality, either containing or contained by external objects. Each particle, says Bion, is felt to be engulfed and encapsulated in a real external object. If the mental apparatus of sight is projected into the 'real' object gramophone, then the patient feels that when the gramophone is played, it is watching the patient. I find it useful to speak about 'fragments of reality' rather than simply fragments of the mental apparatus, which is none the less a complementary notion. I developed these ideas in a seminar, which I was invited to give in Arles, France (Resnik, 1989a). Concerning the psychic apparatus, Freud (1940, p. 145) in *An Outline of Psycho-Analysis* writes: 'Mental life is the function of an apparatus to which we ascribe the characteristics of being extended in space and of being made up of several portions – which we imagine, that is, as resembling a telescope or microscope or something of this kind.'[5]

In this same seminar, I suggested that fragments of reality imply an ensemble of different parts and functions of a broken, rather than a dismantled mental apparatus, whose effect is to change the whole landscape of inner and outer reality in a very bizarre way. During the acute, catastrophic crisis, each piece or fragment of the broken psychic apparatus becomes a confused amalgamation of 'fragments of reality' composed of broken particles of internal objects, fractured links, parts of the ego, and vision-parts or landscape-parts of an apparently incomprehensible puzzle of reality. These fragments or minute fragmentations that have been projected on to reality, become confused or amalgamated, as Bion stresses, with 'real' objects. But each fragment of reality projected into a particular real object obeys a certain specificity.

In my experience I have found that the projection of a fragment coincides with the nature of the object, into which it has been ejected. In German, Freud used the words *Verwerfung* and *verwerft* for ejection and ejected. For instance if the fragment of unconscious is a vegetating fantasy the subject will project it into a vegetable or vegetable-like object or a tree. In the group itself, an intentional fantasy of cutting the link between two members was equated to a crucifixion. They will, therefore, look for a cross as the place of projection, and thereby camouflage this intention. These ideas are discussed in my paper 'Funzione del padre e spazio mentale' (Resnik, 1989b, p. 97). In this paper, I examined, among other things, the concept of foreclosure in Lacan (1971), regarding his ideas on psychosis. For Lacan, what is ejected, *verwerft* (foreclosed or repudiated) out into the world is what he refers to as 'the Name of the Father', a failure of the paternal metaphor. According to him, during the psychotic crisis, it is the Name of the Father that is being rejected and then ejected and enclosed in an external object, and then denied. I suggest that what is being expelled is a broken fragment of inner reality, in which the paternal super-ego – or a piece of it – is amalgamated with other internal objects and broken parts of the mental apparatus. As a 'result', a bizarre, extravagant picture of the world is revealed.

What I find important to stress concerning this reality or *Wirklichkeit* is the idea of strange forms of objects whether in motion or not (petrified). The idea of movement (*Wirkung* in German, which comes from *wirken* to operate or to work, and which is found in the word *Wirklichkeit*) implies that during a crisis or during a catastrophic change, the patient's vision of the world will move contrarily – it stops or becomes frozen.

Life is normally composed of objects or particles moving and vibrating in harmony with the human landscape (beings and objects). But when reality is felt to be unpleasant, unbearable and persecuting, the living world becomes motionless and life turns out to be paralysed, devitalized and petrified. I call this phenomenon the 'a-motional state' as opposed to the emotional state. This relates to the psychopathology of the schizo-paranoid position and the ego's capacity, mainly in psychotic patients, to tolerate affectivity in motion and emotion (see Resnik, 1989a).

Before finishing, I should like to discuss briefly the material from Rossana's diaries, which revealed either her own vision of the group or the vision that the group expressed through her. She in fact became a sort of enigmatic priestess translator or scribe of the hieroglyphic, hidden, personal language of the group. I should like to point out that she was not only the anchor of the boat-group but also by turning the anchor upside down, the inverted cross – a diabolic personification of a delusional, Antichrist, rival ideology, which sometimes changed into a messianic illusion. Further, she wrote in her diary that an inner, hallucinated voice had once said to her, 'Jesus Christ, you should leave the group.' She also wrote in her diary in many places about God and about a diabolic bomb that was going to kill the group and *Resnica o Resnieg* – which was me as a maternal figure, a part of her group personality who wanted to kill, blow up or negate (*Res-nieg*).

Beyond or 'behind' these persecuting and vengeful feelings against the mother figure or the containing function of the group or the institution as a whole, she expressed in different ways her wish, as the spokesperson of the group's unconscious, of wanting an ideal father, a messianic, therapeutic one and sometimes a less idealized and more human one: a messianic father able to fulfil the paternal function of integrating and matching the dispersed and bizarre particles and fragments of reality in order to attain normality, and therefore to achieve desirable object relationships. To accomplish this, the psychoanalyst must reconstruct together with the patients the mutilated basic network of the group mental or emotional apparatus.

My aim in writing this chapter was to trace the psychodynamic itinerary of a group which became therapeutic, and which has become the basis of a learning and training experience both for me and for the hospital staff.

I am convinced that the correct psychoanalytic training to comprehend psychotic phenomena in institutions and the development of our methods of observation will contribute effectively to the theoretical and clinical understanding of severely psychotic patients. And in these hopes, this piece of work or research should be useful for the social, psychoanalytic understanding of the daily life of a psychiatric clinic.

## SUMMARY AND CONCLUSION

I regard this research as a piece of field work, in Kurt Lewin's sense of the word. It has been a co-existing experience in which the patients, the staff and myself were able to interact and exchange views and feelings concerning the same environmental, institutional life. In discussing an environmental situation and the vicissitudes of daily life in a mental hospital, we were trying to share a learning experience.

As far as our roles and institutional conditions are concerned, I remember Stanton and Schwartz's (1954) work in their book *The Mental Hospital*, where they describe the position of all the staff as participant observers. In psychoanalytic terms, to be able to use our position as 'living', participant observers, as potential witnesses, means having a dynamic understanding about institutional transference and countertransference 'movement.'

Our discussion meetings also meant exchanging feelings and personal views concerning the impact of the patients' anxiety and their manipulations of our own mental apparatus. It also meant trying to discuss, up to a point, our own feelings and intentions and our unconscious 'actings', in relation both to the patients and to the psychopathology of everyday institutional life.

During the group session with the patients, envy of communication and attacks on linking took place whenever there was an attempt to establish a dialogue either between two patients or between a patient and myself. In these cases Marco would always speak in biblical terms about the cross, which finally enabled us to understand that the attacks on linking were a sort of repetitive crucifixion. But where was the scapegoat? Who was crucified? The answer is that the attack and the hatred are directed at any link, any 'bridge', any 'bridging experience'. I have spoken in this chapter about the psychotic attacks on the father's linking function. The primitive child, the violent creature who cannot stand the primal scene, directs aggression at the parental relationship, which means attacking a model of creative or procreative communication. Sometimes the role of the scapegoat is dominated by a narcissistic cathexis, which is a sign of destructive narcissism as described by Herbert Rosenfeld.

Sometimes the incapacity to take in or to introject other people's projections acquires a sporting quality of denial, thereby treating other people's messages or presentations as a devalued basketball, football or tennis ball. The destiny of the object is to always to be sent back and returned to the other (to get rid of). This reminds me of one of Beckett's characters in *Waiting for Godot*. Lucky, a silent character during most of the play, begins to talk and tries to express himself. But he is impeded by the accumulated, indigested speech which other people have projected on to him. It is at this moment that he speaks about tennis and stones coming out of his mouth as if he is returning or sending back what is being said by the others with a mental racket – as if the answering balls had become aggressive and as hard as stones.

Freud in the *New Introductory Lectures on Psycho-Analysis* compares the psychotic ego to a crystal. He says, 'If we throw a crystal on the floor, it breaks, but not into haphazard pieces. It falls apart along its lines of cleavage into fragments whose boundaries, although they were invisible, were predetermined by the crystal's structure. Mental patients are split and broken structures of that kind' (Freud, 1933, p. 59). Then he adds, speaking about those patients, 'They have turned away from external reality, but for that very reason they know more about internal, psychic reality and can reveal to us a number of things that would otherwise be inaccessible to us' (ibid.).

Analysing this experiment from another viewpoint, we can see it as a labyrinthine landscape, whose peripatetic, wandering line of psychoanalytic phenomena is in progress. From this standpoint, then, we can contemplate different views or stages of development and of regression oscillating between warm periods of integration and emotional communication – that is, living time – and cold periods of non-integration or freezing time – that is, feelings and thoughts of non-living time. The latter corresponds to what Freud himself suggests in *Inhibitions, Symptoms and Anxiety* as being regression to a 'geological glacial era in mind' (Freud, 1926, p. 155). Freud speaks about interruption or geological congelation or glaciation of the sexual development of the individual as a historical precipitate: 'This factor owes its pathogenic significance,' he says, 'to the fact that the majority of the instinctual demands of this infantile sexuality are treated by the Ego as dangers and fended off as such' (ibid.). We can expand Freud's views by adding an ancient atomistic point of view whereby, concerning matter and substantial changes in psychotic regression, the fragile or broken ego cannot confront life and needs to use hibernation techniques in order to avoid pain and suffering. How can we help psychotic regressive patients liberate themselves from 'glacial times' individually, in groups, institutionally, or through working with the family? Can we give them something better than anaesthetic glaciation? Deglaciation can become a flooding and catastrophic solution if we fail to provide a good containing, holding and caring approach. A therapeutic, psychoanalytic attitude also means a careful archaeological inquiry into old wounds and scars. Therefore, we must take into account the advice of the patient who said that, before making an interpretation or decision, one should be informed about the blood coagulation time. When bleeding mental time is increased, after a long emotional clot retraction, which is the case in chronic psychotics, we should be very careful. In order to deal appropriately with a patient or a group of patients or an institution, we need to take into account the reaction and capacity to respond to mental bleeding and mourning process, which is a constitutive part of any sensitive – and therefore fragile – organism.

## NOTES

1  I use the word 'metaphysical' to express the atmosphere illustrated in some of De Chirico's metaphysical paintings. Furthermore, meta-physics means beyond the physical world. The impression of the group and myself was of a sort of experience which goes beyond ordinary common sensory experience. Perhaps the appropriate word would be something equivalent to the German term 'das Unheimliche', which was translated into English as 'the uncanny', in Freud's 1919 paper (Freud, 1925).

2  Freud uses this expression in the Schreber case history (Freud, 1911; *SE* 1925 vol. 12).

3  Metempsychosis has to do with the myth of transmigration of the soul. The Pythagoreans borrowed from the Egyptians the belief that the human soul is an independent substance which, after death, can be reborn within another body or nature.

4  Antinomic is from the Greek *anti* against, and *nomos* norm: against the norm and the law. This implies an inner contradiction which is usually found in psychotic patients. J. Gabel, a pupil of Lukács's, in his book, *La Fausse Conscience* (1962), speaks about schizophrenic patients suffering from antinomic or antithetic inner feelings, a sort of hatred of dialectic and synthetic thinking.

5  Portion, which was translated from the German word *Stücke*, can also mean pieces or fragments.

# REFERENCES

Bion, W.R. (1956) 'Development of schizophrenic thought', *International Journal of Psycho-Analysis* 37.
—— (1961) *Experiences in Groups*, London: Tavistock.
—— (1970) 'The mystic and the group', in *Attention and Interpretation*, London: Tavistock.
—— (1984) 'Attacks on linking', in *Second Thoughts*, London: Maresfield Reprints.
Canetti, E. (1991) *The Secret Heart of the Clock*, London: André Deutsch.
Devereux, G (1980) *De L'angoisse à la méthode dans les sciences du comportement*, Paris: Flammarion.
Federn, P. (1953) *Ego Psychology and the Psychoses*, London: Imago.
Foulkes, S.H. and Anthony, E.J. (1957) *Group Psychotherapy. A Psychoanalytic Approach*, London: Karnac.
Freud, S. (1896a) 'Further remarks on the neuro-psychoses of defence', in James Strachey (ed.), *The Standard Edition of the Complete Psychological Works of Sigmund Freud*, 24 vols, London: Hogarth, 1953–73, vol. 3.
—— (1896b) *Heredity and the Aetiology of Neurosis*, *S.E.* 3.
—— (1905) *Three Essays on the Theory of Sexuality*, *S.E.* 7.
—— (1911) 'Psycho-analytic notes upon an autobiographical account of a case of paranoia (dementia paranoides)', *S.E.* 12.
—— (1914) 'On narcissism: an introduction', *S.E.* 14.
—— (1915) *A Phylogenetic Fantasy: Overview of the Transference Neuroses*, ed. I. Grubrich-Simitis, transl. A. and P.T. Hoffer, Cambridge, MA: Harvard University Press.
—— (1917) *Mourning and Melancholia*, *S.E.* 14.
—— (1921) *Group Psychology and the Analysis of the Ego*, *S.E.* 18.
—— (1925) 'The "Uncanny" ', *S.E.* 17.
—— (1926) *Inhibitions, Symptoms and Anxiety*, *S.E.* 20.
—— (1933) *New Introductory Lectures on Psycho-Analysis*, *S.E.* 22.
—— (1940) *An Outline of Psycho-Analysis*, *S.E.* 23.
Gabel, J. (1962) *La Fausse Conscience*, Paris: Minuit.
Goldstein, K. (1951) *Human Nature in the Light of Psychopathology*, Cambridge, MA: Harvard University Press.
Klein, M. (1975) *Envy and Gratitude*, 3 vols, London: Hogarth.
Lacan, J. (1971) *Écrits*, vol. 2, Paris: Seuil.
Lewin, K. (1952) *Field Theory in Social Science*, London: Tavistock.
Money-Kyrle, R. (1978) *The Collected Papers of Roger Money-Kyrle*, ed. Donald Meltzer, Strath Tay, Perthshire: Clunie.
Pines, M. (1990) 'Group analytic psychotherapy of the borderline patient', in B.E. Roth, W.N. Stone and H.D. Kibel (eds) *The Difficult Patient in Group*, Madison, CT: International Universities Press.
Resnik, S. (ed.) (1973) *Personne et psychose*, Paris: Payot.
—— (1980) 'À propos de la dépression narcissique', in *Regard, Acceuil et présence: mélanges en l'honneur de G. Daumézon*, Toulouse: Privat.
—— (1981) 'Nosferatu ou l'épouvante', in *Bestario* 1 (2), Rome: Kappa.
—— (1985) 'The psychotic crisis', *British Journal of Psychotherapy* 2.
—— (1986) *L'esperienza psicotica*, Turin: Bollati-Boringhieri.
—— (1989a) 'Fragments de réalité', unpublished paper.

—— (1989b) 'Funzione del padre e spazio mentale', in David Meghnagi (ed.), *Studi Freudiani*, Milan: Guerini.

—— (1990) *Spazio mentale*, Turin: Bollati-Boringhieri.

—— (1992) 'The space of madness', in M. Pines (ed.), *Bion and Group Psychotherapy*, London: Routledge.

Rosenfeld, H. (1965) *Psychotic States: A Psychoanalytical Approach*, London: Hogarth.

—— (1987) *Impasse and Interpretation*, London: Routledge.

Stanton, A. and Schwartz, M. (1954) *The Mental Hospital*, New York: Basic Books.

Thienemann, T. (1967) *The Subconscious Language*, New York: Washington Square Press.

# Author index

# Subject index